ENQUIRIES

CONCERNING THE HUMAN UNDERSTANDING
AND CONCERNING THE PRINCIPLES OF MORALS
BY DAVID HUME

HENRY FROWDE, M.A.

PUBLISHER TO THE UNIVERSITY OF OXFORD

LONDON, EDINBURGH

NEW YORK 18|19 Irg

18-19

ENQUIRIES

CONCERNING THE HUMAN UNDERSTANDING
AND CONCERNING THE PRINCIPLES OF MORALS

BY DAVID HUME

REPRINTED FROM THE POSTHUMOUS EDITION OF 1777
AND EDITED WITH INTRODUCTION, COMPARATIVE
TABLES OF CONTENTS, AND ANALYTICAL INDEX BY

L. A. SELBY-BIGGE, M.A.
LATE FELLOW OF UNIVERSITY COLLEGE, OXFORD

SECOND EDITION

OXFORD
AT THE CLARENDON PRESS
MDCCCCII

OXFORD
PRINTED AT THE CLARENDON PRESS
BY HORACE HART, M.A.
PRINTER TO THE UNIVERSITY

NOTE TO THE FIRST EDITION

THIS edition is a reprint of the second volume of the posthumous edition of 1777, omitting 'A Dissertation on the Passions,' 'A Dialogue,' 'The Natural History of Religion,' and a long note (L) to § x. *Of Miracles*, in the 'Enquiry concerning Human Understanding.'

The marginal sections have been introduced merely for convenience of reference, and for the clearer articulation of the argument, and do not correspond to anything in the original edition.

Three comparative tables of contents are given at the end of the Introduction, showing the relation of the two Enquiries and the Dissertation on the Passion to the three books of the Treatise.

In these tables, and also in the Index and Introduction, the references to the Enquiries are made by means of the marginal sections of the present edition, those to the Dissertation by means of the pages of the edition of 1777, and those to the Treatise by means of the pages of the Clarendon Press edition, Oxford, 1888.

NOTE TO THE SECOND EDITION

THIS edition contains 'A Dialogue' and the note to § x. which were omitted in the first edition.

EDITOR'S INTRODUCTION

——•+•——

1   HUME's philosophic writings are to be read with great caution. His pages, especially those of the Treatise, are so full of matter, he says so many different things in so many different ways and different connexions, and with so much indifference to what he has said before, that it is very hard to say positively that he taught, or did not teach, this or that particular doctrine. He applies the same principles to such a great variety of subjects that it is not surprising that many verbal, and some real inconsistencies can be found in his statements. He is ambitious rather than shy of saying the same thing in different ways, and at the same time he is often slovenly and indifferent about his words and formulae. This makes. it easy to find all philosophies in Hume, or, by setting up one statement against another, none at all. Of Professor Green's criticism of Hume it is impossible to speak, here in Oxford, without the greatest respect. Apart from its philosophic import- ance, it is always serious and legitimate; but it is also impossible not to feel that it would have been quite as important and· a good deal shorter, if it had contained fewer of the verbal victories which are so easily won over Hume.

2   The question whether Hume's philosophy is to be judged by his Treatise or his Enquiries is of some interest, and

this Introduction aims chiefly at making clear the relation between them.

Hume composed his Treatise between the ages of twenty-one and twenty-five, finishing it in the year 1736. The first two books were published in 1739, and the third book in 1740. The first edition of the *Enquiry into the Human Understanding* appeared in 1748; the *Enquiry concerning the Principles of Morals* appeared in 1751, and the *Dissertation on the Passions* (corresponding to Bk. II of the Treatise) in 1757 [1].

Hume says himself that the Treatise 'fell dead-born from the press without reaching such distinction as even to excite a murmur among the zealots.' That distinction was, to the end of his life, particularly dear to Hume; and it will be seen that in the Enquiries he made a bold bid for it in his quite superfluous section on Miracles and a Particular Providence. He entertained the notion, however, that his want of success in publishing the Treatise 'had proceeded

---

[1] At the time when the Treatise was published, Locke, Berkeley, Clarke, Shaftesbury, and Mandeville were already classics. Hutcheson had published his *Enquiry* in 1725, and his *Essay* and *Illustrations* in 1728. Butler's sermons were published in 1726, and his *Analogy* and *Dissertations* in 1736. Wollaston's *Religions of Nature Delineated* was first printed in 1722, and Cudworth's *Eternal and Immutable Morality* did not appear till 1731, more than forty years after the author's death. The first edition of H Home's (Lord Kames) *Essays* appeared in 1751, and that of Price's *Review* in 1758. There is not much direct criticism of other philosophers in Hume's books. Locke's distinction of primary and secondary qualities, and Wollaston's theory of 'truth' in morals, are directly handled in the Treatise; but whereas Hume's contemporaries were much stronger in criticism of one another's principles than in the establishment of their own, Hume's writings are from the first distinguished by a great detachment from particular controversies. The close internal relation of the Treatise to Locke's essay as the philosopher's bible of the time has been pointed out by Mr. Grose. *Hume's Philosophical Works,* iii. 36. London: Longmans, 1875.

more from the manner than the matter,' and that he had
been 'guilty of a very usual indiscretion in going to the
press too early.' He therefore ' cast the first part of that
work anew in the *Enquiry concerning the Human Understanding*,' and afterwards continued the same process in
his *Enquiry concerning the Principles of Morals*, which, he
says, 'in my own opinion is of all my writings, historical,
philosophical, or literary, incomparably the best.' In the
posthumous edition of his Collected Essays of 1777, the
Advertisement, on which so much stress has been laid, first
appeared. It is printed at the beginning of this reprint,
and declares the author's desire that 'the following pieces
may alone be regarded as . containing his philosophical
sentiments and principles'

This declaration has not only been taken seriously by
some writers, but they have even complied with it and
duly ignored the Treatise. By others it has been treated
as an interesting indication of the character of a man who
had long ago given up philosophy, who always had a passion
for applause, and little respect or generosity for his own
failures. By Mr. Grose the Advertisement is regarded as
'the posthumous utterance of a splenetic invalid,' and
Mr. Green's elaborate criticism is directed almost entirely
against the Treatise.

3   To discuss a question of literary justice would be out of
place in an Introduction which aims at estimating philosophic importance. Two remarks, however, may be made
before passing on.

The first is, that even in Hume's philosophical writings
the author's personal character continually excites our
interest. The Treatise, as was noticed at the time of its
publication, is full of egoisms. Even in this severe work,

together with a genuine ardour and enthusiasm, there is an occasional note of insincerity, arrogance or wantonness which strikes the serious student painfully. The following pages will perhaps show that Hume, in re-casting the Treatise into its new form, displayed the less admirable sides of his temper rather freely.

In the second place, it is undeniable that Hume's own judgement on the style of his earlier work was quite correct. The Treatise was ill-proportioned, incoherent, ill-expressed. There are ambiguities and obscurities of expression in important passages which are most exasperating. Instead of the easy language, familiar and yet precise, of the Enquiries, we have an amount of verbal vagueness and slovenliness for which it is hard to excuse even 'a solitary Scotchman.' How far the difference between the two works is merely one of style is considered below, but whether it be due to matter or manner, it remains that the Enquiries are an easy book and the Treatise a very hard one. In the Treatise he revels in minutiae, in difficulties, in paradoxes: he heaps questions upon himself, and complicates argument by argument: he is pedantic and captious. In the Enquiry he ignores much with which he had formerly vexed his own and his readers' souls, and like a man of the world takes the line of least resistance (except as touching the 'zealots'). He gives us elegance, lucidity and proportion.

4   Perhaps it may be allowed the writer here to record his own adherence to those who judge Hume's philosophy by his Treatise. Bk. I of the Treatise is beyond doubt a work of first-rate philosophic importance, and in some ways the most important work of philosophy in the English language. It would be impossible to say the same of the Enquiries, and although in one sense the *Enquiry concerning the*

Principles of Morals is the best thing Hume ever wrote, to ignore the Treatise is to deprive him of his place among the great thinkers of Europe.

At the same time it is perhaps well worth while to examine rather closely the actual relations between the contents of the earlier and later works. The comparative tables of contents which are printed at the end of this Introduction may perhaps save the student some ungrateful labour, and show, in a graphic form, at all events the relative amount of space assigned to various subjects in the two works. The difference in the method of treatment, conclusions, and general tone can of course only be gathered ˙ by reading the different passages side by side. The results of such a reading are presented in the following pages.

5   Taking the ENQUIRY CONCERNING THE HUMAN UNDERSTANDING separately, we are at once struck by the entire omission of Bk. I, part ii of the Treatise. Space and time are not treated of at all in the Enquiry as independent subjects interesting in themselves; they are only introduced incidentally in §§ 124–5 of the Enquiry, as illustrating the absurdity of the abstract sciences and in support of a sceptical position.

We are also struck by the introduction of the two theological sections (x–xi) of the Enquiry, and by the very small space given to the general questions concerning knowledge and the relation of subject and object.

Sections 116–132, covering only seventeen pages in all, do duty in the Enquiry for the whole of Bk. I, part iv of the ˙ Treatise, where ninety-four pages are devoted to the same topics.

This wholesale omission and insertion cannot well be due to philosophical discontent with the positions or arguments, or to a general desire to fill up a gap in the system, but must be ascribed rather to a general desire, to make the Enquiry readable.   Parts ii and iv are certainly the hardest in the Treatise, and the least generally interesting to the *habitués* of coffee-houses, especially at a period when 'the greatest part of men have agreed to convert reading into an amusement;' whereas a lively and sceptical discussion of miracles and providence could hardly fail to find readers, attract attention, and excite that 'murmur among the zealots' by which the author desired to be distinguished.

Taking the two works rather more in detail, we find these notable differences :—

6   *Psychology.*   Even in the Treatise we feel that the introductory psychology is rather meagre and short to serve as a foundation for so large a system, but in the Enquiry it is still more cut down.

Thus the Enquiry omits the distinction between simple and complex ideas ; between impressions of sensation and reflexion, which is of importance afterwards for the explanation of the idea of necessary connexion; between ideas of memory and imagination : in the treatment of association little is said about causation as a principle of association, and the account of the products of association, the three classes of complex ideas, relations, modes and substances, and abstract ideas, disappears.

Thus the list of philosophic relations and the distinction between philosophic and natural relation are omitted, and do not appear at all in the Enquiry.   The question of abstraction is only alluded to incidentally near the end of the Enquiry (§§ 122 and 125 *n*).   Substance is passed

over, as it is also in § xii of the Enquiry, probably both
from the difficulty of the subject, and because in the
Enquiry Hume is not nearly so anxious to show that
the fundamental popular conceptions are fictitious. There
is something solid to which the popular conception of
causation can be reduced, but when substance and body
are analyzed, as they are in the Treatise, the importance
of the materials out of which they are said to be formed
is out of all proportion to the place which the finished
products occupy in thought and language.

The slight treatment of association again is quite characteristic of the temper of the Enquiry. The details of
psychical mechanism, which are rather tiresomely paraded
in the Treatise, are consistently passed over in the Enquiry,
notably so in the case of sympathy.

7 *Space and Time.* It must be admitted that the subject
of space and time, as treated in the Treatise, is not very
attractive. There is nothing in the Enquiry corresponding
to the forty-two pages of the Treatise, in which space and
time are treated, except two pages in § xii.

Of the philosophical importance of Hume's treatment
of them in the Treatise it is unnecessary to speak, it is
apparent from the large amount of criticism which Professor
Green thought fit to bestow on it. It is to be noted, however, that the account of causation which Hume gives afterwards in the Enquiry, is left hanging in the air when the
support of the theory of succession has been withdrawn.
The omission of the section on the ideas of existence and
external existence is, like the omission of the various
accounts of substance, only a part of Hume's avoidance of
the general question of the relation of knowledge and reality.

8 *Causation.* In the account of causation Hume passes

over the very interesting and fundamental question raised
in the Treatise of the position of cause in the fabric of
our knowledge. On p. 78 of the Treatise (Bk. I, iii, § 3;
cf. p. 157), he asks why a cause is always necessary, and
concludes that there is no reason for the presumption that
everything must have a cause. This conclusion he supports by his analysis of the idea of a particular cause, and
asserts again (p. 172) that there is 'no absolute metaphysical necessity' that one object should have another
associated with it in such a way that its idea shall determine the mind to form the idea of the other. This
conclusion is of the gravest importance for Hume's theory
of causation in general, and is difficult to reconcile with
his negation of the reality of chance and his assumption of
secret causes (Treatise, pp. 130, 132). His failure in the
Enquiry to take the opportunity of treating this question
over again is significant of the lower philosophic standard
of the later work, especially as he does take the opportunity
to add a good deal to his previous discussion of the origin
of the idea of power (Enquiry, §§ 51-3, 60 *n*; cf. Treatise,
p. 632, Appendix). In the same spirit the distinction
between essential and accidental circumstances, and the
question of the employment of general rules (Treatise,
pp. 145f, 173f), subjects of great speculative as well as
practical interest, are ignored in the Enquiry.

9   A good deal of psychological detail is omitted in the
Enquiry. Thus §§ v, ix, x and xiii of Bk. I, part iii, of the
Treatise are omitted bodily, partly no doubt to shorten
the discussion, and partly on Hume's new principle of
not trying to penetrate beneath the obvious explanations
of phenomena. He adds, however, a detailed discussion
(Enquiry, §§ 51-3) of the possibility of deriving the idea of

power from an internal impression, such as the feeling of
initiative or effort accompanying a bodily or mental movement. These sections would appear to be occasioned by
contemporary discussions, and are excellently expressed.
On the same footing stands the discussion of the theory of
occasional causes, which is very well done in §§ 54-7 of the
Enquiry (cf. Treatise, p. 171). The omission of the practical § xv of the Treatise, on the rules by which to judge of
causes and effects, appears rather strange, unless we regard
it as raising a difficult general question which Hume has
already shown his anxiety to avoid in his omission of § iii.
With regard to the account of the origin, in particular cases,
of the idea of cause and effect, there is little difference
between the Treatise and Enquiry, except that in the
Enquiry 'contiguity' practically drops out altogether. A
good deal was said about contiguity in § ix of the Treatise,
which disappears in the Enquiry; and again in the final
definitions of cause given in § xiv, pp. 170-172 of the
Treatise, contiguity appears on the same level as resemblance, whereas in the definitions given in the Enquiry,
§ 60, no mention is made of it at all.

10   A comparison of the definitions given on pp. 170-2 of
the Treatise and § 60 of the Enquiry, shows that in the
Enquiry the distinction between causation as a philosophical and a natural relation is altogether dropped. In
the Treatise this distinction is very hard to follow, and there
is little doubt that the sacrifice of it in the Enquiry is
deliberate. In the Enquiry Hume asserts more clearly
than in the Treatise (though with some of the old inconsistencies) that there is nothing at the bottom of causation
except a mental habit of transition or expectation, or, in
other words, a 'natural relation.' Thus the omission of the

chapter on the rules by which to judge of cause and effect and the sacrifice of contiguity are both part of the same policy : succession cannot be got rid of altogether, and this, it is true, is a philosophical relation ('Treatise, p. 14), but it is one which is a matter of perception rather than reasoning (Treatise, p. 73), and is not one which raises much dis-cussion—we 'seldom have much difficulty in discovering whether A or B came first, and you cannot strictly say that B was *more* consequent on A than C was, or vice versa. But men of science are very curious about contiguity, and the examination of it as a philosophical relation would often run counter to the connexions established by contiguity as a natural relation. Contiguity therefore drops out of the Enquiry as a philosophical relation, though it must be supposed to exert its influence as a natural relation (cf. Treatise, p. 92).

Resemblance was not treated in the Treatise as a philosophical relation, in connexion with causation, but rather as a natural relation, i. e. not as a relation between A and B which men of science would take into consideration, but as the relation between $a^1 b^1$, $a^2 b^2$, $a^3 b^3$, &c., which was the foundation of the unconscious habit of proceeding to assert $a^4 b^4$ or A B. This position is still more clearly given to resemblance in the Enquiry, where Hume asserts roundly that one instance is as good philosophically (or as we should say, 'scientifically') as a thousand (cf. Enquiry, § 31). The only effect of resemblance or repetition is to produce a habit.

Philosophical relations are those which a man of science perceives or establishes when he consciously compares one object with another. Natural relations are those which unconsciously join one idea to another in his mind. In the case of causation, therefore, a philosophical relation must be between A and B, a¹ and b¹, a² and b²: natural relation must be between one particular case of A B and another, e. g. between a¹ b¹ and a² b², a³ b³, &c. The philosophical relation of causation is what a man of science sees in one case of A B taken by itself, and that is nothing but succession and contiguity. Hume feeling the difficulty of maintaining philosophical relations at all, wisely says nothing in the Enquiry about their difference from natural relations, and says as little as possible about those elements of causation which he cannot spare, and which in the Treatise appeared as philosophical relations. The distinction in the Treatise is indeed most bewildering, but, with its disappearance in the Enquiry, the relation of causation becomes more completely subjective, and it becomes even more hard than in the Treatise to see how there can be any difference between real and apparent causes, or any room for concealed causes. On the other hand, it may be said that, so long as natural was opposed to philosophical relation, there was still possible an invidious contrast between the subjectivity of the one and the objectivity of the other, while in the Enquiry some credit is restored to causation, because nothing is said about its seven philosophical rivals. Both in the Enquiry and Treatise the operations of resemblance, contiguity and succession, are described in language which is far from precise and clear, and which justifies many of the lively strictures passed on the association theory by Mr. Bradley in his Principles of Logic; but it is certainly easier to grasp Hume's meaning in the Enquiry than in the Treatise, and a comparison of the passages containing the definitions is decidedly instructive.

11   It will be noted that in the Enquiry, §60, Hume interjects

a curious little explanation of his first definition : ' We may
define a cause to be an object followed by another, and
when all the objects similar to the first are followed by
objects similar to the second, *or, in other words, where if
the first object had not been, the second never had existed.*'
The words in italics can hardly be regarded as a paraphrase
or equivalent of the main definition, and must be added to
the rather large collection of unassimilated dicta which so
much occupied Professor Green.

12   *Liberty and necessity.*—Hume has certainly effected an
improvement in the Enquiry by bringing this subject into
closer connexion with his theory of causation.   In the
Treatise he deals with it under the general heading of the
'will and direct passions,' and with an interval of more
than 200 pages from the main treatment of cause.   The
only important differences between the two discussions of
the freedom of the will are (*a*) the omission in the Enquiry
of the preliminary definition of the will (Treatise, p. 399),
(*b*) the insertion in the Enquiry of the definition of ' liberty,'
§ 73, (*c*) the more emphatic assertion in the Enquiry that
the whole dispute is one of words, and that all men have really
been always agreed on the matter.   (Cf. Enquiry, §§ 62–3, 71,
73, and Treatise, pp. 399, 407, 409.)   (*d*) The development
of the religious aspect of the question, Enquiry, §§ 76–81.
To this nothing corresponds in the Treatise, and like the
following sections in the Enquiry it may be ascribed to
Hume's ambition to disturb ' the zealots ' at all costs.

The discussion has been carefully re-written in the
Enquiry, many of the illustrations used are different and
more elegant, and the whole section in the Enquiry is an
excellent instance of the general improvement in style and
construction which appears in the later work.

Miracles, providence, and a future state. §§ x and xi of the Enquiry, in which these subjects are treated, belong to Hume's applied philosophy, and, important and interesting as they are in themselves, they do not add anything to his general speculative position. Their insertion in the Enquiry is due doubtless rather to other considerations than to a simple desire to illustrate or draw corollaries from the philosophical principles laid down in the original work.

13 *Knowledge and reality.* § 12 of the Enquiry very inadequately represents the whole of Book I, part iv of the Treatise, occupying as it does only seventeen pages as against ninety-four in the earlier work. In details the correspondence is necessarily very imperfect.

Brevity is, it is true, legitimately attained in some cases by compression. Thus the rather rambling general discussions of Scepticism in the Treatise contained in § i and § vii (some eighteen pages) are fairly represented by § 116 and §§ 126-132 of the Enquiry (some nine pages). So also there is not much reason to complain of the abbreviation to one page of the criticism of the distinction between primary and secondary qualities (Treatise, § iv, pp. 225-231 ; Enquiry, § 122, pp. 154-5), this part of the Treatise being undeniably cumbrous. Two pages more in the Enquiry are occupied with an illustration of the absurdity of the abstract sciences, drawn from their doctrine of infinite divisibility, this having originally appeared in Book I, p. ii, § ii of the Treatise.

This leaves only §§ 117-121 and 123 of the Enquiry (about four pages) to do duty for the whole of §§ ii, iii, v, vi of the Treatise (some sixty-nine pages).

In the Enquiry Hume merely confines himself to asserting the opposition between the vulgar belief, based on instinct and natural propensity, in external objects on the one side, and the conclusions of philosophy, that we know nothing but perceptions in the mind, on the other side. He does not attempt any further investigation beyond rejecting an appeal to the veracity of God which was not mentioned in the Treatise (Enquiry, § 120), but simply falls back on the position that sceptical arguments, if they admit of no answer, at all events produce no conviction. Perhaps the most interesting part of the whole Treatise is that in which Hume tried to explain (§ ii, pp. 187–218) our belief in the existence of body, which he reduced to the continued and distinct existence of perceptions, by the influence of their constancy and coherence on our imagination. This is entirely dropped in the Enquiry, together with the account of our idea of substance (Treatise, § iii, 'Of the antient philosophy'), and of our idea of mind (Treatise, § vi, 'Of personal identity'). A considerable part of the discussion on the immateriality of the soul (Treatise, § v), may appear to us antiquated, just as it may fairly have appeared to Hume too dry for a popular work, and not absolutely necessary to his system. But it is not too much to say on the whole, that the omissions in § 12 of the Enquiry are alone amply sufficient to render it quite impossible to comply with Hume's wish and treat the Enquiry as representing the whole of his philosophic system.

14 THE DISSERTATION ON THE PASSIONS, first published in 1757, together with the Natural History of Religion and two essays on tragedy and taste, and printed in the edition of 1777 between the two Enquiries, is not reprinted in this volume.

It consists largely, as Mr. Grose says, of verbatim extracts from Bk. II of the Treatise, with some trifling verbal alterations.

As it stands, the Dissertation is a very uninteresting and unsatisfactory work. The portion of Bk. II of the Treatise which was perhaps of most general interest, namely the discussion of Liberty and Necessity, had been previously transferred to the Enquiry into Human Understanding, and so was no longer available for the Dissertation. But the Dissertation suffers, not only by this transference of matter, but also by omissions of other really important matters.

(1) In the Treatise an elaborate account was given of pride and humility, love and hatred, and an attempt was made to explain the mechanism of the passions, by the relation of impressions and ideas, which was at all events a serious essay towards something less superficial than the prevalent psychology. Its bearing on Hume's general system is, it is true, not very great and not at all clear, and it is easy to understand how, as a matter of literary policy, it was omitted by Hume. But in connexion with other omissions it has a decided philosophical significance.

(2) The psychology of *sympathy*, which occupies so much space in Bk. II, and on which so much depends in Bk. III of the Treatise, is almost entirely ignored in the Enquiry. How it is possible to find room for sympathy in so atomistic or individualistic a psychology as Hume's, is one of the most interesting questions which are raised by his system. How I can not only know but enter into the feelings of another person, when I can only know my own feelings, is indeed a problem worthy of grave consideration. When we come to consider the treatment of sympathy in the Enquiry concerning the Principles of Morals by the side of its treatment in the Treatise, we shall see reason to think

that Hume has very considerably modified his views, not only as to the functions of sympathy, but also as to the proper limits of psychological analysis.

(3) The discussion in the Treatise, Bk. II, § iii, of the relation of passion to reason is of great importance for the subsequent question of the source of moral distinctions, as also are the distinction between calm and violent passions and the identification of reason with the former; but the Dissertation is contented with the barest mention of them.

In general, we may say that, whereas Bk. II of the Treatise was not only valuable as an independent essay in psychology, and interesting from its wealth of observation and illustration, but also important from its preliminary treatment of questions which were going to be of vital importance in Bk. III, the Dissertation is neither interesting in itself nor of any assistance for the interpretation or criticism of the Enquiry concerning the Principles of Morals. The extent of its correspondence with Bk. II of the Treatise is shown in the accompanying comparative Table of Contents.

15 ENQUIRY CONCERNING THE PRINCIPLES OF MORALS.
Hume has recorded his own opinion that the Enquiry concerning the Principles of Morals was, of all his writings, 'historical, philosophical, or literary, incomparably the best.' It was first published in 1751, the corresponding book in the Treatise having been published in 1740. Hume himself considered that the failure of the Treatise 'had proceeded more from the manner than the matter,' and in this Enquiry it is evident that he has given the greatest attention to the style, and with such success as to justify Mr. Grose's estimate of him as 'the one master of philosophic English.'

It is far less easy to compare the matter of this Enquiry with that of Bk. III of the Treatise, because the earlier work has, in this case, been really re-written. The comparative Table of Contents will show in a graphic form the difficulty of making out a correspondence between them. The arrangement is largely different. The omissions are not in this case so important as the additions, and there is a great change in the proportions and emphasis with which various subjects are treated. There is also, the writer ventures to believe, a very remarkable change of tone or temper, which, even more than particular statements, leads him to suppose that the system of Morals in the Enquiry is really and essentially different from that in the Treatise.

16 In the Treatise nothing is more clear than his intention to reduce the various principles of human nature, which appear distinct to ordinary men, to some more general and underlying principle, and indeed his philosophy differed from that of the moral sense school, represented by Hutcheson, in precisely that particular. In other words, he attempted a philosophical explanation of human nature, and was not content to accept the ordinary distinctions of 'faculties' and 'senses' as final. Thus the temper of the Treatise is well expressed by his emphatic declaration (Bk. III, part iii, § 1, p. 578), that it is 'an inviolable maxim in philosophy, that where any particular cause is sufficient for an effect, we ought to rest satisfied with it, and ought not to multiply causes without necessity'; and again (Bk. II, part i, § iii, p. 282), 'we find in the course of nature that though the effects be many, the principles from which they arise are commonly but few and simple, and that it is the sign of an unskilful naturalist to have recourse to a different quality in order to explain every different operation. How much

more must this be true with regard to the human mind?'
(Cf. also Treatise, Bk. III, part iii, § ii, p. 473.)

With these passages we may compare, observing the
caution inculcated at the beginning of this Introduction,
§ 250 of the Enquiry, where speaking of self-love, he says,
'The obvious appearance of things ... must be admitted
till some hypothesis be discovered which, by penetrating
deeper into human nature, may prove the former affections to be nothing but modifications of the latter. All
attempts of this kind have hitherto proved fruitless, and
seem to have *proceeded entirely from that love of simplicity
which has been the source of so much false reasoning in philosophy.*' (Cf. § 9, 'Philosophers have sometimes carried
the matter too far by their passion for some one general
principle.')

Without laying undue stress on these express statements
(which go for less in Hume than in most authors), we can
hardly help feeling that Hume is approximating to the
position of Hutcheson, as expressed in his Preface to the
Essay on the Nature and Conduct of the Passions (p. ix,
ed. 3, Lond. 1742): 'Some strange love of simplicity in the
structure of human nature ... has engaged many writers to
pass over a great many simple Perceptions which we may
find in ourselves: ... had they ∴ considered our affections
without a previous notion that they were all from self-love,
they might have felt an ultimate desire of the happiness of
others as easily conceivable and as certainly implanted in
the human breast, though perhaps not so strong as self-
love.' (Cf. ib. p. xiv: 'This difficulty probably arises from
our previous notions of a small number of senses, so that
we are unwilling to have recourse in our theories to any
more; and rather strain out some explication of Moral

Ideas, with relation to some of the natural Powers of Perception universally acknowledged.')

17 This change of attitude is, I think, seen in several points, some of which have been already pointed out in dealing with the Dissertation on the Passions, and which are here only distinguished for convenience of reference.

Benevolence. In the Treatise there are passages, it is true, which seem to admit an original unaccountable instinct of benevolence (Treatise, Bk. II, part iii, § iii, p. 417; ib. § ix, p. 439; Bk. II, part ii, § vi, p. 368; cf. Bk. III, part ii, § i, p. 478). There are also passages which sternly limit its extent and influence. Thus he says (Treatise, Bk. III, part ii, § i, p. 481), 'In general it may be affirmed that there is no such passion in human minds as the love of mankind merely as such, independent of personal qualities, of services, or of relation to oneself. It is true there is no human and indeed no sensible creature whose happiness does not, in some measure, affect us, when brought near to us and represented in lively colours. But this proceeds merely from sympathy, and is no proof of such an universal affection to mankind, since this concern extends itself beyond our own species.' (Cf. Bk. III, part ii, § ii, p. 496.) With this we may compare the Enquiry, § 184, where he speaks of 'our natural philanthropy'; § 135, 'a feeling for the happiness of mankind and a resentment of their misery'; § 252, 'these and a thousand other instances are marks of a general benevolence in human nature.' (Cf. § 178 *n*; § 250 *n*.)

The fact that in the Enquiry Hume inserts a section on Benevolence (§ 2) before the treatment of Justice is in itself significant. In the Treatise benevolence is treated among the natural virtues and vices (Treatise, Bk. III, part iii,

§ iii, p. 602) immediately before 'natural abilities.' In the Enquiry it is treated as the chief of the social virtues, and though a main object of its treatment is to show its 'utility,' its independence is fully recognized.

18 But the impression produced by the comparison of such passages as the above is very much strengthened when we consider the functions and position of *Sympathy* in the Treatise and Enquiry respectively. It has been already noticed that in the Dissertation on the Passions sympathy was almost ignored, though it was perhaps the most important subject of Bk. II of the Treatise.

Speaking broadly, we may say that in the Treatise nothing more is clear than that sympathy is used as a solvent to reduce complex feelings to simpler elements. In the Enquiry sympathy is another name for social feeling, humanity, benevolence, natural philanthropy, rather than the name of the process by which the social feeling has been constructed out of non-social or individual feeling (§§ 180, 182, 186, 199, 203, 210, 221–3). Hume may have felt that the machinery assigned to sympathy in Bk. II of the Treatise did not work very well, and so have decided to get rid of it, but in so doing he may be said to have abandoned perhaps the most distinctive feature of his moral system as expounded in the Treatise, so that in the Enquiry there is little to distinguish his theory from the ordinary moral-sense theory, except perhaps a more destructive use of 'utility.' In the Treatise his difference from the moral-sense school lay precisely in his attempt to resolve social feeling into a simple sensitivity to pleasure and pain, which has become complicated and transformed by sympathy. In reading Hutcheson we feel that he makes out a good case for his 'benevolence' against Hobbes and Mandeville and the more insidious selfishness of Shaftesbury, but that it would fall an easy prey to the 'sympathy' of Hume's Treatise.

19   *Self-love* is much more fully and fairly dealt with by Hume in the Enquiry than in the Treatise.   He had declined, even in the Treatise, with excellent good sense, to accept the popular reduction of benevolence as given by the selfish school, but he certainly tried to reduce benevolence to something which was neither selfish nor unselfish, but rather physical.

In the Enquiry (Bk. V, §§ 173-8, and App. ii, §§ 247-254) he carries the war into the enemy's camp, and introduces the conception of self-love which we find in·Hutcheson's later works, and especially in Butler.   Section 253 is especially remarkable, insisting as it does on the necessity of appetites antecedent to self-love.   The germ of the same thought is perhaps to be found in an obscure passage in the Treatise (Bk. III, part ii, § i, p. 478), though it is used for a significantly different purpose.

Benevolence is suggested in the Enquiry as the primary, and self-love as the secondary passion, and the suggestion is supported by the appeal to accept 'the simplest and most obvious cause which can be assigned' for any passion or operation of the human mind.

It is true that he makes even freer use of *Utility* in the Enquiry than in the Treatise, and that it would be easy to draw consequences from this principle which would neutralize the concessions made to benevolence, but he is content himself to leave it without developement, and to say in effect that utility pleases simply because it does please.

20   His tenderness towards benevolence is also seen in his treatment of *Justice*.   In the Treatise he insisted vigorously,

though not very intelligibly, that justice was not a natural but only an artificial virtue, and it is pretty plain that he meant to be offensive in doing so. His argument in the Treatise was, to say the least, awkward, and he may have been glad to get rid of an ungainly and unnecessary discussion. In the Enquiry he dismisses the question in a few words as a vain one. (§ 258), and contents himself with pointing out the superior sociality of justice as compared with benevolence (§§ 255-6).

21   *Reason.* He devotes much less space in the Enquiry to proving that moral distinctions are not derived from reason, than to showing that they are derived from a sentiment of humanity. He is more tolerant to the claims of reason, and shows some approach to the indifference of Butler. 'These arguments on each side are so plausible that I am apt to suspect they may, the one as well as the other, be solid and satisfactory, and that reason and sentiment concur in almost all moral determinations and conclusions' (§ 137). In the same place he gives reason an important function in the correction of our sentiments of moral and natural beauty, a point which is of great importance in the moral philosophy of that time, and indeed was not ignored in the Treatise. Similarly in the Treatise he laid some stress on the identity of what was usually called 'reason' with the calm passions (Bk. II, part iii, § iii, p. 417; ib. § viii, p. 437), whereas he only mentions it incidentally in the Enquiry in connexion with strength of mind (§ 196).

22   The old difficulty about '*general rules,*' 'the general and unalterable point of view,' re-appears in the Enquiry, though I think it is dealt with in a manner quite foreign to the Treatise. In the Treatise the universality of our moral judgements and their detachment from private interest was

accounted for by sympathy (Treatise, Bk. III, part ii, § ii, p. 500; Bk. III, part iii, § i, p. 577; § vi, p. 618). But sympathy itself varies with time, place and person, and consequently requires correction, which is supplied by the use of general rules (Bk. III, part iii, § i, pp. 581-5). How these corrective rules are obtained he does not explain in the Treatise, and indeed they seem to work in a circle with sympathy. In the Enquiry they again appear, and are in the first place ascribed to the 'intercourse of sentiments in society and conversation' (§ 186), arising apparently in the same way as 'general ideas,' which are really only particular ideas with their particularity rubbed off by wear and tear. But in §§ 221-2 of the Enquiry he asserts the universality of moral judgements in quite a new style. 'The notion of morals implies some sentiment common to all mankind which recommends the same object to general approbation and makes every man, or most men, agree in the same opinion or decision concerning it. It also implies some sentiment, so universal and comprehensive as to extend to all mankind, and render the actions and conduct even of persons the most remote, an object of applause and censure. . . . These two requisites belong alone to the sentiment of Humanity.' This sentiment is the only ' universal principle of the human frame,' and ' can alone be the foundation of morals or of any general system of blame or praise.' 'One man's ambition is not another's ambition, nor will the same event or object satisfy both: but the humanity of one man is the humanity of every one, and the same object touches the passion in all human creatures.' This may not be the 'moral sense,' but it certainly is not the doctrine of the Treatise.

23   There does not seem to be any trace in the Enquiry of

the appeal to the 'natural and *usual* force of the passions,' as the standard of morals, of which considerable use is made in the Treatise, and which has been considered to brand Hume's moral system as one of sheer respectability (Treatise, Bk. III, part ii, § i, pp. 483–4 ; § ii, p. 488 ; § v, p. 518 ; § vi, p. 532).

24   The interest of Hume's philosophical writings must not be judged by the dryness of the foregoing discussion of them. The question of the relation of the two versions with which Hume himself has endowed and puzzled us, appears of sufficient general interest to warrant a serious examination. But such questions cannot be decided by general impressions, and this Introduction aims at supplying, or rather indicating, the material for a more exact determination of Hume's relations to himself, than has been previously attempted.   The writer has also had the temerity to relieve the rather mechanical toil of tabulating differences and correspondences by attempts to distinguish the purely philosophical from the non-philosophical and personal considerations which influenced a philosopher who was often both more and less than a philosopher.   How much in the matter and manner of Hume's work is due to peculiarities of his character is hard to say, but the personal element continually challenges, even if it eludes, our appreciation.

The Introduction undoubtedly supposes that the reader has some acquaintance with the Treatise, and may serve as a guide to those students who wish to see for themselves what Hume's last word on philosophy was.   The present Edition also is intended rather as a recognition of that wish than as a concession to those who would substitute the Enquiries for the Treatise as the authoritative exposition of

Hume's system. It would be a considerable misfortune for our native philosophy if the Treatise were left unread. But the Treatise is hard, and many of us are weak, and it is better to read Hume in the Enquiries than not to read him at all. By those who begin on the Enquiries the Introduction may be read, as it were, backwards, and it may, perhaps, serve to point out the road to a fuller knowledge of a philosopher, who, at his greatest, is very great indeed.

OXFORD, *Nov.* 1893.

Comparative Tables of the Contents of the Treatise *and of the* Enquiries *and* Dissertation on the Passions.

TABLE I.

Comparison of the Enquiry Concerning Human Understanding (*according to the marginal sections of the present edition*), *with Book I of the* Treatise on Human Nature (*according to the pages of the* Clarendon Press *edition, Oxford,* 1888 *and* 1896).

Enquiry.	Section	Page.	Treatise.
§ i. Of the different species of philosophy.	1–10	xvii–xxiii	Introduction.
			Part i. Of ideas, their origin, composition, connexion, abstraction, &c., pp. 1–25.
§ ii. Of the origin of ideas.	11–20	1–7	§ i. Of the origin of our ideas.
		7, 8	§ ii. Division of the subject.
		8–10	§ iii. Of the ideas of the memory and imagination.
§ iii. Of the association of ideas.	18–19	10–13	§ iv. Of the connexion or association of ideas.
		13–15	§ v. Of relations.
		15–17	§ vi. Of modes and substances.
	122–125 n.	17–26	§ vii. Of abstract ideas.
			Part ii. Of the ideas of space and time, pp. 26–68
		26–28	§ i. Of the infinite divisibility of our ideas of space and time.
	(124–5)	29–33	§ ii. Of the infinite divisibility of space and time
		33–39	§ iii. Of the other qualities of our ideas of space and time.
		39–53	§ iv. Objections answered.

c

TABLE I.   XXXV

Enquiry.	Section.	Page.	Treatise.
	117–123	187–218	§ ii. Of scepticism with regard to the senses. (Body, and continued and distinct existence of perceptions; constancy and coherence.)
		219–225	§ iii. Of the antient philosophy. (Substance and quality.)
	122	225–231	§ iv. Of the modern philosophy. (Primary and secondary qualities.)
Part ii, 124–129. (Space and time.) '	124,125 {	(Book I, part ii, § 2.)	
		232–251	§ v. Of the immateriality of the soul (Existence and perception.)
		251–263	§ vi. Of personal identity.
Part iii, 129–132.	126–132	263–274	§ vii. Conclusion of this book.

TABLE II.

Comparison of Book II of the Treatise on Human Nature (*according to the pages of the Clarendon Press edition*), *with the* Dissertation on the Passions (*according to the pages of the collected edition of* 1777, *London, vol.* ii).

	Treatise page.	Dissertation page.
Treatise, Book II. ' Of the Passions,' pp. 275–454		
Part i. Of Pride and Humility, pp. 275–328		
§ i. Division of the subject.	275–277	
§ii. Of Pride and Humility : their objects and causes	277–279	
§ iii. Whence their objects and causes are derived.	280–282	
§ iv. Of the relations of impressions and ideas.	282–284	184–186

TABLE II. xxxvii

TABLE III.

Comparison of the Enquiry Concerning the Principles of Morals *with* Book III of the Treatise on Human Nature.

Enquiry.	Section.	Page.	Treatise.
An Enquiry concerning the principles of morals.	133–299	455–621	*Book III. Of morals.*
			Part i. Of virtue and vice in general, pp 455–476.
§ i. Of the general principles of morals.	133–38	455–470	§ i. Moral distinctions not derived from reason
Appendix i. Concerning moral sentiment.	234–46	470–476	§ ii. Moral distinction derived from a moral sense.
	136	457	
	236, 237	6–468 (458	
	238	463	
	239	(475	
	240		
	241	459	
	242		
	243	466, 467	
	244, 245		
	246	(465)	
§ ii. Of benevolence.	139–144	(602–6)	
§ iii. Of justice. Part i, 145-153 Part ii. 154-163. Appendix iii. Some further considerations with regard to justice.	145–63 255–60	477–573	*Part ii. Of justice and injustice.*
	258	477–484	§ i Justice whether a natural or artificial virtue
	(253)	477–480	
	(254, cf 235)	480–483	
	255	(481, 82)	
		484–501	§ ii. Of the origin of justice and property.
	145–149	484–489 495, 496	
	150, 151	493	

TABLE III. xxxix

Enquiry.	Section.	Page.	Treatise.
	152		
	153	(493)	
	256	{ 497, cf. 532	
	174	498	
	257	490	
	173	500	
	154–162	501–513	§ iii. Of the rules which determine property.
	259, 260	514 516	§ iv. Of the transference of property by consent.
	(257)	{ 516–525 (cf. 490)	§ v. Of the obligation of promises.
		526–534	§ vi. Some further reflections concerning justice and injustice.
	(160–62)	528, 529	
	256	532	
§ iv. Of political society.	164–171		
		534–539	§ vii. Of the origin of government.
		539–549	§ viii. Of the sources of allegiance.
	164	549–553	§ ix. Of the measures of allegiance.
		553–567	§ x. Of the objects of allegiance.
	165	567–569	§ xi. Of the laws of nations.
	166–168	570–573	§ xii Of chastity and modesty.
			Part iii. Of the other Virtues and Vices, pp. 574–621.
§ v. Why utility pleases. Part i, 172–177. Part ii, 178–190.	172–190	574–591	§ i. Of the origin of the natural virtues and vices.
	173–190	577–591	
	173	500, 578	
	174	498–501	
	257	579	
	185, 186	580–583	
	175	581, 582	
	176		
	177		
	178–181	575	
	182	585	

Enquiry.	Section.	Page.	Treatise.
	182, 183	576, 577	
	184		
	185	580–584	
	185 n.	584, 585	
	186	581, 603	
	187–190		
Appendix ii. Of self-love.	247–254		
§ vi. Of qualities useful to ourselves.	191–202		
Part i, 191–199			
Part ii, 200–202.	198	610, 612	
§ vii. Of qualities immediately agreeable to ourselves.	203–210	592–606	§ ii. Of greatness of mind.
	203	592, 611	
	204	599	
	205	600	
	207	604	
	208		
§ viii. Of qualities immediately agreeable to others.	(139–44) 211–216	602–606	§ iii. Of goodness and benevolence.
		606–614	§ iv. Of natural abilities.
	212	611	
	211, 213 214	596, 597	
	215, 216	611, 612 (617)	
Appendix iv. Of some verbal disputes.	261–267	606–610	
	261–264	606, 607	
	265	607, 608	
	266	609	
	267	608, 609	
	268	609	
§ ix. Conclusion.	217–233		
Part i, 217–227.		614–617	§ v. Some further reflections concerning the natural virtues.
	(217–19)	614, 615 618–621	§ vi. Conclusion of this book.
	220–227	618	
Part ii, 228–233	228–233	619–621	

ESSAYS

AND

TREATISES

ON

SEVERAL SUBJECTS.

By DAVID HUME, Efq;

VOL. II.

CONTAINING

An ENQUIRY concerning HUMAN
UNDERSTANDING;

A DISSERTATION on the PASSIONS;

An ENQUIRY concerning the PRINCIPLES
of MORALS;

AND

The NATURAL HISTORY of RELIGION.

A NEW EDITION.

LONDON:

Printed for T. CADELL, in the Strand: and
A. DONALDSON, and W. CREECH, at Edinburgh.
MDCCLXXVII.

ADVERTISEMENT

Most of the principles, and reasonings, contained in this volume, were published in a work in three volumes, called A Treatise of Human Nature: *A work which the Author had projected before he left College, and which he wrote and published not long after. But not finding it successful, he was sensible of his error in going to the press too early, and he cast the whole anew in the following pieces, where some negligences in his former reasoning and more in the expression, are, he hopes, corrected. Yet several writers, who have honoured the Author's Philosophy with answers, have taken care to direct all their batteries against that juvenile work, which the Author never acknowledged, and have affected to triumph in any advantages, which, they imagined, they had obtained over it: A practice very contrary to all rules of candour and fair-dealing, and a strong instance of those polemical artifices, which a bigotted zeal thinks itself authorized to employ. Henceforth, the Author desires, that the following Pieces may alone be regarded as containing his philosophical sentiments and principles.*

THE

CONTENTS

AN ENQUIRY CONCERNING HUMAN UNDERSTANDING.

AN ENQUIRY CONCERNING THE PRINCIPLES OF MORALS.

B 2

4   *CONTENTS.*

AN ENQUIRY

CONCERNING

HUMAN UNDERSTANDING

—◆—

SECTION I.

OF THE DIFFERENT SPECIES OF PHILOSOPHY.

1   MORAL philosophy, or the science of human nature, may
be treated after two different manners; each of which has
its peculiar merit, and may contribute to the entertainment,
instruction, and reformation of mankind. The one considers man chiefly as born for action; and as influenced in
his measures by taste and sentiment; pursuing one object,
and avoiding another, according to the value which these
objects seem to possess, and according to the light in
which they present themselves. As virtue, of all objects,
is allowed to be the most valuable, this species of philosophers paint her in the most amiable colours; borrowing
all helps from poetry and eloquence, and treating their
subject in an easy and obvious manner, and such as is
best fitted to please the imagination, and engage the
affections. They select the most striking observations and
instances from common life; place opposite characters in
a proper contrast; and alluring us into the paths of virtue
by the views of glory and happiness, direct our steps in

these paths by the soundest precepts and most illustrious examples. They make us *feel* the difference between vice and virtue; they excite and regulate our sentiments; and so they can but bend our hearts to the love of probity and true honour, they think, that they have fully attained the end of all their labours.

2   The other species of philosophers consider man in the light of a reasonable rather than an active being, and endeavour to form his understanding more than cultivate his manners. They regard human nature as a subject of speculation; and with a narrow scrutiny examine it, in order to find those principles, which regulate our understanding, excite our sentiments, and make us approve or blame any particular object, action, or behaviour. They think it a reproach to all literature, that philosophy should not yet have fixed, beyond controversy, the foundation of morals, reasoning, and criticism; and should for ever talk of truth and falsehood, vice and virtue, beauty and deformity, without being able to determine the source of these distinctions. While they attempt this arduous task, they are deterred by no difficulties; but proceeding from particular instances to general principles, they still push on their enquiries to principles more general, and rest not satisfied till they arrive at those original principles, by which, in every science, all human curiosity must be bounded. Though their speculations seem abstract, and even unintelligible to common readers, they aim at the approbation of the learned and the wise; and think themselves sufficiently compensated for the labour of their whole lives, if they can discover some hidden truths, which may contribute to the instruction of posterity.

3   It is certain that the easy and obvious philosophy will always, with the generality of mankind, have the preference above the accurate and abstruse; and by many will be recommended, not only as more agreeable, but more useful

than the other. It enters more into common life; moulds the heart and affections; and, by touching those principles which actuate men, reforms their conduct, and brings them nearer to that model of perfection which it describes. On the contrary, the abstruse philosophy, being founded on a turn of mind, which cannot enter into business and action, vanishes when the philosopher leaves the shade, and comes into open day; nor can its principles easily retain any influence over our conduct and behaviour. The feelings of our heart, the agitation of our passions, the vehemence of our affections, dissipate all its conclusions, and reduce the profound philosopher to a mere plebeian.

4   This also must be confessed, that the most durable, as well as justest fame, has been acquired by the easy philosophy, and that abstract reasoners seem hitherto to have enjoyed only a momentary reputation, from the caprice or ignorance of their own age, but have not been able to support their renown with more equitable posterity. It is easy for a profound philosopher to commit a mistake in his subtile reasonings; and one mistake is the necessary parent of another, while he pushes on his consequences, and is not deterred from embracing any conclusion, by its unusual appearance, or its contradiction to popular opinion. But a philosopher, who purposes only to represent the common sense of mankind in more beautiful and more engaging colours, if by accident he falls into error, goes no farther; but renewing his appeal to common sense, and the natural sentiments of the mind, returns into the right path, and secures himself from any dangerous illusions. The fame of Cicero flourishes at present; but that of Aristotle is utterly decayed. La Bruyere passes the seas, and still maintains his reputation: But the glory of Malebranche is confined to his own nation, and to his own age. And Addison, perhaps, will be read with pleasure, when Locke shall be entirely forgotten.

The mere philosopher is a character, which is commonly but little acceptable in the world, as being supposed to contribute nothing either to the advantage or pleasure of society; while he lives remote from communication with mankind, and is wrapped up in principles and notions equally remote from their comprehension. On the other hand, the mere ignorant is still more despised; nor is any thing deemed a surer sign of an illiberal genius in an age and nation where the sciences flourish, than to be entirely destitute of all relish for those noble entertainments. The most perfect character is supposed to lie between those extremes; retaining an equal ability and taste for books, company, and business; preserving in conversation that discernment and delicacy which arise from polite letters; and in business, that probity and accuracy which are the natural result of a just philosophy. In order to diffuse and cultivate so accomplished a character, nothing can be more useful than compositions of the easy style and manner, which draw not too much from life, require no deep application or retreat to be comprehended, and send back the student among mankind full of noble sentiments and wise precepts, applicable to every exigence of human life. By means of such compositions, virtue becomes amiable, science agreeable, company instructive, and retirement entertaining.

Man is a reasonable being; and as such, receives from science his proper food and nourishment: But so narrow are the bounds of human understanding, that little satisfaction can be hoped for in this particular, either from the extent of security or his acquisitions. Man is a sociable, no less than a reasonable being: But neither can he always enjoy company agreeable and amusing, or preserve the proper relish for them. Man is also an active being; and from that disposition, as well as from the various necessities of human life, must submit to business and occupation:

But the mind requires some relaxation, and cannot always support its bent to care and industry. It seems, then, that nature has pointed out a mixed kind of life as most suitable to the human race, and secretly admonished them to allow none of these biasses to *draw* too much, so as to incapacitate them for other occupations and entertainments. Indulge your passion for science, says she, but let your science be human, and such as may have a direct reference to action and society. Abstruse thought and profound researches I prohibit, and will severely punish, by the pensive melancholy which they introduce, by the endless uncertainty in which they involve you, and by the cold reception which your pretended discoveries shall meet with, when communicated. Be a philosopher; but, amidst all your philosophy, be still a man.

5   Were the generality of mankind contented to prefer the easy philosophy to the abstract and profound, without throwing any blame or contempt on the latter, it might not be improper, perhaps, to comply with this general opinion, and allow every man to enjoy, without opposition, his own taste and sentiment. But as the matter is often carried farther, even to the absolute rejecting of all profound reasonings, or what is commonly called *metaphysics*, we shall now proceed to consider what can reasonably be pleaded in their behalf.

We may begin with observing, that one considerable advantage, which results from the accurate and abstract philosophy, is, its subserviency to the easy and humane; which, without the former, can never attain a sufficient degree of exactness in its sentiments, precepts, or reasonings. All polite letters are nothing but pictures of human life in various attitudes and situations; and inspire us with different sentiments, of praise or blame, admiration or ridicule, according to the qualities of the object, which they set before us. An artist must be better qualified to succeed in this undertaking, who, besides a delicate taste and a quick apprehension, possesses an accurate knowledge of the internal fabric, the operations of the understanding, the workings of the passions, and the various species of sentiment which discriminate vice and virtue. How painful soever this inward search or enquiry may appear, it becomes, in some measure, requisite to those, who would describe with success the obvious and outward appearances of life and manners. The anatomist presents to the eye the most hideous and disagreeable objects; but his science is useful to the painter in delineating even a Venus or an Helen. While the latter employs all the richest colours of his art, and gives his figures the most graceful and engaging airs; he must still carry his attention to the inward structure of the human body, the position of the muscles, the fabric of the bones, and the use and figure of every part or organ. Accuracy is, in every case, advantageous to beauty, and just reasoning to delicate sentiment. In vain would we exalt the one by depreciating the other.

Besides, we may observe, in every art or profession, even those which most concern life or action, that a spirit of accuracy, however acquired, carries all of them nearer their perfection, and renders them more subservient to the interests of society. And though a philosopher may live remote from business, the genius of philosophy, if carefully cultivated by several, must gradually diffuse itself throughout the whole society, and bestow a similar correctness on every art and calling. The politician will acquire greater foresight and subtility, in the subdividing and balancing of power; the lawyer more method and finer principles in his reasonings; and the general more regularity in his discipline, and more caution in his plans and operations. The stability of modern governments above the ancient, and the accuracy of modern philosophy, have improved, and probably will still improve, by similar gradations.

6 Were there no advantage to be reaped from these studies, beyond the gratification of an innocent curiosity, yet ought not even this to be despised; as being one accession to those few safe and harmless pleasures, which are bestowed on human race. The sweetest and most inoffensive path of life leads through the avenues of science and learning; and whoever can either remove any obstructions in this way, or open up any new prospect, ought so far to be esteemed a benefactor to mankind. And though these researches may appear painful and fatiguing, it is with some minds as with some bodies, which being endowed with vigorous and florid health, require severe exercise, and reap a pleasure from what, to the generality of mankind, may seem burdensome and laborious. Obscurity, indeed, is painful to the mind as well as to the eye; but to bring light from obscurity, by whatever labour, must needs be delightful and rejoicing.

But this obscurity in the profound and abstract philosophy, is objected to, not only as painful and fatiguing, but as the inevitable source of uncertainty and error. Here indeed lies the justest and most plausible objection against a considerable part of metaphysics, that they are not properly a science; but arise either from the fruitless efforts of human vanity, which would penetrate into subjects utterly inaccessible to the understanding, or from the craft of popular superstitions, which, being unable to defend themselves on fair ground, raise these intangling brambles to cover and protect their weakness. Chaced from the open country, these robbers fly into the forest, and lie in wait to break in upon every unguarded avenue of the mind, and overwhelm it with religious fears and prejudices. The stoutest antagonist, if he remit his watch a moment, is oppressed. And many, through cowardice and folly, open the gates to the enemies, and willingly receive them with reverence and submission, as their legal sovereigns.

But is this a sufficient reason, why philosophers should desist from such researches, and leave superstition still in possession of her retreat? Is it not proper to draw an opposite conclusion, and perceive the necessity of carrying the war into the most secret recesses of the enemy? In vain do we hope, that men, from frequent disappointment, will at last abandon such airy sciences, and discover the proper province of human reason. For, besides, that many persons find too sensible an interest in perpetually recalling such topics; besides this, I say, the motive of blind despair can never reasonably have place in the sciences; since, however unsuccessful former attempts may have proved, there is still room to hope, that the industry, good fortune, or improved sagacity of succeeding generations may reach discoveries unknown to former ages. Each adventurous genius will still leap at the arduous prize, and find himself stimulated, rather that discouraged, by the failures of his predecessors; while he hopes that the glory of achieving so hard an adventure is reserved for him alone. The only method of freeing learning, at once, from these abstruse questions, is to enquire seriously into the nature of human understanding, and show, from an exact analysis of its powers and capacity, that it is by no means fitted for such remote and abstruse subjects. We must submit to this fatigue, in order to live at ease ever after: And must cultivate true metaphysics with some care, in order to destroy the false and adulterate. Indolence, which, to some persons, affords a safeguard against this deceitful philosophy, is, with others, overbalanced by curiosity; and despair, which, at some moments, prevails, may give place afterwards to sanguine hopes and expectations. Accurate and just reasoning is the only catholic remedy, fitted for all persons and all dispositions; and is alone able to subvert that abstruse philosophy and metaphysical jargon, which, being mixed up with popular superstition, renders it in a manner impenetrable to careless reasoners, and gives it the air of science and wisdom.

8   Besides this advantage of rejecting, after deliberate enquiry, the most uncertain and disagreeable part of learning, there are many positive advantages, which result from an accurate scrutiny into the powers and faculties of human nature. It is remarkable concerning the operations of the mind, that, though most intimately present to us, yet, whenever they become the object of reflexion, they seem involved in obscurity; nor can the eye readily find those lines and boundaries, which discriminate and distinguish them. The objects are too fine to remain long in the same aspect or situation; and must be apprehended in an instant, by a superior penetration, derived from nature, and improved by habit and reflexion. It becomes, therefore, no inconsiderable part of science barely to know the different operations of the mind, to separate them from each other, to class them under their proper heads, and to correct all that seeming disorder, in which they lie involved, when made the object of reflexion and enquiry. This talk of ordering and distinguishing, which has no merit, when performed with regard to external bodies, the objects of our senses, rises in its value, when directed towards the operations of the mind, in proportion to the difficulty and labour, which we meet with in performing it. And if we can go no farther than this mental geography, or delineation of the distinct parts and powers of the mind, it is at least a satisfaction to go so far; and the more obvious this science may appear (and it is by no means obvious) the more contemptible still must the ignorance of it be esteemed, in all pretenders to learning and philosophy.

Nor can there remain any suspicion, that this science is uncertain and chimerical; unless we should entertain such a scepticism as is entirely subversive of all speculation, and even action. It cannot be doubted, that the mind

is endowed with several powers and faculties, that these
powers are distinct from each other, that what is really
distinct to the immediate perception may be distinguished
by reflexion; and consequently, that there is a truth and
falsehood in all propositions on this subject, and a truth
and falsehood, which lie not beyond the compass of human
understanding. There are many obvious distinctions of
this kind, such as those between the will and understanding,
the imagination and passions, which fall within the comprehension of every human creature; and the finer and
more philosophical distinctions are no less real and certain,
though more difficult to be comprehended. Some instances,
especially late ones, of success in these enquiries, may give
us a juster notion of the certainty and solidity of this branch
of learning. And shall we esteem it worthy the labour of
a philosopher to give us a true system of the planets, and
adjust the position and order of those remote bodies;
while we affect to overlook those, who, with so much
success, delineate the parts of the mind, in which we are so
intimately concerned?

But may we not hope, that philosophy, if cultivated with
care, and encouraged by the attention of the public, may
carry its researches still farther, and discover, at least in
some degree, the secret springs and principles, by which the
human mind is actuated in its operations? Astronomers
had long contented themselves with proving, from the
phaenomena, the true motions, order, and magnitude of
the heavenly bodies: Till a philosopher, at last, arose,
who seems, from the happiest reasoning, to have also determined the laws and forces, by which the revolutions of the
planets are governed and directed. The like has been
performed with regard to other parts of nature. And there
is no reason to despair of equal success in our enquiries
concerning the mental powers and economy, if prosecuted
with equal capacity and caution. It is probable, that one

operation and principle of the mind depends on another; which, again, may be resolved into one more general and universal: And how far these researches may possibly be carried, it will be difficult for us, before, or even after, a careful trial, exactly to determine. This is certain, that attempts of this kind are every day made even by those who philosophize the most negligently: And nothing can be more requisite than to enter upon the enterprize with thorough care and attention; that, if it lie within the compass of human understanding, it may at last be happily achieved; if not, it may, however, be rejected with some confidence and security. This last conclusion, surely, is not desirable; nor ought it to be embraced too rashly. For how much must we diminish from the beauty and value of this species of philosophy, upon such a supposition? Moralists have hitherto been accustomed, when they considered the vast multitude and diversity of those actions that excite our approbation or dislike, to search for some common principle, on which this variety of sentiments might depend. And though they have sometimes carried the matter too far, by their passion for some one general principle; it must, however, be confessed, that they are excusable in expecting to find some general principles, into which all the vices and virtues were justly to be resolved. The like has been the endeavour of critics, logicians, and even politicians: Nor have their attempts been wholly unsuccessful; though perhaps longer time, greater accuracy, and more ardent application may bring these sciences still nearer their perfection. To throw up at once all pretensions of this kind may justly be deemed more rash, precipitate, and dogmatical, than even the boldest and most affirmative philosophy, that has ever attempted to impose its crude dictates and principles on mankind.

10　　What though these reasonings concerning human nature seem abstract, and of difficult comprehension? This affords

no presumption of their falsehood. On the contrary,
seems impossible, that what has hitherto escaped so ma
wise and profound philosophers can be very obvious ai
easy. And whatever pains these researches may cost us, '
may think ourselves sufficiently rewarded, not only in poi
of profit but of pleasure, if, by that means, we can ma
any addition to our stock of knowledge, in subjects
such unspeakable importance.

But as, after all, the abstractedness of these speculatio
is no recommendation, but rather a disadvantage to the
and as this difficulty may perhaps be surmounted by ca
and art, and the avoiding of all unnecessary detail, we hav
in the following enquiry, attempted to throw some lig
upon subjects, from which uncertainty has hitherto deterr
the wise, and obscurity the ignorant. Happy, if we c
unite the boundaries of the different species of philosopt
by reconciling profound enquiry with clearness, and tru
with novelty ! And still more happy, if, reasoning in tl
easy manner, we can undermine the foundations of
abstruse philosophy, which seems to have hitherto serv
only as a shelter to superstition, and a cover to absurdi
and error !

SECTION II.

OF THE ORIGIN OF IDEAS.

11   EVERY one will readily allow, that there is a considerable difference between the perceptions of the mind, when a man feels the pain of excessive heat, or the pleasure of moderate warmth, and when he afterwards recalls to his memory this sensation, or anticipates it by his imagination. These faculties may mimic or copy the perceptions of the senses; but they never can entirely reach the force and vivacity of the original sentiment. The utmost we say of them, even when they operate with greatest vigour, is, that they represent their object in so lively a manner, that we could *almost* say we feel or see it: But, except the mind be disordered by disease or madness, they never can arrive at such a pitch of vivacity, as to render these perceptions altogether undistinguishable. All the colours of poetry, however splendid, can never paint natural objects in such a manner as to make the description be taken for a real landskip. The most lively thought is still inferior to the dullest sensation.

We may observe a like distinction to run through all the other perceptions of the mind. A man in a fit of anger, is actuated in a very different manner from one who only thinks of that emotion. If you tell me, that any person is in love, I easily understand your meaning, and form a just conception of his situation; but never can mistake that conception for the real disorders and agitations of the passion. When we reflect on our past sentiments and

c

affections, our thought is a faithful mirror, and co]
objects truly; but the colours which it employs ar
and dull, in comparison of those in which our origir
ceptions were clothed. It requires no nice discernn
metaphysical head to mark the distinction between t]

12   Here therefore we may divide all the perceptions
mind into two classes or species, which are disting
by their different degrees of force and vivacity. T
forcible and lively are commonly denominated *Thou
Ideas.* The other species want a name in our lai
and in most others; I suppose, because it was not r
for any, but philosophical purposes, to rank them
a general term or appellation. Let us, therefore, use
freedom, and call them *Impressions*; employing tha
in a sense somewhat different from the usual. By tl
impression, then, I mean all our more lively perce
when we hear, or see, or feel, or love, or hate, or
or will. And impressions are distinguished from
which are the less lively perceptions, of which '
conscious, when we reflect on any of those sensat.
movements above mentioned.

13   Nothing, at first view, may seem more unbounde
the thought of man, which not only escapes all
power and authority, but is not even restrained witl
limits of nature and reality. To form monsters, ai
incongruous shapes and appearances, costs the imag
no more trouble than to conceive the most natui
familiar objects. And while the body is confined
planet, along which it creeps with pain and difficul
thought can in an instant transport us into the most
regions of the universe; or even beyond the univer:
the unbounded chaos, where nature is supposed tc
total confusion. What never was seen, or heard (
yet be conceived; nor is any thing beyond the pc
thought, except what implies an absolute contradictic

But though our thought seems to possess this unbounded liberty, we shall find, upon a nearer examination, that it is really confined within very narrow limits, and that all this creative power of the mind amounts to no more than the faculty of compounding, transposing, augmenting, or diminishing the materials afforded us by the senses and experience. When we think of a golden mountain, we only join two consistent ideas, *gold*, and *mountain*, with which we were formerly acquainted. A virtuous horse we can conceive; because, from our own feeling, we can conceive virtue; and this we may unite to the figure and shape of a horse, which is an animal familiar to us. In short, all the materials of thinking are derived either from our outward or inward sentiment: the mixture and composition of these belongs alone to the mind and will. Or, to express myself in philosophical language, all our ideas or more feeble perceptions are copies of our impressions or more lively ones.

14   To prove this, the two following arguments will, I hope, be sufficient. First, when we analyze our thoughts or ideas, however compounded or sublime, we always find that they resolve themselves into such simple ideas as were copied from a precedent feeling or sentiment. Even those ideas, which, at first view, seem the most wide of this origin, are found, upon a nearer scrutiny, to be derived from it. The idea of God, as meaning an infinitely intelligent, wise, and good Being, arises from reflecting on the operations of our own mind, and augmenting, without limit, those qualities of goodness and wisdom. We may prosecute this enquiry to what length we please; where we shall always find, that every idea which we examine is copied from a similar impression. Those who would assert that this position is not universally true nor without exception, have only one, and that an easy method of refuting it; by producing that idea, which, in their opinion, is not derived from this source.

It will then be incumbent on us, if we would maintain
doctrine, to produce the impression, or lively percept
which corresponds to it.

15   Secondly. If it happen, from a defect of the org
that a man is not susceptible of any species of sensat
we always find that he is as little susceptible of the
respondent ideas. A blind man can form no notion
colours; a deaf man of sounds. Restore either of tl
that sense in which he is deficient; by opening this i
inlet for his sensations, you also open an inlet for the id
and he finds no difficulty in conceiving these objects. '
case is the same, if the object, proper for exciting
sensation, has never been applied to the organ. A I
lander or Negro has no notion of the relish of w
And though there are few or no instances of a
deficiency in the mind, where a person has never felt
is wholly incapable of a sentiment or passion that belc
to his species; yet we find the same observation to 1
place in a less degree. A man of mild manners can f
no idea of inveterate revenge or cruelty; nor can a sel
heart easily conceive the heights of friendship and genero;
It is readily allowed, that other beings may possess m
senses of which we can have no conception; because
ideas of them have never been introduced to us in
only manner by which an idea can have access to the m
to wit, by the actual feeling and sensation.

16   There is, however, one contradictory phenomenon, wl
may prove that it is not absolutely impossible for ic
to arise, independent of their correspondent impressi
I believe it will readily be allowed, that the several dist
ideas of colour, which enter by the eye, or those of sou
which are conveyed by the ear, are really different f
each other; though, at the same time, resembling. I
if this be true of different colours, it must be no less s
the different shades of the same colour; and each sh

produces a distinct idea, independent of the rest. For if this should be denied, it is possible, by the continual gradation of shades, to run a colour insensibly into what is most remote from it; and if you will not allow any of the means to be different, you cannot, without absurdity, deny the extremes to be the same. Suppose, therefore, a person to have enjoyed his sight for thirty years, and to have become perfectly acquainted with colours of all kinds except one particular shade of blue, for instance, which it never has been his fortune to meet with. Let all the different shades of that colour, except that single one, be placed before him, descending gradually from the deepest to the lightest; it is plain that he will perceive a blank, where that shade is wanting, and will be sensible that there is a greater distance in that place between the contiguous colours than in any other. Now I ask, whether it be possible for him, from his own imagination, to supply this deficiency, and raise up to himself the idea of that particular shade, though it had never been conveyed to him by his senses? I believe there are few but will be of opinion that he can: and this may serve as a proof that the simple ideas are not always, in every instance, derived from the correspondent impressions; though this instance is so singular, that it is scarcely worth our observing, and does not merit that for it alone we should alter our general maxim.

17   Here, therefore, is a proposition, which not only seems, in itself, simple and intelligible; but, if a proper use were made of it, might render every dispute equally intelligible, and banish all that jargon, which has so long taken possession of metaphysical reasonings, and drawn disgrace upon them. All ideas, especially abstract ones, are naturally faint and obscure: the mind has but a slender hold of them: they are apt to be confounded with other resembling ideas; and when we have often employed any

term, though without a distinct meaning, we are apt
imagine it has a determinate idea annexed to it. On
contrary, all impressions, that is, all sensations, eit
outward or inward, are strong and vivid: the li
between them are more exactly determined : nor is it (
to fall into any error or mistake with regard to them. W
we entertain, therefore, any suspicion that a philosoph
term is employed without any meaning or idea (as is
too frequent), we need but enquire, *from what impres.
is that supposed idea derived?* And if it be impossibl
assign any, this will serve to confirm our suspicion.
bringing ideas into so clear a light we may reasonably h
to remove all dispute, which may arise, concerning t
nature and reality [1].

[1] It is probable that no more was meant by those, who denied in
ideas, than that all ideas were copies of our impressions; thoug
must be confessed, that the terms, which they employed, were
chosen with such caution, nor so exactly defined, as to prevent
mistakes about their doctrine. For what is meant by *innate?*
innate be equivalent to natural, then all the perceptions and ideas o
mind must be allowed to be innate or natural, in whatever sense
take the latter word, whether in opposition to what is uncomr
artificial, or miraculous. If by innate be meant, contemporary to
birth, the dispute seems to be frivolous ; nor is it worth while to enc
at what time thinking begins, whether before, at, or after our b
Again, the word *idea,* seems to be commonly taken in a very l
sense, by LOCKE and others; as standing for any of our percept
our sensations and passions, as well as thoughts. Now in this s
I should desire to know, what can be meant by asserting, that self-l
or resentment of injuries, or the passion between the sexes is not inn

But admitting these terms, *impressions* and *ideas,* in the sense al
explained, and understanding by *innate,* what is original or copied f
no precedent perception, then may we assert that all our impress
are innate, and our ideas not innate.

To be ingenuous, I must own it to be my opinion, that LOCKE
betrayed into this question by the schoolmen, who, making us
undefined terms, draw out their disputes to a tedious length, wit
ever touching the point in question. A like ambiguity and circuml
tion seem to run through that philosopher's reasonings on this as
as most other subjects.

SECTION III.

OF THE ASSOCIATION OF IDEAS.

18 IT is evident that there is a principle of connexion between the different thoughts or ideas of the mind, and that, in their appearance to the memory or imagination, they introduce each other with a certain degree of method and regularity. In our more serious thinking or discourse this is so observable that any particular thought, which breaks in upon the regular tract or chain of ideas, is immediately remarked and rejected. And even in our wildest and most wandering reveries, nay in our very dreams, we shall find, if we reflect, that the imagination ran not altogether at adventures, but that there was still a connexion upheld among the different ideas, which succeeded each other. Were the loosest and freest conversation to be transcribed, there would immediately be observed something which connected it in all its transitions. Or where this is wanting, the person who broke the thread of discourse might still inform you, that there had secretly revolved in his mind a succession of thought, which had gradually led him from the subject of conversation. Among different languages, even where we cannot suspect the least connexion or communication, it is found, that the words, expressive of ideas, the most compounded, do yet nearly correspond to each other: a certain proof that the simple ideas, comprehended in the compound ones, were bound together by some universal principle, which had an equal influence on all mankind.

19 Though it be too obvious to escape observation, 1
different ideas are connected together; I do not find 1
any philosopher has attempted to enumerate or class
the principles of association; a subject, however, 1
seems worthy of curiosity. To me, there appear to
only three principles of connexion among ideas, nam
Resemblance, Contiguity in time or place, and *Cause*
Effect.

That these principles serve to connect ideas will 1
I believe, be much doubted. A picture naturally le
our thoughts to the original[1]: the mention of one ap
ment in a building naturally introduces an enquiry
discourse concerning the others[2]: and if we think
a wound, we can scarcely forbear reflecting on the 1
which follows it[3]. But that this enumeration is compl
and that there are no other principles of association exc
these, may be difficult to prove to the satisfaction of
reader, or even to a man's own satisfaction. All we can
in such cases, is to run over several instances, and exan
carefully the principle which binds the different thou
to each other, never stopping till we render the principl
general as possible[2]. The more instances we examine,
the more care we employ, the more assurance shall
acquire, that the enumeration, which we form from
whole, is complete and entire.

[1] Resemblance.　　　　[2] Contiguity.　　　　[3] Canse and effe
[4] For instance, Contrast or Contrariety is also a connexion ac
Ideas: but it may, perhaps, be considered as a mixture of *Caus*
and *Resemblance*. Where two objects are contrary, the one destroy
other; that is, the cause of its annihilation, and the idea of the anni
tion of an object, implies the idea of its former existence.

SECTION IV.

PART I.

20 ALL the objects of human reason or enquiry may naturally be divided into two kinds, to wit, *Relations of Ideas*, and *Matters of Fact*. Of the first kind are the sciences of Geometry, Algebra, and Arithmetic; and in short, every affirmation which is either intuitively or demonstratively certain. *That the square of the hypothenuse is equal to the square of the two sides*, is a proposition which expresses a relation between these figures. *That three times five is equal to the half of thirty*, expresses a relation between these numbers. Propositions of this kind are discoverable by the mere operation of thought, without dependence on what is anywhere existent in the universe. Though there never were a circle or triangle in nature, the truths demonstrated by Euclid would for ever retain their certainty and evidence.

21 Matters of fact, which are the second objects of human reason, are not ascertained in the same manner; nor is our evidence of their truth, however great, of a like nature with the foregoing. The contrary of every matter of fact is still possible; because it can never imply a contradiction, and is conceived by the mind with the same facility and distinctness, as if ever so conformable to reality. *That the* *sun will not rise to-morrow* is no less intelligible a position, and implies no more contradiction than affirmation, *that it will rise.* We should in vain, theref attempt to demonstrate its falsehood. Were it dem stratively false, it would imply a contradiction, and co never be distinctly conceived by the mind.

It may, therefore, be a subject worthy of curiosity, enquire what is the nature of that evidence which assu us of any real existence and matter of fact, beyond present testimony of our senses, or the records of memory. This part of philosophy, it is observable, been little cultivated, either by the ancients or moder and therefore our doubts and errors, in the prosecution so important an enquiry, may be the more excusal while we march through such difficult paths without guide or direction. They may even prove useful, by excit curiosity, and destroying that implicit faith and secu which is the bane of all reasoning and free enquiry. discovery of defects in the common philosophy, if any s there be, will not, I presume, be a discouragement, rather an incitement, as is usual, to attempt someth more full and satisfactory than has yet been proposed the public.

22 All reasonings concerning matter of fact seem to founded on the relation of *Cause and Effect.* By mean that relation alone we can go beyond the evidence of memory and senses. If you were to ask a man, why believes any matter of fact, which is absent ; for instar that his friend is in the country, or in France ; he wo give you a reason ; and this reason would be some of fact ; as a letter received from him, or the knowledge of former resolutions and promises. A man finding a wa or any other machine in a desert island, would conch that there had once been men in that island. All reasonings concerning fact are of the same nature. *E* here it is constantly supposed that there is a connexion between the present fact and that which is inferred from it. Were there nothing to bind them together, the inference would be entirely precarious. The hearing of an articulate voice and rational discourse in the dark assures us of the presence of some person : Why ? because these are the effects of the human make and fabric, and closely connected with it. If we anatomize all the other reasonings of this nature, we shall find that they are founded on the relation of cause and effect, and that this relation is either near or remote, direct or collateral. Heat and light are collateral effects of fire, and the one effect may justly be inferred from the other.

23　　If we would satisfy ourselves, therefore, concerning the nature of that evidence, which assures us of matters of fact, we must enquire how we arrive at the knowledge of cause and effect.

I shall venture to affirm, as a general proposition, which admits of no exception, that the knowledge of this relation is not, in any instance, attained by reasonings *a priori*; but arises entirely from experience, when we find that any particular objects are constantly conjoined with each other. Let an object be presented to a man of ever so strong natural reason and abilities; if that object be entirely new to him, he will not be able, by the most accurate examination of its sensible qualities, to discover any of its causes or effects. Adam, though his rational faculties be supposed, at the very first, entirely perfect, could not have inferred from the fluidity and transparency of water that it would suffocate him, or from the light and warmth of fire that it would consume him. No object ever discovers, by the qualities which appear to the senses, either the causes which produced it, or the effects which will arise from it ; nor can our reason, unassisted by experience, ever draw any inference concerning real existence and matter of fact.

24　This proposition, *that causes and effects are discor not by reason but by experience*, will readily be admitte
regard to such objects, as we remember to have onc
altogether unknown to us ; since we must be consciou:
utter inability, which we then lay under, of foretellin
would arise from them.　Present two smooth pie
marble to a man who has no tincture of natural philo:
he will never discover that they will adhere toget
such a manner as to require great force to separate tl
a direct line, while they make so small a resista
a lateral pressure.　Such events, as bear little anal
the common course of nature, are also readily cor
to be known only by experience ; nor does any man ii
that the explosion of gunpowder, or the attraction of
stone, could ever be discovered by arguments *a prio*
like manner, when an effect is supposed to depend uj
intricate machinery or secret structure of parts, we m.
difficulty in attributing all our knowledge of it to expe
Who will assert that he can give the ultimate reaso
milk or bread is proper nourishment for a man, r
a lion or a tiger ?

But the same truth may not appear, at first sight, t
the same evidence with regard to events, which have b
familiar to us from our first appearance in the world,
bear a close analogy to the whole course of nature, and
are supposed to depend on the simple qualities of o
without any secret structure of parts.　We are apt to ii
that we could discover these effects by the mere opera
our reason, without experience.　We fancy, that w
brought on a sudden into this world, we could at firs
inferred that one Billiard-ball would communicate i
to another upon impulse ; and that we needed not t
waited for the event, in order to pronounce with ce
concerning it.　Such is the influence of custom, that,
it'is strongest, it not only covers our natural ignoranc

even conceals itself, and seems not to take place, merely
because it is found in the highest degree.

25   But to convince us that all the laws of nature, and all
the operations of bodies without exception, are known only
by experience, the following reflections may, perhaps, suffice.
Were any object presented to us, and were we required to
pronounce concerning the effect, which will result from it,
without consulting past observation; after what manner,
I beseech you, must the mind proceed in this operation?
It must invent or imagine some event, which it ascribes to
the object as its effect; and it is plain that this invention
must be entirely arbitrary. The mind can never possibly
find the effect in the supposed cause, by the most accurate
scrutiny and examination. For the effect is totally different
from the cause, and consequently can never be discovered
in it. Motion in the second Billiard-ball is a quite distinct
event from motion in the first; nor is there anything in the
one to suggest the smallest hint of the other. A stone or
piece of metal raised into the air, and left without any
support, immediately falls: but to consider the matter
a priori, is there anything we discover in this situation
which can beget the idea of a downward, rather than an
upward, or any other motion, in the stone or metal?

And as the first imagination or invention of a particular
effect, in all natural operations, is arbitrary, where we consult not experience; so must we also esteem the supposed
tie or connexion between the cause and effect, which binds
them together, and renders it impossible that any other
effect could result from the operation of that cause. When
I see, for instance, a Billiard-ball moving in a straight line
towards another; even suppose motion in the second ball
should by accident be suggested to me, as the result of their
contact or impulse; may I not conceive, that a hundred
different events might as well follow from that cause? May
not both these balls remain at absolute rest? May not the

first ball return in a straight line, or leap off from the sec
in any line or direction? All these suppositions are
sistent and conceivable. Why then should we give
preference to one, which is no more consistent or conceiv
than the rest? All our reasonings *a priori* will neve
able to show us any foundation for this preference.

In a word, then, every effect is a distinct event from
cause. It could not, therefore, be discovered in the ca
and the first invention or conception of it, *a priori*, mus
entirely arbitrary. And even after it is suggested, the
junction of it with the cause must appear equally arbitr
since there are always many other effects, which, to rea
must seem fully as consistent and natural. In vain, th
fore, should we pretend to determine any single event
infer any cause or effect, without the assistance of obse
tion and experience.

26   Hence we may discover the reason why no philosop
who is rational and modest, has ever pretended to as
the ultimate cause of any natural operation, or to s
distinctly the action of that power, which produces
single effect in the universe. It is confessed, that the utr
effort of human reason is to reduce the principles, pro
tive of natural phenomena, to a greater simplicity, anc
resolve the many particular effects into a few general cau
by means of reasonings from analogy, experience,
observation. But as to the causes of these general cau
we should in vain attempt their discovery; nor shall
ever be able to satisfy ourselves, by any particular explica
of them. These ultimate springs and principles are tot
shut up from human curiosity and enquiry. Elasti
gravity, cohesion of parts, communication of motion
impulse; these are probably the ultimate causes and f
ciples which we shall ever discover in nature; and we
esteem ourselves sufficiently happy, if, by accurate enq
and reasoning, we can trace up the particular phenon

to, or near to, these general principles. The most perfect
philosophy of the natural kind only staves off our ignorance
a little longer : as perhaps the most perfect philosophy of
the moral or metaphysical kind serves only to discover larger
portions of it. Thus the observation of human blindness
and weakness is the result of all philosophy, and meets us at
every turn, in spite of our endeavours to elude or avoid it.

27   Nor is geometry, when taken into the assistance of natural
philosophy, ever able to remedy this defect, or lead us into
the knowledge of ultimate causes, by all that accuracy of
reasoning for which it is so justly celebrated. Every part
of mixed mathematics proceeds upon the supposition that
certain laws are established by nature in her operations;
and abstract reasonings are employed, either to assist experience in the discovery of these laws, or to determine
their influence in particular instances, where it depends
upon any precise degree of distance and quantity. Thus, it
is a law of motion, discovered by experience, that the moment
or force of any body in motion is in the compound ratio or
proportion of its solid contents and its velocity ; and consequently, that a small force may remove the greatest obstacle
or raise the greatest weight, if, by any contrivance or
machinery, we can increase the velocity of that force, so as
to make it an overmatch for its antagonist. Geometry assists
us in the application of this law, by giving us the just dimensions of all the parts and figures which can enter into any
species of machine ; but still the discovery of the law itself
is owing merely to experience, and all the abstract reasonings
in the world could never lead us one step towards the knowledge of it. When we reason *a priori*, and consider merely any
object or cause, as it appears to the mind, independent of
all observation, it never could suggest to us the notion of
any distinct object, such as its effect ; much less, show us
the inseparable and inviolable connexion between them.
A man must be very sagacious who could discover by

reasoning that crystal is the effect of heat, and ice of co
without being previously acquainted with the operation
these qualities.

PART II.

28   But we have not yet attained any tolerable satisfact
with regard to the question first proposed. Each solut
still gives rise to a new question as difficult as the foregoi
and leads us on to farther enquiries. When it is ask
*What is the nature of all our reasonings concerning matter
fact?* the proper answer seems to be, that they are foun
on the relation of cause and effect. When again it is ask
*What is the foundation of all our reasonings and conclusi
concerning that relation?* it may be replied in one wo
Experience. But if we still carry on our sifting humour, a
ask, *What is the foundation of all conclusions from experien*
this implies a new question, which may be of more diffi
solution and explication. Philosophers, that give themsel
airs of superior wisdom and sufficiency, have a hard t
when they encounter persons of inquisitive dispositions, v
push them from every corner to which they retreat, and v
are sure at last to bring them to some dangerous dilem
The best expedient to prevent this confusion, is to be mod
in our pretensions; and even to discover the difficulty c
selves before it is objected to us. By this means, we n
make a kind of merit of our very ignorance.

I shall content myself, in this section, with an easy ta
and shall pretend only to give a negative answer to
question here proposed. I say then, that, even after
have experience of the operations of cause and effect,
conclusions from that experience are *not* founded on reas
ing, or any process of the understanding. This answer
must endeavour both to explain and to defend.

29   It must certainly be allowed, that nature has kept
at a great distance from all her secrets, and has affor

us only the knowledge of a few superficial qualities of objects; while she conceals from us those powers and principles on which the influence of those objects entirely depends. Our senses inform us of the colour, weight, and consistence of bread; but neither sense nor reason can ever inform us of those qualities which fit it for the nourishment and support of a human body. Sight or feeling conveys an idea of the actual motion of bodies; but as to that wonderful force or power, which would carry on a moving body for ever in a continued change of place, and which bodies never lose but by communicating it to others; of this we cannot form the most distant conception. But notwithstanding this ignorance of natural powers[1] and principles, we always presume, when we see like sensible qualities, that they have like secret powers, and expect that effects, similar to those which we have experienced, will follow from them. If a body of like colour and consistence with that bread, which we have formerly eat, be presented to us, we make no scruple of repeating the experiment, and foresee, with certainty, like nourishment and support. Now this is a process of the mind or thought, of which I would willingly know the foundation. It is allowed on all hands that there is no known connexion between the sensible qualities and the secret powers; and consequently, that the mind is not led to form such a conclusion concerning their constant and regular conjunction, by anything which it knows of their nature. As to past *Experience*, it can be allowed to give *direct* and *certain* information of those precise objects only, and that precise period of time, which fell under its cognizance: but why this experience should be extended to future times, and to other objects, which for aught we know, may be only in

---

[1] The word, Power, is here used in a loose and popular sense. The more accurate explication of it would give additional evidence to this argument. See Sect. 7.

appearance similar; this is the main question on w
I would insist. The bread, which I formerly eat, nouri
me; that is, a body of such sensible qualities was, at
time, endued with such secret powers : but does it fo
that other bread must also nourish me at another time,
that like sensible qualities must always be attended
like secret powers? The consequence seems nowise n
sary. At least, it must be acknowledged that there is
a consequence drawn by the mind; that there is a ce
step taken; a process of thought, and an inference, v
wants to be explained, These two propositions ar
from being the same, *I have found that such an objec
always been attended with such an effect,* and *I foresee
other objects, which are, in appearance, similar, w
attended with similar effects.* I shall allow, if you p
that the one proposition may justly be inferred fron
other : I know, in fact, that it always is inferred. But :
insist that the inference is made by a chain of reasc
I desire you to produce that reasoning. · The conn
between these propositions is not intuitive. There
quired' a medium, which may enable the mind to
such an inference, if indeed it be drawn by reasonin̨
argument. What that medium is, I must confess, ȷ
my comprehension; and it is incumbent on those to
duce it, who assert that it really exists, and is the ori
all our conclusions concerning matter of fact.

30   This negative argument must certainly, in proce
time, become altogether convincing, if many penet
and able philosophers shall turn their enquiries thi̧
and no one be ever able to discover any connecting
position or intermediate step, which supports the ι
standing in this conclusion. But as the question :
new, every reader may not trust so far to his own
tration, as to conclude, because an argument escape
enquiry, that therefore it does not really exist. Fc

reason it may be requisite to venture upon a more difficult task; and enumerating all the branches of human knowledge, endeavour to show that none of them can afford such an argument.

All reasonings may be divided into two kinds, namely, demonstrative reasoning, or that concerning relations of ideas, and moral reasoning, or that concerning matter of fact and existence. That there are no demonstrative arguments in the case seems evident; since it implies no contradiction that the course of nature may change, and that an object, seemingly like those which we have experienced, may be attended with different or contrary effects. May I not clearly and distinctly conceive that a body, falling from the clouds, and which, in all other respects, resembles snow, has yet the taste of salt or feeling of fire? Is there any more intelligible proposition than to affirm, that all the trees will flourish in December and January, and decay in May and June? Now whatever is intelligible, and can be distinctly conceived, implies no contradiction, and can never be proved false by any demonstrative argument or abstract reasoning *à priori*.

If we be, therefore, engaged by arguments to put trust in past experience, and make it the standard of our future judgement, these arguments must be probable only, or such as regard matter of fact and real existence, according to the division above mentioned. But that there is no argument of this kind, must appear, if our explication of that species of reasoning be admitted as solid and satisfactory. We have said that all arguments concerning existence are founded on the relation of cause and effect; that our knowledge of that relation is derived entirely from experience; and that all our experimental conclusions proceed upon the supposition that the future will be conformable to the past. To endeavour, therefore, the proof of this last supposition by probable arguments, or arguments regarding

existence, must be evidently going in a circle, and tal
that for granted, which is the very point in question.

31   In reality, all arguments from experience are founded
the similarity which we discover among natural obj(
and by which we are induced to expect effects simila
those which we have found to follow from such obj(
And though none but a fool or madman will ever pret
to dispute the authority of experience, or to reject
great guide of human life, it may surely be allowed a pl
sopher to have so much curiosity at least as to examine
principle of human nature, which gives this mighty authc
to experience, and makes us draw advantage from
similarity which nature has placed among different obj(
From causes which appear *similar* we expect similar eff(
This is the sum of all our experimental conclusions.   I
it seems evident that, if this conclusion were formed
reason, it would be as perfect at first, and upon
instance, as after ever so long a course of experience.
the case is far otherwise.   Nothing so like as eggs ; ye
one, on account of this appearing similarity, expects
same taste and relish in all of them.   It is only after a l
course of uniform experiments in any kind, that we at
a firm reliance and security with regard to a partic
event.   Now where is that process of reasoning wh
from one instance, draws a conclusion, so different f
that which it infers from a hundred instances that
nowise different from that single one?   This ques
I propose as much for the sake of information, as witl
intention of raising difficulties.   I cannot find, I car
imagine any such reasoning.   But I keep my mind
open to instruction, if any one will vouchsafe to bes
it on me.

32   Should it be said that, from a number of uniform ex[
ments, we *infer* a connexion between the sensible quali
and the secret powers; this, I must confess, seems

same difficulty, couched in different terms. The question still recurs, on what process of argument this *inference* is founded? Where is the medium, the interposing ideas, which join propositions so very wide of each other? It is confessed that the colour, consistence, and other sensible qualities of bread appear not, of themselves, to have any connexion with the secret powers of nourishment and support. For otherwise we could infer these secret powers from the first appearance of these sensible qualities, without the aid of experience; contrary to the sentiment of all philosophers, and contrary to plain matter of fact. Here, then, is our natural state of ignorance with regard to the powers and influence of all objects. How is this remedied by experience? It only shows us a number of uniform effects, resulting from certain objects, and teaches us that those particular objects, at that particular time, were endowed with such powers and forces. When a new object, endowed with similar sensible qualities, is produced, we expect similar powers and forces, and look for a like effect. From a body of like colour and consistence with bread we expect like nourishment and support. But this surely is a step or progress of the mind, which wants to be explained. When a man says, *I have found, in all past instances, such sensible qualities conjoined with such secret powers*: And when he says, *Similar sensible qualities will always be conjoined with similar secret powers*, he is not guilty of a tautology, nor are these propositions in any respect the same. You say that the one proposition is an inference from the other. But you must confess that the inference is not intuitive; neither is it demonstrative: Of what nature is it, then? To say it is experimental, is begging the question. For all inferences from experience suppose, as their foundation, that the future will resemble the past, and that similar powers will be conjoined with similar sensible qualities. If there be any suspicion that the course of nature may

change, and that the past may be no rule for the future
experience becomes useless, and can give rise to no
ference or conclusion.   It is impossible, therefore, that
arguments from experience can prove this resembla
of the past to the future; since all these arguments
founded on the supposition of that resemblance.   Let
course of things be allowed hitherto ever so regular;
alone, without some new argument or inference, pro
not that, for the future, it will continue so.   In vain
you pretend to have learned the nature of bodies from y
past experience.   Their secret nature, and conseque
all their effects and influence, may change, without
change in their sensible qualities.   This happens so
times, and with regard to some objects : Why may it
happen always, and with regard to all objects ?   What lc
what process of argument secures you against this supp
tion ?   My practice, you say, refutes my doubts.   But
mistake the purport of my question.   As an agent, I
quite satisfied in the point; but as a philosopher, who
some share of curiosity, I will not say scepticism, I wan
learn the foundation of this inference.   No reading,
enquiry has yet been able to remove my difficulty, or ;
me satisfaction in a matter of such importance.   Can I
better than propose the difficulty to the public, even thoi
perhaps, I have small hopes of obtaining a solution ?
shall at least, by this means, be sensible of our ignora:
if we do not augment our knowledge.

33   I must confess that a man is guilty of unpardon:
arrogance who concludes, because an argument
escaped his own investigation, that therefore it does
really exist.   I must also confess that, though all
learned, for several ages, should have employed themse
in fruitless search upon any subject, it may still, perhaps
rash to conclude positively that the subject must, theref
pass all human comprehension.   Even though we exan

all the sources of our knowledge, and conclude them unfit for such a subject, there may still remain a suspicion, that the enumeration is not complete, or the examination not accurate. But with regard to the present subject, there are some considerations which seem to remove all this accusation of arrogance or suspicion of mistake.

It is certain that the most ignorant and stupid peasants— nay infants, nay even brute beasts—improve by experience, and learn the qualities of natural objects, by observing the effects which result from them. When a child has felt the sensation of pain from touching the flame of a candle, he will be careful not to put his hand near any candle; but will expect a similar effect from a cause which is similar in its sensible qualities and appearance. If you assert, there- fore, that the understanding of the child is led into this conclusion by any process of argument or ratiocination, I may justly require you to produce that argument; nor have you any pretence to refuse so equitable a demand. You cannot say that the argument is abstruse, and may possibly escape your enquiry; since you confess that it is obvious to the capacity of a mere infant. If you hesitate, therefore, a moment, or if, after reflection, you produce any intricate or profound argument, you, in a manner, give up the question, and confess that it is not reasoning which engages us to suppose the past resembling the future, and to expect similar effects from causes which are, to appear- ance, similar. This is the proposition which I intended to enforce in the present section. If I be right, I pretend not to have made any mighty discovery. And if I be wrong, I must acknowledge myself to be indeed a very backward scholar; since I cannot now discover an argument which, it seems, was perfectly familiar to me long before I was out of my cradle.

SECTION V.

SCEPTICAL SOLUTION OF THESE DOUBTS.

PART I.

34 THE passion for philosophy, like that for religion, se
liable to this inconvenience, that, though it aims at
correction of our manners, and extirpation of our vi
it may only serve, by imprudent management, to fc
a predominant inclination, and push the mind, with n
determined resolution, towards that side which alre
draws too much, by the bias and propensity of the nat
temper. It is certain that, while we aspire to the n
nanimous firmness of the philosophic sage, and endea\
to confine our pleasures altogether within our own mil
we may, at last, render our philosophy like that of Epicte
and other *Stoics*, only a more refined system of selfishn
and reason ourselves out of all virtue as well as sc
enjoyment. While we study with attention the vanit
human life, and turn all our thoughts towards the en
and transitory nature of riches and honours, we
perhaps, all the while flattering our natural indole:
which, hating the bustle of the world, and drudger
business, seeks a pretence of reason to give itself a
and uncontrolled indulgence. There is, however,
species of philosophy which seems little liable to
inconvenience, and that because it strikes in with
disorderly passion of the human mind, nor can mil
itself with any natural affection or propensity ; and tha

the Academic or Sceptical philosophy. The academics always talk of doubt and suspense of judgement, of danger in hasty determinations, of confining to very narrow bounds the enquiries of the understanding, and of renouncing all speculations which lie not within the limits of common life and practice. Nothing, therefore, can be more contrary than such a philosophy to the supine indolence of the mind, its rash arrogance, its lofty pretensions, and its superstitious credulity. Every passion is mortified by it, except the love of truth; and that passion never is, nor can be, carried to too high a degree. It is surprising, therefore, that this philosophy, which, in almost every instance, must be harmless and innocent, should be the subject of so much groundless reproach and obloquy. But, perhaps, the very circumstance which renders it so innocent is what chiefly exposes it to the public hatred and resentment. By flattering no irregular passion, it gains few partizans: By opposing so many vices and follies, it raises to itself abundance of enemies, who stigmatize it as libertine, profane, and irreligious.

Nor need we fear that this philosophy, while it endeavours to limit our enquiries to common life, should ever undermine the reasonings of common life, and carry its doubts so far as to destroy all action, as well as speculation. Nature will always maintain her rights, and prevail in the end over any abstract reasoning whatsoever. Though we should conclude, for instance, as in the foregoing section, that, in all reasonings from experience, there is a step taken by the mind which is not supported by any argument or process of the understanding; there is no danger that these reasonings, on which almost all knowledge depends, will ever be affected by such a discovery. If the mind be not engaged by argument to make this step, it must be induced by some other principle of equal weight and authority; and that principle will preserve its influence as long as human

nature remains the same. What that principle is may v
be worth the pains of enquiry.

35   Suppose a person, though endowed with the strong
faculties of reason and reflection, to be brought on a sudd
into this world; he would, indeed, immediately obse
a continual succession of objects, and one event follow
another; but he would not be able to discover anyth
farther. He would not, at first, by any reasoning, be a
to reach the idea of cause and effect; since the partici
powers, by which all natural operations are perform
never appear to the senses; nor is it reasonable to conclu
merely because one event, in one instance, precedes anotl
that therefore the one is the cause, the other the eff
Their conjunction may be arbitrary and casual. Th
may be no reason to infer the existence of one from
appearance of the other. And in a word, such a pers
without more experience, could never employ his conject
or reasoning concerning any matter of fact, or be assu
of anything beyond what was immediately present to
memory and senses.

Suppose, again, that he has acquired more experier
and has lived so long in the world as to have obser
familiar objects or events to be constantly conjoii
together; what is the consequence of this experience?
immediately infers the existence of one object from
appearance of the other. Yet he has not, by all
experience, acquired any idea or knowledge of the se
power by which the one object produces the other;
is it, by any process of reasoning, he is engaged to d
this inference. But still he finds himself determined
draw it: And though he should be convinced that
understanding has no part in the operation, he wc
nevertheless continue in the same course of think
There is some other principle which determines him
form such a conclusion.

36   This principle is Custom or Habit.   For wherever the
repetition of any particular act or operation produces a
propensity to renew the same act or operation, without
being impelled by any reasoning or process of the understanding, we always say, that this propensity is the effect
of *Custom.*   By employing that word, we pretend not to
have given the ultimate reason of such a propensity.   We
only point out a principle of human nature, which is
universally acknowledged, and which is well known by its
effects.   Perhaps we can push our enquiries no farther, or
pretend to give the cause of this cause; but must rest
contented with it as the ultimate principle, which we can
assign, of all our conclusions from experience.   It is
sufficient satisfaction,. that we can go so far, without
repining at the narrowness of our faculties because they
will carry us no farther.   And it is certain we here advance
'a very intelligible proposition at least, if not a true one,
when we assert that, after the constant conjunction of two
objects—heat and flame, for instance, weight and solidity—
we are determined by custom alone to expect the one from
the appearance of the other.   This hypothesis seems even
the only one which explains the difficulty, why we draw,
from a thousand instances, an inference which we are not
able to draw from one instance, that is, in no respect,
different from them.   Reason is incapable of any such
variation.   The conclusions which it draws from considering one circle are the same which it would form upon
surveying all the circles in the universe.   But no man,
having seen only one body move after being impelled by
another, could infer that every other body will move after
a like impulse.   All inferences from experience, therefore,
are effects of custom, not of reasoning

1 Nothing is more useful than for writers, even, on *moral, political,* or
physical subjects, to distinguish between *reason* and *experience,* and to
suppose, that these species of argumentation are entirely different from

Custom, then, is the great guide of human life. It
that principle alone which renders our experience use
to us, and makes us expect, for the future, a similar tra
of events with those which have appeared in the pa

each other. The former are taken for the mere result of our intellect
faculties, which, by considering *à priori* the nature of things, a
examining the effects, that must follow from their operation, establ
particular principles of science and philosophy. The latter are suppos
to be derived entirely from sense and observation, by which we lea
what has actually resulted from the operation of particular objects, a
are thence able to infer, what will, for the future, result from the
Thus, for instance, the limitations and restraints of civil governme
and a legal constitution, may be defended, either from *reason*, who
reflecting on the great frailty and corruption of human nature, teach
that no man can safely be trusted with unlimited authority; or fro
experience and history, which inform us of the enormous abuses, th
ambition, in every age and country, has been found to make of
imprudent a confidence.

The same distinction between reason and experience is maintained
all our deliberations concerning the conduct of life; while the experienc
statesman, general, physician, or merchant is trusted and followed; a
the unpractised novice, with whatever natural talents endowed, neglect
and despised. Though it be allowed, that reason may form ve
plausible conjectures with regard to the consequences of such a pa
ticular conduct in such particular circumstances; it is still suppos
imperfect, without the assistance of experience, which is alone al
to give stability and certainty to the maxims, derived from study a
reflection.

But notwithstanding that this distinction be thus universally receive
both in the active speculative scenes of life, I shall not scruple
pronounce, that it is, at bottom, erroneous, at least, superficial.

If we examine those arguments, which, in any of the sciences abc
mentioned, are supposed to be the mere effects of reasoning a
reflection, they will be found to terminate, at last, in some gene
principle or conclusion, for which we can assign no reason but obser
tion and experience. The only difference between them and th
maxims, which are vulgarly esteemed the result of pure experience,
that the former cannot be established without some process of thoug
and some reflection on what we have observed, in order to distingui
its circumstances, and trace its consequences: Whereas in the latter, t
experienced event is exactly and fully familiar to that which we infer
the result of any particular situation. The history of a TIBERIUS
a NERO makes us dread a like tyranny, were our monarchs freed fro
the restraints of laws and senates: But the observation of any fraud

Without the influence of custom, we should be entirely ignorant of every matter of fact beyond what is immediately present to the memory and senses. We should never know how to adjust means to ends, or to employ our natural powers in the production of any effect. There would be an end at once of all action, as well as of the chief part of speculation.

37   But here it may be proper to remark, that though our conclusions from experience carry us beyond our memory and senses, and assure us of matters of fact which happened in the most distant places and most remote ages, yet some fact must always be present to the senses or memory, from which we may first proceed in drawing these conclusions. A man, who should find in a desert country the remains of pompous buildings, would conclude that the country had, in ancient times, been cultivated by civilized inhabitants ; but did nothing of this nature occur

cruelty in private life is sufficient, with the aid of a little thought, to give us the same apprehension ; while it serves as an instance of the general corruption of human nature, and shows us the danger which we must incur by reposing an entire confidence in mankind. In both cases, it is experience which is ultimately the foundation of our inference and conclusion.

There is no man so young and unexperienced, as not to have formed, from observation, many general and just maxims concerning human affairs and the conduct of life ; but it must be confessed, that, when a man comes to put these in practice, he will be extremely liable to error, till time and farther experience both enlarge these maxims, and teach him their proper use and application. In every situation or incident, there are many particular and seemingly minute circumstances, which the man of greatest talent is, at first, apt to overlook, though on them the justness of his conclusions, and consequently the prudence of his conduct, entirely depend. Not to mention, that, to a young beginner, the general observations and maxims occur not always on the proper occasions, nor can be immediately applied with due calmness and distinction. The truth is, an unexperienced reasoner could be no reasoner at all, were he absolutely unexperienced; and when we assign that character to any one, we mean it only in a comparative sense, and suppose him possessed of experience, in a smaller and more imperfect degree.

to him, he could never form such an inference. We le
the events of former ages from history; but then we n
peruse the volumes in which this instruction is contain
and thence carry up our inferences from one testimon}
another, till we arrive at the eyewitnesses and spectator:
these distant events. In a word, if we proceed not uj
some fact, present to the memory or senses, our reasoni
would be merely hypothetical; and however the partict
links might be connected with each other, the whcle ch
of inferences would have nothing to support it, nor co
we ever, by its means, arrive at the knowledge of any i
existence. If I ask why you believe any particular ma
of fact, which you relate, you must tell me some reas:
and this reason will be some other fact, connected with
But as you cannot proceed after this manner, *in infiniti*
you must at last terminate in some fact, which is presen
your memory or senses; or must allow that your belie
entirely without foundation.

38   What, then, is the conclusion of the whole matter?
simple one; though, it must be confessed, pretty rem
from the common theories of philosophy. All belief
matter of fact or real existence is derived merely from sc
object, present to the memory or senses, and a custom
conjunction between that and some other object. O1
other words; having found, in many instances, that
two kinds of objects—flame and heat, snow and cold—h
always been conjoined together; if flame or snow be]
sented anew to the senses, the mind is carried by cust
to expect heat or cold, and to *believe* that such a qua
does exist, and will discover itself upon a nearer approa
This belief is the necessary result of placing the mind
such circumstances. It is an operation of the soul, wl
we are so situated, as unavoidable as to feel the passion
love, when we receive benefits; or hatred, when we m
with injuries. All these operations are a species of natu

instincts, which no reasoning or process of the thought and understanding is able either to produce or to prevent.

At this point, it would be very allowable for us to stop our philosophical researches. In most questions we can never make a single step farther; and in all questions we must terminate here at last, after our most restless and curious enquiries. But still our curiosity will be pardonable, perhaps commendable, if it carry us on to still farther researches, and make us examine more accurately the nature of this *belief,* and of the *customary conjunction,* whence it is derived. By this means we may meet with some explications and analogies that will give satisfaction; at least to such as love the abstract sciences, and can be entertained with speculations, which, however accurate, may still retain a degree of doubt and uncertainty. As to readers of a different taste; the remaining part of this section is not calculated for them, and the following enquiries may well be understood, though it be neglected.

PART II.

39 (Nothing is more free than the imagination of man; and though it cannot exceed that original stock of ideas furnished by the internal and external senses, it has un-limited power of mixing, compounding, separating, and dividing these ideas, in all the varieties of fiction and vision. It can feign a train of events, with all the appearance of reality, ascribe to them a particular time and place, conceive them as existent, and paint them out to itself with every circumstance, that belongs to any historical fact, which it believes with the greatest certainty. Wherein, therefore, consists the difference between such a fiction and belief? It lies not merely in any peculiar idea, which is annexed to such a conception as commands our assent, and which is wanting to every known fiction. For as the mind has

authority over all its ideas, it could voluntarily annex th particular idea to any fiction, and consequently be able believe whatever it pleases; contrary to what we find l daily experience. We can, in our conception, join the hea of a man to the body of a horse; but it is not in o power to believe that such an animal has ever real existed.

/   It follows, therefore, that the difference between *ficti* and *belief* lies in some sentiment or feeling, which annexed to the latter, not to the former, and which depen‹ not on the will, nor can be commanded at pleasure. must be excited by nature, like all other sentiments; ar must arise from the particular situation, in which the mir is placed at any particular juncture. Whenever any obje is presented to the memory or senses, it immediately, by th force of custom, carries the imagination to conceive th object, which is usually conjoined to it; and this conceptic is attended with a feeling or sentiment, different from th loose reveries of the fancy. In this consists the who nature of belief. For as there is no matter of fact which v believe so firmly that we cannot conceive the contrar there would be no difference between the conceptic assented to and that which is rejected, were it not for son sentiment which distinguishes the one from the other. I see a billiard-ball moving towards another, on a smoo‹ table, I can easily conceive it to stop upon contact. Th conception implies no contradiction; but still it feels ve differently from that conception by which I represent myself the impulse and the communication of motic from one ball to another.

40   Were we to attempt a *definition* of this sentiment, v should, perhaps, find it a very difficult, if not an impossib task; in the same manner as if we should endeavour ‹ define the feeling of cold or passion of anger, to a creatu who never had any experience of these sentiments. Beli

is the true and proper name of this feeling; and no one is
ever at a loss to know the meaning of that term; because
every man is every moment conscious of the sentiment
represented by it. It may not, however, be improper to
attempt a *description* of this sentiment; in hopes we may,
by that means, arrive at some analogies, which may afford
a more perfect explication of it. I say, then, that belief is
nothing but a more vivid, lively, forcible, firm, steady conception of an object, than what the imagination alone is
ever able to attain. This variety of terms, which may
seem so unphilosophical, is intended only to express that
act of the mind, which renders realities, or what is taken for
such, more present to us than fictions, causes them to
weigh more in the thought, and gives them a superior
influence on the passions and imagination. Provided we
agree about the thing, it is needless to dispute about the
terms. The imagination has the command over all its
ideas, and can join and mix and vary them, in all the
ways possible. It may conceive fictitious objects with all
the circumstances of place and time. It may set them,
in a manner, before our eyes, in their true colours, just
as they might have existed. But as it is impossible that
this faculty of imagination can ever, of itself, reach belief,
it is evident that belief consists not in the peculiar nature
or order of ideas, but in the *manner* of their conception,
and in their *feeling* to the mind. I confess, that it is
impossible perfectly to explain this feeling or manner of
conception. We may make use of words which express
something near it. But its true and proper name, as we
observed before, is *belief*; which is a term that every one
sufficiently understands in common life. And in philosophy, we can go no farther than assert, that *belief* is
something felt by the mind, which distinguishes the ideas
of the judgement from the fictions of the imagination. It
gives them more weight and influence; makes them appear

E

of greater importance; enforces them in the mind; i
renders them the governing principle of our actions.   I h
at present, for instance, a person's voice, with whom I
acquainted; and the sound comes as from the next roi
This impression of my senses immediately conveys
thought to the person, together with all the surround
objects.   I paint them out to myself as existing at pres(
with the same qualities and relations, of which I form(
knew them possessed.   These ideas take faster hold of
mind than ideas of an enchanted castle.   They are ν
different to the feeling, and have a much greater influenc(
every kind, either to give pleasure or pain, joy or sorrow

Let us, then, take in the whole compass of this doctr
and allow, that the sentiment of belief is nothing
a conception more intense and steady than what atte
the mere fictions of the imagination, and that this *maη*
of conception arises from a customary conjunction
the object with something present to the memory
senses: I believe that it will not be difficult, upon tl
suppositions, to find other operations of the mind analog
to it, and to trace up these phenomena to principles
more general.

41   We have already observed that nature has establis
connexions among particular ideas, and that no soc
one idea occurs to our thoughts than it introduces its
relative, and carries our attention towards it, by a ge
and insensible movement.   These principles of conneι
or association we have reduced to three, namely, *Re.
blance, Contiguity* and *Causation*; which are the ι
bonds that unite our thoughts together, and beget
regular train of reflection or discourse, which, in a gre
or less degree, takes place among all mankind.   Now I
arises a question, on which the solution of the pre
difficulty will depend.   Does it happen, in all these ι
tions, that, when one of the objects is presented to

senses or memory, the mind is not only carried to the conception of the correlative, but reaches a steadier and stronger conception of it than what otherwise it would have been able to attain? This seems to be the case with that belief which arises from the relation of cause and effect. And if the case be the same with the other relations or principles of associations, this may be established as a general law, which takes place in all the operations of the mind.

We may, therefore, observe, as the first experiment to our present purpose, that, upon the appearance of the picture of an absent friend, our idea of him is evidently enlivened by the *resemblance*, and that every passion, which that idea occasions, whether of joy or sorrow, acquires new force and vigour. In producing this effect, there concur both a relation and a present impression. Where the picture bears him no resemblance, at least was not intended for him, it never so much as conveys our thought to him : And where it is absent, as well as the person, though the mind may pass from the thought of the one to that of the other, it feels its idea to be rather weakened than enlivened by that transition. We take a pleasure in viewing the picture of a friend, when it is set before us ; but when it is removed, rather choose to consider him directly than by reflection in an image, which is equally distant and obscure.

The ceremonies of the Roman Catholic religion may be considered as instances of the same nature. The devotees of that superstition usually plead in excuse for the mummeries, with which they are upbraided, that they feel the good effect of those external motions, and postures, and actions, in enlivening their devotion and quickening their fervour, which otherwise would decay, if directed entirely to distant and immaterial objects. We shadow out the objects of our faith, say they, in sensible

types and images, and render them more present tc
by the immediate presence of these types, than it is
sible for us to do merely by an intellectual view
contemplation. Sensible objects have always a gre
influence on the fancy than any other; and this influe
they readily convey to those ideas to which they
related, and which they resemble. I shall only infer f
these practices, and this reasoning, that the effect of res
blance in enlivening the ideas is very common; and a
every case a resemblance and a present impression n
concur, we are abundantly supplied with experiment:
prove the reality of the foregoing principle.

42   We may add force to these experiments by other:
a different kind, in considering the effects of *contiguit)*
well as of *resemblance*. It is certain that distance dir
ishes the force of every idea, and that, upon our appro
to any object; though it does not discover itself to
senses; it operates upon the mind with an influence, wl
imitates an immediate impression. The thinking on
object readily transports the mind to what is contiguc
but it is only the actual presence of an object, that tr:
ports it with a superior vivacity. When I am a few m
from home, whatever relates to it touches me more ne
than when I am two hundred leagues distant; though e
at that distance the reflecting on any thing in the ne
bourhood of my friends or family naturally produces
idea of them. But as in this latter case, both the obj
of the mind are ideas; notwithstanding there is an e
transition between them; that transition alone is not abl
give a superior vivacity to any of the ideas, for want of sc
immediate impression[1].

[1] 'Naturane nobis, inquit, datum dicam, an errore quodam, ut,
ea loca videamus, in quibus memoria dignos viros acceperimus mul
esse versatos, magis moveamur, quam siquando eorum ipsorum aut 1
audiamus aut scriptum aliquod legamus? Velut ego nunc mov

43 No one can doubt but causation has the same influence as the other two relations of resemblance and contiguity. Superstitious people are fond of the reliques of saints and holy men, for the same reason, that they seek after types or images, in order to enliven their devotion, and give them a more intimate and strong conception of those exemplary lives, which they desire to imitate. Now it is evident, that one of the best reliques, which a devotee could procure, would be the handywork of a saint; and if his cloaths and furniture are ever to be considered in this light, it is because they were once at his disposal, and were moved and affected by him; in which respect they are to be considered as imperfect effects, and as connected with him by a shorter chain of consequences than any of those, by which we learn the reality of his existence.

Suppose, that the son of a friend, who had been long dead or absent, were presented to us; it is evident, that this object would instantly revive its correlative idea, and recal to our thoughts all past intimacies and familiarities, in more lively colours than they would otherwise have appeared to us. This is another phaenomenon, which seems to prove the principle above mentioned.

44 We may observe, that, in these phaenomena, the belief of the correlative object is always presupposed; without · which the relation could have no effect. The influence of the picture supposes, that we *believe* our friend to have

Venit enim mihi Plato in mentem, quem accepimus primum hic disputare solitum : cuius etiam illi hortuli propinqui non memoriam solum mihi afferunt, sed ipsum videntur in conspectu meo hic ponere. Hic Spensippus, hic Xenocrates, hic eius auditor Polemo; cuius ipsa illa sessio fuit, quam videmus. Equidem etiam curiam nostram, Hostiliam dico, non hanc novam, quae mihi minor esse videtur postquam est maior, solebam intuens, Scipionem, Catonem, Laelium, nostrum vero in primis avum cogitare. Tanta vis admonitionis est in locis; ut non sine causa ex his memoriae deducta sit disciplina.'

Cicero de Finibus. Lib. v.

once existed. Contiguity to home can never excite o
ideas of home, unless we *believe* that it really exists. N(
I assert, that this belief, where it reaches beyond t
memory or senses, is of a similar nature, and arises fro
similar causes, with the transition of thought and vivacity
conception here explained. When I throw a piece of d
wood into a fire, my mind is immediately carried to co
ceive, that it augments, not extinguishes the flame. Tl
transition of thought from the cause to the effect procee
not from reason. It derives its origin altogether fro
custom and experience. And as it first begins from :
object, present to the senses, it renders the idea or co
ception of flame more strong and lively than any loos
floating reverie of the imagination. That idea arises ii
mediately. The thought moves instantly towards it, ai
conveys to it all that force of conception, which is deriv(
from the impression present to the senses. When a swo
is levelled at my breast, does not the idea of wound ai
pain strike me more strongly, than when a glass of wii
is presented to me, even though by accident this id(
should occur after the appearance of the latter objec
But what is there in this whole matter to cause such a stroi
conception, except only a present object and a customa
transition to the idea of another object, which we ha'
been accustomed to conjoin with the former? This is tl
whole operation of the mind, in all our conclusions co
cerning matter of fact and existence; and it is a satisfacti(
to find some analogies, by which it may be explaine
The transition from a present object does in all cases gi'
strength and solidity to the related idea.

Here, then, is a kind of pre-established harmony betwe(
the course of nature and the succession of our idea
and though the powers and forces, by which the former
governed, be wholly unknown to us; yet our thoughts ar
conceptions have still, we find, gone on in the same tra

with the other works of nature. Custom is that principle, by which this correspondence has been effected; so necessary to the subsistence of our species, and the regulation of our conduct, in every circumstance and occurrence of human life. Had not the presence of an object, instantly excited the idea of those objects, commonly conjoined with it, all our knowledge must have been limited to the narrow sphere of our memory and senses; and we should never have been able to adjust means to ends, or employ our natural powers, either to the producing of good, or avoiding of evil. Those, who delight in the discovery and contemplation of *final causes*, have here ample subject to employ their wonder and admiration.

45   I shall add, for a further confirmation of the foregoing theory, that, as this operation of the mind, by which we infer like effects from like causes, and *vice versa*, is so essential to the subsistence of all human creatures, it is not probable, that it could be trusted to the fallacious deductions of our reason, which is slow in its operations; appears not, in any degree, during the first years of infancy; and at best is, in every age and period of human life, extremely liable to error and mistake. It is more conformable to the ordinary wisdom of nature to secure so necessary an act of the mind, by some instinct or mechanical tendency, which may be infallible in its operations, may discover itself at the first appearance of life and thought, and may be independent of all the laboured deductions of the understanding. As nature has taught us the use of our limbs, without giving us the knowledge of the muscles and nerves, by which they are actuated; so has she implanted in us an instinct, which carries forward the thought in a correspondent course to that which she has established among external objects; though we are ignorant of those powers and forces, on which this regular course and succession of objects totally depends.

SECTION VI.

OF PROBABILITY[1].

46 THOUGH there be no such thing as *Chance* in the world; our ignorance of the real cause of any event has the same influence on the understanding, and begets a like species of belief or opinion.

There is certainly a probability, which arises from a superiority of chances on any side; and according as this superiority encreases, and surpasses the opposite chances, the probability receives a proportionable encrease, and begets still a higher degree of belief or assent to that side, in which we discover the superiority. If a dye were marked with one figure or number of spots on four sides, and with another figure or number of spots on the two remaining sides, it would be more probable, that the former would turn up than the latter; though, if it had a thousand sides marked in the same manner, and only one side different, the probability would be much higher, and our belief or expectation of the event more steady and secure. This process of the thought or reasoning may seem trivial and obvious; but to those who

---

[1] Mr. Locke divides all arguments into demonstrative and probable. In this view, we must say, that it is only probable all men must die, or that the sun will rise to-morrow. But to conform our language more to common use, we ought to divide arguments into *demonstrations, proofs,* and *probabilities.* By proofs meaning such arguments from experience as leave no room for doubt or opposition.

consider it more narrowly, it may, perhaps, afford matter for curious speculation.

It seems evident, that, when the mind looks forward to discover the event, which may result from the throw of such a dye, it considers the turning up of each particular side as alike probable; and this is the very nature of chance, to render all the particular events, comprehended in it, entirely equal. But finding a greater number of sides concur in the one event than in the other, the mind is carried more frequently to that event, and meets it oftener, in revolving the various possibilities or chances, on which the ultimate result depends. This concurrence of several views in one particular event begets immediately, by an inexplicable contrivance of nature, the sentiment of belief, and gives that event the advantage over its antagonist, which is supported by a smaller number of views, and recurs less frequently to the mind. If we allow, that belief is nothing but a firmer and stronger conception of an object than what attends the mere fictions of the imagination, this operation may, perhaps, in some measure, be accounted for. The concurrence of these several views or glimpses imprints the idea more strongly on the imagination; gives it superior force and vigour; renders its influence on the passions and affections more sensible; and in a word, begets that reliance or security, which constitutes the nature of belief and opinion.

47 The case is the same with the probability of causes, as with that of chance. There are some causes, which are entirely uniform and constant in producing a particular effect; and no instance has ever yet been found of any failure or irregularity in their operation. Fire has always burned, and water suffocated every human creature: The production of motion by impulse and gravity is an universal law, which has hitherto admitted of no exception. But there are other causes, which have been found more irregular and uncertain; nor has rhubarb always proved a purge, or

opium a soporific to every one, who has taken these medicines. It is true, when any cause fails of producing its usual effect, philosophers ascribe not this to any irregularity in nature; but suppose, that some secret causes, in the particular structure of parts, have prevented the operation. Our reasonings, however, and conclusions concerning the event are the same as if this principle had no place. Being determined by custom to transfer the past to the future, in all our inferences; where the past has been entirely regular and uniform, we expect the event with the greatest assurance, and leave no room for any contrary supposition. But where different effects have been found to follow from causes, which are to *appearance* exactly similar, all these various effects must occur to the mind in transferring the past to the future, and enter into our consideration, when we determine the probability of the event. Though we give the preference to that which has been found most usual, and believe that this effect will exist, we must not overlook the other effects, but must assign to each of them a particular weight and authority, in proportion as we have found it to be more or less frequent. ·
It is more probable, in almost every country of Europe, that there will be frost sometime in January, than that the weather will continue open throughout that whole month; though this probability varies according to the different climates, and approaches to a certainty in the more northern kingdoms. Here then it seems evident, that, when we transfer the past to the future, in order to determine the effect, which will result from any cause, we transfer all the different events, in the same proportion as they have appeared in the past, and conceive one to have existed a hundred times, for instance, another ten times, and another once. As a great number of views do here concur in one event, they fortify and confirm it to the imagination, beget that sentiment which we call *belief*, and give its object the preference above the contrary event, which is not supported by an equal number of

experiments, and recurs not so frequently to the thought in transferring the past to the future. Let any one try to account for this operation of the mind upon any of the received systems of philosophy, and he will be sensible of the difficulty. For my part, I shall think it sufficient, if the present hints excite the curiosity of philosophers, and make them sensible how defective all common theories are in treating of such curious and such sublime subjects.

SECTION VII.

PART I.

48   THE great advantage of the mathematical sciences above the moral consists in this, that the ideas of the former, being sensible, are always clear and determinate, the smallest distinction between them is immediately perceptible, and the same terms are still expressive of the same ideas, without ambiguity or variation. An oval is never mistaken for a circle, nor an hyperbola for an ellipsis. The isosceles and scalenum are distinguished by boundaries more exact than vice and virtue, right and wrong. If any term be defined in geometry, the mind readily, of itself, substitutes, on all occasions, the definition for the term defined : Or even when no definition is employed, the object itself may be presented to the senses, and by that means be steadily and clearly apprehended. But the finer sentiments of the mind, the operations of the understanding, the various agitations of the passions, though really in themselves distinct, easily escape us, when surveyed by reflection ; nor is it in our power to recal the original object, as often as we have occasion to contemplate it. Ambiguity, by this means, is gradually introduced into our reasonings : Similar objects are readily taken to be the same : And the conclusion becomes at last very wide of the premises.

One may safely, however, affirm, that, if we consider these

sciences in a proper light, their advantages and disadvantages nearly compensate each other, and reduce both of them to a state of equality.   If the mind, with greater facility, retains the ideas of geometry clear and determinate, it must carry on a much longer and more intricate chain of reasoning, and compare ideas much wider of each other, in order to reach the abstruser truths of that science.   And if moral ideas are apt, without extreme care, to fall into obscurity and confusion, the inferences are always much shorter in these disquisitions, and the intermediate steps, which lead to the conclusion, much fewer than in the sciences which treat of quantity and number.   In reality, there is scarcely a proposition in Euclid so simple, as not to consist of more parts, than are to be found in any moral reasoning which runs not into chimera and conceit.   Where we trace the principles of the human mind through a few steps, we may be very well satisfied with our progress ; considering how soon nature throws a bar to all our enquiries concerning causes, and reduces us to an acknowledgment of our ignorance.   The chief obstacle, therefore, to our improvement in the moral or metaphysical sciences is the obscurity of the ideas, and ambiguity of the terms.   The principal difficulty in the mathematics is the length of inferences and compass of thought, requisite to the forming of any conclusion.   And, perhaps, our progress in natural philosophy is chiefly retarded by the want of proper experiments and phaenomena, which are often discovered by chance, and cannot always be found, when requisite, even by the most diligent and prudent enquiry.   As moral philosophy seems hitherto to have received less improvement than either geometry or physics, we may conclude, that, if there be any difference in this respect among these sciences, the difficulties, which obstruct the progress of the former, require superior care and capacity to be surmounted.

49   There are no ideas, which occur in metaphysics, more

obscure and uncertain, than those of *power, force, energy* or *necessary connexion,* of which it is every moment necessary for us to treat in all our disquisitions. We shall, therefore, endeavour, in this section, to fix, if possible, the precise meaning of these terms, and thereby remove some part of that obscurity, which is so much complained of in this species of philosophy.

It seems a proposition, which will not admit of much dispute, that all our ideas are nothing but copies of our impressions, or, in other words, that it is impossible for us to *think* of any thing, which we have not antecedently *felt*, either by our external or internal senses. I have endeavoured [1] to explain and prove this proposition, and have expressed my hopes, that, by a proper application of it, men may reach a greater clearness and precision in philosophical reasonings, than what they have hitherto been able to attain. Complex ideas may, perhaps, be well known by definition, which is nothing but an enumeration of those parts or simple ideas, that compose them. But when we have pushed up definitions to the most simple ideas, and find still some ambiguity and obscurity; what resource are we then possessed of? By what invention can we throw light upon these ideas, and render them altogether precise and determinate to our intellectual view? Produce the impressions or original sentiments, from which the ideas are copied. These impressions are all strong and sensible. They admit not of ambiguity. They are not only placed in a full light themselves, but may throw light on their correspondent ideas, which lie in obscurity. And by this means, we may, perhaps, attain a new microscope or species of optics, by which, in the moral sciences, the most minute, and most simple ideas may be so enlarged as to fall readily under our apprehension, and be equally known with the grossest and most sensible ideas, that can be the object of our enquiry.

[1] Section II.

50   To be fully acquainted, therefore, with the idea of power or necessary connexion, let us examine its impression ; and in order to find the impression with greater certainty, let us search for it in all the sources, from which it may possibly be derived.

When we look about us towards external objects, and consider the operation of causes, we are never able, in a single instance, to discover any power or necessary connexion ; any quality, which binds the effect to the cause, and renders the one an infallible consequence of the other. We only find, that the one does actually, in fact, follow the other. The impulse of one billiard-ball is attended with motion in the second. This is the whole that appears to the *outward* senses. The mind feels no sentiment or *inward* impression from this succession of objects : Consequently, there is not, in any single, particular instance of cause and effect, any thing which can suggest the idea of power or necessary connexion.

From the first appearance of an object, we never can conjecture what effect will result from it. But were the power or energy of any cause discoverable by the mind, we could foresee the effect, even without experience ; and might, at first, pronounce with certainty concerning it, by mere dint of thought and reasoning.

In reality, there is no part of matter, that does ever, by its sensible qualities, discover any power or energy, or give us ground to imagine, that it could produce any thing, or be followed by any other object, which we could denominate its effect. Solidity, extension, motion ; these qualities are all complete in themselves, and never point out any other event which may result from them. The scenes of the universe are continually shifting, and one object follows another in an uninterrupted succession ; but the power of force, which actuates the whole machine, is entirely concealed from us, and never discovers itself in any of the sensible

qualities of body. We know, that, in fact, heat is a constant
attendant of flame; but what is the connexion between
them, we have no room so much as to conjecture or imagine.
It is impossible, therefore, that the idea of power can be
derived from the contemplation of bodies, in single instances
of their operation; because no bodies ever discover any
power, which can be the original of this idea[1].

51   Since, therefore, external objects as they appear to the
senses, give us no idea of power or necessary connexion, by
their operation in particular instances, let us see, whether
this idea be derived from reflection on the operations of our
own minds, and be copied from any internal impression.
It may be said, that we are every moment conscious of
internal power; while we feel, that, by the simple command
of our will, we can move the organs of our body, or direct
the faculties of our mind. An act of volition produces
motion in our limbs, or raises a new idea in our imagination.
This influence of the will we know by consciousness. Hence
we acquire the idea of power or energy; and are certain,
that we ourselves and all other intelligent beings are possessed of power. This idea, then, is an idea of reflection,
since it arises from reflecting on the operations of our own
mind, and on the command which is exercised by will, both
over the organs of the body and faculties of the soul.

52   We shall proceed to examine this pretension; and first
with regard to the influence of volition over the organs of
the body. This influence, we may observe, is a fact, which,
like all other natural events, can be known only by experience, and can never beforeseen from any apparent energy

---

[1] Mr. Locke, in his chapter of power, says that, finding from experience, that there are several new productions in matter, and concluding
that there must somewhere be a power capable of producing them, we
arrive at last by this reasoning at the idea of power. But no reasoning
can ever give us a new, original, simple idea; as this philosopher himself
confesses. This, therefore, can never be the origin of that idea.

or power in the cause, which connects it with the effect, and renders the one an infallible consequence of the other. The motion of our body follows upon the command of our will. Of this we are every moment conscious. But the means, by which this is effected ; the energy, by which the will performs so extraordinary an operation ; of this we are so far from being immediately conscious, that it must for ever escape our most diligent enquiry.

For *first*; is there any principle in all nature more mysterious than the union of soul with body; by which a supposed spiritual substance acquires such an influence over a material one, that the most refined thought is able to actuate the grossest matter? Were we empowered, by a secret wish, to remove mountains, or control the planets in their orbit ; this extensive authority would not be more extraordinary, nor more beyond our comprehension. But if by consciousness we perceived any power or energy in the will, we must know this power; we must know its connexion with the effect ; we must know the secret union of soul and body, and the nature of both these substances ; by which the one is able to operate, in so many instances, upon the other.

Secondly, We are not able to move all the organs of the body with a like authority ; though we cannot assign any reason besides experience, for so remarkable a difference between one and the other. Why has the will an influence over the tongue and fingers, not over the heart or liver ? This question would never embarrass us, were we conscious of a power in the former case, not in the latter. We should then perceive, independent of experience, why the authority of will over the organs of the body is circumscribed within such particular limits. Being in that case fully acquainted with the power or force, by which it operates, we should also know, why its influence reaches precisely to such boundaries, and no farther.

F

A man, suddenly struck with palsy in the leg or arm, or who had newly lost those members, frequently endeavours, at first to move them, and employ them in their usual offices. Here he is as much conscious of power to command such limbs, as a man in perfect health is conscious of power to actuate any member which remains in its natural state and condition. But consciousness never deceives. Consequently, neither in the one case nor in the other, are we ever conscious of any power. We learn the influence of our will from experience alone. And experience only teaches us, how one event constantly follows another; without instructing us in the secret connexion, which binds them together, and renders them inseparable.

Thirdly, We learn from anatomy, that the immediate object of power in voluntary motion, is not the member itself which is moved, but certain muscles, and nerves, and animal spirits, and, perhaps, something still more minute and more unknown, through which the motion is successively propagated, ere it reach the member itself whose motion is the immediate object of volition. Can there be a more certain proof, that the power, by which this whole operation is performed, so far from being directly and fully known by an inward sentiment or consciousness, is, to the last degree, mysterious and unintelligible? Here the mind wills a certain event: Immediately another event, unknown to ourselves, and totally different from the one intended, is produced: This event produces another, equally unknown: Till at last, through a long succession, the desired event is produced. But if the original power were felt, it must be known: Were it known, its effect also must be known; since all power is relative to its effect. And *vice versa*, if the effect be not known, the power cannot be known nor felt. How indeed can we be conscious of a power to move our limbs, when we have no such power; but only that to move certain animal spirits, which, though they produce at last the motion of our limbs, yet operate in such a manner as is wholly beyond our comprehension?

We may, therefore, conclude from the whole, I hope, without any temerity, though with assurance; that our idea of power is not copied from any sentiment or consciousness of power within ourselves, when we give rise to animal motion, or apply our limbs to their proper use and office. That their motion follows the command of the will is a matter of common experience, like other natural events: But the power or energy by which this is effected, like that in other natural events, is unknown and inconceivable [1].

53   Shall we then assert, that we are conscious of a power or energy in our own minds, when, by an act or command of our will, we raise up a new idea, fix the mind to the contemplation of it, turn it on all sides, and at last dismiss it for some other idea, when we think that we have surveyed it with sufficient accuracy? I believe the same arguments will prove, that even this command of the will gives us no real idea of force or energy.

First, It must be allowed, that, when we know a power, we know that very circumstance in the cause, by which it is

[1] It may be pretended, that the resistance which we meet with in bodies, obliging us frequently to exert our force, and call up all our power, this gives us the idea of force and power. It is this *nisus*, or strong endeavour, of which we are conscious, that is the original impression from which this idea is copied. But, first, we attribute power to a vast number of objects, where we never can suppose this resistance or exertion of force to take place; to the Supreme Being, who never meets with any resistance; to the mind in its command over its ideas and limbs, in common thinking and motion, where the effect follows immediately upon the will, without any exertion or summoning up of force; to inanimate matter, which is not capable of this sentiment. *Secondly*, This sentiment of an endeavour to overcome resistance has no known connexion with any event: What follows it, we know by experience; but could not know it *à priori*. It must, however, be confessed, that the animal *nisus*, which we experience, though it can afford no accurate precise idea of power, enters very much into that vulgar, inaccurate idea, which is formed of it.

enabled to produce the effect : For these are supposed to be synonimous. We must, therefore, know both the cause and effect, and the relation between them. But do we pretend to be acquainted with the nature of the human soul and the nature of an idea, or the aptitude of the one to produce the other? This is a real creation ; a production of something out of nothing : Which implies a power so great, that it may seem, at first sight, beyond the reach of any being, less than infinite. At least it must be owned, that such a power is not felt, nor known, nor even conceivable by the mind. We only feel the event, namely, the existence of an idea, consequent to a command of the will : But the manner, in which this operation is performed, the power by which it is produced, is entirely beyond our comprehension.

Secondly, The command of the mind over itself is limited, as well as its command over the body ; and these limits are not known by reason, or any acquaintance with the nature of cause and effect, but only by experience and observation, as in all other natural events and in the operation of external objects. Our authority over our sentiments and passions is much weaker than that over our ideas ; and even the latter authority is circumscribed within very narrow boundaries. Will any one pretend to assign the ultimate reason of these boundaries, or show why the power is deficient in one case, not in another.

Thirdly, This self-command is very different at different times. A man in health possesses more of it than one languishing with sickness. We are more master of our thoughts in the morning than in the evening : Fasting, than after a full meal. Can we give any reason for these variations, except experience? Where then is the power, of which we pretend to be conscious? Is there not here, either in a spiritual or material substance, or both, some secret mechanism or structure of parts, upon which the effect depends, and which, being entirely unknown to us, renders the power or energy of the will equally unknown and incomprehensible?

Volition is surely an act of the mind, with which we are sufficiently acquainted. Reflect upon it. Consider it on all sides. Do you find anything in it like this creative power, by which it raises from nothing a new idea, and with a kind of *Fiat*, imitates the omnipotence of its Maker, if I may be allowed so to speak, who called forth into existence all the various scenes of nature? So far from being conscious of this energy in the will, it requires as certain experience as that of which we are possessed, to convince us that such extraordinary effects do ever result from a simple act of volition.

54 The generality of mankind never find any difficulty in accounting for the more common and familiar operations of nature—such as the descent of heavy bodies, the growth of plants, the generation of animals, or the nourishment of bodies by food: But suppose that, in all these cases, they perceive the very force or energy of the cause, by which it is connected with its effect, and is for ever infallible in its operation. They acquire, by long habit, such a turn of mind, that, upon the appearance of the cause, they immediately expect with assurance its usual attendant, and hardly conceive it possible that any other event could result from it. It is only on the discovery of extraordinary phaenomena, such as earthquakes, pestilence, and prodigies of any kind, that they find themselves at a loss to assign a proper cause, and to explain the manner in which the effect is produced by it. It is usual for men, in such difficulties, to have recourse to some invisible intelligent principle[1] as the immediate cause of that event which surprises them, and which, they think, cannot be accounted for from the common powers of nature. But philosophers, who carry their scrutiny

---

[1] Θεὸς ἀπὸ μηχανῆς.

a little farther, immediately perceive that, even in the most familiar events, the energy of the cause is as unintelligible as in the most unusual, and that we only learn by experience the frequent *Conjunction* of objects, without being ever able to comprehend anything like *Connexion* between them.

55 Here, then, many philosophers think themselves obliged by reason to have recourse, on all occasions, to the same principle, which the vulgar never appeal to but in cases that appear miraculous and supernatural. They acknowledge mind and intelligence to be, not only the ultimate and original cause of all things, but the immediate and sole cause of every event which appears in nature. They pretend that those objects which are commonly denominated *causes*, are in reality nothing but *occasions*; and that the true and direct principle of every effect is not any power or force in nature, but a volition of the Supreme Being, who wills that such particular objects should for ever be conjoined with each other. Instead of saying that one billiard-ball moves another by a force which it has derived from the author of nature, it is the Deity himself, they say, who, by a particular volition, moves the second ball, being determined to this operation by the impulse of the first ball, in consequence of those general laws which he has laid down to himself in the government of the universe. But philosophers advancing still in their inquiries, discover that, as we are totally ignorant of the power on which depends the mutual operation of bodies, we are no less ignorant of that power on which depends the operation of mind on body, or of body on mind; nor are we able, either from our senses or consciousness, to assign the ultimate principle in one case more than in the other. The same ignorance, therefore, reduces them to the same conclusion. They assert that the Deity is the immediate cause of the union between soul and body; and that they are not the organs of sense, which, being agitated by external objects, produce sensations in the mind;

but that it is a particular volition of our omnipotent Maker, which excites such a sensation, in consequence of such a motion in the organ. In like manner, it is not any energy in the will that produces local motion in our members : It is God himself, who is pleased to second our will, in itself impotent, and to command that motion which we erroneously attribute to our own power and efficacy. Nor do philosophers stop at this conclusion. They sometimes extend the same inference to the mind itself, in its internal operations. Our mental vision or conception of ideas is nothing but a revelation made to us by our Maker. When we voluntarily turn our thoughts to any object, and raise up its image in the fancy, it is not the will which creates that idea : It is the universal Creator, who discovers it to the mind, and renders it present to us.

56   Thus, according to these philosophers, every thing is full of God. Not content with the principle, that nothing exists but by his will, that nothing possesses any power but by his concession : They rob nature, and all created beings, of every power, in order to render their dependence on the Deity still more sensible and immediate. They consider not that, by this theory, they diminish, instead of magnifying, the grandeur of those attributes, which they affect so much to celebrate. It argues surely more power in the Deity to delegate a certain degree of power to inferior creatures than to produce every thing by his own immediate volition. It argues more wisdom to contrive at first the fabric of the world with such perfect foresight that, of itself, and by its proper operation, it may serve all the purposes of providence, than if the great Creator were obliged every moment to adjust its parts, and animate by his breath all the wheels of that stupendous machine.

But if we would have a more philosophical confutation of this theory, perhaps the two following reflections may suffice.

57   *First*, it seems to me that this theory of the universal energy and operation of the Supreme Being is too bold ever to carry conviction with it to a man, sufficiently apprized of the weakness of human reason, and the narrow limits to which it is confined in all its operations.   Though the chain of arguments which conduct to it were ever so logical, there must arise a strong suspicion, if not an absolute assurance, that it has carried us quite beyond the reach of our faculties, when it leads to conclusions so extraordinary, and so remote from common life and experience.   We are got into fairy land, long ere we have reached the last steps of our theory; and *there* we have no reason to trust our common methods of argument, or to think that our usual analogies and probabilities have any authority.   Our line is too short to fathom such immense abysses.   And however we may flatter ourselves that we are guided, in every step which we take, by a kind of verisimilitude and experience, we may be assured that this fancied experience has no authority when we thus apply it to subjects that lie entirely out of the sphere of experience.   But on this we shall have occasion to touch afterwards[1].

Secondly, I cannot perceive any force in the arguments on which this theory is founded.   We are ignorant, it is true, of the manner in which bodies operate on each other: Their force or energy is entirely incomprehensible: But are we not equally ignorant of the manner or force by which a mind, even the supreme mind, operates either on itself or on body?   Whence, I beseech you, do we acquire any idea of it?   We have no sentiment or consciousness of this power in ourselves.   We have no idea of the Supreme Being but what we learn from reflection on our own faculties.   Were our ignorance, therefore, a good reason for rejecting any

[1] Section XII.

thing, we should be led into that principle of denying all energy in the Supreme Being as much as in the grossest matter. We surely comprehend as little the operations of one as of the other. Is it more difficult to conceive that motion may arise from impulse than that it may arise from volition? All we know is our profound ignorance in both cases [1].

PART II.

58 But to hasten to a conclusion of this argument, which is already drawn out to too great a length: We have sought in vain for an idea of power or necessary connexion in all the sources from which we could suppose it to be derived. It appears that, in single instances of the operation of bodies, we never can, by our utmost scrutiny, discover any thing but one event following another, without being able to comprehend any force or power by which the cause

[1] I need not examine at length the *vis inertiae* which is so much talked of in the new philosophy, and which is ascribed to matter. We find by experience, that a body at rest or in motion continues for ever in its present state, till put from it by some new cause; and that a body impelled takes as much motion from the impelling body as it acquires itself. These are facts. When we call this a *vis inertiae*, we only mark these facts, without pretending to have any idea of the inert power; in the same manner as, when we talk of gravity, we mean certain effects, without comprehending that active power. It was never the meaning of Sir Isaac Newton to rob second causes of all force or energy; though some of his followers have endeavoured to establish that theory upon his authority. On the contrary, that great philosopher had recourse to an etherial active fluid to explain his universal attraction; though he was so cautious and modest as to allow, that it was a mere hypothesis, not to be insisted on, without more experiments. I must confess, that there is something in the fate of opinions a little extraordinary. Des Cartes insinuated that doctrine of the universal and sole efficacy of the Deity, without insisting on it. Malebranche and other Cartesians made it the foundation of all their philosophy. It had, however, no authority in England. Locke, Clarke, and Cudworth, never so much as take notice of it, but suppose all along, that matter has a real, though subordinate and derived power. By what means has it become so prevalent among our modern metaphysicians?

operates, or any connexion between it and its supposed effect. The same difficulty occurs in contemplating the operations of mind on body—where we observe the motion of the latter to follow upon the volition of the former, but are not able to observe or conceive the tie which binds together the motion and volition, or the energy by which the mind produces this effect. The authority of the will over its own faculties and ideas is not a whit more comprehensible: So that, upon the whole, there appears not, throughout all nature, any one instance of connexion which is conceivable by us. All events seem entirely loose and separate. One event follows another; but we never can observe any tie between them. They seem *conjoined*, but never *connected*. And as we can have no idea of any thing which never appeared to our outward sense or inward sentiment, the necessary conclusion *seems* to be that we have no idea of connexion or power at all, and that these words are absolutely without any meaning, when employed either in philosophical reasonings or common life.

59   But there still remains one method of avoiding this conclusion, and one source which we have not yet examined. When any natural object or event is presented, it is impossible for us, by any sagacity or penetration, to discover, or even conjecture, without experience, what event will result from it, or to carry our foresight beyond that object which is immediately present to the memory and senses. Even after one instance or experiment where we have observed a particular event to follow upon another, we are not entitled to form a general rule, or foretell what will happen in like cases; it being justly esteemed an unpardonable temerity to judge of the whole course of nature from one single experiment, however accurate or certain. But when one particular species of event has always, in all instances, been conjoined with another, we make no longer

any scruple of foretelling one upon the appearance of the
other, and of employing that reasoning, which can alone
assure us of any matter of fact or existence. We then
call the one object, *Cause*; the other, *Effect*. We suppose that there is some connexion between them; some
power in the one, by which it infallibly produces the other,
and operates with the greatest certainty and strongest
necessity.

It appears, then, that this idea of a necessary connexion
among events arises from a number of similar instances
which occur of the constant conjunction of these events;
nor can that idea ever be suggested by any one of these
instances, surveyed in all possible lights and positions.
But there is nothing in a number of instances, different
from every single instance, which is supposed to be exactly
similar; except only, that after a repetition of similar
instances, the mind is carried by habit, upon the appearance of one event, to expect its usual attendant, and to
believe that it will exist. This connexion, therefore, which
we *feel* in the mind, this customary transition of the
imagination from one object to its usual attendant, is the
sentiment or impression from which we form the idea of
power or necessary connexion. Nothing farther is in the
case. Contemplate the subject on all sides; you will never
find any other origin of that idea. This is the sole difference
between one instance, from which we can never receive the
idea of connexion, and a number of similar instances, by
which it is suggested. The first time a man saw the
communication of motion by impulse, as by the shock of
two billiard balls, he could not pronounce that the one
event was *connected*: but only that it was *conjoined* with
the other. After he has observed several instances of this
nature, he then pronounces them to be *connected*. What
alteration has happened to give rise to this new idea of
connexion? Nothing but that he now *feels* these events to

be *connected* in his imagination, and can readily foretell the
existence of one from the appearance of the other.   When
we say, therefore, that one object is connected with another,
we mean only that they have acquired a connexion in our
thought, and give rise to this inference, by which they
become proofs of each other's existence : A conclusion
which is somewhat extraordinary, but which seems founded
on sufficient evidence.   Nor will its evidence be weakened
by any general diffidence of the understanding, or sceptical
suspicion concerning every conclusion which is new and
extraordinary.   No conclusions can be more agreeable to
scepticism than such as make discoveries concerning the
weakness and narrow limits of human reason and capacity.

60   And what stronger instance can be produced of the
surprising ignorance and weakness of the understanding
than the present?   For surely, if there be any relation
among objects which it imports to us to know perfectly,
it is that of cause and effect.   On this are founded all
our reasonings concerning matter of fact or existence.   By
means of it alone we attain any assurance concerning
objects which are removed from the present testimony of
our memory and senses.   The only immediate utility of
all sciences, is to teach us, how to control and regulate
future events by their causes.   Our thoughts and enquiries
are, therefore, every moment, employed about this relation :
Yet so imperfect are the ideas which we form concerning
it, that it is impossible to give any just definition of cause,
except what is drawn from something extraneous and
foreign to it.   Similar objects are always conjoined with
similar.   Of this we have experience.   Suitably to this
experience, therefore, we may define a cause to be *an
object, followed by another, and where all the objects similar
to the first are followed by objects similar to the second.*   Or
in other words *where, if the first object had not been, the
second never had existed.*   The appearance of a cause always

conveys the mind, by a customary transition, to the idea of the effect. Of this also we have experience. We may, therefore, suitably to this experience, form another definition of cause, and call it, *an object followed by another, and whose appearance always conveys the thought to that other.* But though both these definitions be drawn from circumstances foreign to the cause, we cannot remedy this inconvenience, or attain any more perfect definition, which may point out that circumstance in the cause, which gives it a connexion with its effect.˙ We have no idea of, this connexion, nor even any distinct notion what it is we desire to know, when we endeavour at a conception of it. We say, for instance, that the vibration of this string is the cause of this particular sound. But what do we mean by that affirmation? We either mean *that this vibration is followed by this sound, and that all similar vibrations have been followed by similar sounds:* Or, *that this vibration is followed by this sound, and that upon the appearance of one the mind anticipates the senses, and forms immediately an idea of the other.* We may consider the relation of cause and effect in either of these two lights; but beyond these, we have no idea of it [1].

---

[1] According to these explications and definitions, the idea of *power* is relative as much as that of *cause*; and both have a reference to an effect, or some other event constantly conjoined with the former. When we consider the *unknown* circumstance of an object, by which the degree or quantity of its effect is fixed and determined, we call that its power: And accordingly, it is allowed by all philosophers, that the effect is the measure of the power. But if they had any idea of power, as it is in itself, why could not they Measure it in itself? The dispute whether the force of a body in motion be as its velocity, or the square of its velocity; this dispute, I say, need not be decided by comparing its effects in equal or unequal times; but by a direct mensuration and comparison.

As to the frequent use of the words, Force, Power, Energy, &c., which every where occur in common conversation, as well as in philosophy; that is no proof, that we are acquainted, in any instance, with the connecting principle between cause and effect, or can account ultimately for the production of one thing to another. These words, as commonly

61   To recapitulate, therefore, the reasonings of this section : Every idea is copied from some preceding impression or sentiment; and where we cannot find any impression, we may be certain that there is no idea. In all single instances of the operation of bodies or minds, there is nothing that produces any impression, nor consequently can suggest any idea of power or necessary connexion. But when many uniform instances appear, and the same object is always followed by the same event; we then begin to entertain the notion of cause and connexion. We then *feel* a new sentiment or impression, to wit, a customary connexion in the thought or imagination between one object and its usual attendant; and this sentiment is the original of that idea which we seek for. For as this idea arises from a number of similar instances, and not from any single instance, it must arise from that circumstance, in which the number of instances differ from every individual instance. But this customary connexion or transition of the imagination is the only circumstance in which they differ. In every other particular they are alike. The first instance which we saw of motion communicated by the shock of two billiard balls (to return to this obvious illustration) is exactly similar to any instance that may, at present, occur to us; except only, that we could not, at first, *infer*

used, have very loose meanings annexed to them; and their ideas are very uncertain and confused. No animal can put external bodies in motion without the sentiment of a *nisus* or endeavour; and every animal has a sentiment or feeling from the stroke or blow of an external object, that is in motion. These sensations, which are merely animal, and from which we can *à priori* draw no inference, we are apt to transfer to inanimate objects, and to suppose, that they have some such feelings, whenever they transfer or receive motion. With regard to energies, which are exerted, without our annexing to them any idea of communicated motion, we consider only the constant experienced conjunction of the events ; and as we *feel* a customary connexion between the ideas, we transfer that feeling to the objects; as nothing is more usual than to apply to external bodies every internal sensation, which they occasion.

one event from the other; which we are enabled to do at present, after so long a course of uniform experience. I know not whether the reader will readily apprehend this reasoning. I am afraid that, should I multiply words about it, or throw it into a greater variety of lights, it would only become more obscure and intricate. In all abstract reasonings there is one point of view which, if we can happily hit, we shall go farther towards illustrating the subject than by all the eloquence and copious expression in the world. This point of view we should endeavour to reach, and reserve the flowers of rhetoric for subjects which are more adapted to them.

SECTION VIII.

OF LIBERTY AND NECESSITY.

PART I.

62 IT might reasonably be expected in questions which have been canvassed and disputed with great eagerness, since the first origin of science and philosophy, that the meaning of all the terms, at least, should have been agreed upon among the disputants; and our enquiries, in the course of two thousand years, been able to pass from words to the true and real subject of the controversy. For how easy may it seem to give exact definitions of the terms employed in reasoning, and make these definitions, not the mere sound of words, the object of future scrutiny and examination? But if we consider the matter more narrowly, we shall be apt to draw a quite opposite conclusion. From this circumstance alone, that a controversy has been long kept on foot, and remains still undecided, we may presume that there is some ambiguity in the expression, and that the disputants affix different ideas to the terms employed in the controversy. For as the faculties of the mind are supposed to be naturally alike in every individual; otherwise nothing could be more fruitless than to reason or dispute together; it were impossible, if men affix the same ideas to their terms, that they could so long form different opinions of the same subject; especially when they communicate their views, and each party turn themselves on all sides, in search of arguments which may give them the victory over their antagonists. It is true, if men attempt the discussion of questions which lie entirely beyond the reach of human capacity, such as those concerning the origin of worlds, or the economy of the intellectual system or region of spirits, they may long beat the air in their fruitless contests, and never arrive at any determinate conclusion. But if the question regard any subject of common life and experience, nothing, one would think, could preserve the dispute so long undecided but some ambiguous expressions, which keep the antagonists still at a distance, and hinder them from grappling with each other.

63   This has been the case in the long disputed question concerning liberty and necessity; and to so remarkable a degree that, if I be not much mistaken, we shall find, that all mankind, both learned and ignorant, have always been of the same opinion with regard to this subject, and that a few intelligible definitions would immediately have put an end to the whole controversy. I own that this dispute has been so much canvassed on all hands, and has led philosophers into such a labyrinth of obscure sophistry, that it is no wonder, if a sensible reader indulge his ease so far as to turn a deaf ear to the proposal of such a question, from which he can expect neither instruction or entertainment. But the state of the argument here proposed may, perhaps, serve to renew his attention; as it has more novelty, promises at least some decision of the controversy, and will not much disturb his ease by any intricate or obscure reasoning.

I hope, therefore, to make it appear that all men have ever agreed in the doctrine both of necessity and of liberty, according to any reasonable sense, which can be put on these terms; and that the whole controversy has hitherto turned merely upon words. We shall begin with examining the doctrine of necessity.

G

64   It is universally allowed that matter, in all its operations, is actuated by a necessary force, and that every natural effect is so precisely determined by the energy of its cause that no other effect, in such particular circumstances, could possibly have resulted from it. The degree and direction of every motion is, by the laws of nature, prescribed with such exactness that a living creature may as soon arise from the shock of two bodies as motion in any other degree or direction than what is actually produced by it. Would we, therefore, form a just and precise idea of *necessity*, we must consider whence that idea arises when we apply it to the operation of bodies.

It seems evident that, if all the scenes of nature were continually shifted in such a manner that no two events bore any resemblance to each other, but every object was entirely new, without any similitude to whatever had been seen before, we should never, in that case, have attained the least idea of necessity, or of a connexion among these objects. We might say, upon such a supposition, that one object or event has followed another; not that one was produced by the other. The relation of cause and effect must be utterly unknown to mankind. Inference and reasoning concerning the operations of nature would, from that moment, be at an end; and the memory and senses remain the only canals, by which the knowledge of any real existence could possibly have access to the mind. Our idea, therefore, of necessity and causation arises entirely from the uniformity observable in the operations of nature, where similar objects are constantly conjoined together, and the mind is determined by custom to infer the one from the appearance of the other. These two circumstances form the whole of that necessity, which we ascribe to matter. Beyond the constant *conjunction* of similar objects, and the consequent *inference* from one to the other, we have no notion of any necessity or connexion.

If it appear, therefore, that all mankind have ever allowed, without any doubt or hesitation, that these two circumstances take place in the voluntary actions of men, and in the operations of mind; it must follow, that all mankind have ever agreed in the doctrine of necessity, and that they have hitherto disputed, merely for not understanding each other.

65   As to the first circumstance, the constant and regular conjunction of similar events, we may possibly satisfy ourselves by the following considerations. It is universally acknowledged that there is a great uniformity among the actions of men, in all nations and ages, and that human nature remains still the same, in its principles and operations. The same motives always produce the same actions: The same events follow from the same causes. Ambition, avarice, self-love, vanity, friendship, generosity, public spirit: these passions, mixed in various degrees, and distributed through society, have been, from the beginning of the world, and still are, the source of all the actions and enterprises, which have ever been observed among mankind. Would you know the sentiments, inclinations, and course of life of the Greeks and Romans? Study well the temper and actions of the French and English: You cannot be much mistaken in transferring to the former *most* of the observations which you have made with regard to the latter. Mankind are so much the same, in all times and places, that history informs us of nothing new or strange in this particular. Its chief use is only to discover the constant and universal principles of human nature, by showing men in all varieties of circumstances and situations, and furnishing us with materials from which we may form our observations and become acquainted with the regular springs of human action and behaviour. These records or wars, intrigues, factions, and revolutions, are so many collections of experiments, by which the politician or moral

philosopher fixes the principles of his science, in the same
manner as the physician or natural philosopher becomes
acquainted with the nature of plants, minerals, and other
external objects, by the experiments which he forms concerning them. Nor are the earth, water, and other elements,
examined by Aristotle, and Hippocrates, more like to those
which at present lie under our observation than the men
described by Polybius and Tacitus are to those who now
govern the world.

Should a traveller, returning from a far country, bring us
an account of men, wholly different from any with whom
we were ever acquainted; men, who were entirely divested
of avarice, ambition, or revenge; who knew no pleasure
but friendship, generosity, and public spirit; we should
immediately, from these circumstances, detect the falsehood, and prove him a liar, with the same certainty as if
he had stuffed his narration with stories of centaurs and
dragons, miracles and prodigies. And if we would explode
any forgery in history, we cannot make use of a more convincing argument, than to prove, that the actions ascribed
to any person are directly contrary to the course of nature,
and that no human motives, in such circumstances, could
ever induce him to such a conduct. The veracity of
Quintus Curtius is as much to be suspected, when he
describes the supernatural courage of Alexander, by which
he was hurried on singly to attack multitudes, as when he
describes his supernatural force and activity, by which he
was able to resist them. So readily and universally do we
acknowledge a uniformity in human motives and actions as
well as in the operations of body.

Hence likewise the benefit of that experience, acquired
by long life and a variety of business and company, in
order to instruct us in the principles of human nature, and
regulate our future conduct, as well as speculation. By
means of this guide, we mount up to the knowledge of

men's inclinations and motives, from their actions, expressions, and even gestures; and again descend to the
interpretation of their actions from our knowledge of
their motives and inclinations. The general observations
treasured up by a course of experience, give us the clue
of human nature, and teach us to unravel all its intricacies.
Pretexts and appearances no longer deceive us. Public
declarations pass for the specious colouring of a cause.
And though virtue and honour be allowed their proper
weight and authority, that perfect disinterestedness, so often
pretended to, is never expected in multitudes and parties;
seldom in their leaders; and scarcely even in individuals
of any rank or station. But were there no uniformity in
human actions, and were every experiment which we could
form of this kind irregular and anomalous, it were impossible to collect any general observations concerning mankind; and no experience, however accurately digested by
reflection, would ever serve to any purpose. Why is the
aged husbandman more skilful in his calling than the young
beginner but because there is a certain uniformity in the
operation of the sun, rain, and earth towards the production of vegetables; and experience teaches the old
practitioner the rules by which this operation is governed
and directed.

66   We must not, however, expect that this uniformity of
human actions should be carried to such a length as that
all men, in the same circumstances, will always act precisely
in the same manner, without making any allowance for
the diversity of characters, prejudices, and opinions. Such
a uniformity in every particular, is found in no part of
nature. On the contrary, from observing the variety of
conduct in different men, we are enabled to form a greater
variety of maxims, which still suppose a degree of uniformity and regularity.

Are the manners of men different in different ages and

countries? We learn thence the great force of custom and education, which mould the human mind from its infancy and form it into a fixed and established character. Is the behaviour and conduct of the one sex very unlike that of the other? Is it thence we become acquainted with the different characters which nature has impressed upon the sexes, and which she preserves with constancy and regularity? Are the actions of the same person much diversified in the different periods of his life, from infancy to old age? This affords room for many general observations concerning the gradual change of our sentiments and inclinations, and the different maxims which prevail in the different ages of human creatures. Even the characters, which are peculiar to each individual, have a uniformity in their influence; otherwise our acquaintance with the persons and our observation of their conduct could never teach us their dispositions, or serve to direct our behaviour with regard to them.

67   I grant it possible to find some actions, which seem to have no regular connexion with any known motives, and are exceptions to all the measures of conduct which have ever been established for the government of men. But if we would willingly know what judgement should be formed of such irregular and extraordinary actions, we may consider the sentiments commonly entertained with regard to those irregular events which appear in the course of nature, and the operations of external objects. All causes are not conjoined to their usual effects with like uniformity. An artificer, who handles only dead matter, may be disappointed of his aim, as well as the politician, who directs the conduct of sensible and intelligent agents.

The vulgar, who take things according to their first appearance, attribute the uncertainty of events to such an uncertainty in the causes as makes the latter often fail of their usual influence; though they meet with no impediment in their operation. But philosophers, observing that, almost in every part of nature, there is contained a vast variety of springs and principles, which are hid, by reason of their minuteness or remoteness, find, that it is at least possible the contrariety of events may not proceed from any contingency in the cause, but from the secret operation of contrary causes. This possibility is converted into certainty by farther observation, when they remark that, upon an exact scrutiny, a contrariety of effects always betrays a contrariety of causes, and proceeds from their mutual opposition. A peasant can give no better reason for the stopping of any clock or watch than to say that it does not commonly go right: But an artist easily perceives that the same force in the spring or pendulum has always the same influence on the wheels; but fails of its usual effect, perhaps by reason of a grain of dust, which puts a stop to the whole movement. From the observation of several parallel instances, philosophers form a maxim that the connexion between all causes and effects is equally necessary, and that its seeming uncertainty in some instances proceeds from the secret opposition of contrary causes.

Thus, for instance, in the human body, when the usual symptoms of health or sickness disappoint our expectation; when medicines operate not with their wonted powers; when irregular events follow from any particular cause; the philosopher and physician are not surprised at the matter, nor are ever tempted to deny, in general, the necessity and uniformity of those principles by which the animal economy is conducted. They know that a human body is a mighty complicated machine: That many secret powers lurk in it, which are altogether beyond our comprehension: That to us it must often appear very uncertain in its operations: And that therefore the irregular events, which outwardly discover themselves, can be no proof that the laws of nature are not observed with the greatest regularity in its internal operations and government.

68   The philosopher, if he be consistent, must apply the same reasoning to the actions and volitions of intelligent agents. The most irregular and unexpected resolutions of men may frequently be accounted for by those who know every particular circumstance of their character and situation. A person of an obliging disposition gives a peevish answer: But he has the toothache, or has not dined. A stupid fellow discovers an uncommon alacrity in his carriage: But he has met with a sudden piece of good fortune. Or even when an action, as sometimes happens, cannot be particularly accounted for, either by the person himself or by others; we know, in general, that the characters of men are, to a certain degree, inconstant and irregular. This is, in a manner, the constant character of human nature; though it be applicable, in a more particular manner, to some persons who have no fixed rule for their conduct, but proceed in a continued course of caprice and inconstancy. The internal principles and motives may operate in a uniform manner, notwithstanding these seeming irregularities; in the same manner as the winds, rain, clouds, and other variations of the weather are supposed to be governed by steady principles; though not easily discoverable by human sagacity and enquiry.

69   Thus it appears, not only that the conjunction between motives and voluntary actions is as regular and uniform as that between the cause and effect in any part of nature; but also that this regular conjunction has been universally acknowledged among mankind, and has never been the subject of dispute, either in philosophy or common life. Now, as it is from past experience that we draw all inferences concerning the future, and as we conclude that objects will always be conjoined together which we find to have always been conjoined; it may seem superfluous to prove that this experienced uniformity in human actions is a source whence we draw *inferences* concerning them. But in order to throw

the argument into a greater variety of lights we shall also insist, though briefly, on this latter topic.

The mutual dependence of men is so great in all societies that scarce any human action is entirely complete in itself, or is performed without some reference to the actions of others, which are requisite to make it answer fully the intention of the agent. The poorest artificer, who labours alone, expects at least the protection of the magistrate, to ensure him the enjoyment of the fruits of his labour. He also expects that, when he carries his goods to market, and offers them at a reasonable price, he shall find purchasers, and shall be able, by the money he acquires, to engage others to supply him with those commodities which are requisite for his subsistence. In proportion as men extend their dealings, and render their intercourse with others more complicated, they always comprehend, in their schemes of life, a greater variety of voluntary actions, which they expect, from the proper motives, to co-operate with their own. In all these conclusions they take their measures from past experience, in the same manner as in their reasonings concerning external objects; and firmly believe that men, as well as all the elements, are to continue, in their operations, the same that they have ever found them. A manufacturer reckons upon the labour of his servants for the execution of any work as much as upon the tools which he employs, and would be equally surprised were his expectations disappointed. In short, this experimental inference and reasoning concerning the actions of others enters so much into human life that no man, while awake, is ever a moment without employing it. Have we not reason, therefore, to affirm that all mankind have always agreed in the doctrine of necessity according to the foregoing definition and explication of it?

70 Nor have philosophers ever entertained a different opinion from the people in this particular. For, not to mention that almost every action of their life supposes that opinion, there

are even few of the speculative parts of learning to which it
is not essential.   What would become of *history*, had we not
a dependence on the veracity of the historian according to
the experience which we have had of mankind?   How could
politics be a science, if laws and forms of goverment had not
a uniform influence upon society?   Where would be the
foundation of *morals*, if particular characters had no certain
or determinate power to produce particular sentiments, and
if these sentiments had no constant operation on actions?
And with what pretence could we employ our *criticism* upon
any poet or polite author, if we could not pronounce the
conduct and sentiments of his actors either natural or unnatural to such characters, and in such circumstances?
It seems almost impossible, therefore, to engage either in
science or action of any kind without acknowledging the
doctrine of necessity, and this *inference* from motive to
voluntary actions, from characters to conduct.

And indeed, when we consider how aptly *natural* and
moral evidence link together, and form only one chain of
argument, we shall make no scruple to allow that they are
of the same nature, and derived from the same principles.
A prisoner who has neither money nor interest, discovers
the impossibility of his escape, as well when he considers
the obstinacy of the gaoler, as the walls and bars with
which he is surrounded; and, in all attempts for his freedom,
chooses rather to work upon the stone and iron of the one,
than upon the inflexible nature of the other.   The same
prisoner, when conducted to the scaffold, foresees his death
as certainly from the constancy and fidelity of his guards, as
from the operation of the axe or wheel.   His mind runs
along a certain train of ideas: The refusal of the soldiers
to consent to his escape; the action of the executioner;
the separation of the head and body; bleeding, convulsive
motions, and death.   Here is a connected chain of natural
causes and voluntary actions; but the mind feels no differ-

ence between them in passing from one link to another:
Nor is less certain of the future event than if it were connected with the objects present to the memory or senses, by
a train of causes, cemented together by what we are pleased
to call a *physical* necessity. The same experienced union
has the same effect on the mind, whether the united
objects be motives, volition, and actions; or figure and
motion. We may change the name of things; but their
nature and their operation on the understanding never
change.

Were a man, whom I know to be honest and opulent,
and with whom I live in intimate friendship, to come into
my house, where I am surrounded with my servants, I rest
assured that he is not to stab me before he leaves it in
order to rob me of my silver standish; and I no more
suspect this event than the falling of the house itself, which
is new, and solidly built and founded.—*But he may have
been seized with a sudden and unknown frenzy.*—So may
a sudden earthquake arise, and shake and tumble my house
about my ears. I shall therefore change the suppositions.
I shall say that I know with certainty that he is not to put
his hand into the fire and hold it there till it be consumed:
And this event, I think I can foretell with the same assurance,
as that, if he throw himself out at the window, and meet
with no obstruction, he will not remain a moment suspended
in the air. No suspicion of an unknown frenzy can give
the least possibility to the former event, which is so contrary to all the known principles of human nature. A man
who at noon leaves his purse full of gold on the pavement
at Charing-Cross, may as well expect that it will fly away
like a feather, as that he will find it untouched an hour after.
Above one half of human reasonings contain inferences of
a similar nature, attended with more or less degrees of certainty proportioned to our experience of the usual conduct
of mankind in such particular situations.

71 I have frequently considered, what could possibly be the reason why all mankind, though they have ever, without hesitation, acknowledged the doctrine of necessity in their whole practice and reasoning, have yet discovered such a reluctance to acknowledge it in words, and have rather shown a propensity, in all ages, to profess the contrary opinion. The matter, I think, may be accounted for after the following manner. If we examine the operations of body, and the production of effects from their causes, we shall find that all our faculties can never carry us farther in our knowledge of this relation than barely to observe that particular objects are *constantly conjoined* together, and that the mind is carried, by a *customary transition,* from the appearance of one to the belief of the other. But though this conclusion concerning human ignorance be the result of the strictest scrutiny of this subject, men still entertain a strong propensity to believe that they penetrate farther into the powers of nature, and perceive something like a necessary connexion between the cause and the effect. When again they turn their reflections towards the operations of their own minds, and *feel* no such connexion of the motive and the action; they are thence apt to suppose, that there is a difference between the effects which result from material force, and those which arise from thought and intelligence. But being once convinced that we know nothing farther of causation of any kind than merely the *constant conjunction* of objects, and the consequent *inference* of the mind from one to another, and finding that these two circumstances are universally allowed to have place in voluntary actions; we may be more easily led to own the same necessity common to all causes. And though this reasoning may contradict the systems of many philosophers, in ascribing necessity to the determinations of the will, we shall find, upon reflection, that they dissent from it in words only, not in their real sentiment. Necessity, according to the

sense in which it is here taken, has never yet been rejected, nor can ever, I think, be rejected by any philosopher. It may only, perhaps, be pretended that the mind can perceive, in the operations of matter, some farther connexion between the cause and effect; and connexion that has not place in voluntary actions of intelligent beings. Now whether it be so or not, can only appear upon examination; and it is incumbent on these philosophers to make good their assertion, by defining or describing that necessity, and pointing it out to us in the operations of material causes.

72   It would seem, indeed, that men begin at the wrong end of this question concerning liberty and necessity, when they enter upon it by examining the faculties of the soul, the influence of the understanding, and the operations of the will. Let them first discuss a more simple question, namely, the operations of body and of brute unintelligent matter; and try whether they can there form any idea of causation and necessity, except that of a constant conjunction of objects, and subsequent inference of the mind from one to another. If these circumstances form, in reality, the whole of that necessity, which we conceive in matter, and if these circumstances be also universally acknowledged to take place in the operations of the mind, the dispute is at an end; at least, must be owned to be thenceforth merely verbal. But as long as we will rashly suppose, that we have some farther idea of necessity and causation in the operations of external objects; at the same time, that we can find nothing farther in the voluntary actions of the mind; there is no possibility of bringing the question to any determinate issue, while we proceed upon so erroneous a supposition. The only method of undeceiving us is to mount up higher; to examine the narrow extent of science when applied to material causes; and to convince ourselves that all we know of them is the constant conjunction and inference above mentioned. We may, perhaps, find that it

is with difficulty we are induced 'to fix such narrow limits to·
human understanding: But we can afterwards find no
difficulty when we come to apply this doctrine to the actions
of the will. For as it is evident that these have a regular
conjunction with motives and circumstances and characters,
and as we always draw inferences from one to the other,
we must be obliged to acknowledge in words that necessity,
which we have already avowed, in every deliberation of our
lives, and in every step of our conduct and behaviour.[1]

[1] The prevalence of the doctrine of liberty may be accounted for, from
another cause, viz. a false sensation or seeming experience which we
have, or may have, of liberty or indifference, in many of our actions.
The necessity of any action, whether of matter or of mind, is not,
properly speaking, a quality in the agent, but in any thinking or
intelligent being, who may consider the action; and it consists chiefly
in the determination of his thoughts to infer the existence of that action
from some preceding objects; as liberty, when opposed to necessity, is
nothing but the want of that determination, and a certain looseness or
indifference, which we feel, in passing, or not passing, from the idea of
one object to that of any succeeding one. Now we may observe, that,
though, in *reflecting* on human actions, we seldom feel such a looseness,
or indifference, but are commonly able to infer them with considerable
certainty from their motives, and from the dispositions of the agent; yet
it frequently happens, that, in *performing* the actions themselves, we
are sensible of something like it: And as all resembling objects are
readily taken for each other, this has been employed as a demonstrative
and even intuitive proof of human liberty. We feel, that our actions are
subject to our will, on most occasions; and imagine we feel, that the
will itself is subject to nothing, because, when by a denial of it we are
provoked to try, we feel, that it moves easily every way, and produces
an image of itself (or a *Velleity*, as it is called in the schools) even on
that side, on which it did not settle. This image, or faint motion, we
persuade ourselves, could, at that time, have been compleated into the
thing itself; because, should that be denied, we find, upon a second
trial, that, at present, it can. We consider not, that the fantastical
desire of shewing liberty, is here the motive of our actions. And it
seems certain, that, however we may imagine we feel a liberty within
ourselves, a spectator can commonly infer our actions from our motives
and character; and even where he cannot, he concludes in general, that
he might, were he perfectly acquainted with every circumstance of our
situation and temper, and the most secret springs of our complexion and
disposition. Now this is the very essence of necessity, according to the
foregoing doctrine.

73 But to proceed in this reconciling project with regard to the question of liberty and necessity; the most contentious question of metaphysics, the most contentious science; it will not require many words to prove, that all mankind have ever agreed in the doctrine of liberty as well as in that of necessity, and that the whole dispute, in this respect also, has been hitherto merely verbal. For what is meant by liberty, when applied to voluntary actions? We cannot surely mean that actions have so little connexion with motives, inclinations, and circumstances, that one does not follow with a certain degree of uniformity from the other, and that one affords no inference by which we can conclude the existence of the other. For these are plain and acknowledged matters of fact. By liberty, then, we can only mean *a power of acting or not acting, according to the determinations of the will;* that is, if we choose to remain at rest, we may; if we choose to move, we also may. Now this hypothetical liberty is universally allowed to belong to every one who is not a prisoner and in chains. Here, then, is no subject of dispute.

74 Whatever definition we may give of liberty, we should be careful to observe two requisite circumstances; *first,* that it be consistent with plain matter of fact; *secondly,* that it be consistent with itself. If we observe these circumstances, and render our definition intelligible, I am persuaded that all mankind will be found of one opinion with regard to it.

It is universally allowed that nothing exists without a cause of its existence, and that chance, when strictly examined, is a mere negative word, and means not any real power which has anywhere a being in nature. But it is pretended that some causes are necessary, some not necessary. Here then is the advantage of definitions. Let any one *define a cause,* without comprehending, as a part of the definition, a *necessary connexion* with its effect; and let him show distinctly the origin of the idea, expressed by the definition; and I shall readily give up the whole controversy. But if the foregoing explication of the matter be received, this must be absolutely impracticable. Had not objects a regular conjunction with each other, we should never have entertained any notion of cause and effect; and this regular conjunction produces that inference of the understanding, which is the only connexion, that we can have any comprehension of. Whoever attempts a definition of cause, exclusive of these circumstances, will be obliged either to employ unintelligible terms or such as are synonymous to the term which he endeavours to define [1]. And if the definition above mentioned be admitted; liberty, when opposed to necessity, not to constraint, is the same thing with chance; which is universally allowed to have no existence.

PART II.

75   THERE is no method of reasoning more common, and yet none more blameable, than, in philosophical disputes, to endeavour the refutation of any hypothesis, by a pretence of its dangerous consequences to religion and morality. When any opinion leads to absurdities, it is certainly false; but it is not certain that an opinion is false, because it is of dangerous consequence. Such topics, therefore, ought entirely to be forborne; as serving nothing to the discovery of truth, but only to make the person of an antagonist odious. This I observe in general, without pretending to

---

[1] Thus, if a cause be defined, *that which produces any thing*; it is easy to observe, that *producing* is synonimous to *causing*. In like manner, if a cause be defined, *that by which any thing exists*; this is liable to the same objection. For what is meant by these words, *by which*? Had it been said, that a cause is *that* after which any thing *constantly exists*; we should have understood the terms. For this is, indeed, all we know of the matter. And this constancy forms the very essence of necessity, nor have we any other idea of it.

draw any advantage from it. I frankly submit to an examination of this kind, and shall venture to affirm that the doctrines, both of necessity and of liberty, as above explained, are not only consistent with morality, but are absolutely essential to its support.

Necessity may be defined two ways, conformably to the two definitions of *cause*, of which it makes an essential part. It consists either in the constant conjunction of like objects, or in the inference of the understanding from one object to another. Now necessity, in both these senses, (which, indeed, are at bottom the same) has universally, though tacitly, in the schools, in the pulpit, and in common life, been allowed to belong to the will of man; and no one has ever pretended to deny that we can draw inferences concerning human actions, and that those inferences are founded on the experienced union of like actions, with like motives, inclinations, and circumstances. The only particular in which any one can differ, is, that either, perhaps, he will refuse to give the name of necessity to this property of human actions : But as long as the meaning is understood, I hope the word can do no harm: Or that he will maintain it possible to discover something farther in the operations of matter. But this, it must be acknowledged, can be of no consequence to morality or religion, whatever it may be to natural philosophy or metaphysics. We may here be mistaken in asserting that there is no idea of any other necessity or connexion in the actions of body : But surely we ascribe nothing to the actions of the mind, but what everyone does, and must readily allow of. We change no circumstance in the received orthodox system with regard to the will, but only in that with regard to material objects and causes. Nothing, therefore, can be more innocent, at least, than this doctrine.

76 All laws being founded on rewards and punishments, it is supposed as a fundamental principle, that these motives

H

have a regular and uniform influence on the mind, and both produce the good and prevent the evil actions. We may give to this influence what name we please; but, as it is usually conjoined with the action, it must be esteemed a *cause*, and be looked upon as an instance of that necessity, which we would here establish.

The only proper object of hatred or vengeance is a person or creature, endowed with thought and conscious-ness; and when any criminal or injurious actions excite that passion, it is only by their relation to the person, or connexion with him. Actions are, by their very nature, temporary and perishing; and where they proceed not from some *cause* in the character and disposition of the person who performed them, they can neither redound to his honour, if good; nor infamy, if evil. The actions themselves may be blameable; they may be contrary to all the rules of morality and religion: But the person is not answerable for them; and as they proceeded from nothing in him that is durable and constant, and leave nothing of that nature behind them, it is impossible he can, upon their account, become the object of punishment or vengeance. According to the principle, therefore, which denies necessity, and consequently causes, a man is as pure and untainted, after having committed the most horrid crime, as at the first moment of his birth, nor is his character anywise concerned in his actions, since they are not derived from it, and the wickedness of the one can never be used as a proof of the depravity of the other.

Men are not blamed for such actions as they perform ignorantly and casually, whatever may be the consequences. Why? but because the principles of these actions are only momentary, and terminate in them alone. Men are less blamed for such actions as they perform hastily and unpre-meditately than for such as proceed from deliberation. For what reason? but because a hasty temper, though a constant cause or principle in the mind, operates only by intervals, and infects not the whole character. Again, repentance wipes off every crime, if attended with a reformation of life and manners. How is this to be accounted for? but by asserting that actions render a person criminal merely as they are proofs of criminal principles in the mind; and when, by an alteration of these principles, they cease to be just proofs, they likewise cease to be criminal. But, except upon the doctrine of necessity, they never were just proofs, and consequently never were criminal.

77   It will be equally easy to prove, and from the same arguments, that *liberty*, according to that definition above mentioned, in which all men agree, is also essential to morality, and that no human actions, where it is wanting, are susceptible of any moral qualities, or can be the objects either of approbation or dislike. For as actions are objects of our moral sentiment, so far only as they are indications of the internal character, passions, and affections; it is impossible that they can give rise either to praise or blame, where they proceed not from these principles, but are derived altogether from external violence.

78   I pretend not to have obviated or removed all objections to this theory, with regard to necessity and liberty. I can foresee other objections, derived from topics which have not here been treated of. It may be said, for instance, that, if voluntary actions be subjected to the same laws of necessity with the operations of matter, there is a continued chain of necessary causes, pre-ordained and pre-determined, reaching from the original cause of all to every single volition of every human creature. No contingency anywhere in the universe; no indifference; no liberty. While we act, we are, at the same time, acted upon. The ultimate Author of all our volitions is the Creator of the world, who first bestowed motion on this immense machine, and placed all beings in that particular position, whence

every subsequent event, by an inevitable necessity, must result. Human actions, therefore, either can have no moral turpitude at all, as proceeding from so good a cause ; or if they have any turpitude, they must involve our Creator in the same guilt, while he is acknowledged to be their ultimate cause and author. For as a man, who fired a mine, is answerable for all the consequences whether the train he employed be long or short ; so wherever a continued chain of necessary causes is fixed, that Being, either finite or infinite, who produces the first, is likewise the author of all the rest, and must both bear the blame and acquire the praise which belong to them. Our clear and unalterable ideas of morality establish this rule, upon unquestionable reasons, when we examine the consequences of any human action ; and these reasons must still have greater force when applied to the volitions and intentions of a Being infinitely wise and powerful. Ignorance or impotence may be pleaded for so limited a creature as man ; but those imperfections have no place in our Creator. He foresaw, he ordained, he intended all those actions of men, which we so rashly pronounce criminal. And we must therefore conclude, either that they are not criminal, or that the Deity, not man, is accountable for them. But as either of these positions is absurd and impious, it follows, that the doctrine from which they are deduced cannot possibly be true, as being liable to all the same objections. An absurd consequence, if necessary, proves the original doctrine to be absurd ; in the same manner as criminal actions render criminal the original cause, if the connexion between them be necessary and evitable.

This objection consists of two parts, which we shall examine separately ; *First*, that, if human actions can be traced up, by a necessary chain, to the Deity, they can never be criminal ; on account of the infinite perfection of that Being from whom they are derived, and who can intend nothing but what is altogether good and laudable. Or, *Secondly*, if they be criminal, we must retract the attribute of perfection, which we ascribe to the Deity, and must acknowledge him to be the ultimate author of guilt and moral turpitude in all his creatures.

79   The answer to the first objection seems obvious and convincing. There are many philosophers who, after an exact scrutiny of all the phenomena of nature, conclude, that the WHOLE, considered as one system, is, in every period of its existence, ordered with perfect benevolence; and that the utmost possible happiness will, in the end, result to all created beings, without any mixture of positive or absolute ill or misery. Every physical ill, say they, makes an essential part of this benevolent system, and could not possibly be removed, even by the Deity himself, considered as a wise agent, without giving entrance to greater ill, or excluding greater good, which will result from it. From this theory, some philosophers, and the ancient *Stoics* among the rest, derived a topic of consolation under all afflictions, while they taught their pupils that those ills under which they laboured were, in reality, goods to the universe; and that to an enlarged view, which could comprehend the whole system of nature, every event became an object of joy and exultation. But though this topic be specious and sublime, it was soon found in practice weak and ineffectual. You would surely more irritate than appease a man lying under the racking pains of the gout by preaching up to him the rectitude of those general laws, which produced the malignant humours in his body, and led them through the proper canals, to the sinews and nerves, where they now excite such acute torments. These enlarged views may, for a moment, please the imagination of a speculative man, who is placed in ease and security; but neither can they dwell with constancy on his mind, even though undisturbed by the emotions of pain or passion;

much less can they maintain their ground when attacked by such powerful antagonists. The affections take a narrower and more natural survey of their object; and by an economy, more suitable to the infirmity of human minds, regard alone the beings around us, and are actuated by such events as appear good or ill to the private system.

80   The case is the same with *moral* as with *physical* ill. It cannot reasonably be supposed, that those remote considerations, which are found of so little efficacy with regard to one, will have a more powerful influence with regard to the other. The mind of man is so formed by nature that, upon the appearance of certain characters, dispositions, and actions, it immediately feels the sentiment of approbation or blame; nor are there any emotions more essential to its frame and constitution. The characters which engage our approbation are chiefly such as contribute to the peace and security of human society; as the characters which excite blame are chiefly such as tend to public detriment and disturbance : Whence it may reasonably be presumed, that the moral sentiments arise, either mediately or immediately, from a reflection of these opposite interests. What though philosophical meditations establish a different opinion or conjecture; that everything is right with regard to the WHOLE, and that the qualities, which disturb society, are, in the main, as beneficial, and are as suitable to the primary intention of nature as those which more directly promote its happiness and welfare? Are such remote and uncertain speculations able to counterbalance the sentiments which arise from the natural and immediate view of the objects? A man who is robbed of a considerable sum; does he find his vexation for the loss anywise diminished by these sublime reflections? Why then should his moral resentment against the crime be supposed incompatible with them? Or why should not the acknowledgment of a real distinction between vice and virtue be reconcileable

to all speculative systems of philosophy, as well as that of a real distinction between personal beauty and deformity? Both these distinctions are founded in the natural sentiments of the human mind: And these sentiments are not to be controuled or altered by any philosophical theory or speculation whatsoever.

81   The *second* objection admits not of so easy and satisfactory an answer; nor is it possible to explain distinctly, how the Deity can be the mediate cause of all the actions of men, without being the author of sin and moral turpitude. These are mysteries, which mere natural and unassisted reason is very unfit to handle; and whatever system she embraces, she must find herself involved in inextricable difficulties, and even contradictions, at every step which she takes with regard to such subjects. To reconcile the indifference and contingency of human actions with prescience; or to defend absolute decrees, and yet free the Deity from being the author of sin, has been found hitherto to exceed all the power of philosophy. Happy, if she be thence sensible of her temerity, when she pries into these sublime mysteries; and leaving a scene so full of obscurities and perplexities, return, with suitable modesty, to her true and proper province, the examination of common life; where she will find difficulties enough to employ her enquiries, without launching into so boundless an ocean of doubt, uncertainty, and contradiction!

SECTION IX.

82 ALL our reasonings concerning matter of fact are founded
on a species of Analogy, which leads us to expect from any
cause the same events, which we have observed to result
from similar causes. Where the causes are entirely similar,
the analogy is perfect, and the inference, drawn from it, is
regarded as certain and conclusive : nor does any man ever
entertain a doubt, where he sees a piece of iron, that it will
have weight and cohesion of parts ; as in all other instances,
which have ever fallen under his observation. But where
the objects have not so exact a similarity, the analogy
is less perfect, and the inference is less conclusive ; though
still it has some force, in proportion to the degree of
similarity and resemblance. The anatomical observations,
formed upon one animal, are, by this species of reasoning,
extended to all animals ; and it is certain, that when the
circulation of the blood, for instance, is clearly proved to
have place in one creature, as a frog, or fish, it forms a strong
presumption, that the same principle has place in all. These
analogical observations may be carried farther, even to this
science, of which we are now treating ; and any theory, by
which we explain the operations of the understanding, or
the origin and connexion of the passions in man, will
acquire additional authority, if we find, that the same theory
is requisite to explain the same phenomena in all other
animals. We shall make trial of this, with regard to the

hypothesis, by which we have, in the foregoing discourse, endeavoured to account for all experimental reasonings; and it is hoped, that this new point of view will serve to confirm all our former observations.

83   *First,* It seems evident, that animals as well as men learn many things from experience, and infer, that the same events will always follow from the same causes. By this principle they become acquainted with the more obvious properties of external objects, and gradually, from their birth, treasure up a knowledge of the nature of fire, water, earth, stones, heights, depths, &c., and of the effects which result from their operation. The ignorance and inexperience of the young are here plainly distinguishable from the cunning and sagacity of the old, who have learned, by long observation, to avoid what hurt them, and to pursue what gave ease or pleasure. A horse, that has been accustomed to the field, becomes acquainted with the proper height which he can leap, and will never attempt what exceeds his force and ability. An old greyhound will trust the more fatiguing part of the chace to the younger, and will place himself so as to meet the hare in her doubles; nor are the conjectures, which he forms on this occasion, founded in any thing but his observation and experience.

This is still more evident from the effects of discipline and education on animals, who, by the proper application of rewards and punishments, may be taught any course of action, and most contrary to their natural instincts and propensities. Is it not experience, which renders a dog apprehensive of pain, when you menace him, or lift up the whip to beat him? Is it not even experience, which makes him answer to his name, and infer, from such an arbitrary sound, that you mean him rather than any of his fellows, and intend to call him, when you pronounce it in a certain manner, and with a certain tone and accent?

In all these cases, we may observe, that the animal infers

some fact beyond what immediately strikes his senses ; and
that this inference is altogether founded on past experience,
while the creature expects from the present object the same
consequences, which it has always found in its observation
to result from similar objects.

84   *Secondly,* It is impossible, that this inference of the animal
can be founded on any process of argument or reasoning,
by which he concludes, that like events must follow like
objects, and that the course of nature will always be regular
in its operations.   For if there be in reality any arguments
of this nature, they surely lie too abstruse for the observation
of such imperfect understandings ; since it may well employ
the utmost care and attention of a philosophic genius to
discover and observe them.   Animals, therefore, are not
guided in these inferences by reasoning: Neither are
children : Neither are the generality of mankind, in their
ordinary actions and conclusions : Neither are philosophers
themselves, who, in all the active parts of life, are, in the
main, the same with the vulgar, and are governed by the
same maxims.   Nature must have provided some other
principle, of more ready, and more general use and application ; nor can an operation of such immense consequence in
life, as that of inferring effects from causes, be trusted to
the uncertain process of reasoning and argumentation.
Were this doubtful with regard to men, it seems to admit
of no question with regard to the brute creation ; and the
conclusion being once firmly established in the one, we have
a strong presumption, from all the rules of analogy, that
it ought to be universally admitted, without any exception
or reserve.   It is custom alone, which engages animals,
from every object, that strikes their senses, to infer its
usual attendant, and carries their imagination, from the
appearance of the one, to conceive the other, in that
particular manner, which we denominate *belief.*   No other
explication can be given of this operation, in all the higher,

as well as lower classes of sensitive beings, which fall under our notice and observation [1].

[1] Since all reasonings concerning facts or causes is derived merely from custom, it may be asked how it happens, that men so much surpass animals in reasoning, and one man so much surpasses another? Has not the same custom the same influence on all?

We shall here endeavour briefly to explain the great difference in human understandings: After which the reason of the difference between men and animals will easily be comprehended.

1. When we have lived any time, and have been accustomed to the uniformity of nature, we acquire a general habit, by which we always transfer the known to the unknown, and conceive the latter to resemble the former. By means of this general habitual principle, we regard even one experiment as the foundation of reasoning, and expect a similar event with some degree of certainty, where the experiment has been made accurately, and free from all foreign circumstances. It is therefore considered as a matter of great importance to observe the consequences of things; and as one man may very much surpass another in attention and memory and observation, this will make a very great difference in their reasoning.

2. Where there is a complication of causes to produce any effect, one mind may be much larger than another, and better able to comprehend the whole system of objects, and to infer justly their consequences.

3. One man is able to carry on a chain of consequences to a greater length than another.

4. Few men can think long without running into a confusion of ideas, and mistaking one for another; and there are various degrees of this infirmity.

5. The circumstance, on which the effect depends, is frequently involved in other circumstances, which are foreign and extrinsic. The separation of it often requires great attention, accuracy, and subtilty.

6. The forming of general maxims from particular observation is a very nice operation; and nothing is more usual, from haste or a narrowness of mind, which sees not on all sides, than to commit mistakes in this particular.

7. When we reason from analogies, the man, who has the greater experience or the greater promptitude of suggesting analogies, will be the better reasoner.

8. Byasses from prejudice, education, passion, party, &c. hang more upon one mind than another.

9. After we have acquired a confidence in human testimony, books and conversation enlarge much more the sphere of one man's experience and thought than those of another.

It would be easy to discover many other circumstances that make a difference in the understandings of men.

85 But though animals learn many parts of their knowledge from observation, there are also many parts of it, which they derive from the original hand of nature ; which much exceed the share of capacity they possess on ordinary occasions ; and in which they improve, little or nothing, by the longest practice and experience. These we denominate Instincts, and are so apt to admire as something very extraordinary, and inexplicable by all the disquisitions of human understanding. But our wonder will, perhaps, cease or diminish, when we consider, that the experimental reasoning itself, which we possess in common with beasts, and on which the whole conduct of life depends, is nothing but a species of instinct or mechanical power, that acts in us unknown to ourselves ; and in its chief operations, is not directed by any such relations or comparisons of ideas, as are the proper objects of our intellectual faculties. Though the instinct be different, yet still it is an instinct, which teaches a man to avoid the fire ; as much as that, which teaches a bird, with such exactness, the art of incubation, and the whole economy and order of its nursery.

SECTION X.

OF MIRACLES.

PART I.

86   THERE is, in Dr. Tillotson's writings, an argument against the *real presence*, which is as concise, and elegant, and strong as any argument can possibly be supposed against a doctrine, so little worthy of a serious refutation. It is acknowledged on all hands, says that learned prelate, that the authority, either of the scripture or of tradition, is founded merely in the testimony of the apostles, who were eye-witnesses to those miracles of our Saviour, by which he proved his divine mission. Our evidence, then, for the truth of the *Christian* religion is less than the evidence for the truth of our senses ; because, even in the first authors of our religion, it was no greater ; and it is evident it must diminish in passing from them to their disciples ; nor can any one rest such confidence in their testimony, as in the immediate object of his senses. But a weaker evidence can never destroy a stronger ; and therefore, were the doctrine of the real presence ever so clearly revealed in scripture, it were directly contrary to the rules of just reasoning to give our assent to it. It contradicts sense, though both the scripture and tradition, on which it is supposed to be built, carry not such evidence with them as sense ; when they are considered merely as external evidences, and are not brought home to every one's breast, by the immediate operation of the Holy Spirit.

Nothing is so convenient as a decisive argument of this kind, which must at least *silence* the most arrogant bigotry and superstition, and free us from their impertinent solicitations. I flatter myself, that I have discovered an argument of a like nature, which, if just, will, with the wise and learned, be an everlasting check to all kinds of superstitious delusion, and consequently, will be useful as long as the world endures. For so long, I presume, will the accounts of miracles and prodigies be found in all history, sacred and profane.

87   Though experience be our only guide in reasoning concerning matters of fact; it must be acknowledged, that this guide is not altogether infallible, but in some cases is apt to lead us into errors. One, who in our climate, should expect better weather in any week of June than in one of December, would reason justly, and conformably to experience; but it is certain, that he may happen, in the event, to find himself mistaken. However, we may observe, that, in such a case, he would have no cause to complain of experience; because it commonly informs us beforehand of the uncertainty, by that contrariety of events, which we may learn from a diligent observation. All effects follow not with like certainty from their supposed causes. Some events are found, in all countries and all ages, to have been constantly conjoined together: Others are found to have been more variable, and sometimes to disappoint our expectations; so that, in our reasonings concerning matter of fact, there are all imaginable degrees of assurance, from the highest certainty to the lowest species of moral evidence.

A wise man, therefore, proportions his belief to the evidence. In such conclusions as are founded on an infallible experience, he expects the event with the last degree of assurance, and regards his past experience as a full *proof* of the future existence of that event. In other cases, he proceeds with more caution: He weighs the opposite experiments: He considers which side is supported by the greater number of experiments: to that side he inclines, with doubt and hesitation; and when at last he fixes his judgement, the evidence exceeds not what we properly call *probability*. All probability, then, supposes an opposition of experiments and observations, where the one side is found to overbalance the other, and to produce a degree of evidence, proportioned to the superiority. A hundred instances or experiments on one side, and fifty on another, afford a doubtful expectation of any event; though a hundred uniform experiments, with only one that is contradictory, reasonably beget a pretty strong degree of assurance. In all cases, we must balance the opposite experiments, where they are opposite, and deduct the smaller number from the greater, in order to know the exact force of the superior evidence.

88   To apply these principles to a particular instance; we may observe, that there is no species of reasoning more common, more useful, and even necessary to human life, than that which is derived from the testimony of men, and the reports of eye-witnesses and spectators. This species of reasoning, perhaps, one may deny to be founded on the relation of cause and effect. I shall not dispute about a word. It will be sufficient to observe that our assurance in any argument of this kind is derived from no other principle than our observation of the veracity of human testimony, and of the usual conformity of facts to the reports of witnesses. It being a general maxim, that no objects have any discoverable connexion together, and that all the inferences, which we can draw from one to another, are founded merely on our experience of their constant and regular conjunction; it is evident, that we ought not to make an exception to this maxim in favour of human testimony, whose connexion with any event seems, in itself, as little necessary as any other.

Were not the memory tenacious to a certain degree; had
not men commonly an inclination to truth and a principle
of probity; were they not sensible to shame, when detected
in a falsehood: Were not these, I say, discovered by
experience to be qualities, inherent in human nature, we
should never repose the least confidence in human testimony. A man delirious, or noted for falsehood and villany,
has no manner of authority with us.

And as the evidence, derived from witnesses and human
testimony, is founded on past experience, so it varies with
the experience, and is regarded either as a *proof* or a *probability*, according as the conjunction between any particular
kind of report and any kind of object has been found to be
constant or variable. There are a number of circumstances
to be taken into consideration in all judgements of this kind;
and the ultimate standard, by which we determine all
disputes, that may arise concerning them, is always derived
from experience and observation. Where this experience
is not entirely uniform on any side, it is attended with an
unavoidable contrariety in our judgements, and with the
same opposition and mutual destruction of argument as in
every other kind of evidence. We frequently hesitate
concerning the reports of others. We balance the opposite
circumstances, which cause any doubt or uncertainty; and
when we discover a superiority on any side, we incline to it;
but still with a diminution of assurance, in proportion to the
force of its antagonist.

89   This contrariety of evidence, in the present case, may be
derived from several different causes; from the opposition
of contrary testimony; from the character or number of the
witnesses; from the manner of their delivering their testimony; or from the union of all these circumstances. We
entertain a suspicion concerning any matter of fact, when
the witnesses contradict each other; when they are but
few, or of a doubtful character; when they have an interest

in what they affirm ; when they deliver their testimony with hesitation, or on the contrary, with too violent asseverations. There are many other particulars of the same kind, which may diminish or destroy the force of any argument, derived from human testimony.

Suppose, for instance, that the fact, which the testimony endeavours to establish, partakes of the extraordinary and the marvellous; in that case, the evidence, resulting from the testimony, admits of a diminution, greater or less, in proportion as the fact is more or less unusual. The reason why we place any credit in witnesses and historians, is not derived from any *connexion*, which we perceive *a priori*, between testimony and reality, but because we are accustomed to find a conformity between them. But when the fact attested is such a one as has seldom fallen under our observation, here is a contest of two opposite experiences; of which the one destroys the other, as far as its force goes, and the superior can only operate on the mind by the force, which remains. The very same principle of experience, which gives us a certain degree of assurance in the testimony of witnesses, gives us also, in this case, another degree of assurance against the fact, which they endeavour to establish ; from which contradition there necessarily arises a counterpoize, and mutual destruction of belief and authority.

I should not believe such a story were it told me by Cato, was a proverbial saying in Rome,·even during the lifetime of that philosophical patriot [1]. The incredibility of a fact, it was allowed, might invalidate so great an authority.

The Indian prince, who refused to believe the first relations concerning the effects of frost, reasoned justly; and it naturally required very strong testimony to engage his assent to facts, that arose from a state of nature, with which he was unacquainted, and which bore so little

[1] Plutarch, in vita Catonis.

I

analogy to those events, of which he had had constant and
uniform experience. Though they were not contrary to his
experience, they were not conformable to it [1].

90   But in order to encrease the probability against the
testimony of witnesses, let us suppose, that the fact, which
they affirm, instead of being only marvellous, is really
miraculous ; and suppose also, that the testimony considered
apart and in itself, amounts to an entire proof; in that
case, there is proof against proof, of which the strongest
must prevail, but still with a diminution of its force, in proportion to that of its antagonist.

A miracle is a violation of the laws of nature; and as
a firm and unalterable experience has established these laws,
the proof against a miracle, from the very nature of the fact,
is as entire as any argument from experience can possibly
be imagined. Why is it more than probable, that all men
must die ; that lead cannot, of itself, remain suspended in
the air ; that fire consumes wood, and is extinguished by
water ; unless it be, that these events are found agreeable

---

[1] No Indian, it is evident, could have experience that water did not
freeze in cold climates. This is placing nature in a situation quite
unknown to him ; and it is impossible for him to tell *a priori* what will
result from it. It is making a new experiment, the consequence of
which is always uncertain. One may sometimes conjecture from
analogy what will follow ; but still this is but conjecture. And it must
be confessed, that, in the present case of freezing, the event follows
contrary to the rules of analogy, and is such as a rational Indian would
not look for. The operations of cold upon water are not gradual,
according to the degrees of cold ; but whenever it comes to the freezing
point, the water passes in a moment, from the utmost liquidity to
perfect hardness. Such an event, therefore, may be denominated *extraordinary*, and requires a pretty strong testimony, to render it credible to
people in a warm climate : But still it is not *miraculous*, nor contrary
to uniform experience of the course of nature in cases where all the
circumstances are the same. The inhabitants of Sumatra have always
seen water fluid in their own climate, and the freezing of their rivers
ought to be deemed a prodigy : But they never saw water in Muscovy
during the winter ; and therefore they cannot reasonably be positive what
would there be the consequence.

to the laws of nature, and there is required a violation of
these laws, or in other words, a miracle to prevent them?
Nothing is esteemed a miracle, if it ever happen in the
common course of nature. It is no miracle that a man,
seemingly in good health, should die on a sudden : because
such a kind of death, though more unusual than any other,
has yet been frequently observed to happen. But it is
a miracle, that a dead man should come to life; because
that has never been observed in any age or country. There
must, therefore, be a uniform experience against every
miraculous event, otherwise the event would not merit that
appellation. And as a uniform experience amounts to a
proof, there is here a direct and full *proof*, from the nature
of the fact, against the existence of any miracle ; nor can
such a proof be destroyed, or the miracle rendered credible,
but by an opposite proof, which is superior [1].

91   The plain consequence is (and it is a general maxim
worthy of our attention), 'That no testimony is sufficient

---

[1] Sometimes an event may not, *in itself, seem* to be contrary to the laws
of nature, and yet, if it were real, it might, by reason of some circumstances, be denominated a miracle; because, in *fact*, it is contrary to
these laws.   Thus if a person, claiming a divine authority, should
command a sick person to be well, a healthful man to fall down dead,
the clouds to pour rain, the winds to blow, in short, should order many
natural events, which immediately follow upon his command ; these
might justly be esteemed miracles, because they are really, in this case,
contrary to the laws of nature.   For if any suspicion remain, that the
event and command concurred by accident, there is no miracle and no
transgression of the laws of nature.   If this suspicion be removed, there
is evidently a miracle, and a transgression of these laws ; because nothing
can be more contrary to nature than that the voice or command of a man
should have such an influence. A miracle may be accurately defined,
*a transgression of a law of nature by a particular volition of the Deity,
or by the interposition of some invisible agent.* A miracle may either be
discoverable by men or not. This alters not its nature and essence.
The raising of a house or ship into the air is a visible miracle. The
raising of a feather, when the wind wants ever so little of a force
requisite for that purpose, is as real a miracle, though not so sensible
with regard to us.

to establish a miracle, unless the testimony be of such
a kind, that its falsehood would be more miraculous, than
the fact, which it endeavours to establish; and even in
that case there is a mutual destruction of arguments, and
the superior only gives us an assurance suitable to that
degree of force, which remains, after deducting the inferior.'
When anyone tells me, that he saw a dead man restored
to life, I immediately consider with myself, whether it be
more probable, that this person should either deceive or be
deceived, or that the fact, which he relates, should really
have happened.   I weigh the one miracle against the other;
and according to the superiority, which I discover, I pronounce my decision, and always reject the greater miracle.
If the falsehood of his testimony would be more miraculous,
than the event which he relates; then, and not till then,
can he pretend to command my belief or opinion.

Part II.

92   In the foregoing reasoning we have supposed, that the
testimony, upon which a miracle is founded, may possibly
amount to an entire proof, and that the falsehood of that
testimony would be a real prodigy: But it is easy to shew,
that we have been a great deal too liberal in our concession,
and that there never was a miraculous event established on
so full an evidence.

For *first*, there is not to be found, in all history, any
miracle attested by a sufficient number of men, of such
unquestioned good-sense, education, and learning, as to
secure us against all delusion in themselves; of such undoubted integrity, as to place them beyond all suspicion of
any design to deceive others; of such credit and reputation
in the eyes of mankind, as to have a great deal to lose in
case of their being detected in any falsehood; and at the
same time, attesting facts performed in such a public manner
and in so celebrated a part of the world, as to render the

detection unavoidable : All which circumstances are requisite to give us a full assurance in the testimony of men.

93   *Secondly.* We may observe in human nature a principle
which, if strictly examined, will be found to diminish
extremely the assurance, which we might, from human
testimony, have, in any kind of prodigy. The maxim, by
which we commonly conduct ourselves in our reasonings,
is, that the objects, of which we have no experience, resembles
those, of which we have ; that what we have found to be,
most usual is always most probable ; and that where there·
is an opposition of arguments, we ought to give the preference
to such as are founded on the greatest number of past
observations. But though, in proceeding by this rule, we·
readily reject any fact which is unusual and incredible in an
ordinary degree ; yet in advancing farther, the mind observes·
not always the same rule ; but when anything is affirmed
utterly absurd and miraculous, it rather the more readily·
admits of such a fact, upon account of that very circumstance, which ought to destroy all its authority. The
passion of *surprise* and *wonder*, arising from miracles, being
an agreeable emotion, gives a sensible tendency towards the
belief of those events, from which it is derived. And this
goes so far, that even those who cannot enjoy this pleasure
immediately, nor can believe those miraculous events, of
which they are informed, yet love to partake of the satisfaction at second-hand or by rebound, and place a pride and
delight in exciting the admiration of others.

With what greediness are the miraculous accounts of
travellers received, their descriptions of sea and land
monsters, their relations of wonderful adventures, strange
men, and uncouth manners ? But if the spirit of religion
join itself to the love of wonder, there is an end of common
sense ; and human testimony, in these circumstances, loses
all pretensions to authority. A religionist may be an
enthusiast, and imagine he sees what has no reality : he may

know his narrative to be false, and yet persevere in it, with
the best intentions in the world, for the sake of promoting
so holy a cause : or even where this delusion has not
place, vanity, excited by so strong a temptation, operates on
him more powerfully than on the rest of mankind in any
other circumstances; and self-interest with equal force.
His auditors may not have, and commonly have not, sufficient judgement to canvass his evidence : what judgement
they have, they renounce by principle, in these sublime
and mysterious subjects : or if they were ever so willing
to employ it, passion and a heated imagination disturb
the regularity of its operations. Their credulity increases
his impudence : and his impudence overpowers their
credulity.

Eloquence, when at its highest pitch, leaves little room
for reason or reflection ; but addressing itself entirely to the
fancy or the affections, captivates the willing hearers, and
subdues their understanding. Happily, this pitch it seldom
attains. But what a Tully or a Demosthenes could scarcely
effect over a Roman or Athenian audience, every *Capuchin*,
every itinerant or stationary teacher can perform over the
generality of mankind, and in a higher degree, by touching
such gross and vulgar passions.

The many instances of forged miracles, and prophecies,
and supernatural events, which, in all ages, have either been
detected by contrary evidence, or which detect themselves
by their absurdity, prove sufficiently the strong propensity
of mankind to the extraoidinary and the marvellous, and
ought reasonably to beget a suspicion against all relations
of this kind. This is our natural way of thinking, even
with regard to the most common and most credible events.
For instance : There is no kind of report which rises so
easily, and spreads so quickly, especially in country places
and provincial towns, as those concerning marriages ; inso-
much that two young persons of equal condition never see

each other twice, but the whole neighbourhood immediately join them together. The pleasure of telling a piece of news so interesting, of propagating it, and of being the first reporters of it, spreads the intelligence. And this is so well known, that no man of sense gives attention to these reports, till he find them confirmed by some greater evidence. Do not the same passions, and others still stronger, incline the generality of mankind to believe and report, with the greatest vehemence and assurance, all religious miracles?

94 *Thirdly.* It forms a strong presumption against all supernatural and miraculous relations, that they are observed chiefly to abound among ignorant and barbarous nations; or if a civilized people has ever given admission to any of them, that people will be found to have received them from ignorant and barbarous ancestors, who transmitted them with that inviolable sanction and authority, which always attend received opinions. When we peruse the first histories of all nations, we are apt to imagine ourselves transported into some new world; where the whole frame of nature is disjointed, and every element performs its operations in a different manner, from what it does at present. Battles, revolutions, pestilence, famine and death, are never the effect of those natural causes, which we experience. Prodigies, omens, oracles, judgements, quite obscure the few natural events, that are intermingled with them. But as the former grow thinner every page, in proportion as we advance nearer the enlightened ages, we soon learn, that there is nothing mysterious or supernatural in the case, but that all proceeds from the usual propensity of mankind towards the marvellous, and that, though this inclination may at intervals receive a check from sense and learning, it can never be thoroughly extirpated from human nature.

It is strange, a judicious reader is apt to say, upon the perusal of these wonderful historians, *that such prodigious*

events never happen in our days. But it is nothing strange,
I hope, that men should lie in all ages. You must surely
have seen instances enough of that frailty. You have yourself heard many such marvellous relations started, which,
being treated with scorn by all the wise and judicious, have
at last been abandoned even by the vulgar. Be assured,
that those renowned lies, which have spread and flourished
to such a monstrous height, arose from like beginnings;
but being sown in a more proper soil, shot up at last into
prodigies almost equal to those which they relate.

It was a wise policy in that false prophet, Alexander, who
though now forgotten, was once so famous, to lay the first
scene of his impostures in Paphlagonia, where, as Lucian
tells us, the people were extremely ignorant and stupid, and
ready to swallow even the grossest delusion. People at
a distance, who are weak enough to think the matter at all
worth enquiry, have no opportunity of receiving better information. The stories come magnified to them by a hundred
circumstances. Fools are industrious in propagating the
imposture; while the wise and learned are contented, in
general, to deride its absurdity, without informing themselves
of the particular facts, by which it may be distinctly refuted.
And thus the impostor above mentioned was enabled to
proceed, from his ignorant Paphlagonians, to the enlisting
of votaries, even among the Grecian philosophers, and men
of the most eminent rank and distinction in Rome : nay,
could engage the attention of that sage emperor Marcus
Aurelius ; so far as to make him trust the success of
a military expedition to his delusive prophecies.

The advantages are so great, of starting an imposture
among an ignorant people, that, even though the delusion
should be too gross to impose on the generality of them
(*which, though seldom, is sometimes the case*) it has a much
better chance for succeeding in remote countries, than if
the first scene had been laid in a city renowned for arts and

knowledge. The most ignorant and barbarous of these barbarians carry the report abroad. None of their country-men have a large correspondence, or sufficient credit and authority to contradict and beat down the delusion. Men's inclination to the marvellous has full opportunity to display itself. And thus a story, which is universally exploded in the place where it was first started, shall pass for certain at a thousand miles distance. But had Alexander fixed his residence at Athens, the philosophers of that renowned mart of learning had immediately spread, throughout the whole Roman empire, their sense of the matter; which, being supported by so great authority, and displayed by all the force of reason and eloquence, had entirely opened the eyes of mankind. It is true; Lucian, passing by chance through Paphlagonia, had an opportunity of performing this good office. But, though much to be wished, it does not always happen, that every Alexander meets with a Lucian, ready to expose and detect his impostures.

95 I may add as a *fourth* reason, which diminishes the authority of prodigies, that there is no testimony for any, even those which have not been expressly detected, that is not opposed by an infinite number of witnesses; so that not only the miracle destroys the credit of testimony, but the testimony destroys itself. To make this the better understood, let us consider, that, in matters of religion, whatever is different is contrary; and that it is impossible the religions of ancient Rome, of Turkey, of Siam, and of China should, all of them, be established on any solid foundation. Every miracle, therefore, pretended to have been wrought in any of these religions (and all of them abound in miracles), as its direct scope is to establish the particular system to which it is attributed; so has it the same force, though more indirectly, to overthrow every other system. In destroying a rival system, it likewise destroys the credit of those miracles, on which that system

was established; so that all the prodigies of different religions are to be regarded as contrary facts, and the evidences of these prodigies, whether weak or strong, as opposite to each other. According to this method of reasoning, when we believe any miracle of Mahomet or his successors, we have for our warrant the testimony of a few barbarous Arabians: And on the other hand, we are to regard the authority of Titus Livius, Plutarch, Tacitus, and, in short, of all the authors and witnesses, Grecian, Chinese, and Roman Catholic, who have related any miracle in their particular religion; I say, we are to regard their testimony in the same light as if they had mentioned that Mahometan miracle, and had in express terms contradicted it, with the same certainty as they have for the miracle they relate. This argument may appear over subtile and refined; but is not in reality different from the reasoning of a judge, who supposes, that the credit of two witnesses, maintaining a crime against any one, is destroyed by the testimony of two others, who affirm him to have been two hundred leagues distant, at the same instant when the crime is said to have been committed.

96   One of the best attested miracles in all profane history, is that which Tacitus reports of Vespasian, who cured a blind man in Alexandria, by means of his spittle, and a lame man by the mere touch of his foot; in obedience to a vision of the god Serapis, who had enjoined them to have recourse to the Emperor, for these miraculous cures. The story may be seen in that fine historian[1]; where every circumstance seems to add weight to the testimony, and might be displayed at large with all the force of argument and eloquence, if any one were now concerned to enforce the evidence of that exploded and idolatrous superstition.

[1] Hist. lib. v. cap. 8. Suetonius gives nearly the same account *in vita* Vesp.

The gravity, solidity, age, and probity of so great an emperor, who, through the whole course of his life, conversed in a familiar manner with his friends and courtiers, and never affected those extraordinary airs of divinity assumed by Alexander and Demetrius. The historian, a cotemporary writer, noted for candour and veracity, and withal, the greatest and most penetrating genius, perhaps, of all antiquity; and so free from any tendency to credulity, that he even lies under the contrary imputation, of atheism and profaneness: The persons, from whose authority he related the miracle, of established character for judgement and veracity, as we may well presume; eye-witnesses of the fact, and confirming their testimony, after the Flavian family was despoiled of the empire, and could no longer give any reward, as the price of a lie. *Utrumque, qui interfuere, nunc quoque memorant, postquam nullum mendacio pretium.* To which if we add the public nature of the facts, as related, it will appear, that no evidence can well be supposed stronger for so gross and so palpable a falsehood.

There is also a memorable story related by Cardinal de Retz, which may well deserve our consideration. When that intriguing politician fled into Spain, to avoid the persecution of his enemies, he passed through Saragossa, the capital of Arragon, where he was shewn, in the cathedral, a man, who had served seven years as a doorkeeper, and was well known to every body in town, that had ever paid his devotions at that church. He had been seen, for so long a time, wanting a leg; but recovered that limb by the rubbing of holy oil upon the stump; and the cardinal assures us that he saw him with two legs. This miracle was vouched by all the canons of the church; and the whole company in town were appealed to for a confirmation of the fact; whom the cardinal found, by their zealous devotion, to be thorough believers of the miracle. Here the relater was also cotemporary to the supposed

prodigy, of an incredulous and libertine character, as well
as of great genius, the miracle of so *singular* a nature as
could scarcely admit of a counterfeit, and the witnesses
very numerous, and all of them, in a manner, spectators of
the fact, to which they gave their testimony. And what
adds mightily to the force of the evidence, and may double
our surprise on this occasion, is, that the cardinal himself,
who relates the story, seems not to give any credit to it, and
consequently cannot be suspected of any concurrence in
the holy fraud. He considered justly, that it was not
requisite, in order to reject a fact of this nature, to be
able accurately to disprove the testimony, and to trace its
falsehood, through all the circumstances of knavery and
credulity which produced it. He knew, that, as this was
commonly altogether impossible at any small distance of
time and place; so was it extremely difficult, even where
one was immediately present, by reason of the bigotry,
ignorance, cunning, and roguery of a great part of mankind. He therefore concluded, like a just reasoner, that
such an evidence carried falsehood upon the very face of it,
and that a miracle, supported by any human testimony, was
more properly a subject of derision than of argument.

There surely never was a greater number of miracles
ascribed to one person, than those, which were lately said
to have been wrought in France upon the tomb of Abbé
Paris, the famous Jansenist, with whose sanctity the people
were so long deluded. The curing of the sick, giving
hearing to the deaf, and sight to the blind, were every
where talked of as the usual effects of that holy sepulchre.
But what is more extraordinary; many of the miracles were
immediately proved upon the spot, before judges of unquestioned integrity, attested by witnesses of credit and
distinction, in a learned age, and on the most eminent
theatre that is now in the world. Nor is this all: a relation
of them was published and dispersed every where; nor were

the *Jesuits*, though a learned body, supported by the civil magistrate, and determined enemies to those opinions, in whose favour the miracles were said to have been wrought, ever able distinctly to refute or detect them[1]. Where shall we find such a number of circumstances, agreeing to the corroboration of one fact? And what have we to oppose to such a cloud of witnesses, but the absolute impossibility or miraculous nature of the events, which they relate? And this surely, in the eyes of all reasonable people, will alone be regarded as a sufficient refutation.

97 Is the consequence just, because some human testimony has the utmost force and authority in some cases, when it relates the battle of Philippi or Pharsalia for instance; that therefore all kinds of testimony must, in all cases, have equal force and authority? Suppose that the Cæsarean and Pompeian factions had, each of them, claimed the victory in these battles, and that the historians of each party had uniformly ascribed the advantage to their own side; how could mankind, at this distance, have been able to determine between them? The contrariety is equally strong between the miracles related by Herodotus or Plutarch, and those delivered by Mariana, Bede, or any monkish historian.

The wise lend a very academic faith to every report which favours the passion of the reporter; whether it magnifies his country, his family, or himself, or in any other way strikes in with his natural inclinations and propensities. But what greater temptation than to appear a missionary, a prophet, an ambassador from heaven? Who would not encounter many dangers and difficulties, in order to attain so sublime a character? Or if, by the help of vanity and a heated imagination, a man has first made a convert of himself, and entered seriously into the delusion; who ever scruples to make use of pious frauds, in support of so holy and meritorious a cause?

[1] For Note, see p. 344.

The smallest spark may here kindle into the greatest flame; because the materials are always prepared for it. The *avidum genus auricularum*[1], the gazing populace, receive greedily, without examination, whatever sooths superstition, and promotes wonder.

How many stories of this nature have, in all ages, been detected and exploded in their infancy? How many more have been celebrated for a time, and have afterwards sunk into neglect and oblivion? Where such reports, therefore, fly about, the solution of the phenomenon is obvious; and we judge in conformity to regular experience and observation, when we account for it by the known and natural principles of credulity and delusion. And shall we, rather than have a recourse to so natural a solution, allow of a miraculous violation of the most established laws of nature?

I need not mention the difficulty of detecting a falsehood in any private or even public history, at the place, where it is said to happen; much more when the scene is removed to ever so small a distance. Even a court of judicature, with all the authority, accuracy, and judgement, which they can employ, find themselves often at a loss to distinguish between truth and falsehood in the most recent actions. But the matter never comes to any issue, if trusted to the common method of altercations and debate and flying rumours; especially when men's passions have taken part on either side.

In the infancy of new religions, the wise and learned commonly esteem the matter too inconsiderable to deserve their attention or regard. And when afterwards they would willingly detect the cheat, in order to undeceive the deluded multitude, the season is now past, and the records and witnesses, which might clear up the matter, have perished beyond recovery.

[1] Lucret.

No means of detection remain, but those which must be drawn from the very testimony itself of the reporters: and these, though always sufficient with the judicious and knowing, are commonly too fine to fall under the comprehension of the vulgar.

98   Upon the whole, then, it appears, that no testimony for any kind of miracle has ever amounted to a probability, much less to a proof; and that, even supposing it amounted to a proof, it would be opposed by another proof; derived from the very nature of the fact, which it would endeavour to establish. It is experience only, which gives authority to human testimony; and it is the same experience, which assures us of the laws of nature. When, therefore, these two kinds of experience are contrary, we have nothing to do but substract the one from the other, and embrace an opinion, either on one side or the other, with that assurance which arises from the remainder. But according to the principle here explained, this substraction, with regard to all popular religions, amounts to an entire annihilation; and therefore we may establish it as a maxim, that no human testimony can have such force as to prove a miracle, and make it a just foundation for any such system of religion.

99   I beg the limitations here made may be remarked, when I say, that a miracle can never be proved, so as to be the foundation of a system of religion. For I own, that otherwise, there may possibly be miracles, or violations of the usual course of nature, of such a kind as to admit of proof from human testimony; though, perhaps, it will be impossible to find any such in all the records of history. Thus, suppose, all authors, in all languages, agree, that, from the first of January 1600, there was a total darkness over the whole earth for eight days: suppose that the tradition of this extraordinary event is still strong and lively among the people: that all travellers, who return from foreign countries, bring us accounts of the same

tradition, without the least variation or contradiction: it is evident, that our present philosophers, instead of doubting the fact, ought to receive it as certain, and ought to search for the causes whence it might be derived. The decay, corruption, and dissolution of nature, is an event rendered probable by so many analogies, that any phenomenon, which seems to have a tendency towards that catastrophe, comes within the reach of human testimony, if that testimony be very extensive and uniform.

But suppose, that all the historians who treat of England, should agree, that, on the first of January 1600, Queen Elizabeth died; that both before and after her death she was seen by her physicians and the whole court, as is usual with persons of her rank; that her successor was acknowledged and proclaimed by the parliament; and that, after being interred a month, she again appeared, resumed the throne, and governed England for three years: I must confess that I should be surprised at the concurrence of so many odd circumstances, but should not have the least inclination to believe so miraculous an event. I should not doubt of her pretended death, and of those other public circumstances that followed it: I should only assert it to have been pretended, and that it neither was, nor possibly could be real. You would in vain object to me the difficulty, and almost impossibility of deceiving the world in an affair of such consequence; the wisdom and solid judgement of that renowned queen; with the little or no advantage which she could reap from so poor an artifice: All this might astonish me; but I would still reply, that the knavery and folly of men are such common phenomena, that I should rather believe the most extraordinary events to arise from their concurrence, than admit of so signal a violation of the laws of nature.

But should this miracle be ascribed to any new system of religion; men, in all ages, have been so much imposed on by ridiculous stories of that kind, that this very circumstance would be a full proof of a cheat, and sufficient, with all men of sense, not only to make them reject the fact, but even reject it without farther examination. Though the Being to whom the miracle is ascribed, be, in this case, Almighty, it does not, upon that account, become a whit more probable; since it is impossible for us to know the attributes or actions of such a Being, otherwise than from the experience which we have of his productions, in the usual course of nature. This still reduces us to past observation, and obliges us to compare the instances of the violation of truth in the testimony of men, with those of the violation of the laws of nature by miracles, in order to judge which of them is most likely and probable. As the violations of truth are more common in the testimony concerning religious miracles, than in that concerning any other matter of fact; this must diminish very much the authority of the former testimony, and make us form a general resolution, never to lend any attention to it, with whatever specious pretence it may be covered.

Lord Bacon seems to have embraced the same principles of reasoning. 'We ought,' says he, 'to make a collection or particular history of all monsters and prodigious births or productions, and in a word of every thing new, rare, and extraordinary in nature. But this must be done with the most severe scrutiny, lest we depart from truth. Above all, every relation must be considered as suspicious, which depends in any degree upon religion, as the prodigies of Livy: And no less so, every thing that is to be found in the writers of natural magic or alchimy, or such authors, who seem, all of them, to have an unconquerable appetite for falsehood and fable [1].'

100 I am the better pleased with the method of reasoning here delivered, as I think it may serve to confound those

[1] Nov. Org. lib. ii. aph. 29.

dangerous friends or disguised enemies to the *Christian Religion*, who have undertaken to defend it by the principles of human reason. Our most holy religion is founded on *Faith*, not on reason; and it is a sure method of exposing it to put it to such a trial as it is, by no means, fitted to endure. To make this more evident, let us examine those miracles, related in scripture; and not to lose ourselves in too wide a field, let us confine ourselves to such as we find in the *Pentateuch*, which we shall examine, according to the principles of these pretended Christians, not as the word or testimony of God himself, but as the production of a mere human writer and historian. Here then we are first to consider a book, presented to us by a barbarous and ignorant people, written in an age when they were still more barbarous, and in all probability long after the facts which it relates, corroborated by no concurring testimony, and resembling those fabulous accounts, which every nation gives of its origin. Upon reading this book, we find it full of prodigies and miracles. It gives an account of a state of the world and of human nature entirely different from the present: Of our fall from that state: Of the age of man, extended to near a thousand years: Of the destruction of the world by a deluge: Of the arbitrary choice of one people, as the favourites of heaven; and that people the countrymen of the author: Of their deliverance from bondage by prodigies the most astonishing imaginable: I desire any one to lay his hand upon his heart, and after a serious consideration declare, whether he thinks that the falsehood of such a book, supported by such a testimony, would be more extraordinary and miraculous than all the miracles it relates; which is, however, necessary to make it be received, according to the measures of probability above established.

101   What we have said of miracles may be applied, without any variation, to prophecies; and indeed, all prophecies are

real miracles, and as such only, can be admitted as proofs of any revelation. If it did not exceed the capacity of human nature to foretell future events, it would be absurd to employ any prophecy as an argument for a divine mission or authority from heaven. So that, upon the whole, we may conclude, that the *Christian Religion* not only was at first attended with miracles, but even at this day cannot be believed by any reasonable person without one. Mere reason is insufficient to convince us of its veracity: And whoever is moved by *Faith* to assent to it, is conscious of a continued miracle in his own person, which subverts all the principles of his understanding, and gives him a determination to believe what is most contrary to custom and experience.

SECTION XI.

OF A PARTICULAR PROVIDENCE AND OF A FUTURE
STATE.

102 I was lately engaged in conversation with a friend who loves sceptical paradoxes; where, though he advanced many principles, of which I can by no means approve, yet as they seem to be curious, and to bear some relation to the chain of reasoning carried on throughout this enquiry, I shall here copy them from my memory as accurately as I can, in order to submit them to the judgement of the reader.

Our conversation began with my admiring the singular good fortune of philosophy, which, as it requires entire liberty above all other privileges, and chiefly flourishes from the free opposition of sentiments and argumentation, received its first birth in an age and country of freedom and toleration, and was never cramped, even in its most extravagant principles, by any creeds, concessions, or penal statutes. For, except the banishment of Protagoras, and the death of Socrates, which last event proceeded partly from other motives, there are scarcely any instances to be met with, in ancient history, of this bigotted jealousy, with which the present age is so much infested. Epicurus lived at Athens to an advanced age, in peace and tranquillity: Epicureans[1] were even admitted to receive the sacerdotal character, and to officiate at the altar, in the most sacred rites of the established religion: And the public encouragement[2] of pensions and

[1] Luciani συμπ. ἡ Λαπίθαι.   [2] Luciani εὐνοῦχος.

salaries was afforded equally, by the wisest of all the Roman
emperors[1], to the professors of every sect of philosophy.
How requisite such kind of treatment was to philosophy, in
her early youth, will easily be conceived, if we reflect, that,
even at present, when she may be supposed more hardy and
robust, she bears with much difficulty the inclemency of the
seasons, and those harsh winds of calumny and persecution,
which blow upon her.

You admire, says my friend, as the singular good fortune
of philosophy, what seems to result from the natural course
of things, and to be unavoidable in every age and nation.
This pertinacious bigotry, of which you complain, as so fatal
to philosophy, is really her offspring, who, after allying with
superstition, separates himself entirely from the interest of
his parent, and becomes her most inveterate enemy and
persecutor. Speculative dogmas of religion, the present
occasions of such furious dispute, could not possibly be
conceived or admitted in the early ages of the world ; when
mankind, being wholly illiterate, formed an idea of religion
more suitable to their weak apprehension, and composed
their sacred tenets of such tales chiefly as were the objects
of traditional belief, more than of argument or disputation.
After the first alarm, therefore, was over, which arose from
the new paradoxes and principles of the philosophers ; these
teachers seem ever after, during the ages of antiquity, to
have lived in great harmony with the established superstition, and to have made a fair partition of mankind between
them ; the former claiming all the learned and wise, the
latter possessing all the vulgar and illiterate.

103   It seems then, say I, that you leave politics entirely out of
the question, and never suppose, that a wise magistrate can
justly be jealous of certain tenets of philosophy, such as
those of Epicurus, which, denying a divine existence, and
consequently a providence and a future state, seem to loosen,

[1] Luciani and Dio.

in a great measure, the ties of morality, and may be supposed, for that reason, pernicious to the peace of civil society.

I know, replied he, that in fact these persecutions never, in any age, proceeded from calm reason, or from experience of the pernicious consequences of philosophy; but arose entirely from passion and prejudice. But what if I should advance farther, and assert, that if Epicurus had been accused before the people, by any of the *sycophants* or informers of those days, he could easily have defended his cause, and proved his principles of philosophy to be as salutary as those of his adversaries, who endeavoured, with such zeal, to expose him to the public hatred and jealousy?

I wish, said I, you would try your eloquence upon so extraordinary a topic, and make a speech for Epicurus, which might satisfy, not the mob of Athens, if you will allow that ancient and polite city to have contained any mob, but the more philosophical part of his audience, such as might be supposed capable of comprehending his arguments.

The matter would not be difficult, upon such conditions, replied he: And if you please, I shall suppose myself Epicurus for a moment, and make you stand for the Athenian people, and shall deliver you such an harangue as will fill all the urn with white beans, and leave not a black one to gratify the malice of my adversaries.

Very well: Pray proceed upon these suppositions.

104   I come hither, O ye Athenians, to justify in your assembly what I maintained in my school, and I find myself impeached by furious antagonists, instead of reasoning with calm and dispassionate enquirers. Your deliberations, which of right should be directed to questions of public good, and the interest of the commonwealth, are diverted to the disquisitions of speculative philosophy; and these magnificent, but perhaps fruitless enquiries, take place of your more familiar

but more useful occupations. But so far as in me lies, I will prevent this abuse. We shall not here dispute concerning the origin and government of worlds. We shall only enquire how far such questions concern the public interest. And if I can persuade you, that they are entirely indifferent to the peace of society and security of government, I hope that you will presently send us back to our schools, there to examine, at leisure, the question the most sublime, but at the same time, the most speculative of all philosophy.

The religious philosophers, not satisfied with the tradition of your forefathers, and doctrine of your priests (in which I willingly acquiesce), indulge a rash curiosity, in trying how far they can establish religion upon the principles of reason ; and they thereby excite, instead of satisfying, the doubts, which naturally arise from a diligent and scrutinous enquiry. They paint, in the most magnificent colours, the order, beauty, and wise arrangement of the universe ; and then ask, if such a glorious display of intelligence could proceed from the fortuitous concourse of atoms, or if chance could produce what the greatest genius can never sufficiently admire. I shall not examine the justness of this argument. I shall allow it to be as solid as my antagonists and accusers can desire. It is sufficient, if I can prove, from this very reasoning, that the question is entirely speculative, and that, when, in my philosophical disquisitions, I deny a providence and a future state, I undermine not the foundations of society, but advance principles, which they themselves, upon their own topics, if they argue consistently, must allow to be solid and satisfactory.

105   You then, who are my accusers, have acknowledged, that the chief or sole argument for a divine existence (which I never questioned) is derived from the order of nature ; where there appear such marks of intelligence and design, that you think it extravagant to assign for its cause, either chance, or the blind and unguided force of matter. You allow, that this

is an argument drawn from effects to causes. From the order of the work, you infer, that there must have been project and forethought in the workman. If you cannot make out this point, you allow, that your conclusion fails; and you pretend not to establish the conclusion in a greater latitude than the phenomena of nature will justify. These are your concessions. I desire you to mark the consequences.

When we infer any particular cause from an effect, we must proportion the one to the other, and can never be allowed to ascribe to the cause any qualities, but what are exactly sufficient to produce the effect. A body of ten ounces raised in any scale may serve as a proof, that the counterbalancing weight exceeds ten ounces; but can never afford a reason that it exceeds a hundred. If the cause, assigned for any effect, be not sufficient to produce it, we must either reject that cause, or add to it such qualities as will give it a just proportion to the effect. But if we ascribe to it farther qualities, or affirm it capable of producing other effects, we can only indulge the licence of conjecture, and arbitrarily suppose the existence of qualities and energies, without reason or authority.

The same rule holds, whether the cause assigned be brute unconscious matter, or a rational intelligent being. If the cause be known only by the effect, we never ought to ascribe to it any qualities, beyond what are precisely requisite to produce the effect: Nor can we, by any rules of just reasoning, return back from the cause, and infer other effects from it, beyond those by which alone it is known to us. No one, merely from the sight of one of Zeuxis's pictures, could know, that he was also a statuary or architect, and was an artist no less skilful in stone and marble than in colours. The talents and taste, displayed in the particular work before us; these we may safely conclude the workman to be possessed of. The cause must be proportioned to the effect; and if we exactly and precisely proportion it, we shall never find in it any qualities, that point farther, or afford an inference concerning any other design or performance. Such qualities must be somewhat beyond what is merely requisite for producing the effect, which we examine.

106 Allowing, therefore, the gods to be the authors of the existence or order of the universe; it follows, that they possess that precise degree of power, intelligence, and benevolence, which appears in their workmanship; but nothing farther can ever be proved, except we call in the assistance of exaggeration and flattery to supply the defects of argument and reasoning. So far as the traces of any attributes, at present, appear, so far may we conclude these attributes to exist. The supposition of farther attributes is mere hypothesis; much more the supposition, that, in distant regions of space or periods of time, there has been, or will be, a more magnificent display of these attributes, and a scheme of administration more suitable to such imaginary virtues. We can never be allowed to mount up from the universe, the effect, to Jupiter, the cause; and then descend downwards, to infer any new effect from that cause; as if the present effects alone were not entirely worthy of the glorious attributes, which we ascribe to that deity. The knowledge of the cause being derived solely from the effect, they must be exactly adjusted to each other; and the one can never refer to anything farther, or be the foundation of any new inference and conclusion.

You find certain phenomena in nature. You seek a cause or author. You imagine that you have found him. You afterwards become so enamoured of this offspring of your brain, that you imagine it impossible, but he must produce something greater and more perfect than the present scene of things, which is so full of ill and disorder. You forget, that this superlative intelligence and benevolence are entirely imaginary, or, at least, without any foundation in reason; and that you have no ground to ascribe to him any qualities, but what you see he has actually exerted and displayed in his productions. Let your gods, therefore, O philosophers, be suited to the present appearances of nature: and presume not to alter these appearances by arbitrary suppositions, in order to suit them to the attributes, which you so fondly ascribe to your deities.

107   When priests and poets, supported by your authority, O Athenians, talk of a golden or silver age, which preceded the present state of vice and misery, I hear them with attention and with reverence. But when philosophers, who pretend to neglect authority, and to cultivate reason, hold the same discourse, I pay them not, I own, the same obsequious submission and pious deference. I ask; who carried them into the celestial regions, who admitted them into the councils of the gods, who opened to them the book of fate, that they thus rashly affirm, that their deities have executed, or will execute, any purpose beyond what has actually appeared? If they tell me, that they have mounted on the steps or by the gradual ascent of reason, and by drawing inferences from effects to causes, I still insist, that they have aided the ascent of reason by the wings of imagination; otherwise they could not thus change their manner of inference, and argue from causes to effects; presuming, that a more perfect production than the present world would be more suitable to such perfect beings as the gods, and forgetting that they have no reason to ascribe to these celestial beings any perfection or any attribute, but what can be found in the present world.

Hence all the fruitless industry to account for the ill appearances of nature, and save the honour of the gods; while we must acknowledge the reality of that evil and disorder, with which the world so much abounds. The obstinate and intractable qualities of matter, we are told, or the observance of general laws, or some such reason, is the sole cause, which controlled the power and benevolence of Jupiter, and obliged him to create mankind and every sensible creature so imperfect and so unhappy. These attributes then, are, it seems, beforehand, taken for granted, in their greatest latitude. And upon that supposition, I own that such conjectures may, perhaps, be admitted as plausible solutions of the ill phenomena. But still I ask; Why take these attributes for granted, or why ascribe to the cause any qualities but what actually appear in the effect? Why torture your brain to justify the course of nature upon suppositions, which, for aught you know, may be entirely imaginary, and of which there are to be found no traces in the course of nature?

The religious hypothesis, therefore, must be considered only as a particular method of accounting for the visible phenomena of the universe : but no just reasoner will ever presume to infer from it any single fact, and alter or add to the phenomena, in any single particular. If you think, that the appearances of things prove such causes, it is allowable for you to draw an inference concerning the existence of these causes. In such complicated and sublime subjects, every one should be indulged in the liberty of conjecture and argument. But here you ought to rest. If you come backward, and arguing from your inferred causes, conclude, that any other fact has existed, or will exist, in the course of nature, which may serve as a fuller display of particular attributes; I must admonish you, that you have departed from the method of reasoning, attached to the present subject, and have certainly added something to the attributes of the cause, beyond what appears in the effect; otherwise you could never, with tolerable sense or propriety, add anything to the effect, in order to render it more worthy of the cause.

108   Where, then, is the odiousness of that doctrine, which

I teach in my school, or rather, which I examine in my gardens? Or what do you find in this whole question, wherein the security of good morals, or the peace and order of society, is in the least concerned?

I deny a providence, you say, and supreme governor of the world, who guides the course of events, and punishes the vicious with infamy and disappointment, and rewards the virtuous with honour and success, in all their undertakings. But surely, I deny not the course itself of events, which lies open to every one's inquiry and examination. I acknowledge, that, in the present order of things, virtue is attended with more peace of mind than vice, and meets with a more favourable reception from the world. I am sensible, that, according to the past experience of mankind, friendship is the chief joy of human life, and moderation the only source of tranquillity and happiness. I never balance between the virtuous and the vicious course of life; but am sensible, that, to a well-disposed mind, every advantage is on the side of the former. And what can you say more, allowing all your suppositions and reasonings? You tell me, indeed, that this disposition of things proceeds from intelligence and design. But whatever it proceeds from, the disposition itself, on which depends our happiness or misery, and consequently our conduct and deportment in life is still the same. It is still open for me, as well as you, to regulate my behaviour, by my experience of past events. And if you affirm, that, while a divine providence is allowed, and a supreme distributive justice in the universe, I ought to expect some more particular reward of the good, and punishment of the bad, beyond the ordinary course of events; I here find the same fallacy, which I have before endeavoured to detect. You persist in imagining, that, if we grant that divine existence, for which you so earnestly contend, you may safely infer consequences from it, and add something to the experienced order of nature, by arguing from the attributes which you ascribe to your gods. You seem not to remember, that all your reasonings on this subject can only be drawn from effects to causes; and that every argument, deducted from causes to effects, must of necessity be a gross sophism; since it is impossible for you to know anything of the cause, but what you have antecedently, not inferred, but discovered to the full, in the effect.

109   But what must a philosopher think of those vain reasoners, who, instead of regarding the present scene of things as the sole object of their contemplation, so far reverse the whole course of nature, as to render this life merely a passage to something farther; a porch, which leads to a greater, and vastly different building; a prologue, which serves only to introduce the piece, and give it more grace and propriety? Whence, do you think, can such philosophers derive their idea of the gods? From their own conceit and imagination surely. For if they derived it from the present phenomena, it would never point to anything farther, but must be exactly adjusted to them. That the divinity may *possibly* be endowed with attributes, which we have never seen exerted; may be governed by principles of action, which we cannot discover to be satisfied: all this will freely be allowed. But still this is mere *possibility* and hypothesis. We never can have reason to *infer* any attributes, or any principles of action in him, but so far as we know them to have been exerted and satisfied.

Are there any marks of a distributive justice in the world? If you answer in the affirmative, I conclude, that, since justice here exerts itself, it is satisfied. If you reply in the negative, I conclude, that you have then no reason to ascribe justice, in our sense of it, to the gods. If you hold a medium between affirmation and negation, by

saying, that the justice of the gods, at present, exerts
itself in part, but not in its full extent; I answer, that
you have no reason to give it any particular extent, but
only so far as you see it, *at present*, exert itself.

110   Thus I bring the dispute, O Athenians, to a short
issue with my antagonists. The course of nature lies
open to my contemplation as well as to theirs. The experienced train of events is the great standard, by which
we all regulate our conduct. Nothing else can be appealed
to in the field, or in the senate. Nothing else ought
ever to be heard of in the school, or in the closet. In
vain would our limited understanding break through those
boundaries, which are too narrow for our fond imagination.
While we argue from the course of nature, and infer
a particular intelligent cause, which first bestowed, and still
preserves order in the universe, we embrace a principle,
which is both uncertain and useless. It is uncertain;
because the subject lies entirely beyond the reach of
human experience. It is useless; because our knowledge
of this cause being derived entirely from the course of
nature, we can never, according to the rules of just reasoning, return back from the cause with any new inference,
or making additions to the common and experienced course
of nature, establish any new principles of conduct and
behaviour.

111   I observe (said I, finding he had finished his harangue)
that you neglect not the artifice of the demagogues of
old ; and as you were pleased to make me stand for the
people, you insinuate yourself into my favour by embracing
those principles, to which, you know, I have always expressed a particular attachment. But allowing you to
make experience (as indeed I think you ought) the only
standard of our judgement concerning this, and all other
questions of fact; I doubt not but, from the very same
experience, to which you appeal, it may be possible to

refute this reasoning, which you have put into the mouth of Epicurus. If you saw, for instance, a half-finished building, surrounded with heaps of brick and stone and mortar, and all the instruments of masonry; could you not *infer* from the effect, that it was a work of design and contrivance? And could you not return again, from this inferred cause, to infer new additions to the effect, and conclude, that the building would soon be finished, and receive all the further improvements, which art could bestow upon it? If you saw upon the sea-shore the print of one human foot, you would conclude, that a man had passed that way, and that he had also left the traces of the other foot, though effaced by the rolling of the sands or inundation of the waters. Why then do you refuse to admit the same method of reasoning with regard to the order of nature? Consider the world and the present life only as an imperfect building, from which you can infer a superior intelligence; and arguing from that superior intelligence, which can leave nothing imperfect; why may you not infer a more finished scheme or plan, which will receive its completion in some distant point of space or time? Are not these methods of reasoning exactly similar? And under what pretence can you embrace the one, while you reject the other?

112   The infinite difference of the subjects, replied he, is a sufficient foundation for this difference in my conclusions. In works of *human* art and contrivance, it is allowable to advance from the effect to the cause, and returning back from the cause, to form new inferences concerning the effect, and examine the alterations, which it has probably undergone, or may still undergo. But what is the foundation of this method of reasoning? Plainly this; that man is a being, whom we know by experience, whose motives and designs we are acquainted with, and whose projects and inclinations have a certain connexion and

coherence, according to the laws which nature has established for the government of such a creature. When, therefore, we find, that any work has proceeded from the skill and industry of man; as we are otherwise acquainted with the nature of the animal, we can draw a hundred inferences concerning what may be expected from him; and these inferences will all be founded in experience and observation. But did we know man only from the single work or production which we examine, it were impossible for us to argue in this manner; because our knowledge of all the qualities, which we ascribe to him, being in that case derived from the production, it is impossible they could point to anything farther, or be the foundation of any new inference. The print of a foot in the sand can only prove, when considered alone, that there was some figure adapted to it, by which it was produced: but the print of a human foot proves likewise, from our other experience, that there was probably another foot, which also left its impression, though effaced by time or other accidents. Here we mount from the effect to the cause; and descending again from the cause, infer alterations in the effect; but this is not a continuation of the same simple chain of reasoning. We comprehend in this case a hundred other experiences and observations, concerning the *usual* figure and members of that species of animal, without which this method of argument must be considered as fallacious and sophistical.

113   The case is not the same with our reasonings from the works of nature. The Deity is known to us only by his productions, and is a single being in the universe, not comprehended under any species or genus, from whose experienced attributes or qualities, we can, by analogy, infer any attribute or quality in him. As the universe shews wisdom and goodness, we infer wisdom and goodness. As it shews a particular degree of these perfections,

we infer a particular degree of them, precisely adapted to the effect which we examine. But farther attributes or farther degrees of the same attributes, we can never be authorised to infer or suppose, by any rules of just reasoning. Now, without some such licence of supposition, it is impossible for us to argue from the cause, or infer any alteration in the effect, beyond what has immediately fallen under our observation. Greater good produced by this Being must still prove a greater degree of goodness: a more impartial distribution of rewards and punishments must proceed from a greater regard to justice and equity. Every supposed addition to the works of nature makes an addition to the attributes of the Author of nature; and consequently, being entirely unsupported by any reason or argument, can never be admitted but as mere conjecture and hypothesis[1].

The great source of our mistake in this subject, and of the unbounded licence of conjecture, which we indulge, is, that we tacitly consider ourselves, as in the place of the Supreme Being, and conclude, that he will, on every

---

[1] In general, it may, I think, be established as a maxim, that where any cause is known only by its particular effects, it must be impossible to infer any new effects from that cause; since the qualities, which are requisite to produce these new effects along with the former, must either be different, or superior, or of more extensive operation, than those which simply produced the effect, whence alone the cause is supposed to be known to us. We can never, therefore, have any reason to suppose the existence of these qualities. To say, that the new effects proceed only from a continuation of the same energy, which is already known from the first effects, will not remove the difficulty. For even granting this to be the case (which can seldom be supposed), the very continuation and exertion of a like energy (for it is impossible it can be absolutely the same), I say, this exertion of a like energy, in a different period of space and time, is a very arbitrary supposition, and what there cannot possibly be any traces of in the effects, from which all our knowledge of the cause is originally derived. Let the *inferred* cause be exactly proportioned (as it should be) to the known effect; and it is impossible that it can possess any qualities, from which new or different effects can be *inferred*.

L

occasion, observe the same conduct, which we ourselves, in his situation, would have embraced as reasonable and eligible. But, besides that the ordinary course of nature may convince us, that almost everything is regulated by principles and maxims very different from ours; besides this, I say, it must evidently appear contrary to all rules of analogy to reason, from the intentions and projects of men, to those of a Being so different, and so much superior. In human nature, there is a certain experienced coherence of designs and inclinations; so that when, from any fact, we have discovered one intention of any man, it may often be reasonable, from experience, to infer another, and draw a long chain of conclusions concerning his past or future conduct. But this method of reasoning can never have place with regard to a Being, so remote and incomprehensible, who bears much less analogy to any other being in the universe than the sun to a waxen taper, and who discovers himself only by some faint traces or outlines, beyond which we have no authority to ascribe to him any attribute or perfection. What we imagine to be a superior perfection, may really be a defect. Or were it ever so much a perfection, the ascribing of it to the Supreme Being, where it appears not to have been really exerted, to the full, in his works, savours more of flattery and panegyric, than of just reasoning and sound philosophy. All the philosophy, therefore, in the world, and all the religion, which is nothing but a species of philosophy, will never be able to carry us beyond the usual course of experience, or give us measures of conduct and behaviour different from those which are furnished by reflections on common life. No new fact can ever be inferred from the religious hypothesis; no event foreseen or foretold; no reward or punishment expected or dreaded, beyond what is already known by practice and observation. So that my apology for Epicurus will still appear solid and satisfactory; nor have the political interests of society any connexion with the philosophical disputes concerning metaphysics and religion.

114   There is still one circumstance, replied I, which you seem to have overlooked. Though I should allow your premises, I must deny your conclusion. You conclude, that religious doctrines and reasonings *can* have no influence on life, because they *ought* to have no influence; never considering, that men reason not in the same manner you do, but draw many consequences from the belief of a divine Existence, and suppose that the Deity will inflict punishments on vice, and bestow rewards on virtue, beyond what appear in the ordinary course of nature. Whether this reasoning of theirs be just or not, is no matter. Its influence on their life and conduct must still be the same. And, those, who attempt to disabuse them of such prejudices, may, for aught I know, be good reasoners, but I cannot allow them to be good citizens and politicians; since they free men from one restraint upon their passions, and make the infringement of the laws of society, in one respect, more easy and secure.

After all, I may, perhaps, agree to your general conclusion in favour of liberty, though upon different premises from those, on which you endeavour to found it. I think, that the state ought to tolerate every principle of philosophy; nor is there an instance, that any government has suffered in its political interests by such indulgence. There is no enthusiasm among philosophers; their doctrines are not very alluring to the people; and no restraint can be put upon their reasonings, but what must be of dangerous consequence to the sciences, and even to the state, by paving the way for persecution and oppression in points, where the generality of mankind are more deeply interested and concerned.

115   But there occurs to me (continued I) with regard to your

main topic, a difficulty, which I shall just propose to you without insisting on it; lest it lead into reasonings of too nice and delicate a nature. In a word, I much doubt whether it be possible for a cause to be known only by its effect (as you have all along supposed) or to be of so singular and particular a nature as to have no parallel and no similarity with any other cause or object, that has ever fallen under our observation. It is only when two *species* of objects are found to be constantly conjoined, that we can infer the one from the other; and were an effect presented, which was entirely singular, and could not be comprehended under any known *species*, I do not see, that we could form any conjecture or inference at all concerning its cause. If experience and observation and analogy be, indeed, the only guides which we can reasonably follow in inferences of this nature; both the effect and cause must bear a similarity and resemblance to other effects and causes, which we know, and which we have found, in many instances, to be conjoined with each other. I leave it to your own reflection to pursue the consequences of this principle. I shall just observe, that, as the antagonists of Epicurus always suppose the universe, an effect quite singular and unparalleled, to be the proof of a Deity, a cause no less singular and unparalleled; your reasonings, upon that supposition, seem, at least, to merit our attention. There is, I own, some difficulty, how we can ever return from the cause to the effect, and, reasoning from our ideas of the former, infer any alteration on the latter, or any addition to it.

SECTION XII.

OF THE ACADEMICAL OR SCEPTICAL PHILOSOPHY.

PART I.

116 THERE is not a greater number of philosophical reasonings, displayed upon any subject, than those, which prove the existence of a Deity, and refute the fallacies of *Atheists*; and yet the most religious philosophers still dispute whether any man can be so blinded as to be a speculative atheist. How shall we reconcile these contradictions? The knights-errant, who wandered about to clear the world of dragons and giants, never entertained the least doubt with regard to the existence of these monsters.

The *Sceptic* is another enemy of religion, who naturally provokes the indignation of all divines and graver philosophers; though it is certain, that no man ever met with any such absurd creature, or conversed with a man, who had no opinion or principle concerning any subject, either of action or speculation. This begets a very natural question; What is meant by a sceptic? And how far it is possible to push these philosophical principles of doubt and uncertainty?

There is a species of scepticism, *antecedent* to all study and philosophy, which is much inculcated by Des Cartes and others, as a sovereign preservative against error and precipitate judgement. It recommends an universal doubt, not only of all our former opinions and principles, but also of our very faculties; of whose veracity, say they, we must assure ourselves, by a chain of reasoning, deduced from some original principle, which cannot possibly be fallacious or deceitful. But neither is there any such original principle, which has a prerogative above others, that are self-evident and convincing : or if there were, could we advance a step beyond it, but by the use of those very faculties, of which we are supposed to be already diffident. The Cartesian doubt, therefore, were it ever possible to be attained by any human creature (as it plainly is not) would be entirely incurable ; and no reasoning could ever bring us to a state of assurance and conviction upon any subject.

It must, however, be confessed, that this species of scepticism, when more moderate, may be understood in a very reasonable sense, and is a necessary preparative to the study of philosophy, by preserving a proper impartiality in our judgements, and weaning our mind from all those prejudices, which we may have imbibed from education or rash opinion. To begin with clear and self-evident principles, to advance by timorous and sure steps, to review frequently our conclusions, and examine accurately all their consequences ; though by these means we shall make both a slow and a short progress in our systems ; are the only methods, by which we can ever hope to reach truth, and attain a proper stability and certainty in our determinations.

117   There is another species of scepticism, *consequent* to science and enquiry, when men are supposed to have discovered, either the absolute fallaciousness of their mental faculties, or their unfitness to reach any fixed determination in all those curious subjects of speculation, about which they are commonly employed. Even our very senses are brought into dispute, by a certain species of philosophers ; and the maxims of common life are subjected to the same doubt as the most profound principles or conclusions of metaphysics and theology. As these paradoxical tenets

(if they may be called tenets) are to be met with in some philosophers, and the refutation of them in several, they naturally excite our curiosity, and make us enquire into the arguments, on which they may be founded.

I need not insist upon the more trite topics, employed by the sceptics in all ages, against the evidence of *sense*; such as those which are derived from the imperfection and fallaciousness of our organs, on numberless occasions ; the crooked appearance of an oar in water ; the various aspects of objects, according to their different distances ; the double images which arise from the pressing one eye ; with many other appearances of a like nature. These sceptical topics, indeed, are only sufficient to prove, that the senses alone are not implicitly to be depended on ; but that we must correct their evidence by reason, and by considerations, derived from the nature of the medium, the distance of the object, and the disposition of the organ, in order to render them, within their sphere, the proper *criteria* of truth and ✓ falsehood. There are other more profound arguments against the senses, which admit not of so easy a solution.

118   It seems evident, that men are carried, by a natural instinct or prepossession, to repose faith in their senses ; and that, without any reasoning, or even almost before the use of reason, we always suppose an external universe, which depends not on our perception, but would exist, though we and every sensible creature were absent or annihilated. Even the animal creation are governed by a like opinion, and preserve this belief of external objects, in all their thoughts, designs, and actions.

It seems also evident, that, when men follow this blind and powerful instinct of nature, they always suppose the very images, presented by the senses, to be the external objects, and never entertain any suspicion, that the one are nothing but representations of the other. This very table, which we see white, and which we feel hard, is believed to exist, independent of our perception, and to be something external to our mind, which perceives it. Our presence bestows not being on it: our absence does not annihilate it. It preserves its existence uniform and entire, independent of the situation of intelligent beings, who perceive or contemplate it.

But this universal and primary opinion of all men is soon destroyed by the slightest philosophy, which teaches us, that nothing can ever be present to the mind but an image or perception, and that the senses are only the inlets, through which these images are conveyed, without being able to produce any immediate intercourse between the mind and the object. The table, which we see, seems to diminish, as we remove farther from it: but the real table, which exists independent of us, suffers no alteration: it was, therefore, nothing but its image, which was present to the mind. These are the obvious dictates of reason; and no man, who reflects, ever doubted, that the existences, which we consider, when we say, *this house* and *that tree*, are nothing but perceptions in the mind, and fleeting copies or representations of other existences, which remain uniform and independent.

119   So far, then, are we necessitated by reasoning to contradict or depart from the primary instincts of nature, and to embrace a new system with regard to the evidence of our senses. But here philosophy finds herself extremely embarrassed, when she would justify this new system, and obviate the cavils and objections of the sceptics. She can no longer plead the infallible and irresistible instinct of nature: for that led us to a quite different system, which is acknowledged fallible and even erroneous. And to justify this pretended philosophical system, by a chain of clear and convincing argument, or even any appearance of argument, exceeds the power of all human capacity.

By what argument can it be proved, that the perceptions

of the mind must be caused by external objects, entirely different from them, though resembling them (if that be possible) and could not arise either from the energy of the mind itself, or from the suggestion of some invisible and unknown spirit, or from some other cause still more unknown to us? It is acknowledged, that, in fact, many of these perceptions arise not from anything external, as in dreams, madness, and other diseases. And nothing can be more inexplicable than the manner, in which body should so operate upon mind as ever to convey an image of itself to a substance, supposed of so different, and even contrary a nature.

It is a question of fact, whether the perceptions of the senses be produced by external objects, resembling them : how shall this question be determined? By experience surely; as all other questions of a like nature. But here experience is, and must be entirely silent. The mind has never anything present to it but the perceptions, and cannot possibly reach any experience of their connexion with objects. The supposition of such a connexion is, therefore, without any foundation in reasoning.

120   To have recourse to the veracity of the supreme Being, in order to prove the veracity of our senses, is surely making a very unexpected circuit. If his veracity were at all concerned in this matter, our senses would be entirely infallible; because it is not possible that he can ever deceive. Not to mention, that, if the external world be once called in question, we shall be at a loss to find arguments, by which we may prove the existence of that Being or any of his attributes.

121   This is a topic, therefore, in which the profounder and more philosophical sceptics will always triumph, when they endeavour to introduce an universal doubt into all subjects of human knowledge and enquiry. Do you follow the instincts and propensities of nature, may they say, in

assenting to the veracity of sense? But these lead you to believe that the very perception or sensible image is the external object. Do you disclaim this principle, in order to embrace a more rational opinion, that the perceptions are only representations of something external? You here depart from your natural propensities and more obvious sentiments; and yet are not able to satisfy your reason, which can never find any convincing argument from experience to prove, that the perceptions are connected with any external objects.

122   There is another sceptical topic of a like nature, derived from the most profound philosophy; which might merit our attention, were it requisite to dive so deep, in order to discover arguments and reasonings, which can so little serve to any serious purpose. It is universally allowed by modern enquirers, that all the sensible qualities of objects, such as hard, soft, hot, cold, white, black, &c. are merely secondary, and exist not in the objects themselves, but are perceptions of the mind, without any external archetype or model, which they represent. If this be allowed, with regard to secondary qualities, it must also follow, with regard to the supposed primary qualities of extension and solidity; nor can the latter be any more entitled to that denomination than the former. The idea of extension is entirely acquired from the senses of sight and feeling; and if all the qualities, perceived by the senses, be in the mind, not in the object, the same conclusion must reach the idea of extension, which is wholly dependent on the sensible ideas or the ideas of secondary qualities. Nothing can save us from this conclusion, but the asserting, that the ideas of those primary qualities are attained by *Abstraction*, an opinion, which, if we examine it accurately, we shall find to be unintelligible, and even absurd. An extension, that is neither tangible nor visible, cannot possibly be conceived: and a tangible or visible extension,

which is neither hard nor soft, black nor white, is equally
beyond the reach of human conception. Let any man try
to conceive a triangle in general, which is neither *Isosceles*
nor *Scalenum*, nor has any particular length or proportion
of sides; and he will soon perceive the absurdity of all the
scholastic notions with regard to abstraction and general
ideas [1].

123   Thus the first philosophical objection to the evidence
of sense or to the opinion of external existence consists
in this, that such an opinion, if rested on natural instinct, is
contrary to reason, and if referred to reason, is contrary to
natural instinct, and at the same time carries no rational
evidence with it, to convince an impartial enquirer. The
second objection goes farther, and represents this opinion
as contrary to reason : at least, if it be a principle of reason,
that all sensible qualities are in the mind, not in the object.
Bereave matter of all its intelligible qualities, both primary
and secondary, you in a manner annihilate it, and leave
only a certain unknown, inexplicable *something*, as the cause
of our perceptions; a notion so imperfect, that no sceptic
will think it worth while to contend against it.

PART II.

124   It may seem a very extravagant attempt of the sceptics
to destroy *reason* by argument and ratiocination; yet is
this the grand scope of all their enquiries and disputes.

---

[1] This argument is drawn from Dr. Berkeley; and indeed most of the
writings of that very ingenious author form the best lessons of scepticism,
which are to be found either among the ancient or modern philosophers,
Bayle not excepted. He professes, however, in his title-page (and
undoubtedly with great truth) to have composed his book against the
sceptics as well as against the atheists and free-thinkers. But that all his
arguments, though otherwise intended, are, in reality, merely sceptical,
appears from this, *that they admit of no answer and produce no conviction*. Their only effect is to cause that momentary amazement and
irresolution and confusion, which is the result of scepticism.

They endeavour to find objections, both to our abstract reasonings, and to those which regard matter of fact and existence.

The chief objection against all *abstract* reasonings is derived from the ideas of space and time; ideas, which, in common life and to a careless view, are very clear and intelligible, but when they pass through the scrutiny of the profound sciences (and they are the chief object of these sciences) afford principles, which seem full of absurdity and contradiction. No priestly *dogmas*, invented on purpose to tame and subdue the rebellious reason of mankind, ever shocked common sense more than the doctrine of the infinitive divisibility of extension, with its consequences; as they are pompously displayed by all geometricians and metaphysicians, with a kind of triumph and exultation. A real quantity, infinitely less than any finite quantity, containing quantities infinitely less than itself, and so on *in infinitum*; this is an edifice so bold and prodigious, that it is too weighty for any pretended demonstration to support, because it shocks the clearest and most natural principles of human reason[1]. But what renders the matter more extraordinary, is, that these seemingly absurd opinions are supported by a chain of reasoning, the clearest and most natural; nor is it possible for us to allow the premises without admitting the consequences. Nothing can be more convincing and satisfactory than all the conclusions

---

[1] Whatever disputes there may be about mathematical points, we must allow that there are physical points; that is, parts of extension, which cannot be divided or lessened, either by the eye or imagination. These images, then, which are present to the fancy or senses, are absolutely indivisible, and consequently must be allowed by mathematicians to be infinitely less than any real part of extension; and yet nothing appears more certain to reason, than that an infinite number of them composes an infinite extension. How much more an infinite number of those infinitely small parts of extension, which are still supposed infinitely divisible.

concerning the properties of circles and triangles; and yet, when these are once received, how can we deny, that the angle of contact between a circle and its tangent is infinitely less than any rectilineal angle, that as you may increase the diameter of the circle *in infinitum*, this angle of contact becomes still less, even *in infinitum*, and that the angle of contact between other curves and their tangents may be infinitely less than those between any circle and its tangent, and so on, *in infinitum*? The demonstration of these principles seems as unexceptionable as that which proves the three angles of a triangle to be equal to two right ones, though the latter opinion be natural and easy, and the former big with contradiction and absurdity. Reason here seems to be thrown into a kind of amazement and suspence, which, without the suggestions of any sceptic, gives her a diffidence of herself, and of the ground on which she treads. She sees a full light, which illuminates certain places; but that light borders upon the most profound darkness. And between these she is so dazzled and confounded, that she scarcely can pronounce with certainty and assurance concerning any one object.

125   The absurdity of these bold determinations of the abstract sciences seems to become, if possible, still more palpable with regard to time than extension. An infinite number of real parts of time, passing in succession, and exhausted one after another, appears so evident a contradiction, that no man, one should think, whose judgement is not corrupted, instead of being improved, by the sciences, would ever be able to admit of it.

Yet still reason must remain restless, and unquiet, even with regard to that scepticism, to which she is driven by these seeming absurdities and contradictions. How any clear, distinct idea can contain circumstances, contradictory to itself, or to any other clear, distinct idea, is absolutely incomprehensible; and is, perhaps, as absurd as any propo-

sition, which can be formed.   So that nothing can be more
sceptical, or more full of doubt and hesitation, than this
scepticism itself, which arises from some of the paradoxical
conclusions of geometry or the science of quantity[1].

126   The sceptical objections to *moral* evidence, or to the
reasonings concerning matter of fact, are either *popular* or
philosophical.   The popular objections are derived from the
natural weakness of human understanding ; the contradictory opinions, which have been entertained in different
ages and nations ; the variations of our judgement in sickness and health, youth and old age, prosperity and adver-
sity; the perpetual contradiction of each particular man's
opinions and sentiments ; with many other topics of that
kind.   It is needless to insist farther on this head.   These
objections are but weak.   For as, in common life, we reason
every moment concerning fact and existence, and cannot
possibly subsist, without continually employing this species
of argument, any popular objections, derived from thence,
must be insufficient to destroy that evidence.   The great
subverter of *Pyrrhonism* or the excessive principles of

---

[1] It seems to me not impossible to avoid these absurdities and
contradictions, if it be admitted, that there is no such thing as abstract
or general ideas, properly speaking; but that all general ideas are, in
reality, particular ones, attached to a general term, which recalls, upon
occasion, other particular ones, that resemble, in certain circumstances,
the idea, present to the mind.   Thus when the term Horse is pronounced,
we immediately figure to ourselves the idea of a black or a white
animal, of a particular size or figure : But as that term is also usually
applied to animals of other colours, figures and sizes, these ideas,
though not actually present to the imagination, are easily recalled ; and
our reasoning and conclusion proceed in the same way, as if they were
actually present.   If this be admitted (as seems reasonable) it follows
that all the ideas of quantity, upon which mathematicians reason, are
nothing but particular, and such as are suggested by the senses and
imagination, and consequently, cannot be infinitely divisible.   It is
sufficient to have dropped this hint at present, without prosecuting it
any farther.   It certainly concerns all lovers of science not to expose
themselves to the ridicule and contempt of the ignorant by their
conclusions; and this seems the readiest solution of these difficulties.

scepticism is action, and employment, and the occupations
of common life. These principles may flourish and triumph
in the schools; where it is, indeed, difficult, if not impossible,
to refute them. But as soon as they leave the shade, and
by the presence of the real objects, which actuate our
passions and sentiments, are put in opposition to the more
powerful principles of our nature, they vanish like smoke,
and leave the most determined sceptic in the same condition
as other mortals.

127　　The sceptic, therefore, had better keep within his proper
sphere, and display those *philosophical* objections, which
arise from more profound researches. Here he seems to
have ample matter of triumph; while he justly insists, that
all our evidence for any matter of fact, which lies beyond the
testimony of sense or memory, is derived entirely from the
relation of cause and effect; that we have no other idea
of this relation than that of two objects, which have been
frequently *conjoined* together; that we have no argument to
convince us, that objects, which have, in our experience,
been frequently conjoined, will likewise, in other instances,
be conjoined in the same manner; and that nothing leads
us to this inference but custom or a certain instinct of our
nature; which it is indeed difficult to resist, but which,
like other instincts, may be fallacious and deceitful. While
the sceptic insists upon these topics, he shows his force, or
rather, indeed, his own and our weakness; and seems, for
the time at least, to destroy all assurance and conviction.
These arguments might be displayed at greater length,
if any durable good or benefit to society could ever be
expected to result from them.

128　　For here is the chief and most confounding objection to
excessive scepticism, that no durable good can ever result
from it; while it remains in its full force and vigour. We
need only ask such a sceptic, *What his meaning is? And
what he proposes by all these curious researches?* He is

immediately at a loss, and knows not what to answer.
A Copernican or Ptolemaic, who supports each his different
system of astronomy, may hope to produce a conviction,
which will remain constant and durable, with his audience.
A Stoic or Epicurean displays principles, which may not
be durable, but which have an effect on conduct and behaviour.   But a Pyrrhonian cannot expect, that his philosophy will have any constant influence on the mind: or if
it had, that its influence would be beneficial to society.   On
the contrary, he must acknowledge, if he will acknowledge
anything, that all human life must perish, were his principles ·
universally and steadily to prevail.   All discourse, all action
would immediately cease; and men remain in a total lethargy,
till the necessities of nature, unsatisfied, put an end to their
miserable existence.   It is true; so fatal an event is very little
to be dreaded.   Nature is always too strong for principle.
And though a Pyrrhonian may throw himself or others into
a momentary amazement and confusion by his profound
reasonings; the first and most trival event in life will
put to flight all his doubts and scruples, and leave him the
same, in every point of action and speculation, with the
philosophers of every other sect, or with those who never
concerned themselves in any philosophical researches.
When he awakes from his dream, he will be the first to join
in the laugh against himself, and to confess, that all his
objections are mere amusement, and can have no other
tendency than to show the whimsical condition of mankind,
who must act and reason and believe; though they are not
able, by their most diligent enquiry, to satisfy themselves
concerning the foundation of these operations, or to remove
the objections, which may be raised against them.

PART III.

129   There is, indeed, a more *mitigated* scepticism or *academical* philosophy, which may be both durable and useful, and which may, in part, be the result of this Pyrrhonism, or *excessive* scepticism, when its undistinguished doubts are, in some measure, corrected by common sense and reflection. The greater part of mankind are naturally apt to be affirmative and dogmatical in their opinions; and while they see objects only on one side, and have no idea of any counterpoising argument, they throw themselves precipitately into the principles, to which they are inclined; nor have they any indulgence for those who entertain opposite sentiments. To hesitate or balance perplexes their understanding, checks their passion, and suspends their action. They are, therefore, impatient till they escape from a state, which to them is so uneasy: and they think, that they could never remove themselves far enough from it, by the violence of their affirmations and obstinacy of their belief. But could such dogmatical reasoners become sensible of the strange infirmities of human understanding, even in its most perfect state, and when most accurate and cautious in its determinations; such a reflection would naturally inspire them with more modesty and reserve, and diminish their fond opinion of themselves, and their prejudice against antagonists. The illiterate may reflect on the disposition of the learned, who, amidst all the advantages of study and reflection, are commonly still diffident in their determinations: and if any of the learned be inclined, from their natural temper, to haughtiness and obstinacy, a small tincture of Pyrrhonism might abate their pride, by showing them, that the few advantages, which they may have attained over their fellows, are but inconsiderable, if compared with the universal perplexity and confusion, which is inherent in human nature. In

M

general, there is a degree of doubt, and caution, and modesty, which, in all kinds of scrutiny and decision, ought for ever to accompany a just reasoner.

130   Another species of *mitigated* scepticism which may be of advantage to mankind, and which may be the natural result of the Pyrrhonian doubts and scruples, is the limitation of our enquiries to such subjects as are best adapted to the narrow capacity of human understanding. The *imagination* of man is naturally sublime, delighted with whatever is remote and extraordinary, and running, without control, into the most distant parts of space and time in order to avoid the objects, which custom has rendered too familiar to it. A correct *Judgement* observes a contrary method, and avoiding all distant and high enquiries, confines itself to common life, and to such subjects as fall under daily practice and experience; leaving the more sublime topics to the embellishment of poets and orators, or to the arts of priests and politicians. To bring us to so salutary a determination, nothing can be more serviceable, than to be once thoroughly convinced of the force of the Pyrrhonian doubt, and of the impossibility, that anything, but the strong power of natural instinct, could free us from it. Those who have a propensity to philosophy, will still continue their researches; because they reflect, that, besides the immediate pleasure, attending such an occupation, philosophical decisions are nothing but the reflections of common life, methodized and corrected. But they will never be tempted to go beyond common life, so long as they consider the imperfection of those faculties which they employ, their narrow reach, and their inaccurate operations. While we cannot give a satisfactory reason, why we believe, after a thousand experiments, that a stone will fall, or fire burn; can we ever satisfy ourselves concerning any determination, which we may form, with regard to the origin of worlds, and the situation of nature, from, and to eternity?

This narrow limitation, indeed, of our enquiries, is, in every respect, so reasonable, that it suffices to make the slightest examination into the natural powers of the human mind and to compare them with their objects, in order to recommend it to us. We shall then find what are the proper subjects of science and enquiry.

131 It seems to me, that the only objects of the abstract science or of demonstration are quantity and number, and that all attempts to extend this more perfect species of knowledge beyond these bounds are mere sophistry and illusion. As the component parts of quantity and number are entirely similar, their relations become intricate and involved; and nothing can be more curious, as well as useful, than to trace, by a variety of mediums, their equality or inequality, through their different appearances. But as all other ideas are clearly distinct and different from each other, we can never advance farther, by our utmost scrutiny, than to observe this diversity, and, by an obvious reflection, pronounce one thing not to be another. Or if there be any difficulty in these decisions, it proceeds entirely from the undeterminate meaning of words, which is corrected by juster definitions. That *the square of the hypothenuse is equal to the squares of the other two sides,* cannot be known, let the terms be ever so exactly defined, without a train of reasoning and enquiry. But to convince us of this proposition, *that where there is no property, there can be no injustice,* it is only necessary to define the terms, and explain injustice to be a violation of property. This proposition is, indeed, nothing but a more imperfect definition. It is the same case with all those pretended syllogistical reasonings, which may be found in every other branch of learning, except the sciences of quantity and number; and these may safely, I think, be pronounced the only proper objects of knowledge and demonstration.

132 All other enquiries of men regard only matter of fact and

existence; and these are evidently incapable of demonstration. Whatever *is* may *not be*. No negation of a fact can involve a contradiction. The non-existence of any being, without exception, is as clear and distinct an idea as its existence. The proposition, which affirms it not to be, however false, is no less conceivable and intelligible, than that which affirms it to be. The case is different with the sciences, properly so called. Every proposition, which is not true, is there confused and unintelligible. That the cube root of 64 is equal to the half of 10, is a false proposition, and can never be distinctly conceived. But that Cæsar, or the angel Gabriel, or any being never existed, may be a false proposition, but still is perfectly conceivable, and implies no contradiction.

The existence, therefore, of any being can only be proved by arguments from its cause or its effect; and these arguments are founded entirely on experience. If we reason *a priori*, anything may appear able to produce anything. The falling of a pebble may, for aught we know, extinguish the sun; or the wish of a man control the planets in their orbits. It is only experience, which teaches us the nature and bounds of cause and effect, and enables us to infer the existence of one object from that of another [1]. Such is the foundation of moral reasoning, which forms the greater part of human knowledge, and is the source of all human action and behaviour.

Moral reasonings are either concerning particular or general facts. All deliberations in life regard the former; as also all disquisitions in history, chronology, geography, and astronomy.

---

[1] That impious maxim of the ancient philosophy, *Ex nihilo, nihil fit,* by which the creation of matter was excluded, ceases to be a maxim, according to this philosophy Not only the will of the supreme Being may create matter; but, for aught we know *a priori*, the will of any other being might create it, or any other cause, that the most whimsical imagination can assign.

The sciences, which treat of general facts, are politics, natural philosophy, physic, chemistry, &c. where the qualities, causes and effects of a whole species of objects are enquired into.

Divinity or Theology, as it proves the existence of a Deity, and the immortality of souls, is composed partly of reasonings concerning particular, partly concerning general facts. It has a foundation in *reason*, so far as it is supported by experience. But its best and most solid foundation is *faith* and divine revelation.

Morals and criticism are not so properly objects of the understanding as of taste and sentiment. Beauty, whether moral or natural, is felt, more properly than perceived. Or if we reason concerning it, and endeavour to fix its standard, we regard a new fact, to wit, the general tastes of mankind, or some such fact, which may be the object of reasoning and enquiry.

When we run over libraries, persuaded of these principles, what havoc must we make? If we take in our hand any volume; of divinity or school metaphysics, for instance; let us ask, *Does it contain any abstract reasoning concerning quantity or number?* No. *Does it contain any experimental reasoning concerning matter of fact and existence?* No. Commit it then to the flames: for it can contain nothing but sophistry and illusion.

AN ENQUIRY

CONCERNING THE

PRINCIPLES OF MORALS

AN ENQUIRY

PRINCIPLES OF MORALS

—+—

SECTION I.

OF THE GENERAL PRINCIPLES OF MORALS.

133 DISPUTES with men, pertinaciously obstinate in their principles, are, of all others, the most irksome; except, perhaps, those with persons, entirely disingenuous, who really do not believe the opinions they defend, but engage in the controversy, from affectation, from a spirit of opposition, or from a desire of showing wit and ingenuity, superior to the rest of mankind. The same blind adherence to their own arguments is to be expected in both; the same contempt of their antagonists; and the same passionate vehemence, in inforcing sophistry and falsehood. And as reasoning is not the source, whence either disputant derives his tenets; it is in vain to expect, that any logic, which speaks not to the affections, will ever engage him to embrace sounder principles.

Those who have denied the reality of moral distinctions, may be ranked among the disingenuous disputants; nor is it conceivable, that any human creature could ever seriously believe, that all characters and actions were alike entitled to the affection and regard of everyone. The difference, which nature has placed between one man and another, is so wide, and this difference is still so much farther widened, by education, example, and habit, that, where the opposite extremes come at once under our apprehension, there is no scepticism so scrupulous, and scarce any assurance so determined, as absolutely to deny all distinction between them. Let a man's insensibility be ever so great, he must often be touched with the images of Right and Wrong; and let his prejudices be ever so obstinate, he must observe, that others are susceptible of like impressions. The only way, therefore, of converting an antagonist of this kind, is to leave him to himself. For, finding that nobody keeps up the controversy with him, it is probable he will, at last, of himself, from mere weariness, come over to the side of common sense and reason.

134   There has been a controversy started of late, much better worth examination, concerning the general foundation of Morals; whether they be derived from Reason, or from Sentiment; whether we attain the knowledge of them by a chain of argument and induction, or by an immediate feeling and finer internal sense; whether, like all sound judgement of truth and falsehood, they should be the same to every rational intelligent being; or whether, like the perception of beauty and deformity, they be founded entirely on the particular fabric and constitution of the human species.

The ancient philosphers, though they often affirm, that virtue is nothing but conformity to reason, yet, in general, seem to consider morals as deriving their existence from taste and sentiment. On the other hand, our modern enquirers, though they also talk much of the beauty of virtue, and deformity of vice, yet have commonly endeavoured to account for these distinctions by metaphysical reasonings, and by deductions from the most abstract principles of the understanding. Such confusion reigned in these subjects, that an opposition of the greatest consequence could prevail between one system and another, and even in the parts of almost each individual system ; and yet nobody, till very lately, was ever sensible of it. The elegant Lord Shaftesbury, who first gave occasion to remark this distinction, and who, in general, adhered to the principles of the ancients, is not, himself, entirely free from the same confusion.

135　　It must be acknowledged, that both sides of the question are susceptible of specious arguments. Moral distinctions, it may be said, are discernible by pure *reason*: else, whence the many disputes that reign in common life, as well as in philosophy, with regard to this subject : the long chain of proofs often produced on both sides ; the examples cited, the authorities appealed to, the analogies employed, the fallacies detected, the inferences drawn, and the several conclusions adjusted to their proper principles. Truth is disputable; not taste : what exists in the nature of things is the standard of our judgement ; what each man feels within himself is the standard of sentiment. Propositions in geometry may be proved, systems in physics may be controverted ; but the harmony of verse, the tenderness of passion, the brilliancy of wit, must give immediate pleasure. No man reasons concerning another's beauty ; but frequently concerning the justice or injustice of his actions. In every criminal trial the first object of the prisoner is to disprove the facts alleged, and deny the actions imputed to him : the second to prove, that, even if these actions were real, they might be justified, as innocent and lawful. It is confessedly by deductions of the understanding, that the first point is ascertained : how can we suppose that a different faculty of the mind is employed in fixing the other?

136　　On the other hand, those who would resolve all moral determinations into *sentiment*, may endeavour to show, that it is impossible for reason ever to draw conclusions of this nature. To virtue, say they, it belongs to be *amiable*, and vice *odious*. This forms their very nature or essence. But can reason or argumentation distribute these different epithets to any subjects, and pronounce beforehand, that this must produce love, and that hatred? Or what other reason can we ever assign for these affections, but the original fabric and formation of the human mind, which is naturally adapted to receive them?

The end of all moral speculations is to teach us our duty; and, by proper representations of the deformity of vice and beauty of virtue, beget correspondent habits, and engage us to avoid the one, and embrace the other. But is this ever to be expected from inferences and conclusions of the understanding, which of themselves have no hold of the affections or set in motion the active powers of men? They discover truths: but where the truths which they discover are indifferent, and beget no desire or aversion, they can have no influence on conduct and behaviour. What is honourable, what is fair, what is becoming, what is noble, what is generous, takes possession of the heart, and animates us to embrace and maintain it. What is intelligible, what is evident, what is probable, what is true, procures only the cool assent of the understanding; and gratifying a speculative curiosity, puts an end to our researches.

Extinguish all the warm feelings and prepossessions in favour of virtue, and all disgust or aversion to vice: render men totally indifferent towards these distinctions; and morality is no longer a practical study, nor has any tendency to regulate our lives and actions.

137   These arguments on each side (and many more might be produced) are so plausible, that I am apt to suspect, they may, the one as well as the other, be solid and satisfactory, and that *reason* and *sentiment* concur in almost all moral determinations and conclusions. The final sentence, it is probable, which pronounces characters and actions amiable or odious, praise-worthy or blameable; that which stamps

on them the mark of honour or infamy, approbation or
censure; that which renders morality an active principle
and constitutes virtue our happiness, and vice our misery:
it is probable, I say, that this final sentence depends on
some internal sense or feeling, which nature has made
universal in the whole species. For what else can have an
influence of this nature? But in order to pave the way for
such a sentiment, and give a proper discernment of its object,
it is often necessary, we find, that much reasoning should
precede, that nice distinctions be made, just conclusions
drawn, distant comparsions formed, complicated relations
examined, and general facts fixed and ascertained. Some
species of beauty, especially the natural kinds, on their first
appearance, command our affection and approbation; and
where they fail of this effect, it is impossible for any reasoning
to redress their influence, or adapt them better to our taste
and sentiment. But in many orders of beauty, particularly
those of the finer arts, it is requisite to employ much reasoning, in order to feel the proper sentiment; and a false relish
may frequently be corrected by argument and reflection.
There are just grounds to conclude, that moral beauty
partakes much of this latter species, and demands the
assistance of our intellectual faculties, in order to give it a
suitable influence on the human mind.

138 . But though this question, concerning the general principles
of morals, be curious and important, it is needless for us, at
present, to employ farther care in our researches concerning
it. For if we can be so happy, in the course of this enquiry,
as to discover the true origin of morals, it will then easily
appear how far either sentiment or reason enters into all
determinations of this nature[1]. In order to attain this
purpose, we shall endeavour to follow a very simple method:
we shall analyse that complication of mental qualities, which
form what, in common life, we call Personal Merit: we shall

[1] See Appendix I.

consider every attribute of the mind, which renders a man an object either of esteem and affection, or of hatred and contempt; every habit or sentiment or faculty, which, if ascribed to any person, implies either praise or blame, and may enter into any panegyric or satire of his character and manners. The quick sensibility, which, on this head, is so universal among mankind, gives a philosopher sufficient assurance, that he can never be considerably mistaken in framing the catalogue, or incur any danger of misplacing the objects of his contemplation: he needs only enter into his own breast for a moment, and consider whether or not he should desire to have this or that quality ascribed to him, and whether such or such an imputation would proceed from a friend or an enemy. The very nature of language guides us almost infallibly in forming a judgement of this nature; and as every tongue possesses one set of words which are taken in a good sense, and another in the opposite, the least acquaintance with the idiom suffices, without any reasoning, to direct us in collecting and arranging the estimable or blameable qualities of men. The only object of reasoning is to discover the circumstances on both sides, which are common to these qualities; to observe that particular in which the estimable qualities agree on the one hand, and the blameable on the other; and thence to reach the foundation of ethics, and find those universal principles, from which all censure or approbation is ultimately derived. As this is a question of fact, not of abstract science, we can only expect success, by following the experimental method, and deducing general maxims from a comparison of particular instances. The other scientific method, where a general abstract principle is first established, and is afterwards branched out into a variety of inferences and conclusions, may be more perfect in itself, but suits less the imperfection of human nature, and is a common source of illusion and mistake in this as well as in other subjects. Men are not cured of their passion for hypotheses and systems in natural philosophy, and will hearken to no arguments but those which are derived from experience. It is full time they should attempt a like reformation in all moral disquisitions; and reject every system of ethics, however subtle or ingenious, which is not founded on fact and observation.

We shall begin our enquiry on this head by the consideration of the social virtues, Benevolence and Justice. The explication of them will probably give us an opening by which the others may be accounted for.

SECTION II.

PART I.

139   It may be esteemed, perhaps, a superfluous task to prove, that the benevolent or softer affections are estimable; and wherever they appear, engage the approbation and good-will of mankind. The epithets *sociable, good-natured, humane, merciful, grateful, friendly, generous, beneficent,* or their equivalents, are known in all languages, and universally express the highest merit, which *human nature* is capable of attaining. Where these amiable qualities are attended with birth and power and eminent abilities, and display themselves in the good government or useful instruction of mankind, they seem even to raise the possessors of them above the rank of *human nature*, and make them approach in some measure to the divine. Exalted capacity, undaunted courage, prosperous success; these may only expose a hero or politician to the envy and ill-will of the public: but as soon as the praises are added of humane and beneficent; when instances are displayed of lenity, tenderness or friendship; envy itself is silent, or joins the general voice of approbation and applause.

When Pericles, the great Athenian statesman and general, was on his death-bed, his surrounding friends, deeming him now insensible, began to indulge their sorrow for their expiring patron, by enumerating his great qualities and successes, his conquests and victories, the unusual length of his administration, and his nine trophies erected over the enemies of the republic. *You forget,* cries the dying hero, who had heard all, *you forget the most eminent of my praises, while you dwell so much on those vulgar advantages, in which fortune had a principal share. You have not observed that no* · *citizen has ever yet worne mourning on my account* [1].

In men of more ordinary talents and capacity, the social virtues become, if possible, still more essentially requisite ; there being nothing eminent, in that case, to compensate for the want of them, or preserve the person from our severest hatred, as well as contempt. A high ambition, an elevated courage, is apt, says Cicero, in less perfect characters, to degenerate into a turbulent ferocity. The more social and softer virtues are there chiefly to be regarded. These are always good and amiable [2].

The principal advantage, which Juvenal discovers in the extensive capacity of the human species, is that it renders our benevolence also more extensive, and gives us larger opportunities of spreading our kindly influence than what are indulged to the inferior creation [3]. It must, indeed, be confessed, that by doing good only, can a man truly enjoy the advantages of being eminent. His exalted station, of itself but the more exposes him to danger and tempest. His sole prerogative is to afford shelter to inferiors, who repose themselves under his cover and protection.

140 But I forget, that it is not my present business to recommend generosity and benevolence, or to paint, in their true colours, all the genuine charms of the social virtues. These, indeed, sufficiently engage every heart, on the first apprehension of them ; and it is difficult to abstain from some sally of panegyric, as often as they occur in discourse or reasoning. But our object here being more the speculative,

[1] Plut. in Pericle.   [2] Cic. de Officiis, lib. 1.
[3] Sat. xv. 139 and seq.

N

than the practical part of morals, it will suffice to remark, (what will readily, I believe, be allowed) that no qualities are more intitled to the general good-will and approbation of mankind than beneficence and humanity, friendship and gratitude, natural affection and public spirit, or whatever proceeds from a tender sympathy with others, and a generous concern for our kind and species. These wherever they appear, seem to transfuse themselves, in a manner, into each beholder, and to call forth, in their own behalf, the same favourable and affectionate sentiments, which they exert on all around.

PART II.

141 —We may observe that, in displaying the praises of any humane, beneficent man, there is one circumstance which never fails to be amply insisted on, namely, the happiness and satisfaction, derived to society from his intercourse and good offices. To his parents, we are apt to say, he endears himself by his pious attachment and duteous care still more than by the connexions of nature. His children never feel his authority, but when employed for their advantage. With him, the ties of love are consolidated by beneficence and friendship. The ties of friendship approach, in a fond observance of each obliging office, to those of love and inclination. His domestics and dependants have in him a sure resource; and no longer dread the power of fortune, but so far as she exercises it over him. From him the hungry receive food, the naked clothing, the ignorant and slothful skill and industry. Like the sun, an inferior minister of providence he cheers, invigorates, and sustains the surrounding world.

If confined to private life, the sphere of his activity is narrower; but his influence is all benign and gentle. If exalted into a higher station, mankind and posterity reap the fruit of his labours.

As these topics of praise never fail to be employed, and with success, where we would inspire esteem for any one; may it not thence be concluded, that the utility, resulting from the social virtues, forms, at least, a *part* of their merit, and is one source of that approbation and regard so universally paid to them?

2   When we recommend even an animal or a plant as *useful* and *beneficial*, we give it an applause and recommendation suited to its nature. As, on the other hand, reflection on the baneful influence of any of these inferior beings always inspires us with the sentiment of aversion. The eye is pleased with the prospect of corn-fields and loaded vineyards; horses grazing, and flocks pasturing: but flies the view of briars and brambles, affording shelter to wolves and serpents.

A machine, a piece of furniture, a vestment, a house well contrived for use and conveniency, is so far beautiful, and is contemplated with pleasure and approbation. An experienced eye is here sensible to many excellencies, which escape persons ignorant and uninstructed.

Can anything stronger be said in praise of a profession, such as merchandize or manufacture, than to observe the advantages which it procures to society; and is not a monk and inquisitor enraged when we treat his order as useless or pernicious to mankind?

The historian exults in displaying the benefit arising from his labours. The writer of romance alleviates or denies the bad consequences ascribed to his manner of composition.

In general, what praise is implied in the simple epithet *useful*! What reproach in the contrary!

Your Gods, says Cicero[1], in opposition to the Epicureans, cannot justly claim any worship or adoration, with whatever imaginary perfections you may suppose them endowed.

[1] De Nat. Deor. lib. i.

They are totally useless and inactive.   Even the Egyptians, whom you so much ridicule, never consecrated any animal but on account of its utility.

The sceptics assert[1], though absurdly, that the origin of all religious worship was derived from the utility of inanimate objects, as the sun and moon, to the support and well-being of mankind.   This is also the common reason assigned by historians, for the deification of eminent heroes and legislators[2].

To plant a tree, to cultivate a field, to beget children; meritorious acts, according to the religion of Zoroaster.

143   In all determinations of morality, this circumstance of public utility is ever principally in view; and wherever disputes arise, either in philosophy or common life, concerning the bounds of duty, the question cannot, by any means, be decided with greater certainty, than by ascertaining, on any side, the true interests of mankind.   If any false opinion, embraced from appearances, has been found to prevail; as soon as farther experience and sounder reasoning have given us juster notions of human affairs, we retract our first sentiment, and adjust anew the boundaries of moral good and evil.

. Giving alms to common beggars is naturally praised; because it seems to carry relief to the distressed and indigent: but when we observe the encouragement thence arising to idleness and debauchery, we regard that species of charity rather as a weakness than a virtue.

Tyrannicide, or the assassination of usurpers and oppressive princes, was highly extolled in ancient times; because it both freed mankind from many of these monsters, and seemed to keep the others in awe, whom the sword or poinard could not reach.   But history and experience having since convinced us, that this practice increases the

[1] Sext. Emp. adversus Math. lib. viii.
[2] Diod. Sic. passim.

jealously and cruelty of princes, a Timoleon and a Brutus, though treated with indulgence on account of the prejudices of their times, are now considered as very improper models for imitation.

Liberality in princes is regarded as a mark of beneficence, but when it occurs, that the homely bread of the honest and industrious is often thereby converted into delicious cates for the idle and the prodigal, we soon retract our heedless praises. The regrets of a prince, for having lost a day, were noble and generous : but had he intended to have spent it in acts of generosity to his greedy courtiers, it was better lost than misemployed after that manner.

Luxury, or a refinement on the pleasures and conveniencies of life, had not long been supposed the source of every corruption in government, and the immediate cause of faction, sedition, civil wars, and the total loss of liberty. It was, therefore, universally regarded as a vice, and was an object of declamation to all satirists, and severe moralists. Those, who prove, or attempt to prove, that such refinements rather tend to the increase of industry, civility, and arts regulate anew our *moral* as well as *political* sentiments, and represent, as laudable or innocent, what had formerly been regarded as pernicious and blameable.

144   Upon the whole, then, it seems undeniable, *that* nothing can bestow more merit on any human creature than the ~sentiment of benevolence in an eminent degree; and *that* a *part*, at least, of its merit arises from its tendency to promote the interests of our species, and bestow happiness on human society. We carry our view into the salutary consequences of such a character and disposition ; and whatever has so benign an influence, and forwards so desirable an end, is beheld with complacency and pleasure. The social virtues are never regarded without their beneficial tendencies, nor viewed as barren and unfruitful. The happiness of mankind, the order of society, the harmony of families, the mutual support of friends, are always considered as the result of their gentle dominion over the breasts of men.

How considerable a *part* of their merit we ought to ascribe to their utility, will better appear from future disquisitions [1]; as well as the reason, why this circumstance has such a command over our esteem and approbation [2].

[1] Sect. III and IV.   [2] Sect. V.

SECTION IIL

OF JUSTICE.

PART I.

145 THAT Justice is useful to society, and consequently that *part* of its merit, at least, must arise from that consideration, it would be a superfluous undertaking to prove. That public utility is the *sole* origin of justice, and that reflections on the beneficial consequences of this virtue are the *sole* foundation of its merit; this proposition, being more curious and important, will better deserve our examination and enquiry.

Let us suppose that nature has bestowed on the human race such profuse *abundance* of all *external* conveniencies, that, without any uncertainty in the event, without any care or industry on our part, every individual finds himself fully provided with whatever his most voracious appetites can want, or luxurious imagination wish or desire. His natural beauty, we shall suppose, surpasses all acquired ornaments: the perpetual clemency of the seasons renders useless all clothes or covering: the raw herbage affords him the most delicious fare; the clear fountain, the richest beverage. No laborious occupation required: no tillage: no navigation. Music, poetry, and contemplation form his sole business: conversation, mirth, and friendship his sole amusement.

It seems evident that, in such a happy state, every other social virtue would flourish, and receive tenfold increase;

but the cautious, jealous virtue of justice would never once have been dreamed of. For what purpose make a partition of goods, where every one has already more than enough? Why give rise to property, where there cannot possibly be any injury? Why call this object *mine*, when upon the seizing of it by another, I need but stretch out my hand to possess myself to what is equally valuable? Justice, in that case, being totally useless, would be an idle ceremonial, and could never possibly have place in the catalogue of virtues.

We see, even in the present necessitous condition of mankind, that, wherever any benefit is bestowed by nature in an unlimited abundance, we leave it always in common among the whole human race, and make no subdivisions of right and property. Water and air, though the most necessary of all objects, are not challenged as the property of individuals; nor can any man commit injustice by the most lavish use and enjoyment of these blessings. In fertile extensive countries, with few inhabitants, land is regarded on the same footing. And no topic is so much insisted on by those, who defend the liberty of the seas, as the unexhausted use of them in navigation. Were the advantages, procured by navigation, as inexhaustible, these reasoners had never had any adversaries to refute; nor had any claims ever been advanced of a separate, exclusive dominion over the ocean.

It may happen, in some countries, at some periods, that there be established a property in water, none in land[1]; if the latter be in greater abundance than can be used by the inhabitants, and the former be found, with difficulty, and in very small quantities.

146   Again; suppose, that, though the necessities of human race continue the same as at present, yet the mind is so enlarged, and so replete with friendship and generosity,

---

[1] Genesis, chaps. xiii and xxi.

that every man has the utmost tenderness for every man,
and feels no more concern for his own interest than for
that of his fellows; it seems evident, that the use of
justice would, in this case, be suspended by such an
extensive benevolence, nor would the divisions and barriers
of property and obligation have ever been thought of. Why
should I bind another, by a deed or promise, to do me any
good office, when I know that he is already prompted, by
the strongest inclination, to seek my happiness, and would,
of himself, perform the desired service; except the hurt, he
thereby receives, be greater than the benefit accruing to me?
in which case, he knows, that, from my innate humanity
and friendship, I should be the first to oppose myself to his
imprudent generosity. Why raise land-marks between my
neighbour's field and mine, when my heart has made no
division between our interests; but shares all his joys and
sorrows with the same force and vivacity as if originally my
own? Every man, upon this supposition, being a second
self to another, would trust all his interests to the discretion
of every man; without jealousy, without partition, without
distinction. And the whole human race would form only
one family; where all would lie in common, and be used
freely, without regard to property; but cautiously too, with
as entire regard to the necessities of each individual, as if
our own interests were most intimately concerned.

In the present disposition of the human heart, it would,
perhaps, be difficult to find complete instances of such
enlarged affections; but still we may observe, that the case
of families approaches towards it; and the stronger the
mutual benevolence is among the individuals, the nearer it
approaches; till all distinction of property be, in a great
measure, lost and confounded among them. Between
married persons, the cement of friendship is by the laws
supposed so strong as to abolish all division of possessions;
and has often, in reality, the force ascribed to it. And it is

observable, that, during the ardour of new enthusiasms, when every principle is inflamed into extravagance, the community of goods has frequently been attempted ; and nothing but experience of its inconveniencies, from the returning or disguised selfishness of men, could make the imprudent fanatics adopt anew the ideas of justice and of separate property. So true is it, that this virtue derives its existence entirely from its necessary use to the intercourse and social state of mankind.

147   To make this truth more evident, let us reverse the foregoing suppositions ; and carrying everything to the opposite extreme, consider what would be the effect of these new situations. Suppose a society to fall into such want of all common necessaries, that the utmost frugality and industry cannot preserve the greater number from perishing, and the whole from extreme misery; it will readily, I believe, be admitted, that the strict laws of justice are suspended, in such a pressing emergence, and give place to the stronger motives of necessity and self-preservation. Is it any crime, after a shipwreck, to seize whatever means or instrument of safety one can lay hold of, without regard to former limitations of property ? Or if a city besieged were perishing with hunger; can we imagine, that men will see any means of preservation before them, and lose their lives, from a scrupulous regard to what, in other situations, would be the rules of equity and justice ? The use and tendency of that virtue is to procure happiness and security, by preserving order in society : but where the society is ready to perish from extreme necessity, no greater evil can be dreaded from violence and injustice ; and every man may now provide for himself by all the means, which prudence can dictate, or humanity permit. The public, even in less urgent necessities, opens granaries, without the consent of proprietors, as justly supposing, that the authority of magistracy may, consistent with equity, extend so far : but were any

number of men to assemble, without the tie of laws or civil
jurisdiction ; would an equal partition of bread in a famine,
though effected by power and even violence, be regarded as
criminal or injurious ?

48   Suppose likewise, that it should be a virtuous man's fate
to fall into the society of ruffians, remote from the protection
of laws and government; what conduct must he embrace
in that melancholy situation ?   He sees such a desperate
rapaciousness prevail ; such a disregard to equity, such contempt of order, such stupid blindness to future consequences,
as must immediately have the most tragical conclusion, and
must terminate in destruction to the greater number, and in
a total dissolution of society to the rest.   He, meanwhile, can
have no other expedient than to arm himself, to whomever
the sword he seizes, or the buckler, may belong : To make
provision of all means of defence and security : And his
particular regard to justice being no longer of use to his own
safety or that of others, he must consult the dictates of
self-preservation alone, without concern for those who no
longer merit his care and attention.

When any man, even in political society, renders himself
by his crimes, obnoxious to the public, he is punished by
the laws in his goods and person ; that is, the ordinary rules
of justice are, with regard to him, suspended for a moment,
and it becomes equitable to inflict on him, for the *benefit* of
society, what otherwise he could not suffer without wrong
or injury.

The rage and violence of public war; what is it but
a suspension of justice among the warring parties, who
perceive, that this virtue is now no longer of any *use* or
advantage to them ?   The laws of war, which then succeed
to those of equity and justice, are rules calculated for the
advantage and *utility* of that particular state, in which men
are now placed.   And were a civilized nation engaged with
barbarians, who observed no rules even of war, the former

must also suspend their observance of them, where they no longer serve to any purpose ; and must render every action or rencounter as bloody and pernicious as possible to the first aggressors.

149   Thus, the rules of equity or justice depend entirely on the particular state and condition in which men are placed, and owe their origin and existence to that utility, which results to the public from their strict and regular observance. Reverse, in any considerable circumstance, the condition of men : Produce extreme abundance or extreme necessity : Implant in the human breast perfect moderation and humanity, or perfect rapaciousness and malice : By rendering justice totally *useless,* you thereby totally destroy its essence, and suspend its obligation upon mankind.

The common situation of society is a medium amidst all these extremes. We are naturally partial to ourselves, and to our friends ; but are capable of learning the advantage resulting from a more equitable conduct. Few enjoyments are given us from the open and liberal hand of nature ; but by art, labour, and industry, we can extract them in great abundance. Hence the ideas of property become necessary in all civil society : Hence justice derives its usefulness to the public : And hence alone arises its merit and moral obligation.

150   These conclusions are so natural and obvious, that they have not escaped even the poets, in their descriptions of the felicity attending the golden age or the reign of Saturn. The seasons, in that first period of nature, were so temperate, if we credit these agreeable fictions, that there was no necessity for men to provide themselves with clothes and houses, as a security against the violence of heat and cold : The rivers flowed with wine and milk · The oaks yielded honey ; and nature spontaneously produced her greatest delicacies. Nor were these the chief advantages of that happy age. Tempests were not alone removed from nature ; but those more furious tempests were unknown to human breasts, which now cause such uproar, and engender such confusion. Avarice, ambition, cruelty, selfishness, were never heard of: Cordial affection, compassion, sympathy, were the only movements with which the mind was yet acquainted. Even the punctilious distinction of *mine* and *thine* was banished from among that happy race of mortals, and carried with it the very notion of property and obligation, justice and injustice.

151 This *poetical* fiction of the *golden age* is, in some respects, of a piece with the *philosophical* fiction of the *state of nature*; only that the former is represented as the most charming and most peaceable condition, which can possibly be imagined; whereas the latter is painted out as a state of mutual war and violence, attended with the most extreme necessity. On the first origin of mankind, we are told, their ignorance and savage nature were so prevalent, that they could give no mutual trust, but must each depend upon himself and his own force or cunning for protection and security. No law was heard of: No rule of justice known: No distinction of property regarded: Power was the only measure of right: and a perpetual war of all against all was the result of men's untamed selfishness and barbarity [1].

[1] This fiction of a state of nature, as a state of war, was not first started by Mr. Hobbes, as is commonly imagined. Plato endeavours to refute an hypothesis very like it in the second, third, and fourth books de republica. Cicero, on the contrary, supposes it certain and universally acknowledged in the following passage. ' Quis enim vestrum, judices, ignorat, ita naturam rerum tulisse, ut quodam tempore homines, nondum neque naturali neque civili jure descripto, fusi per agros ac dispersi vagarentur tantumque haberent quantum manu ac viribus, per caedem ac vulnera, aut eripere aut retinere potuissent? Qui igitur primi virtute & consilio praestanti extiterunt, ii perspecto genere humanae docilitatis atque ingenii, dissipatos unum in locum congregarunt, eosque ex feritate illa ad justitiam ac mansuetudinem transduxerunt. Tum res ad communem utilitatem, quas publicas appellamus, tum conventicula hominum, quae postea civitates nominatae sunt, tum domicilia conjuncta, quas urbes dicamus, invento & divino & humano

Whether such a condition of human nature could ever exist, or if it did, could continue so long as to merit the appellation of a *state*, may justly be doubted. Men are necessarily born in a family-society, at least; and are trained up by their parents to some rule of conduct and behaviour. But this must be admitted, that, if such a state of mutual war and violence was ever real, the suspension of all laws of justice, from their absolute inutility, is a necessary and infallible consequence.

152   The more we vary our views of human life, and the newer and more unusual the lights are in which we survey it, the more shall we be convinced, that the origin here assigned for the virtue of justice is real and satisfactory.

Were there a species of creatures intermingled with men, which, though rational, were possessed of such inferior strength, both of body and mind, that they were incapable of all resistance, and could never, upon the highest provocation, make us feel the effects of their resentment; the necessary consequence, I think, is that we should be bound by the laws of humanity to give gentle usage to these creatures, but should not, properly speaking, lie under any restraint of justice with regard to them, nor could they possess any right or property, exclusive of such arbitrary lords. Our intercourse with them could not be called society, which supposes a degree of equality; but absolute command on the one side, and servile obedience on the other. Whatever we covet, they must instantly resign: Our permission is the only tenure, by which they hold their possessions : Our compassion and kindness the only check,

jure, moenibus sepserunt. Atque inter hanc vitam, perpolitam humanitate, & illam immanem, nihil tam interest quam JUS atque VIS. Horum utro uti nolimus, altero est utendum. Vim volumus extingui Jus valeat necesse est, id est, judicia, quibus omne jus continetur. Judicia displicent, aut nulla sunt. Vis dominetur necesse est. Haec vident omnes.' *Pro Sext.* §. 42.

by which they curb our lawless will : And as no inconvenience ever results from the exercise of a power, so firmly
established in nature, the restraints of justice and property,
being totally *useless*, would never have place in so unequal
a confederacy.

This is plainly the situation of men, with regard to
animals ; and how far these may be said to possess reason,
I leave it to others to determine.   The great superiority of
civilized Europeans above barbarous Indians, tempted us
to imagine ourselves on the same footing with regard to
them, and made us throw off all restraints of justice, and
even of humanity, in our treatment of them.   In many
nations, the female sex are reduced to like slavery, and are
rendered incapable of all property, in opposition to their
lordly masters.   But though the males, when united, have
in all countries bodily force sufficient to maintain this
severe tyranny, yet such are the insinuation, address, and
charms of their fair companions, that women are commonly
able to break the confederacy, and share with the other sex
in all the rights and privileges of society.

3   Were the human species so framed by nature as that
each individual possessed within himself every faculty, requisite both for his own preservation and for the propagation
of his kind : Were all society and intercourse cut off between
man and man, by the primary intention of the supreme
Creator : It seems evident, that so solitary a being would be
as much incapable of justice, as of social discourse and conversation. Where mutual regards and forbearance serve to
no manner of purpose, they would never direct the conduct
of any reasonable man.   The headlong course of the
passions would be checked by no reflection on future consequences.   And as each man is here supposed to love himself alone, and to depend only on himself and his own activity
for safety and happiness, he would, on every occasion, to
the utmost of his power, challenge the preference above

every other being, to none of which he is bound by any ties, either of nature or of interest.

But suppose the conjunction of the sexes to be established in nature, a family immediately arises ; and particular rules being found requisite for its subsistence, these are immediately embraced ; though without comprehending the rest of mankind within their prescriptions. Suppose that several families unite together into one society, which is totally disjoined from all others, the rules, which preserve peace and order, enlarge themselves to the utmost extent of that society ; but becoming then entirely useless, lose their force when carried one step farther. But again suppose, that several distinct societies maintain a kind of intercourse for mutual convenience and advantage, the boundaries of justice still grow larger, in proportion to the largeness of men's views, and the force of their mutual connexions. History, experience, reason sufficiently instruct us in this natural progress of human sentiments, and in the gradual enlargement of our regards to justice, in proportion as we become acquainted with the extensive utility of that virtue.

PART II.

54   If we examine the *particular* laws, by which justice is directed, and property determined ; we shall still be presented with the same conclusion. The good of mankind is the only object of all these laws and regulations. Not only it is requisite, for the peace and interest of society, that men's possessions should be separated ; but the rules, which we follow, in making the separation, are such as can best be contrived to serve farther the interests of society.

We shall suppose that a creature, possessed of reason, but unacquainted with human nature, deliberates with himself what rules of justice or property would best promote public interest, and establish peace and security among mankind : His most obvious thought would be, to assign the largest possessions to the most extensive virtue, and give every one the power of doing good, proportioned to his inclination. In a perfect theocracy, where a being, infinitely intelligent, governs by particular volitions, this rule would certainly have place, and might serve to the wisest purposes : But were mankind to execute such a law, so great is the uncertainty of merit, both from its natural obscurity, and from the self-conceit of each individual, that no determinate rule of conduct would ever result from it; and the total dissolution of society must be the immediate consequence. Fanatics may suppose, *that dominion is founded on grace*, and *that saints alone inherit the earth*; but the civil magistrate very justly puts these sublime theorists on the same footing with common robbers, and teaches them by the severest discipline, that a rule, which, in speculation, may seem the most advantageous to society, may yet be found, in practice, totally pernicious and destructive.

That there were *religious* fanatics of this kind in England, during the civil wars, we learn from history; though it is probable, that the obvious *tendency* of these principles excited such horror in mankind, as soon obliged the dangerous enthusiasts to renounce, or at least conceal their tenets. Perhaps the *levellers*, who claimed an equal distribution of property, were a kind of *political* fanatics, which arose from the religious species, and more openly avowed their pretensions; as carrying a more plausible appearance, of being practicable in themselves, as well as useful to human society.

155   It must, indeed, be confessed, that nature is so liberal to mankind, that, were all her presents equally divided among the species, and improved by art and industry, every individual would enjoy all the necessaries, and even most of the comforts of life; nor would ever be liable to any ills, but such as might accidentally arise from the sickly frame and

constitution of his body. It must also be confessed, that, wherever we depart from this equality, we rob the poor of more satisfaction than we add to the rich, and that the slight gratification of a frivolous vanity, in one individual, frequently costs more than bread to many families, and even provinces. It may appear withal, that the rule of equality, as it would be highly *useful*, is not altogether *impracticable*; but has taken place, at least in an imperfect degree, in some republics; particularly that of Sparta; where it was attended, it is said, with the most beneficial consequences. Not to mention that the Agrarian laws, so frequently claimed in Rome, and carried into execution in many Greek cities, proceeded, all of them, from a general idea of the utility of this principle.

But historians, and even common sense, may inform us, that, however specious these ideas of *perfect* equality may seem, they are really, at bottom, *impracticable*; and were they not so, would be extremely *pernicious* to human society. Render possessions ever so equal, men's different degrees of art, care, and industry will immediately break that equality. Or if you check these virtues, you reduce society to the most extreme indigence; and instead of preventing want and beggary in a few, render it unavoidable to the whole community. The most rigorous inquisition too is requisite to watch every inequality on its first appearance; and the most severe jurisdiction, to punish and redress it. But besides, that so much authority must soon degenerate into tyranny, and be exerted with great partialities; who can possibly be possessed of it, in such a situation as is here supposed? Perfect equality of possessions, destroying all subordination, weakens extremely the authority of magistracy, and must reduce all power nearly to a level, as well as property.

156   We may conclude, therefore, that, in order to establish laws for the regulation of property, we must be acquainted with the nature and situation of man; must reject appearances, which may be false, though specious; and must search for those rules, which are, on the whole, most *useful* and *beneficial.* Vulgar sense and slight experience are sufficient for this purpose; where men give not way to too selfish avidity, or too extensive enthusiasm.

Who sees not, for instance, that whatever is produced or improved by a man's art or industry ought, for ever, to be secured to him, in order to give encouragement to such *useful* habits and accomplishments? That the property ought also to descend to children and relations, for the same *useful* purpose? That it may be alienated by consent, in order to beget that commerce and intercourse, which is so *beneficial* to human society? And that all contracts and promises ought carefully to be fulfilled, in order to secure mutual trust and confidence, by which the general *interest* of mankind is so much promoted?

Examine the writers on the laws of nature; and you will always find, that, whatever principles they set out with, they are sure to terminate here at last, and to assign, as the ultimate reason for every rule which they establish, the convenience and necessities of mankind. A concession thus extorted, in opposition to systems, has more authority than if it had been made in prosecution of them.

What other reason, indeed, could writers ever give, why this must be *mine* and that *yours*; since uninstructed nature surely never made any such distinction? The objects which receive those appellations are, of themselves, foreign to us; they are totally disjoined and separated from us; and nothing but the general interests of society can form the connexion.

7 Sometimes the interests of society may require a rule of justice in a particular case; but may not determine any particular rule, among several, which are all equally beneficial. In that case, the slightest *analogies* are laid hold of, in order to prevent that indifference and ambiguity, which would be

the source of perpetual dissension. Thus possession alone, and first possession, is supposed to convey property, where no body else has any preceding claim and pretension. Many of the reasonings of lawyers are of this analogical nature, and depend on very slight connexions of the imagination.

Does any one scruple, in extraordinary cases, to violate all regard to the private property of individuals, and sacrifice to public interest a distinction, which had been established for the sake of that interest? The safety of the people is the supreme law: All other particular laws are subordinate to it, and dependent on it: And if, in the *common* course of things, they be followed and regarded; it is only because the public safety and interest *commonly* demand so equal and impartial an administration.

Sometimes both *utility* and *analogy* fail, and leave the laws of justice in total uncertainty. Thus, it is highly requisite, that prescription or long possession should convey property; but what number of days or months or years should be sufficient for that purpose, it is impossible for reason alone to determine. *Civil laws* here supply the place of the natural *code*, and assign different terms for prescription, according to the different *utilities*, proposed by the legislator. Bills of exchange and promissory notes, by the laws of most countries, prescribe sooner than bonds, and mortgages, and contracts of a more formal nature.

158   In general we may observe that all questions of property are subordinate to the authority of civil laws, which extend, restrain, modify, and alter the rules of natural justice, according to the particular *convenience* of each community. The laws have, or ought to have, a constant reference to the constitution of government, the manners, the climate, the religion, the commerce, the situation of each society. A late author of genius, as well as learning, has prosecuted this subject at large, and has established, from these prin-

ciples, a system of political knowledge, which abounds in ingenious and brilliant thoughts, and is not wanting in solidity [1].

What is a man's property? Anything which it is lawful for him, and for him alone, to use. *But what rule have we, by which we can distinguish these objects?* Here we must have recourse to statutes, customs, precedents, analogies, and a hundred other circumstances; some of which are constant and inflexible, some variable and arbitrary. But

---

[1] The author of *L'Esprit des Loix.* This illustrious writer, however, sets out with a different theory, and supposes all right to be founded on certain *rapports* or relations; which is a system, that, in my opinion, never will be reconciled with true philosophy. Father Malebranche, as far as I can learn, was the first that started this abstract theory of morals, which was afterwards adopted by Cudworth, Clarke, and others; and as it excludes all sentiment, and pretends to found everything on reason, it has not wanted followers in this philosophic age. See Section I, Appendix I. With regard to justice, the virtue here treated of, the inference against this theory seems short and conclusive. Property is allowed to be dependent on civil laws; civil laws are allowed to have no other object, but the interest of society: This therefore must be allowed to be the sole foundation of property and justice. Not to mention, that our obligation itself to obey the magistrate and his laws is founded on nothing but the interests of society.

If the ideas of justice, sometimes, do not follow the dispositions of civil law; we shall find, that these cases, instead of objections, are confirmations of the theory delivered above. Where a civil law is so perverse as to cross all the interests of society, it loses all its authority, and men judge by the ideas of natural justice, which are conformable to those interests. Sometimes also civil laws, for useful purposes, require a ceremony or form to any deed; and where that is wanting, their decrees run contrary to the usual tenour of justice; but one who takes advantage of such chicanes, is not commonly regarded as an honest man. Thus, the interests of society require, that contracts be fulfilled; and there is not a more material article either of natural or civil justice: But the omission of a trifling circumstance will often, by law, invalidate a contract, *in foro humano*, but not *in foro conscientiae*, as divines express themselves. In these cases, the magistrate is supposed only to withdraw his power of enforcing the right, not to have altered the right. Where his intention extends to the right, and is conformable to the interests of society; it never fails to alter the right; a clear proof of the origin of justice and of property, as assigned above.

the ultimate point, in which they all professedly terminate, is the interest and happiness of human society: Where this enters not into consideration, nothing can appear more whimsical, unnatural, and even superstitious, than all or most of the laws of justice and of property.

Those who ridicule vulgar superstitions, and expose the folly of particular regards to meats, days, places, postures, apparel, have an easy task; while they consider all the qualities and relations of the objects, and discover no adequate cause for that affection or antipathy, veneration or horror, which have so mighty an influence over a considerable part of mankind. A Syrian would have starved rather than taste pigeon; an Egyptian would not have approached bacon: But if these species of food be examined by the senses of sight, smell, or taste, or scrutinized by the sciences of chemistry, medicine, or physics, no difference is ever found between them and any other species, nor can that precise circumstance be pitched on, which may afford a just foundation for the religious passion. A fowl on Thursday is lawful food; on Friday abominable: Eggs in this house and in this diocese, are permitted during Lent; a hundred paces farther, to eat them is a damnable sin. This earth or building, yesterday was profane; to-day, by the muttering of certain words, it has become holy and sacred. Such . reflections as these, in the mouth of a philosopher, one may safely say, are too obvious to have any influence; because they must always, to every man, occur at first sight; and where they prevail not, of themselves, they are surely obstructed by education, prejudice, and passion, not by ignorance or mistake.

159   It may appear to a careless view, or rather a too abstracted reflection, that there enters a like superstition into all the sentiments of justice; and that, if a man expose its object, or what we call property, to the same scrutiny of sense and science, he will not, by the most accurate enquiry, find

any foundation for the difference made by moral sentiment. I may lawfully nourish myself from this tree; but the fruit of another of the same species, ten paces off, it is criminal for me to touch. Had I worn this apparel an hour ago, I had merited the severest punishment; but a man, by pronouncing a few magical syllables, has now rendered it fit for my use and service. Were this house placed in the neighbouring territory, it had been immoral for me to dwell in it; but being built on this side the river, it is subject to a different municipal law, and by its becoming mine I incur no blame or censure. The same species of reasoning it may be thought, which so successfully exposes superstition, is also applicable to justice; nor is it possible, in the one case more than in the other, to point out, in the object, that precise quality or circumstance, which is the foundation of the sentiment.

But there is this material difference between *superstition* and *justice*, that the former is frivolous, useless, and burdensome; the latter is absolutely requisite to the well-being of mankind and existence of society. When we abstract from this circumstance (for it is too apparent ever to be overlooked) it must be confessed, that all regards to right and property, seem entirely without foundation, as much as the grossest and most vulgar superstition. Were the interests of society nowise concerned, it is as unintelligible why another's articulating certain sounds implying consent, should change the nature of my actions with regard to a particular object, as why the reciting of a liturgy by a priest, in a certain habit and posture, should dedicate a heap of brick and timber, and render it, thenceforth and for ever, sacred[1].

---

[1] It is evident, that the will or consent alone never transfers property, nor causes the obligation of a promise (for the same reasoning extends to both) but the will must be expressed by words or signs, in order to impose a tie upon any man. The expression being once brought in as subservient to the will, soon becomes the principal part of the promise; nor will a man be less bound by his word, though he secretly

These reflections are far from weakening the obligations of justice, or diminishing anything from the most sacred

give a different direction to his intention, and withhold the assent of his mind. But though the expression makes, on most occasions, the whole of the promise, yet it does not always so ; and one who should make use of any expression, of which he knows not the meaning, and which he uses without any sense of the consequences, would not certainly be bound by it. Nay, though he know its meaning, yet if he use it in jest only, and with such signs as evidently show, that he has no serious intention of binding himself, he would not lie under any obligation of performance; but it is necessary, that the words be a perfect expression of the will, without any contrary signs. Nay, even this we must not carry so far as to imagine, that one, whom, by our quickness of understanding, we conjecture, from certain signs, to have an intention of deceiving us, is not bound by his expression or verbal promise, if we accept of it; but must limit this conclusion to those cases where the signs are of a different nature from those of deceit. All these contradictions are easily accounted for, if justice arise entirely from its usefulness to society; but will never be explained on any other hypothesis.

It is remarkable, that the moral decisions of the *Jesuits* and other relaxed casuists, were commonly formed in prosecution of some such subtilties of reasoning as are here pointed out, and proceed as much from the habit of scholastic refinement as from any corruption of the heart, if we may follow the authority of Mons. Bayle. See his Dictionary, article LOYOLA. And why has the indignation of mankind risen so high against these casuists; but because every one perceived, that human society could not subsist were such practices authorized, and that morals must always be handled with a view to public interest, more than philosophical regularity? If the secret direction of the intention, said every man of sense, could invalidate a contract ; where is our security? And yet a metaphysical schoolman might think, that, where an intention was supposed to be requisite, if that intention really had not place, no consequence ought to follow, and no obligation be imposed. The casuistical subtilties may not be greater than the subtilties of lawyers, hinted at above ; but as the former are *pernicious*, and the latter *innocent* and even *necessary*, this is the reason of the very different reception they meet with from the world.

It is a doctrine of the Church of Rome, that the priest, by a secret direction of his intention, can invalidate any sacrament This position is derived from a strict and regular prosecution of the obvious truth, that empty words alone, without any meaning or intention in the speaker, can never be attended with any effect. If the same conclusion be not admitted in reasonings concerning civil contracts, where the affair is allowed to be of so much less consequence than the eternal attention to property. On the contrary, such sentiments must acquire new force from the present reasoning. For what stronger foundation can be desired or conceived for any duty, than to observe, that human society, or even human nature, could not subsist without the establishment of it; and will still arrive at greater degrees of happiness and perfection, the more inviolable the regard is, which is paid to that duty?

0   The dilemma seems obvious: As justice evidently tends to promote public utility and to support civil society, the sentiment of justice is either derived from our reflecting on that tendency, or like hunger, thirst, and other appetites, resentment, love of life, attachment to offspring, and other passions, arises from a simple original instinct in the human breast, which nature has implanted for like salutary purposes. If the latter be the case, it follows, that property, which is the object of justice, is also distinguished by a simple original instinct, and is not ascertained by any argument or reflection. But who is there that ever heard of such an instinct? Or is this a subject in which new discoveries can be made? We may as well expect to discover, in the body, new senses, which had before escaped the observation of all mankind.

1   But farther, though it seems a very simple proposition to say, that nature, by an instinctive sentiment, distinguishes property, yet in reality we shall find, that there are required for that purpose ten thousand different instincts, and these employed about objects of the greatest intricacy and nicest discernment. For when a definition of *property* is required,

salvation of thousands, it proceeds entirely from men's sense of the danger and inconvenience of the doctrine in the former case: And we may thence observe, that however positive, arrogant, and dogmatical any superstition may appear, it never can convey any thorough persnasion of the reality of its objects, or put them, in any degree, on a balance with the common incidents of life, which we learn from daily observation and experimental reasoning.

that relation is found to resolve itself into any possession acquired by occupation, by industry, by prescription, by inheritance, by contract, &c. Can we think that nature, by an original instinct, instructs us in all these methods of acquisition?

These words too, inheritance and contract, stand for ideas infinitely complicated; and to define them exactly, a hundred volumes of laws, and a thousand volumes of commentators, have not been found sufficient. Does nature, whose instincts in men are all simple, embrace such complicated and artificial objects, and create a rational creature, without trusting anything to the operation of his reason?

But even though all this were admitted, it would not be satisfactory. Positive laws can certainly transfer property. It is by another original instinct, that we recognize the authority of kings and senates, and mark all the boundaries of their jurisdiction? Judges too, even though their sentence be erroneous and illegal, must be allowed, for the sake of peace and order, to have decisive authority, and ultimately to determine property. Have we original innate ideas of praetors and chancellors and juries? Who sees not, that all these institutions arise merely from the necessities of human society?

All birds of the same species in every age and country, built their nests alike: In this we see the force of instinct. Men, in different times and places, frame their houses differently: Here we perceive the influence of reason and custom. A like inference may be drawn from comparing the instinct of generation and the institution of property.

How great soever the variety of municipal laws, it must be confessed, that their chief out-lines pretty regularly concur; because the purposes, to which they tend, are everywhere exactly similar. In like manner, all houses have a roof and walls, windows and chimneys; though diversified in their shape, figure, and materials. The purposes of the latter, directed to the conveniencies of human life, discover not more plainly their origin from reason and reflection, than do those of the former, which point all to a like end.

I need not mention the variations, which all the rules of property receive from the finer turns and connexions of the imagination, and from the subtilties and abstractions of law-topics and reasonings. There is no possibility of reconciling this observation to the notion of original instincts.

162   What alone will beget a doubt concerning the theory, on which I insist, is the influence of education and acquired habits, by which we are so accustomed to blame injustice, that we are not, in every instance, conscious of any immediate reflection on the pernicious consequences of it. The views the most familiar to us are apt, for that very reason, to escape us ; and what we have very frequently performed from certain motives, we are apt likewise to continue mechanically, without recalling, on every occasion, the reflections, which first determined us. The convenience, or rather necessity, which leads to justice is so universal, and everywhere points so much to the same rules, that the habit takes place in all societies ; and it is not without some scrutiny, that we are able to ascertain its true origin. The matter, however, is not so obscure, but that even in common life we have every moment recourse to the principle of public utility, and ask, *What must become of the world, if such practices prevail? How could society subsist under such disorders?* Were the distinction or separation of possessions entirely useless, can any one conceive, that it ever should have obtained in society?

163   Thus we seem, upon the whole, to have attained a knowledge of the force of that principle here insisted on, and can determine what degree of esteem or moral approbation may result from reflections on public interest and utility. The necessity of justice to the support of society is the sole foundation of that virtue ; and since no moral excellence is

more highly esteemed, we may conclude that this circumstance of usefulness has, in general, the strongest energy, and
most entire command over our sentiments. It must, therefore, be the source of a considerable part of the merit ascribed
to humanity, benevolence, friendship, public spirit, and other
social virtues of that stamp; as it is the sole source of the
moral approbation paid to fidelity, justice, veracity, integrity,
and those other estimable and useful qualities and principles.
It is entirely agreeable to the rules of philosophy, and even
of common reason; where any principle has been found to
have a great force and energy in one instance, to ascribe
to it a like energy in all similar instances. This indeed is
Newton's chief rule of philosophizing[1].

[1] Principia, Lib. iii.

SECTION IV.

OF POLITICAL SOCIETY.

164   HAD every man sufficient *sagacity* to perceive, at all times, the strong interest which binds him to the observance of justice and equity, and *strength of mind* sufficient to persevere in a steady adherence to a general and a distant interest, in opposition to the allurements of present pleasure and advantage; there had never, in that case, been any such thing as government or political society, but each man, following his natural liberty, had lived in entire peace and harmony with all others. What need of positive law where natural justice is, of itself, a sufficient restraint? Why create magistrates, where there never arises any disorder or iniquity? Why abridge our native freedom, when, in every instance, the utmost exertion of it is found innocent and beneficial? It is evident, that, if government were totally useless, it never could have place, and that the sole foundation of the duty of allegiance is the *advantage*, which it procures to society, by preserving peace and order among mankind.

165   When a number of political societies are erected, and maintain a great intercourse together, a new set of rules are immediately discovered to be *useful* in that particular situation; and accordingly take place under the title of Laws of Nations. Of this kind are, the sacredness of the person of ambassadors, abstaining from poisoned arms, quarter in war, with others of that kind, which are plainly calculated for the *advantage* of states and kingdoms in their intercourse with each other.

The rules of justice, such as prevail among individuals, are not entirely suspended among political societies. All princes pretend a regard to the rights of other princes; and some, no doubt, without hypocrisy. Alliances and treaties are every day made between independent states, which would only be so much waste of parchment, if they were not found by experience to have *some* influence and authority. But here is the difference between kingdoms and individuals. Human nature cannot by any means subsist, without the association of individuals; and that association never could have place, were no regard paid to the laws of equity and justice. Disorder, confusion, the war of all against all, are the necessary consequences of such a licentious conduct. But nations can subsist without intercourse. They may even subsist, in some degree, under a general war. The observance of justice, though useful among them, is not guarded by so strong a necessity as among individuals; and the *moral obligation* holds proportion with the *usefulness*. All politicians will allow, and most philosophers, that reasons of state may, in particular emergencies, dispense with the rules of justice, and invalidate any treaty or alliance, where the strict observance of it would be prejudicial, in a considerable degree, to either of the contracting parties. But nothing less than the most extreme necessity, it is confessed, can justify individuals in a breach of promise, or an invasion of the properties of others.

In a confederated commonwealth, such as the Achaean republic of old, or the Swiss Cantons and United Provinces in modern times; as the league has here a peculiar *utility*, the conditions of union have a peculiar sacredness and authority, and a violation of them would be regarded as no less, or even as more criminal, than any private injury or injustice.

166   The long and helpless infancy of man requires the combination of parents for the subsistence of their young; and that combination requires the virtue of chastity or fidelity to the marriage bed. Without such a *utility*, it will readily be owned, that such a virtue would never have been thought of [1].

An infidelity of this nature is much more *pernicious* in *women* than in *men*. Hence the laws of chastity are much stricter over the one sex than over the other.

167 These rules have all a reference to generation; and yet women past child-bearing are no more supposed to be exempted from them than those in the flower of their youth and beauty. *General rules* are often extended beyond the principle whence they first arise; and this in all matters of taste and sentiment. It is a vulgar story at Paris, that, during the rage of the Mississippi, a hump-backed fellow went every day into the Rue de Quincempoix, where the stock-jobbers met in great crowds, and was well paid for allowing them to make use of his hump as a desk, in order to sign their contracts upon it. Would the fortune, which he raised by this expedient, make him a handsome fellow; though it be confessed, that personal beauty arises very much from ideas of utility? The imagination is influenced by associations of ideas; which, though they arise at first from the judgement, are not easily altered by every particular exception that occurs to us. To which we may add, in the present case of chastity, that the example of the old would be pernicious

---

[1] The only solution, which Plato gives to all the objections that might be raised against the community of women, established in his imaginary commonwealth, is, Κάλλιστα γὰρ δὴ τοῦτο καὶ λέγεται καὶ λελέξεται, ὅτι τὸ μὲν ὠφέλιμον καλόν, τὸ δὲ βλαβερὸν αἰσχρόν. *Scite enim istud et dicitur et dicetur, Id quod utile sit honestum esse, quod autem inutile sit turpe esse.* De Rep. lib v. p. 457. ex edit. Ser. And this maxim will admit of no doubt, where public utility is concerned; which is Plato's meaning. And indeed to what other purpose do all the ideas of chastity and modesty serve? *Nisi utile est quod facimus, frustra est gloria*, says Phaedrus. Καλὸν τῶν βλαβερῶν οὐδέν, says Plutarch, *de vitioso pudore.* Nihil eorum quae damnosa sunt, pulchrum est. The same was the opinion of the Stoics. Φασὶν οὖν οἱ Στωικοὶ ἀγαθὸν εἶναι ὠφέλειαν ἢ οὐχ ἕτερον ὠφελείας, ὠφέλειαν μὲν λέγοντες τὴν ἀρετὴν καὶ τὴν σπουδαίαν πρᾶξιν. Sept. Emp. lib. iii. cap. 20.

to the young ; and that women, continually foreseeing that a certain time would bring them the liberty of indulgence, would naturally advance that period, and think more lightly of this whole duty, so requisite to society.

168   Those who live in the same family have such frequent opportunities of licence of this kind, that nothing could preserve purity of manners, were marriage allowed, among the nearest relations, or any intercourse of love between them ratified by law and custom. Incest, therefore, being *pernicious* in a superior degree, has also a superior turpitude and moral deformity annexed to it.

What is the reason, why, by the Athenian laws, one might marry a half-sister by the father, but not by the mother ? Plainly this : The manners of the Athenians were so reserved, that a man was never permitted to approach the women's apartment, even in the same family, unless where he visited his own mother. His step-mother and her children were as much shut up from him as the women of any other family, and there was as little danger of any criminal correspondence between them. Uncles and nieces, for a like reason, might marry at Athens ; but neither these, nor half-brothers and sisters, could contract that alliance at Rome, where the intercourse was more open between the sexes. Public utility is the cause of all these variations.

169   To repeat, to a man's prejudice, anything that escaped him in private conversation, or to make any such use of his private letters, is highly blamed. The free and social intercourse of minds must be extremely checked, where no such rules of fidelity are established.

Even in repeating stories, whence we can foresee no ill consequences to result, the giving of one's author is regarded as a piece of indiscretion, if not of immorality. These stories, in passing from hand to hand, and receiving all the usual variations, frequently come about to the persons concerned, and produce animosities and quarrels among people, whose intentions are the most innocent and in-offensive.

To pry into secrets, to open or even read the letters of others, to play the spy upon their words and looks and actions; what habits more inconvenient in society? What habits, of consequence, more blameable?

This principle is also the foundation of most of the laws of good manners; a kind of lesser morality, calculated for the ease of company and conversation. Too much or too little ceremony are both blamed, and everything, which promotes ease, without an indecent familiarity, is useful and laudable.

Constancy in friendships, attachments, and familiarities, is commendable, and is requisite to support trust and good correspondence in society. But in places of general, though casual concourse, where the pursuit of health and pleasure brings people promiscuously together, public conveniency has dispensed with this maxim; and custom there promotes an unreserved conversation for the time, by indulging the privilege of dropping afterwards every indifferent acquaint-ance, without breach of civility or good manners.

Even in societies, which are established on principles the most immoral, and the most destructive to the interests of the general society, there are required certain rules, which a species of false honour, as well as private interest, engages the members to observe. Robbers and pirates, it has often been remarked, could not maintain their pernicious confederacy, did they not establish a new distributive justice among themselves, and recall those laws of equity, which they have violated with the rest of mankind.

I hate a drinking companion, says the Greek proverb, who never forgets. The follies of the last debauch should be buried in eternal oblivion, in order to give full scope to the follies of the next.

171   Among nations, where an immoral gallantry, if covered
with a thin veil of mystery, is, in some degree, authorized
by custom, there immediately arise a set of rules, calculated
for the conveniency of that attachment. The famous court
or parliament of love in Provence formerly decided all
difficult cases of this nature.

In societies for play, there are laws required for the
conduct of the game ; and these laws are different in each
game. The foundation, I own, of such societies is frivolous ;
and the laws are, in a great measure, though not altogether,
capricious and arbitrary. So far is there a material difference
between them and the rules of justice, fidelity, and loyalty.
The general societies of men are absolutely requisite for the
subsistence of the species ; and the public conveniency,
which regulates morals, is inviolably established in the nature
of man, and of the world, in which he lives. The comparison, therefore, in these respects, is very imperfect. We
may only learn from it the necessity of rules, wherever men
have any intercourse with each other.

They cannot even pass each other on the road without
rules. Waggoners, coachmen, and postilions have principles,
by which they give the way; and these are chiefly founded
on mutual ease and convenience. Sometimes also they are
arbitrary, at least dependent on a kind of capricious analogy
like many of the reasonings of lawyers [1].

To carry the matter farther, we may observe, that it
is impossible for men so much as to murder each other
without statutes, and maxims, and an idea of justice and

[1] That the lighter machine yield to the heavier, and, in machines of
the same kind, that the empty yield to the loaded ; this rule is founded
on convenience. That those who are going to the capital take place of
those who are coming from it ; this seems to be founded on some idea of
the dignity of the great city, and of the preference of the future to the
past. From like reasons, among foot-walkers, the right-hand entitles
a man to the wall, and prevents jostling, which peaceable people find
very disagreeable and inconvenient.

honour. War has its laws as well as peace ; and even that sportive kind of war, carried on among wrestlers, boxers, cudgel-players, gladiators, is regulated by fixed principles. Common interest and utility beget infallibly a standard of right and wrong among the parties concerned.

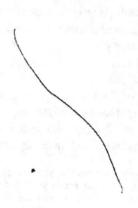

SECTION V.

WHY UTILITY PLEASES.

PART I.

172 IT seems so natural a thought to ascribe to their utility
the praise, which we bestow on the social virtues, that one
would expect to meet with this principle everywhere in
moral writers, as the chief foundation of their reasoning
and enquiry. In common life, we may observe, that the
circumstance of utility is always appealed to; nor is it
supposed, that a greater eulogy can be given to any man,
than to display his usefulness to the public, and enumerate
the services, which he has performed to mankind and
society. What praise, even of an inanimate form, if the
regularity and elegance of its parts destroy not its fitness for
any useful purpose! And how satisfactory an apology for
any disproportion-or seeming deformity, if we can show the
necessity of that particular construction for the use intended!
A ship appears more beautiful to an artist, or one moderately
skilled in navigation, where its prow is wide and swelling
beyond its poop, than if it were framed with a precise
geometrical regularity, in contradiction to all the laws of
mechanics. A building, whose doors and windows were
exact squares, would hurt the eye by that very proportion;
as ill adapted to the figure of a human creature, for whose

service the fabric was intended. What wonder then, that a man, whose habits and conduct are hurtful to society, and dangerous or pernicious to every one who has an intercourse with him, should, on that account, be an object of disapprobation, and communicate to every spectator the strongest sentiment of disgust and hatred[1].

But perhaps the difficulty of accounting for these effects of usefulness, or its contrary, has kept philosophers from admitting them into their systems of ethics, and has induced them rather to employ any other principle, in explaining the origin of moral good and evil. But it is no just reason for rejecting any principle, confirmed by experience, that we cannot give a satisfactory account of its origin, nor are able to resolve it into other more general principles. And if we would employ a little thought on the present subject, we need be at no loss to account for the influence of utility, and to deduce it from principles, the most known and avowed in human nature.

[1] We ought not to imagine, because an inanimate object may be useful as well as a man, that therefore it ought also, according to this system, to merit the appellation of *virtuous*. The sentiments, excited by utility, are, in the two cases, very different; and the one is mixed with affection, esteem, approbation, &c., and not the other. In like manner, an inanimate object may have good colour and proportions as well as a human figure. But can we ever be in love with the former? There are a numerous set of passions and sentiments, of which thinking rational beings are, by the original constitution of nature, the only proper objects : and though the very same qualities be transferred to an insensible, inanimate being, they will not excite the same sentiments. The beneficial qualities of herbs and minerals are, indeed, sometimes called their *virtues*; but this is an effect of the caprice of language, which ought not to be regarded in reasoning. For though there be a species of approbation attending even inanimate objects, when beneficial, yet this sentiment is so weak, and so different from that which is directed to beneficent magistrates or statesmen ; that they ought not to be ranked under the same class or appellation.

A very small variation of the object, even where the same qualities are preserved, will destroy a sentiment. Thus, the same beauty, transferred to a different sex, excites no amorous passion, where nature is not extremely perverted.

173   From the apparent usefulness of the social virtues, it has
readily been inferred by sceptics, both ancient and modern,
that all moral distinctions arise from education, and were,
at first, invented, and afterwards encouraged, by the art of
politicians, in order to render men tractable, and subdue
their natural ferocity and selfishness, which incapacitated
them for society.   This principle, indeed, of precept and
education, must so far be owned to have a powerful influence,
that it may frequently increase or diminish, beyond their
natural standard, the sentiments of approbation or dislike;
and may even, in particular instances, create, without any
natural principle, a new sentiment of this kind; as is
evident in all superstitious practices and observances : But
that *all* moral affection or dislike arises from this origin,
will never surely be allowed by any judicious enquirer.
Had nature made no such distinction, founded on the
original constitution of the mind, the words, *honourable*
and *shameful*, *lovely* and *odious*, *noble* and *despicable*, had
never had place in any language; nor could politicians,
had they invented these terms, ever have been able to
render them intelligible, or make them convey any idea
to the audience.   So that nothing can be more superficial than this paradox of the sceptics ; and it were well,
if, in the abstruser studies of logic and metaphysics, we
could as easily obviate the cavils of that sect, as in the
practical and more intelligible sciences of politics and
morals.

The social virtues must, therefore, be allowed to have
a natural beauty and amiableness, which, at first, antecedent
to all precept or education, recommends them to the esteem
of uninstructed mankind, and engages their affections.   And
as the public utility of these virtues is the chief circumstance, whence they derive their merit, it follows, that the
end, which they have a tendency to promote, must be some
way agreeable to us, and take hold of some natural affection.

It must please, either from considerations of self-interest, or from more generous motives and regards.

174 ❧ It has often been asserted, that, as every man has a strong connexion with society, and perceives the impossibility of his solitary subsistence, he becomes, on that account, favourable to all those habits or principles, which promote order in society, and insure to him the quiet possession of so inestimable a blessing.❡ As much as we value our own happiness and welfare, as much must we applaud the practice of justice and humanity, by which alone the social confederacy can be maintained, and every man reap the fruits of mutual protection and assistance.

This deduction of morals from self-love, or a regard to private interest, is an obvious thought, and has not arisen wholly from the wanton sallies and sportive assaults of the sceptics. To mention no others, Polybius, one of the gravest and most judicious, as well as most moral writers of antiquity, has assigned this selfish origin to all our sentiments of virtue [1].   But though the solid practical sense of that author, and his aversion to all vain subtilties, render his authority on the present subject very considerable; yet is not this an affair to be decided by authority, and the voice of nature and experience seems plainly to oppose the selfish theory.

175   We frequently bestow praise on virtuous actions, performed in very distant ages and remote countries; where

---

[1] Undutifulness to parents is disapproved of by mankind, προορωμένους τὸ μέλλον, καὶ συλλογιζομένους ὅτι τὸ παραπλήσιον ἑκάστοις αὐτῶν συγκυρήσει.   Ingratitude for a like reason (though he seems there to mix a more generous regard) συναγανακτοῦντας μὲν τῷ πέλας, ἀναφέροντας δ᾽ ἐπ᾽ αὐτοὺς τὸ παραπλήσιον, ἐξ ὧν ὑπογίγνεταί τις ἔννοια παρ᾽ ἑκάστῳ τῆς τοῦ καθήκοντος δυνάμεως καὶ θεωρίας. Lib. vi. cap. 4 (ed. Gronovius). Perhaps the historian only meant, that our sympathy and humanity was more enlivened, by our considering the similarity of our case with that of the person suffering; which is a just sentiment.

the utmost subtilty of imagination would not discover any appearance of self-interest, or find any connexion of our present happiness and security with events so widely separated from us.

A generous, a brave, a noble deed, performed by an adversary, commands our approbation; while in its consequences it may be acknowledged prejudicial to our particular interest.

Where private advantage concurs with general affection for virtue, we readily perceive and avow the mixture of these distinct sentiments, which have a very different feeling and influence on the mind. We praise, perhaps, with more alacrity, where the generous humane action contributes to our particular interest; But the topics of praise, which we insist on, are very wide of this circumstance. And we may attempt to bring over others to our sentiments, without endeavouring to convince them, that they reap any advantage from the actions which we recommend to their approbation and applause.

Frame the model of a praiseworthy character, consisting of all the most amiable moral virtues: Give instances, in which these display themselves after an eminent and extraordinary manner: You readily engage the esteem and approbation of all your audience, who never so much as enquire in what age and country the person lived, who possessed these noble qualities: A circumstance, however, of all others, the most material to self-love, or a concern for our own individual happiness.

Once on a time, a statesman, in the shock and contest of parties, prevailed so far as to procure, by his eloquence, the banishment of an able adversary; whom he secretly followed, offering him money for his support during his exile, and soothing him with topics of consolation in his misfortunes. *Alas !* cries the banished statesman, *with what regret must I leave my friends in this city, where even enemies*

are so generous! Virtue, though in an enemy, here pleased
.him: And we also give it the just tribute of praise and
approbation; nor do we retract these sentiments, when we
hear, that the action passed at Athens, about two thousand
years ago, and that the persons names were Eschines and
Demosthenes.

What is that to me? There are few occasions, when this
question is not pertinent: And had it that universal, infallible influence supposed, it would turn into ridicule every
composition, and almost every conversation, which contain
any praise or censure of men and manners.

176   It is but a weak subterfuge, when pressed by these facts
and arguments, to say, that we transport ourselves, by the
force of imagination, into distant ages and countries, and
consider the advantage, which we should have reaped from
these characters, had we been contemporaries, and had any
commerce with the persons. It is not conceivable, how
a *real* sentiment or passion can ever arise from a known
imaginary interest; especially when our *real* interest is still
kept in view, and is often acknowledged to be entirely
distinct from the imaginary, and even sometimes opposite
to it.

A man, brought to the brink of a precipice, cannot look
down without trembling; and the sentiment of *imaginary*
danger actuates him, in opposition to the opinion and
belief of *real* safety. But the imagination is here assisted
by the presence of a striking object; and yet prevails not,
except it be also aided by novelty, and the unusual appearance of the object. Custom soon reconciles us to heights
and precipices, and wears off these false and delusive terrors.
The reverse is observable in the estimates which we form
of characters and manners; and the more we habituate
ourselves to an accurate scrutiny of morals, the more
delicate feeling do we acquire of the most minute distinctions between vice and virtue. Such frequent occasion,

indeed, have we, in common life, to pronounce all kinds of moral determinations, that no object of this kind can be new or unusual to us; nor could any *false* views or pre-possessions maintain their ground against an experience, so common and familiar. Experience being chiefly what forms the associations of ideas, it is impossible that any association could establish and support itself, in direct opposition to that principle.

177   Usefulness is agreeable, and engages our approbation. This is a matter of fact, confirmed by daily observation. But, *useful?* For what? For somebody's interest, surely. Whose interest then? Not our own only: For our approbation frequently extends farther. It must, therefore, be the interest of those, who are served by the character or action approved of; and these we may conclude, however remote, are not totally indifferent to us. By opening up this principle, we shall discover one great source of moral distinctions.

Part II.

178   Self-love is a principle in human nature of such extensive energy, and the interest of each individual is, in general, so closely connected with that of the community, that those philosophers were excusable, who fancied that all our concern for the public might be resolved into a concern for our own happiness and preservation. They saw every moment, instances of approbation or blame, satisfaction or displeasure towards characters and actions; they denominated the objects of these sentiments, *virtues*, or *vices*; they observed, that the former had a tendency to increase the happiness, and the latter the misery of mankind; they asked, whether it were possible that we could have any general concern for society, or any disinterested resentment of the welfare or injury of others; they found it simpler to consider all these sentiments as modifications of self-love; and they discovered a pretence, at least, for this unity of principle, in that close union of interest, which is so observable between the public and each individual.

But notwithstanding this frequent confusion of interests, it is easy to attain what natural philosophers, after Lord Bacon, have affected to call the *experimentum crucis*, or that experiment which points out the right way in any doubt or ambiguity. We have found instances, in which private interest was separate from public; in which it was even contrary: And yet we observed the moral sentiment to continue, notwithstanding this disjunction of interests. And wherever these distinct interests sensibly concurred, we always found a sensible increase of the sentiment, and a more warm affection to virtue, and detestation of vice, or what we properly call, *gratitude* and *revenge*. Compelled by these instances, we must renounce the theory, which accounts for every moral sentiment by the principle of self-love. We must adopt a more public affection, and allow, that the interests of society are not, even on their own account, entirely indifferent to us. Usefulness is only a tendency to a certain end; and it is a contradiction in terms, that anything pleases as means to an end, where the end itself no wise affects us. If usefulness, therefore, be a source of moral sentiment, and if this usefulness be not always considered with a reference to self; it follows, that everything, which contributes to the happiness of society, recommends itself directly to our approbation and good-will. Here is a principle, which accounts, in great part, for the origin of morality: And what need we seek for abstruse and remote systems, when there occurs one so obvious and natural [1]?

---

[1] It is needless to push our researches so far as to ask, why we have humanity or a fellow-feeling with others. It is sufficient, that this is experienced to be a principle in human nature. We must stop some-

179 Have we any difficulty to comprehend the force of humanity and benevolence? Or to conceive, that the very aspect of happiness, joy, prosperity, gives pleasure; that of pain, suffering, sorrow, communicates uneasiness? The human countenance, says Horace [1], borrows smiles or tears from the human countenance. Reduce a person to solitude, and he loses all enjoyment, except either of the sensual or speculative kind; and that because the movements of his heart are not forwarded by correspondent movements in his fellow-creatures. The signs of sorrow and mourning, though arbitrary, affect us with melancholy; but the natural symptoms, tears and cries and groans, never fail to infuse compassion and uneasiness. And if the effects of misery touch us in so lively a manner; can we be supposed altogether insensible or indifferent towards its causes; when a malicious or treacherous character and behaviour are presented to us?

We enter, I shall suppose, into a convenient, warm, well-contrived apartment: We necessarily receive a pleasure from its very survey; because it presents us with the pleasing ideas of ease, satisfaction, and enjoyment. The hospitable, good-humoured, humane landlord appears. This circumstance surely must embellish the whole; nor can we easily forbear reflecting, with pleasure, on the satisfaction

where in our examination of causes; and there are, in every science, some general principles, beyond which we cannot hope to find any principle more general. No man is absolutely indifferent to the happiness and misery of others. The first has a natural tendency to give pleasure; the second, pain. This every one may find in himself. It is not probable, that these principles can be resolved into principles more simple and universal, whatever attempts may have been made to that purpose. But if it were possible, it belongs not to the present subject; and we may here safely consider these principles as original: happy, if we can render all the consequences sufficiently plain and perspicuous!

[1] 'Uti ridentibus arrident, ita flentibus adflent
Humani vultus.'—Hor.

which results to every one from his intercourse and good-offices.

His whole family, by the freedom, ease, confidence, and calm enjoyment, diffused over their countenances, sufficiently express their happiness. I have a pleasing sympathy in the prospect of so much joy, and can never consider the source of it, without the most agreeable emotions.

He tells me, that an oppressive and powerful neighbour had attempted to dispossess him of his inheritance, and had long disturbed all his innocent and social pleasures. I feel an immediate indignation arise in me against such violence and injury.

But it is no wonder, he adds, that a private wrong should proceed from a man, who had enslaved provinces, depopulated cities, and made the field and scaffold stream with human blood. I am struck with horror at the prospect of so much misery, and am actuated by the strongest antipathy against its author.

180   In general, it is certain, that, wherever we go, whatever we reflect on or converse about, everything still presents us with the view of human happiness or misery, and excites in our breast a sympathetic movement of pleasure or uneasiness. In our serious occupations, in our careless amusements, this principle still exerts its active energy.

A man who enters the theatre, is immediately struck with the view of so great a multitude, participating of one common amusement; and experiences, from their very aspect, a superior sensibility or disposition of being affected with every sentiment, which he shares with his fellow-creatures.

He observes the actors to be animated by the appearance of a full audience, and raised to a degree of enthusiasm, which they cannot command in any solitary or calm moment.

Every movement of the theatre, by a skilful poet, is

communicated, as it were by magic, to the spectators; who weep, tremble, resent, rejoice, and are inflamed with all the variety of passions, which actuate the several personages of the drama.

Where any event crosses our wishes, and interrupts the happiness of the favourite characters, we feel a sensible anxiety and concern. But where their sufferings proceed from the treachery, cruelty, or tyranny of an enemy, our breasts are affected with the liveliest resentment against the author of these calamities.

It is here esteemed contrary to the rules of art to represent anything cool and indifferent. A distant friend, or a confident, who has no immediate interest in the catastrophe, ought, if possible, to be avoided by the poet; as communicating a like indifference to the audience, and checking the progress of the passions.

Few species of poetry are more entertaining than *pastoral*; and every one is sensible, that the chief source of its pleasure arises from those images of a gentle and tender tranquillity, which it represents in its personages, and of which it communicates a like sentiment to the reader. Sannazarius, who transferred the scene to the sea-shore, though he presented the most magnificent object in nature, is confessed to have erred in his choice. The idea of toil, labour, and danger, suffered by the fishermen, is painful; by an unavoidable sympathy, which attends every conception of human happiness or misery.

When I was twenty, says a French poet, Ovid was my favourite: Now I am forty, I declare for Horace. We enter, to be sure, more readily into sentiments, which resemble those we feel every day: But no passion, when well represented, can be entirely indifferent to us; because there is none, of which every man has not, within him, at least the seeds and first principles. It is the business of poetry to bring every affection near to us by lively imagery and representation, and make it look like truth and reality : A certain proof, that, wherever that reality is found, our minds are disposed to be strongly affected by it.

181   Any recent event or piece of news, by which the fate of states, provinces, or many individuals is affected, is extremely interesting even to those whose welfare is not immediately engaged. Such intelligence is propagated with celerity, heard with avidity, and enquired into with attention and concern. The interest of society appears, on this occasion, to be in some degree the interest of each individual. The imagination is sure to be affected ; though the passions excited may not always be so strong and steady as to have great influence on the conduct and behaviour.

The perusal of a history seems a calm entertainment ; but would be no entertainment at all, did not our hearts beat with correspondent movements to those which are described by the historian.

Thucydides and Guicciardin support with difficulty our attention ; while the former describes the trivial rencounters of the small cities of Greece, and the latter the harmless wars of Pisa. The few persons interested and the small interest fill not the imagination, and engage not the affections. The deep distress of the numerous Athenian army before Syracuse ; the danger which so nearly threatens Venice ; these excite compassion ; these move terror and anxiety.

The indifferent, uninteresting style of Suetonius, equally with the masterly pencil of Tacitus, may convince us of the cruel depravity of Nero or Tiberius : But what a difference of sentiment ! While the former coldly relates the facts ; and the latter sets before our eyes the venerable figures of a Soranus and a Thrasea, intrepid in their fate, and only moved by the melting sorrows of their friends and kindred. What sympathy then touches every human heart ! What indignation against the tyrant, whose cause-

less fear or unprovoked malice gave rise to such detestable
barbarity !

182   If we bring these subjects nearer: If we remove all
suspicion of fiction and deceit: What powerful concern
is excited, and how much superior, in many instances, to
the narrow attachments of self-love and private interest!
Popular sedition, party zeal, a devoted obedience to
factious leaders; these are some of the most visible,
though less laudable effects of this social sympathy in
human nature.

The frivolousness of the subject too, we may observe, is
not able to detach us entirely from what carries an image of
human sentiment and affection.

When a person stutters, and pronounces with difficulty,
we even sympathize with this trivial uneasiness, and suffer
for him.   And it is a rule in criticism, that every combination of syllables or letters, which gives pain to the organs of
speech in the recital, appears also from a species of sympathy
harsh and disagreeable to the ear.   Nay, when we run over
a book with our eye, we are sensible of such unharmonious
composition; because we still imagine, that a person recites
it to us, and suffers from the pronunciation of these jarring
sounds.   So delicate is our sympathy!

Easy and unconstrained postures and motions are always
beautiful: An air of health and vigour is agreeable : Clothes
which warm, without burthening the body; which cover,
without imprisoning the limbs, are well-fashioned.   In every
judgement of beauty, the feelings of the person affected enter
into consideration, and communicate to the spectator similar
touches of pain or pleasure[1].   What wonder, then, if we

---

[1] 'Decentior equus cujus astricta sunt ilia; sed idem velocior. Pulcher
aspectu sit athleta, cujus lacertos exercitatio expressit; idem certamini
paratior.   Nunquam enim *species* ab *utilitate* dividitur.   Sed hoc
quidem discernere modici judicii est.'—Quintilian, *Inst.* lib. viii..
cap. 3.

can pronounce no judgement concerning the character and conduct of men, without considering the tendencies of their actions, and the happiness or misery which thence arises to society? What association of ideas would ever operate, were that principle here totally unactive [1].

B   If any man from a cold insensibility, or narrow selfishness of temper, is unaffected with the images of human happiness or misery, he must be equally indifferent to the images of vice and virtue: As, on the other hand, it is always found, that a warm concern for the interests of our species is attended with a delicate feeling of all moral distinctions; a strong resentment of injury done to men; a lively approbation of their welfare. In this particular, though great superiority is observable of one man above another; yet none are so entirely indifferent to the interest of their fellow-creatures, as to perceive no distinctions of moral good and evil, in consequence of the different tendencies of actions and principles. How, indeed, can we suppose it possible in any one, who wears a human heart, that if there be subjected to his censure, one character or system of conduct, which is beneficial, and another which is pernicious to his species or

---

[1] In proportion to the station which a man possesses, according to the relations in which he is placed; we always expect from him a greater or less degree of good, and when disappointed, blame his inutility; and much more do we blame him, if any ill or prejudice arise from his conduct and behaviour. When the interests of one country interfere with those of another, we estimate the merits of a statesman by the good or ill, which results to his own country from his measures and councils, without regard to the prejudice which he brings on its enemies and rivals. His fellow-citizens are the objects, which lie nearest the eye, while we determine his character. And as nature has implanted in every one a superior affection to his own country, we never expect any regard to distant nations, where a competition arises. Not to mention, that, while every man consults the good of his own community, we are sensible, that the general interest of mankind is better promoted, than by any loose indeterminate views to the good of a species, whence no beneficial action could ever result, for want of a duly limited object, on which they could exert themselves.

Q

community, he will not so much as give a cool preference to
the former, or ascribe to it the smallest merit or regard?
Let us suppose such a person ever so selfish; let private
interest have ingrossed ever so much his attention; yet in
instances, where that is not concerned, he must unavoidably
feel *some* propensity to the good of mankind, and make it an
object of cho ce, if everything else be equal.   Would any
man, who is walking along, tread as willingly on another's
gouty toes, whom he has no quarrel with, as on the hard
flint and pavement?   There is here surely a difference in
the case.   We surely take into consideration the happiness
and misery of others, in weighing the several motives of
action, and incline to the former, where no private regards
draw us to seek our own promotion or advantage by the
injury of our fellow-creatures.   And if the principles of
humanity are capable, in many instances, of influencing our
actions, they must, at all times, have *some* authority over
our sentiments, and give us a general approbation of what
is useful to society, and blame of what is dangerous or
pernicious.   The degrees of these sentiments may be the
subject of controversy; but the reality of their existence,
one should think, must be admitted in every theory or
system.

184   A creature, absolutely malicious and spiteful, were there
any such in nature, must be worse than indifferent to the
images of vice and virtue.   All his sentiments must be
inverted, and directly opposite to those, which prevail in the
human species.   Whatever contributes to the good of mankind, as it crosses the constant bent of his wishes and desires,
must produce uneasiness and disapprobation; and on the
contrary, whatever is the source of disorder and misery in
society, must, for the same reason, be regarded with pleasure
and complacency.   Timon, who probably from his affected
spleen more than any inveterate malice, was denominated
the manhater, embraced Alcibiades with great fondness.

Go on my boy ! cried he, *acquire the confidence of the people :
You will one day, I foresee, be the cause of great calamities to
them*[1]. Could we admit the two principles of the Manicheans,
it is an infallible consequence, that their sentiments of
human actions, as well as of everything else, must be totally
opposite, and that every instance of justice and humanity,
from its necessary tendency, must please the one deity and
displease the other. All mankind so far resemble the good
principle, that, where interest or revenge or envy perverts not
our disposition, we are always inclined, from our natural
philanthropy, to give the preference to the happiness of
society, and consequently to virtue above its opposite.
Absolute, unprovoked, disinterested malice has never perhaps
place in any human breast ; or if it had, must there pervert
all the sentiments of morals, as well as the feelings of
humanity. If the cruelty of Nero be allowed entirely
voluntary, and not rather the effect of constant fear and
resentment ; it is evident that Tigellinus, preferably to
Seneca or Burrhus, must have possessed his steady and
uniform approbation.

A statesman or patriot, who serves our own country in our
own time, has always a more passionate regard paid to him,
than one whose beneficial influence operated on distant
ages or remote nations ; where the good, resulting from his
generous humanity, being less connected with us, seems
more obscure, and affects us with a less lively sympathy.
We may own the merit to be equally great, though our
sentiments are not raised to an equal height, in both cases.
The judgement here corrects the inequalities of our internal
emotions and perceptions ; in like manner, as it preserves
us from error, in the several variations of images, presented
to our external senses. The same object, at a double
distance, really throws on the eye a picture of but half the

[1] Plutarch *in vita Alc.*

bulk; yet we imagine that it appears of the same size in both situations; because we know that on our approach to it, its image would expand on the eye, and that the difference consists not in the object itself, but in our position with regard to it. And, indeed, without such a correction of appearances, both in internal and external sentiment, men could never think or talk steadily on any subject; while their fluctuating situations produce a continual variation on objects, and throw them into such different and contrary lights and positions [1].

186   The more we converse with mankind, and the greater social intercourse we maintain, the more shall we be familiarized to these general preferences and distinctions, without which our conversation and discourse could scarcely be rendered intelligible to each other. Every man's interest is peculiar to himself, and the aversions and desires, which result from it, cannot be supposed to affect others in a like degree. General language, therefore, being formed for general use, must be moulded on some more general views, and must affix the epithets of praise or blame, in conformity to sentiments, which arise from the general interests of the community. And if these sentiments, in most men, be not

[1] For a like reason, the tendencies of actions and characters, not their real accidental consequences, are alone regarded in our moral determinations or general judgements; though in our real feeling or sentiment, we cannot help paying greater regard to one whose station, joined to virtue, renders him really useful to society, than to one, who exerts the social virtues only in good intentions and benevolent affections. Separating the character from the fortune, by an easy and necessary effort of thought, we pronounce these persons alike, and give them the same general praise. The judgement corrects or endeavours to correct the appearance: But is not able entirely to prevail over sentiment.

Why is this peach-tree said to be better than that other; but because it produces more or better fruit? And would not the same praise be given it, though snails or vermin had destroyed the peaches, before they came to full maturity? In morals too, is not *the tree known by the fruit?* And cannot we easily distinguish between nature and accident, in the one case as well as in the other?

so strong as those, which have a reference to private good ; yet still they must make some distinction, even in persons the most depraved and selfish ; and must attach the notion of good to a beneficent conduct, and of evil to the contrary. Sympathy, we shall allow, is much fainter than our concern for ourselves, and sympathy with persons remote from us much fainter than that with persons near and contiguous ; but for this very reason it is necessary for us, in our calm judgements and discourse concerning the characters of men, to neglect all these differences, and render our sentiments more public and social. Besides, that we ourselves often change our situation in this particular, we every day meet with persons who are in a situation different from us, and who could never converse with us were we to remain constantly in that position and point of view, which is peculiar to ourselves. The intercourse of sentiments, there-fore, in society and conversation, makes us form some general unalterable standard, by which we may approve or disapprove of characters and manners. And though the heart takes not part entirely with those general notions, nor regulates all its love and hatred by the universal abstract differences of vice and virtue, without regard to self, or the persons with whom we are more intimately connected ; yet have these moral differences a considerable influence, and being sufficient, at least for discourse, serve all our purposes in company, in the pulpit, on the theatre, and in the schools [1].

[1] It is wisely ordained by nature, that private connexions should commonly prevail over universal views and considerations ; otherwise our affections and actions would be dissipated and lost, for want of a proper limited object. Thus a small benefit done to ourselves, or our near friends, excites more lively sentiments of love and approbation than a great benefit done to a distant commonwealth : But still we know here, as in all the senses, to correct these inequalities by reflection, and retain a general standard of vice and virtue, founded chiefly on general usefulness.

187   Thus, in whatever light we take this subject, the merit,
ascribed to the social virtues, appears still uniform, and
arises chiefly from that regard, which the natural sentiment of
benevolence engages us to pay to the interests of mankind
and society.   If we consider the principles of the human
make, such as they appear to daily experience and observation, we must, *a priori*, conclude it impossible for such
a creature as man to be totally indifferent to the well or
ill-being of his fellow-creatures, and not readily, of himself,
to pronounce, where nothing gives him any particular bias,
that what promotes their happiness is good, what tends to
their misery is evil, without any farther regard or consideration.   Here then are the faint rudiments, at least, or out-
lines, of a *general* distinction between actions ; and in proportion as the humanity of the person is supposed to encrease,
his connexion with those who are injured or benefited, and
his lively conception of their misery or happiness ; his consequent censure or approbation acquires proportionable
vigour.   There is no necessity, that a generous action,
barely mentioned in an old history or remote gazette, should
communicate any strong feelings of applause and admiration.
Virtue, placed at such a distance, is like a fixed star, which,
though to the eye of reason it may appear as luminous as
the sun in his meridian, is so infinitely removed as to
affect the senses, neither with light nor heat.   Bring this
virtue nearer, by our acquaintance or connexion with the
persons, or even by an eloquent recital of the case ; our
hearts are immediately caught, our sympathy enlivened, and
our cool approbation converted into the warmest sentiments
of friendship and regard.   These seem necessary and
infallible consequences of the general principles of human
nature, as discovered in common life and practice.

188   Again ; reverse these views and reasonings : Consider the
matter *a posteriori* ; and weighing the consequences, enquire
if the merit of social virtue be not, in a great measure,

derived from the feelings of humanity, with which it affects the spectators. It appears to be matter of fact, that the circumstance of *utility*, in all subjects, is a source of praise and approbation : That it is constantly appealed to in all moral decisions concerning the merit and demerit of actions: That it is the *sole* source of that high regard paid to justice, fidelity, honour, allegiance, and chastity : That it is inseparable from all the other social virtues, humanity, generosity, charity, affability, lenity, mercy, and moderation: And, in a word, that it is a foundation of the chief part of morals, which has a reference to mankind and our fellow-creatures.

189   It appears also, that, in our general approbation of characters and manners, the useful tendency of the social virtues moves us not by any regards to self-interest, but has an influence much more universal and extensive. It appears that a tendency to public good, and to the promoting of peace, harmony, and order in society, does always, by affecting the benevolent principles of our frame, engage us on the side of the social virtues. And it appears, as an additional confirmation, that these principles of humanity and sympathy enter so deeply into all our sentiments, and have so powerful an influence, as may enable them to excite the strongest censure and applause. The present theory is the simple result of all these inferences, each of which seems founded on uniform experience and observation.

190   Were it doubtful, whether there were any such principle in our nature as humanity or a concern for others, yet when we see, in numberless instances, that whatever has a tendency to promote the interests of society, is so highly approved of, we ought thence to learn the force of the benevolent principle ; since it is impossible for anything to please as means to an end, where the end is totally indifferent. On the other hand, were it doubtful, whether there were, implanted in our nature, any general principle of moral blame and

approbation, yet when we see, in numberless instances, the influence of humanity, we ought thence to conclude, that it is impossible, but that everything which promotes the interest of society must communicate pleasure, and what is pernicious give uneasiness. But when these different reflections and observations concur in establishing the same conclusion, must they not bestow an undisputed evidence upon it?

It is however hoped, that the progress of this argument will bring a farther confirmation of the present theory, by showing the rise of other sentiments of esteem and regard from the same or like principles.

SECTION VI.

OF QUALITIES USEFUL TO OURSELVES.

PART I.

191 IT seems evident, that where a quality or habit is subjected to our examination, if it appear in any respect prejudicial to the person possessed of it, or such as incapacitates him for business and action, it is instantly blamed, and ranked among his faults and imperfections. Indolence, negligence, want of order and method, obstinacy, fickleness, rashness, credulity; these qualities were never esteemed by any one indifferent to a character; much less, extolled as accomplishments or virtues. The prejudice, resulting from them, immediately strikes our eye, and gives us the sentiment of pain and disapprobation.

No quality, it is allowed, is absolutely either blameable or praise-worthy. It is all according to its degree. A due medium, says the Peripatetics, is the characteristic of virtue. But this medium is chiefly determined by utility. A proper celerity, for instance, and dispatch in business, is commendable. When defective, no progress is ever made in the execution of any purpose: When excessive, it engages us in precipitate and ill-concerted measures and enterprises: By such reasonings, we fix the proper and commendable mediocrity in all moral and prudential disquisitions; and never lose view of the advantages, which result from any character or habit.

Now as these advantages are enjoyed by the person possessed of the character, it can never be *self-love* which renders the prospect of them agreeable to us, the spectators, and prompts our esteem and approbation. No force of imagination can convert us into another person, and make us fancy, that we, being that person, reap benefit from those valuable qualities, which belong to him. Or if it did, no celerity of imagination could immediately transport us back, into ourselves, and make us love and esteem the person, as different from us. Views and sentiments, so opposite to known truth and to each other, could never have place, at the same time, in the same person. All suspicion, therefore, of selfish regards, is here totally excluded. It is a quite different principle, which actuates our bosom, and interests us in the felicity of the person whom we contemplate. Where his natural talents and acquired abilities give us the prospect of elevation, advancement, a figure in life, prosperous success, a steady command over fortune, and the execution of great or advantageous undertakings; we are struck with such agreeable images, and feel a complacency and regard immediately arise towards him. The ideas of happiness, joy, triumph, prosperity, are connected with every circumstance of his character, and diffuse over our minds a pleasing sentiment of sympathy and humanity [1].

---

[1] One may venture to affirm, that there is no human creature, to whom the appearance of happiness (where envy or revenge has no place) does not give pleasure, that of misery, uneasiness. This seems inseparable from our make and constitution. But they are only the more generous minds, that are thence prompted to seek zealously the good of others, and to have a real passion for their welfare. With men of narrow and ungenerous spirits, this sympathy goes not beyond a slight feeling of the imagination, which serves only to excite sentiments of complacency or censure, and makes them apply to the object either honourable or dishonourable appellations. A griping miser, for instance, praises extremely *industry* and *frugality* even in others, and sets them, in his estimation, above all the other virtues. He knows the good that

192 Let us suppose a person originally framed so as to have no manner of concern for his fellow-creatures, but to regard the happiness and misery cf all sensible beings with greater indifference than even two contiguous shades of the same colour.   Let us suppose, if the prosperity of nations were laid on the one hand, and their ruin on the other, and he were desired to choose; that he would stand like the schoolman's ass, irresolute and undetermined, between equal motives; or rather, like the same ass between two pieces of wood or marble, without any inclination or propensity to either side. The consequence, I believe, must be allowed just, that such a person, being absolutely unconcerned, either for the public good of a community or the private utility of others, would look on every quality, however pernicious, or however beneficial, to society, or to its possessor, with the same indifference as on the most common and uninteresting object.

But if, instead of this fancied monster, we suppose a *man* to form a judgement or determination in the case, there is to him a plain foundation of preference, where everything else is equal; and however cool his choice may be, if his heart be selfish, or if the persons interested be remote from him; there must still be a choice or distinction between what is useful, and what is pernicious. Now this distinction is the same in all its parts, with the *moral distinction,* whose foundation has been so often, and so much in vain, enquired after. The same endowments of the mind, in every circumstance, are agreeable to the sentiment of morals and to that of humanity; the same temper is susceptible of high degrees of the one sentiment and of the other; and the same alteration in the objects,

results from them, and feels that species of happiness with a more lively sympathy, than any other you could represent to him; though perhaps he would not part with a shilling to make the fortune of the industrious man, whom he praises so highly.

by their nearer approach or by connexions, enlivens the one and the other. By all the rules of philosophy, therefore, we must conclude, that these sentiments are originally the same; since, in each particular, even the most minute, they are governed by the same laws, and are moved by the same objects.

Why do philosophers infer, with the greatest certainty, that the moon is kept in its orbit by the same force of gravity, that makes bodies fall near the surface of the earth, but because these effects are, upon computation, found similar and equal? And must not this argument bring as strong conviction, in moral as in natural disquisitions?

193 To prove, by any long detail, that all the qualities, useful to the possessor, are approved of, and the contrary censured, would be superfluous. The least reflection on what is every day experienced in life, will be sufficient. We shall only mention a few instances, in order to remove, if possible, all doubt and hesitation.

The quality, the most necessary for the execution of any useful enterprise, is discretion; by which we carry on a safe intercourse with others, give due attention to our own and to their character, weigh each circumstance of the business which we undertake, and employ the surest and safest means for the attainment of any end or purpose. To a Cromwell, perhaps, or a Dè Retz, discretion may appear an alderman-like virtue, as Dr. Swift calls it; and being incompatible with those vast designs, to which their courage and ambition prompted them, it might really, in them, be a fault or imperfection. But in the conduct of ordinary life, no virtue is more requisite, not only to obtain success, but to avoid the most fatal miscarriages and disappointments. The greatest parts without it, as observed by an elegant writer, may be fatal to their owner; as Polyphemus, deprived of his eye, was only the more exposed, on account of his enormous strength and stature.

The best character, indeed, were it not rather too perfect for human nature, is that which is not swayed by temper of any kind; but alternately employs enterprise and caution, as each is *useful* to the particular purpose intended. Such is the excellence which St. Evremond ascribes to Mareschal Turenne, who displayed every campaign, as he grew older, more temerity in his military enterprises; and being now, from long experience, perfectly acquainted with every incident in war, he advanced with greater firmness and security, in a road so well known to him. Fabius, says Machiavel, was cautious; Scipio enterprising: And both succeeded, because the situation of the Roman affairs, during the command of each, was peculiarly adapted to his genius; but both would have failed, had these situations been reversed. He is happy, whose circumstances suit his temper; but he is more excellent, who can suit his temper to any circumstances.

194 What need is there to display the praises of industry, and to extol its advantages, in the acquisition of power and riches, or in raising what we call a *fortune* in the world? The tortoise, according to the fable, by his perseverance, gained the race of the hare, though possessed of much superior swiftness. A man's time, when well husbanded, is like a cultivated field, of which a few acres produce more of what is useful to life, than extensive provinces, even of the richest soil, when over-run with weeds and brambles.

But all prospect of success in life, or even of tolerable subsistence, must fail, where a reasonable frugality is wanting. The heap, instead of encreasing, diminishes daily, and leaves its possessor so much more unhappy, as, not having been able to confine his expences to a large revenue, he will still less be able to live contentedly on a small one.

The souls of men, according to Plato[1], inflamed with impure appetites, and losing the body, which alone afforded means of satisfaction, hover about the earth, and haunt the places, where their bodies are deposited ; possessed with a longing desire to recover the lost organs of sensation.   So may we see worthless prodigals, having consumed their fortune in wild debauches, thrusting themselves into every plentiful table, and every party of pleasure, hated even by the vicious, and despised even by fools.

The one extreme of frugality is *avarice*, which, as it both deprives a man of all use of his riches, and checks hospitality and every social enjoyment, is justly censured on a double account.   *Prodigality*, the other extreme, is commonly more hurtful to a man himself; and each of these extremes is blamed above the other, according to the temper of the person who censures, and according to his greater or less sensibility to pleasure, either social or sensual.

185   Qualities often derive their merit from complicated sources.   *Honesty, fidelity, truth,* are praised for their immediate tendency to promote the interests of society; but after those virtues are once established upon this foundation, they are also considered as advantageous to the person himself, and as the source of that trust and confidence, which can alone give a man any consideration in life.   One becomes contemptible, no less than odious, when he forgets the duty, which, in this particular, he owes to himself as well as to society.

Perhaps, this consideration is one *chief* source of the high blame, which is thrown on any instance of failure among women in point of *chastity*.   The greatest regard, which can be acquired by that sex, is derived from their fidelity; and a woman becomes cheap and vulgar, loses her rank, and is exposed to every insult, who is deficient

[1] *Phaedo.*

in this particular. The smallest failure is here sufficient to blast her character. A female has so many opportunities of secretly indulging these appetites, that nothing can give us security but her absolute modesty and reserve; and where a breach is once made, it can scarcely ever be fully repaired. If a man behave with cowardice on one occasion, a contrary conduct reinstates him in his character. But by what action can a woman, whose behaviour has once been dissolute, be able to assure us, that she has formed better resolutions, and has self-command enough to carry them into execution?

196 All men, it is allowed, are equally desirous of happiness; but few are successful in the pursuit: One considerable cause is the want of strength of mind, which might enable them to resist the temptation of present ease or pleasure, and carry them forward in the search of more distant profit and enjoyment. Our affections, on a general prospect of their objects, form certain rules of conduct, and certain measures of preference of one above another: and these decisions, though really the result of our calm passions and propensities, (for what else can pronounce any object eligible or the contrary?) are yet said, by a natural abuse of terms, to be the determinations of pure *reason* and reflection. But when some of these objects approach nearer to us, or acquire the advantages of favourable lights and positions, which catch the heart or imagination; our general resolutions are frequently confounded, a small enjoyment preferred, and lasting shame and sorrow entailed upon us. And however poets may employ their wit and eloquence, in celebrating present pleasure, and rejecting all distant views to fame, health, or fortune; it is obvious, that this practice is the source of all dissoluteness and disorder, repentance and misery. A man of a strong and determined temper adheres tenaciously to his general resolutions, and is neither seduced by the allurements of pleasure, nor terrified by the menaces of pain; but keeps still in view those distant pursuits, by which he, at once, ensures his happiness and his honour.

197   Self-satisfaction, at least in some degree, is an advantage, which equally attends the fool and the wise man: But it is the only one; nor is there any other circumstance in the conduct of life, where they are upon an equal footing. Business, books, conversation; for all of these, a fool is totally incapacitated, and except condemned by his station to the coarsest drudgery, remains a *useless* burthen upon the earth.   Accordingly, it is found, that men are extremely jealous of their character in this particular; and many instances are seen of profligacy and treachery, the most avowed and unreserved; none of bearing patiently the imputation of ignorance and stupidity.   Dicaearchus, the Macedonian general, who, as Polybius tells us[1], openly erected one altar to impiety, another to injustice, in order to bid defiance to mankind; even he, I am well assured, would have started at the epithet of *fool*, and have meditated revenge for so injurious an appellation.   Except the affection of parents, the strongest and most indissoluble bond in nature, no connexion has strength sufficient to support the disgust arising from this character.   Love itself, which can subsist under treachery, ingratitude, malice, and infidelity, is immediately extinguished by it, when perceived and acknowledged; nor are deformity and old age more fatal to the dominion of that passion.   So dreadful are the ideas of an utter incapacity for any purpose or undertaking, and of continued error and misconduct in life!

198   When it is asked, whether a quick or a slow apprehension be most valuable?   Whether one, that, at first view, penetrates far into a subject, but can perform nothing upon study; or a contrary character, which must work out everything by dint of application?   Whether a clear head or

---

[1] Lib. xvii. cap. 35.

a copious invention? Whether a profound genius or a sure judgement? In short, what character, or peculiar turn of understanding, is more excellent than another? It is evident, that we can answer none of these questions, without considering which of those qualities capacitates a man best for the world, and carries him farthest in any undertaking.

If refined sense and exalted sense be not so *useful* as common sense, their rarity, their novelty, and the nobleness of their objects make some compensation, and render them the admiration of mankind : As gold, though less service-able than iron, acquires from its scarcity a value which is much superior.

The defects of judgement can be supplied by no art or invention ; but those of memory frequently may, both in business and in study, by method and industry, and by diligence in committing everything to writing ; and we scarcely ever hear a short memory given as a reason for a man's failure in any undertaking. But in ancient times, when no man could make a figure without the talent of speaking, and when the audience were too delicate to bear such crude, undigested harangues as our extemporary orators offer to public assemblies ; the faculty of memory was then of the utmost consequence, and was accordingly much more valued than at present. Scarce any great genius is mentioned in antiquity, who is not celebrated for this talent ; and Cicero enumerates it among the other sublime qualities of Caesar himself[1].

199   Particular customs and manners alter the usefulness of qualities : they also alter their merit. Particular situations and accidents have, in some degree, the same influence. He will always be more esteemed, who possesses those

[1] Fuit in illo ingenium, ratio, memoria, literae, cura, cogitatio, dili-gentia, &c. Philip. 2.

talents and accomplishments, which suit his station and profession, than he whom fortune has misplaced in the part which she has assigned him. The private or selfish virtues are, in this respect, more arbitrary than the public and social. In other respects they are, perhaps, less liable to doubt and controversy.

In this kingdom, such continued ostentation, of late years, has prevailed among men in *active* life with regard to *public spirit*, and among those in *speculative* with regard to *benevolence*; and so many false pretensions to each have been, no doubt, detected, that men of the world are apt, without any bad intention, to discover a sullen incredulity on the head of those moral endowments, and even sometimes absolutely to deny their existence and reality. In like manner I find, that, of old, the perpetual cant of the *Stoics* and *Cynics* concerning *virtue*, their magnificent professions and slender performances, bred a disgust in mankind; and Lucian, who, though licentious with regard to pleasure, is yet in other respects a very moral writer, cannot sometimes talk of virtue, so much boasted, without betraying symptoms of spleen and irony [1]. But surely this peevish delicacy, whence-ever it arises, can never be carried so far as to make us deny the existence of every species of merit, and all distinction of manners and behaviour. Besides *discretion, caution, enterprise, industry, assiduity, frugality, economy, good-sense, prudence, discernment*; besides these endowments, I say, whose very names force an avowal of their merit, there are many others, to which the most determined scepticism cannot for a moment refuse the tribute of

---

[1] Ἀρετήν τινα, καὶ ἀσώματα, καὶ λήρους μεγάλῃ τῇ φωνῇ ξυνειρόντων. Luc. Timon. 9. Again, Καὶ συναγαγόντες (οἱ φιλόσοφοι) εὐεξαπάτητα μειράκια τήν τε πολυθρύλητον ἀρετὴν τραγῳδοῦσι. Icaro-men. In another place, Ἦ ποῦ γάρ ἐστιν ἡ πολυθρύλητος ἀρετή, καὶ φύσις, καὶ εἱμαρμένη, καὶ τύχη, ἀνυπόστατα καὶ κενὰ πραγμάτων ὀνόματα; Deor. Concil. 13.

praise and approbation. *Temperance, sobriety, patience, constancy, perseverance, forethought, considerateness, secrecy, order, insinuation, address, presence of mind, quickness of conception, facility of expression*; these, and a thousand more of the same kind, no man will ever deny to be excellencies and perfections. As their merit consists in their tendency to serve the person, possessed of them, without any magnificent claim to public and social desert, we are the less jealous of their pretensions, and readily admit them into the catalogue of laudable qualities. We are not sensible that, by this concession, we have paved the way for all the other moral excellencies, and cannot consistently hesitate any longer, with regard to disinterested benevolence, patriotism, and humanity.

It seems, indeed, certain, that first appearances are here, as usual, extremely deceitful, and that it is more difficult, in a speculative way, to resolve into self-love the merit which we ascribe to the selfish virtues above mentioned, than that even of the social virtues, justice and beneficence. For this latter purpose, we need but say, that whatever conduct promotes the good of the community is loved, praised, and esteemed by the community, on account of that utility and interest, of which every one partakes; and though this affection and regard be, in reality, gratitude, not self-love, yet a distinction, even of this obvious nature, may not readily be made by superficial reasoners; and there is room, at least, to support the cavil and dispute for a moment. But as qualities, which tend only to the utility of their possessor, without any reference to us, or to the community, are yet esteemed and valued; by what theory or system can we account for this sentiment from self-love, or deduce it from that favourite origin? There seems here a necessity for confessing that the happiness and misery of others are not spectacles entirely indifferent to us; but that the view of the former, whether in its causes or effects, like sunshine or the prospect of well-cultivated plains (to carry our pretensions no higher), communicates a secret joy and satisfaction; the appearance of the latter, like a lowering cloud or barren landscape, throws a melancholy damp over the imagination. And this concession being once made, the difficulty is over; and a natural unforced interpretation of the phenomena of human life will afterwards, we may hope, prevail among all speculative enquirers.

Part II.

200   It may not be improper, in this place, to examine the influence of bodily endowments, and of the goods of fortune, over our sentiments of regard and esteem, and to consider whether these phenomena fortify or weaken the present theory. It will naturally be expected, that the beauty of the body, as is supposed by all ancient moralists, will be similar, in some respects, to that of the mind; and that every kind of esteem, which is paid to a man, will have something similar in its origin, whether it arise from his mental endowments, or from the situation of his exterior circumstances.

It is evident, that one considerable source of *beauty* in all animals is the advantage which they reap from the particular structure of their limbs and members, suitably to the particular manner of life, to which they are by nature destined. The just proportions of a horse, described by Xenophon and Virgil, are the same that are received at this day by our modern jockeys; because the foundation of them is the same, namely, experience of what is detrimental or useful in the animal.

Broad shoulders, a lank belly, firm joints, taper legs; all these are beautiful in our species, because signs of force and vigour. Ideas of utility and its contrary, though they do not entirely determine what is handsome or deformed, are evidently the source of a considerable part of approbation or dislike.

In ancient times, bodily strength and dexterity, being of greater *use* and importance in war, was also much more esteemed and valued, than at present. Not to insist on Homer and the poets, we may observe, that historians scruple not to mention *force of body* among the other accomplishments even of Epaminondas, whom they acknowledge to be the greatest hero, statesman, and general of all the Greeks[1]. A like praise is given to Pompey, one of the greatest of the Romans[2]. This instance is similar to what we observed above with regard to memory.

What derision and contempt, with both sexes, attend *impotence*; while the unhappy object is regarded as one deprived of so capital a pleasure in life, and at the same time, as disabled from communicating it to others. *Barrenness* in women, being also a species of *inutility*, is a reproach, but not in the same degree: of which the reason is very obvious, according to the present theory.

There is no rule in painting or statuary more indispensible than that of balancing the figures, and placing them with the greatest exactness on their proper centre of gravity. A figure, which is not justly balanced, is ugly; because it conveys the disagreeable ideas of fall, harm, and pain[3].

---

[1] *Cum alacribus, saltu; cum velocibus, cursu; cum validis recte certabat.* Sallust apud Veget.

[2] Diodorus Siculus, lib. xv. It may not be improper to give the character of Epaminondas, as drawn by the historian, in order to show the ideas of perfect merit, which prevailed in those ages. In other illustrious men, says he, you will observe, that each possessed some one shining quality, which was the foundation of his fame: In Epaminondas all the *virtues* are found united; force of body, eloquence of expression, vigour of mind, contempt of riches, gentleness of disposition, and *what is chiefly to be regarded,* courage and conduct in war.

[3] All men are equally liable to pain and disease and sickness; and may again recover health and ease. These circumstances, as they make no distinction between one man and another, are no source of pride or

201 A disposition or turn of mind, which qualifies a man to rise in the world and advance his fortune, is entitled to esteem and regard, as has already been explained. It may, therefore, naturally be supposed, that the actual possession of riches and authority will have a considerable influence over these sentiments.

Let us examine any hypothesis by which we can account for the regard paid to the rich and powerful; we shall find none satisfactory, but that which derives it from the enjoyment communicated to the spectator by the images of prosperity, happiness, ease, plenty, authority, and the gratification of every appetite. Self-love, for instance, which some affect so much to consider as the source of every sentiment, is plainly insufficient for this purpose. Where no good-will or friendship appears, it is difficult to conceive on what we can found our hope of advantage from the riches of others; though we naturally respect the rich, even before they discover any such favourable disposition towards us.

We are affected with the same sentiments, when we lie so much out of the sphere of their activity, that they cannot even be supposed to possess the power of serving us. A prisoner of war, in all civilized nations, is treated with a regard suited to his condition; and riches, it is evident, go far towards fixing the condition of any person. If birth and quality enter for a share, this still affords us an argument to our present purpose. For what is it we call a man

humility, regard or contempt. But comparing our own species to superior ones, it is a very mortifying consideration, that we should all be so liable to diseases and infirmities; and divines accordingly employ this topic, in order to depress self-conceit and vanity. They would have more success, if the common bent of our thoughts were not perpetually turned to compare ourselves with others. The infirmities of old age are mortifying; because a comparison with the young may take place. The king's evil is industriously concealed, because it affects others, and is often transmitted to posterity. The case is nearly the same with such diseases as convey any nauseous or frightful images; the epilepsy, for instance, ulcers, sores, scabs, &c.

of birth, but one who is descended from a long succession of rich and powerful ancestors, and who acquires our esteem by his connexion with persons whom we esteem? His ancestors, therefore, though dead, are respected, in some measure, on account of their riches; and consequently, without any kind of expectation.

But not to go so far as prisoners of war or the dead, to find instances of this disinterested regard for riches; we may only observe, with a little attention, those phenomena which occur in common life and conversation. A man, who is himself, we shall suppose, of a competent fortune, and of no profession, being introduced to a company of strangers, naturally treats them with different degrees of respect, as he is informed of their different fortunes and conditions; though it is impossible that he can so suddenly propose, and perhaps he would not accept of, any pecuniary advantage from them. A traveller is always admitted into company, and meets with civility, in proportion as his train and equipage speak him a man of great or moderate fortune. In short, the different ranks of men are, in a great measure, regulated by riches; and that with regard to superiors as well as inferiors, strangers as well as acquaintance.

202 What remains, therefore, but to conclude, that, as riches are desired for ourselves only as the means of gratifying our appetites, either at present or in some imaginary future period, they beget esteem in others merely from their having that influence. This indeed is their very nature or offence: they have a direct reference to the commodities, conveniences, and pleasures of life. The bill of a banker, who is broke, or gold in a desert island, would otherwise be full as valuable. When we approach a man who is, as we say, at his ease, we are presented with the pleasing ideas of plenty, satisfaction, cleanliness, warmth; a cheerful house, elegant furniture, ready service, and whatever is desirable in meat, drink, or apparel. On the contrary, when a poor man appears, the disagreeable images of want, penury, hard labour, dirty furniture, coarse or ragged clothes, nauseous meat and distasteful liquor, immediately strike our fancy. What else do we mean by saying that one is rich, the other poor? And as regard or contempt is the natural consequence of those different situations in life, it is easily seen what additional light and evidence this throws on our preceding theory, with regard to all moral distinctions [1].

A man who has cured himself of all ridiculous prepossessions, and is fully, sincerely, and steadily convinced, from experience as well as philosophy, that the difference of fortune makes less difference in happiness than is vulgarly imagined; such a one does not measure out degrees of esteem according to the rent-rolls of his acquaintance. He may, indeed, externally pay a superior deference to the great lord above the vassal; because riches are the most convenient, being the most fixed and determinate, source of distinction. But his internal sentiments are more regulated by the personal characters of men, than by the accidental and capricious favours of fortune.

In most countries of Europe, family, that is, hereditary riches, marked with titles and symbols from the sovereign, is the chief source of distinction. In England, more regard

---

[1] There is something extraordinary, and seemingly unaccountable in the operation of our passions, when we consider the fortune and situation of others. Very often another's advancement and prosperity produces envy, which has a strong mixture of hatred, and arises chiefly from the comparison of ourselves with the person. At the very same time, or at least in very short intervals, we may feel the passion of respect, which is a species of affection or good-will, with a mixture of humility. On the other hand, the misfortunes of our fellows often cause pity, which has in it a strong mixture of good-will. This sentiment of pity is nearly allied to contempt, which is a species of dislike, with a mixture of pride. I only point out these phenomena, as a subject of speculation to such as are curious with regard to moral enquiries. It is sufficient for the present purpose to observe in general, that power and riches commonly cause respect, poverty and meanness contempt, though particular views and incidents may sometimes raise the passions of envy and of pity.

is paid to present opulence and plenty. Each practice has its advantages and disadvantages. Where birth is respected, unactive, spiritless minds remain in haughty indolence, and dream of nothing but pedigrees and genealogies: the generous and ambitious seek honour and authority, and reputation and favour. Where riches are the chief idol, corruption, venality, rapine prevail: arts, manufactures, commerce, agriculture flourish. The former prejudice, being favourable to military virtue, is more suited to monarchies. The latter, being the chief spur to industry, agrees better with a republican government. And we accordingly find that each of these forms of government, by varying the *utility* of those customs, has commonly a proportionable effect on the sentiments of mankind.

SECTION VII.

203 WHOEVER has passed an evening with serious melancholy
people, and has observed how suddenly the conversation
was animated, and what sprightliness diffused itself over
the countenance, discourse, and behaviour of every one, on
the accession of a good-humoured, lively companion; such
a one will easily allow that cheerfulness carries great merit
with it, and naturally conciliates the good-will of mankind.
No quality, indeed, more readily communicates itself to all
around; because no one has a greater propensity to display
itself, in jovial talk and pleasant entertainment. The flame
spreads through the whole circle; and the most sullen and
morose are often caught by it. That the melancholy hate
the merry, even though Horace says it, I have some difficulty
to allow; because I have always observed that, where the
jollity is moderate and decent, serious people are so much
the more delighted, as it dissipates the gloom with which
they are commonly oppressed, and gives them an unusual
enjoyment.

From this influence of cheerfulness, both to communicate
itself and to engage approbation, we may perceive that
there is another set of mental qualities, which, without any
utility or any tendency to farther good, either of the
community or of the possessor, diffuse a satisfaction on the
beholders, and procure friendship and regard. Their imme-

diate sensation, to the person possessed of them, is agreeable. Others enter into the same humour, and catch the sentiment, by a contagion or natural sympathy; and as we cannot forbear loving whatever pleases, a kindly emotion arises towards the person who communicates so much satisfaction. He is a more animating spectacle; his presence diffuses over us more serene complacency and enjoyment; our imagination, entering into his feelings and disposition, is affected in a more agreeable manner than if a melancholy, dejected, sullen, anxious temper were presented to us. Hence the affection and probation which attend the former: the aversion and disgust, with which we regard the latter[1].

Few men would envy the character which Caesar gives of Cassius :

> He loves no play,
> As thou do'st, Anthony: he hears no music:
> Seldom he smiles; and smiles in such a sort,
> As if he mock'd himself, and scorn'd his spirit
> That could be mov'd to smile at any thing.

Not only such men, as Caesar adds, are commonly *dangerous*, but also, having little enjoyment within themselves, they can never become agreeable to others, or contribute to social entertainment. In all polite nations and ages, a relish for pleasure, if accompanied with temperance and decency, is esteemed a considerable merit, even in the greatest men; and becomes still more requisite in those of inferior rank and character. It is an agreeable representation, which a French writer gives of the situation of his own mind in this particular,

---

[1] There is no man, who, on particular occasions, is not affected with all the disagreeable passions, fear, anger, dejection, grief, melancholy, anxiety, &c. But these, so far as they are natural, and universal, make no difference between one man and another, and can never be the object of blame. It is only when the disposition gives a *propensity* to any of these disagreeable passions, that they disfigure the character, and by giving uneasiness, convey the sentiment of disapprobation to the spectator.

Virtue I love, says he, *without austerity: Pleasure without effeminacy: And life, without fearing its end*[1].

204   Who is not struck with any signal instance of greatness of mind or dignity of character; with elevation of sentiment, disdain of slavery, and with that noble pride and spirit, which arises from conscious virtue? The sublime, says Longinus, is often nothing but the echo or image of magnanimity; and where this quality appears in any one, even though a syllable be not uttered, it excites our applause and admiration; as may be observed of the famous silence of Ajax in the Odyssey, which expresses more noble disdain and resolute indignation than any language can convey[2].

Were I Alexander, said Parmenio, *I would accept of these offers made by* Darius. *So would I too*, replied Alexander, *were I* Parmenio. This saying is admirable, says Longinus, from a like principle[3].

Go! cries the same hero to his soldiers, when they refused to follow him to the Indies, *go tell your countrymen, that you left* Alexander *completing the conquest of the world.* 'Alexander,' said the Prince of Condé, who always admired this passage, 'abandoned by his soldiers, among barbarians, not yet fully subdued, felt in himself such a dignity and right of empire, that he could not believe it possible that any one would refuse to obey him. Whether in Europe or in Asia, among Greeks or Persians, all was indifferent to him: wherever he found men, he fancied he should find subjects.'

The confident of Medea in the tragedy recommends caution and submission; and enumerating all the distresses of that unfortunate heroine, asks her, what she has to support her against her numerous and implacable enemies. *Myself,*

---

[1] 'J'aime la vertu, sans rudesse;
    J'aime le plaisir, sans molesse;
    J'aime la vie, et n'en crains point la fin.'—*St. Evremond.*
[2] Cap. 9.   [3] Idem.

replies she; *Myself I say, and it is enough.* Boileau justly recommends this passage as an instance of true sublime [1].

When Phocion, the modest, the gentle Phocion, was led to execution, he turned to one of his fellow-sufferers, who was lamenting his own hard fate, *Is it not glory enough for you,* says he, *that you die with* Phocion [2]?

Place in opposition the picture which Tacitus draws of Vitellius, fallen from empire, prolonging his ignominy from a wretched love of life, delivered over to the merciless rabble; tossed, buffeted, and kicked about; constrained, by their holding a poinard under his chin, to raise his head, and expose himself to every contumely. What abject infamy! What low humilation! Yet even here, says the historian, he discovered some symptoms of a mind not wholly degenerate. To a tribune, who insulted him, he replied, *I am still your emperor* [3].

We never excuse the absolute want of spirit and dignity of character, or a proper sense of what is due to one's self, in society and the common intercourse of life. This vice constitutes what we properly call *meanness*; when a man can submit to the basest slavery, in order to gain his ends; fawn upon those who abuse him; and degrade himself by intimacies and familiarities with undeserving inferiors. A certain degree of generous pride or self-value is so requisite, that the absence of it in the mind displeases, after the same manner as the want of a nose, eye, or any of the most material feature of the face or member of the body [4].

---

[1] Réflexion 10 sur Longin.   [2] Plutarch in Phoc.

[3] Tacit. hist. lib. iii. The author entering upon the narration, says, *Laniata veste, foedum spectaculum ducebatur, multis increpantibus, nullo inlacrimante.* deformitas exitus misericordiam abstulerat To enter thoroughly into this method of thinking, we must make allowance for the ancient maxims, that no one ought to prolong his life after it became dishonourable; but, as he had always a right to dispose of it, it then became a duty to part with it.

[4] The absence of virtue may often be a vice; and that of the highest kind; as in the instance of ingratitude, as well as meanness. Where we

205   The utility of courage, both to the public and to the person possessed of it, is an obvious foundation of merit. But to any one who duly considers of the matter, it will appear that this quality has a peculiar lustre, which it derives wholly from itself, and from that noble elevation inseparable from it. Its figure, drawn by painters and by poets, displays, in each feature, a sublimity and daring confidence; which catches the eye, engages the affections, and diffuses, by sympathy, a like sublimity of sentiment over every spectator.

Under what shining colours does Demosthenes [1] represent Philip; where the orator apologizes for his own administration, and justifies that pertinacious love of liberty, with which he had inspired the Athenians. 'I beheld Philip,' says he, 'he with whom was your contest, resolutely, while in pursuit of empire and dominion, exposing himself to every wound; his eye gored, his neck wrested, his arm, his thigh pierced, what ever part of his body fortune should seize on, that cheerfully relinquishing; provided that, with what remained, he might live in honour and renown. And shall it be said that he, born in Pella, a place heretofore mean and ignoble, should be inspired with so high an ambition and thirst of fame: while you, Athenians, &c.' These praises excite the most lively admiration; but the views presented by the orator, carry us not, we see, beyond the hero himself, nor ever regard the future advantageous consequences of his valour.

The martial temper of the Romans, inflamed by continual wars, had raised their esteem of courage so high, that, in

expect a beauty, the disappointment gives an uneasy sensation, and produces a real deformity. An abjectness of character, likewise, is disgustful and contemptible in another view. Where a man has no sense of value in himself, we are not likely to have any higher esteem of him. And if the same person, who crouches to his superiors, is insolent to his inferiors (as often happens), this contrariety of behaviour, instead of correcting the former vice, aggravates it extremely by the addition of a vice still more odious. See Sect. VIII.   [1] De Corona.

their language, it was called *virtue*, by way of excellence and of distinction from all other moral qualities. *The* Suevi, in the opinion of Tacitus [1], *dressed their hair with a laudable intent: not for the purpose of loving or being loved; they adorned themselves only for their enemies, and in order to appear more terrible.* A sentiment of the historian, which would sound a little oddly in other nations and other ages.

The Scythians, according to Herodotus [2], after scalping their enemies, dressed the skin like leather, and used it as a towel; and whoever had the most of those towels was most esteemed among them. So much had martial bravery, in that nation, as well as in many others, destroyed the sentiments of humanity; a virtue surely much more useful and engaging.

It is indeed observable, that, among all uncultivated nations, who have not as yet had full experience of the advantages attending beneficence, justice, and the social virtues, courage is the predominant excellence; what is most celebrated by poets, recommended by parents and instructors, and admired by the public in general. The ethics of Homer are, in this particular, very different from those of Fénélon, his elegant imitator; and such as were well suited to an age, when one hero, as remarked by Thucydides [3], could ask another, without offence, whether he were a robber or not. Such also very lately was the system of ethics which prevailed in many barbarous parts of Ireland; if we may credit Spenser, in his judicious account of the state of that kingdom [4].

[1] De moribus Germ.   [2] Lib. iv.   [3] Lib. i.

[4] It is a common use, says he, amongst their gentlemen's sons, that, as soon as they are able to use their weapons, they strait gather to themselves three or four stragglers or kern, with whom wandering a while up and down idly the country, taking only meat, he at last falleth into some bad occasion, that shall be offered; which being once made known, he is thenceforth counted a man of worth, in whom there is courage.

206   Of the same class of virtues with courage is that undisturbed philosophical tranquillity, superior to pain, sorrow, anxiety, and each assault of adverse fortune. Conscious of his own virtue, say the philosophers, the sage elevates himself above every accident of life; and securely placed in the temple of wisdom, looks down on inferior mortals engaged in pursuit of honours, riches, reputation, and every frivolous enjoyment. These pretensions, no doubt, when stretched to the utmost, are by far too magnificent for human nature. They carry, however, a grandeur with them, which seizes the spectator, and strikes him with admiration. And the nearer we can approach in practice to this sublime tranquillity and indifference (for we must distinguish it from a stupid insensibility), the more secure enjoyment shall we attain within ourselves, and the more greatness of mind shall we discover to the world. The philosophical tranquillity may, indeed, be considered only as a branch of magnanimity.

Who admires not Socrates; his perpetual serenity and contentment, amidst the greatest poverty and domestic vexations; his resolute contempt of riches, and his magnanimous care of preserving liberty, while he refused all assistance from his friends and disciples, and avoided even the dependence of an obligation? Epictetus had not so much as a door to his little house or hovel; and therefore, soon lost his iron lamp, the only furniture which he had worth taking. But resolving to disappoint all robbers for the future, he supplied its place with an earthen lamp, of which he very peacefully kept possession ever after.

Among the ancients, the heroes in philosophy, as well as those in war and patriotism, have a grandeur and force of sentiment, which astonishes our narrow souls, and is rashly rejected as extravagant and supernatural. They, in their turn, I allow, would have had equal reason to consider as romantic and incredible, the degree of humanity, clemency, order, tranquillity, and other social virtues, to which, in the administration of government, we have attained in modern times, had any one been then able to have made a fair representation of them. Such is the compensation, which nature, or rather education, has made in the distribution of excellencies and virtues, in those different ages.

207 The merit of benevolence, arising from its utility, and its tendency to promote the good of mankind, has been already explained, and is, no doubt, the source of a *considerable* part of that esteem, which is so universally paid to it. But it will also be allowed, that the very softness and tenderness of the sentiment, its engaging endearments, its fond expressions, its delicate attentions, and all that flow of mutual confidence and regard, which enters into a warm attachment of love and friendship : it will be allowed, I say, that these feelings, being delightful in themselves, are necessarily communicated to the spectators, and melt them into the same fondness and delicacy. The tear naturally starts in our eye on the apprehension of a warm sentiment of this nature : our breast heaves, our heart is agitated, and every humane tender principle of our frame is set in motion, and gives us the purest and most satisfactory enjoyment.

When poets form descriptions of Elysian fields, where the blessed inhabitants stand in no need of each other's assistance, they yet represent them as maintaining a constant intercourse of love and friendship, and sooth our fancy with the pleasing image of these soft and gentle passions. The idea of tender tranquillity in a pastoral Arcadia is agreeable from a like principle, as has been observed above [1].

Who would live amidst perpetual wrangling, and scolding, and mutual reproaches? The roughness and harshness of these emotions disturb and displease us: we suffer by

---

[1] Sect. v. Part 2.

contagion and sympathy; nor can we remain indifferent spectators, even though certain that no pernicious consequences would ever follow from such angry passions.

208   As a certain proof that the whole merit of benevolence is not derived from its usefulness, we may observe, that in a kind way of blame, we say, a person is *too good*; when he exceeds his part in society, and carries his attention for others beyond the proper bounds.   In like manner, we say a man is *too high-spirited, too intrepid, too indifferent about fortune*: reproaches, which really, at bottom, imply more esteem than many panegyrics.   Being accustomed to rate the merit and demerit of characters chiefly by their useful or pernicious tendencies, we cannot forbear applying the epithet of blame, when we discover a sentiment, which rises to a degree, that is hurtful; but it may happen, at the same time, that its noble elevation, or its engaging tenderness so seizes the heart, as rather to increase our friendship and concern for the person [1].

The amours and attachments of Harry the IVth of France, during the civil wars of the league, frequently hurt his interest and his cause; but all the young, at least, and amorous, who can sympathize with the tender passions, will allow that this very weakness, for they will readily call it such, chiefly endears that hero, and interests them in his fortunes.

The excessive bravery and resolute inflexibility of Charles the.XIIth ruined his own country, and infested all his neighbours; but have such splendour and greatness in their appearance, as strikes us with admiration; and they might, in some degree, be even approved of, if they betrayed not sometimes too evident symptoms of madness and disorder.

---

[1] Cheerfulness could scarce admit of blame from its excess, were it not that dissolute mirth, without a proper cause or subject, is a sure symptom and characteristic of folly, and on that account disgustful.

209 The Athenians pretended to the first invention of agriculture and of laws : and always valued themselves extremely on the benefit thereby procured to the whole race of mankind. They also boasted, and with reason, of their warlike enterprises ; particularly against those innumerable fleets and armies of Persians, which invaded Greece during the reigns of Darius and Xerxes. But though there be no comparison in point of utility, between these peaceful and military honours ; yet we find, that the orators, who have writ such elaborate panegyrics on that famous city, have chiefly triumphed in displaying the warlike achievements. Lysias, Thucydides, Plato, and Isocrates discover, all of them, the same partiality ; which, though condemned by calm reason and reflection, appears so natural in the mind of man.

It is observable, that the great charm of poetry consists in lively pictures of the sublime passions, magnanimity, courage, disdain of fortune; or those of the tender affections, love and friendship; which warm the heart, and diffuse over it similar sentiments and emotions. And though all kinds of passion, even the most disagreeable, such as grief and anger, are observed, when excited by poetry, to convey a satisfaction, from a mechanism of nature, not easy to be explained : Yet those more elevated or softer affections have a peculiar influence, and please from more than one cause or principle. Not to mention that they alone interest us in the fortune of the persons represented, or communicate any esteem and affection for their character.

And can it possibly be doubted, that this talent itself of poets, to move the passions, this pathetic and sublime of sentiment, is a very considerable merit ; and being enhanced by its extreme rarity, may exalt the person possessed of it, above every character of the age in which he lives? The prudence, address, steadiness, and benign government of Augustus, adorned with all the splendour of his noble birth and imperial crown, render him but an unequal competitor for fame with Virgil, who lays nothing into the opposite scale but the divine beauties of his poetical genius.

The very sensibility to these beauties, or a delicacy of taste, is itself a beauty in any character; as conveying the purest, the most durable, and most innocent of all enjoyments.

210   These are some instances of the several species of merit, that are valued for the immediate pleasure which they communicate to the person possessed of them. No views of utility or of future beneficial consequences enter into this sentiment of approbation; yet is it of a kind similar to that other sentiment, which arises from views of a public or private utility. The same social sympathy, we may observe, or fellow-feeling with human happiness or misery, gives rise to both; and this analogy, in all the parts of the present theory, may justly be regarded as a confirmation of it.

SECTION VIII.

OF QUALITIES IMMEDIATELY AGREEABLE TO OTHERS[1].

211   As the mutual shocks, in *society*, and the oppositions of interest and self-love have constrained mankind to establish the laws of *justice*, in order to preserve the advantages of mutual assistance and protection : in like manner, the eternal contrarieties, in *company*, of men's pride and self-conceit, have introduced the rules of Good Manners or Politeness, in order to facilitate the intercourse of minds, and an undisturbed commerce and conversation. Among well-bred people, a mutual deference is affected ; contempt of others disguised ; authority concealed ; attention given to each in his turn ; and an easy stream of conversation maintained, without vehemence, without interruption, without eagerness for victory, and without any airs of superiority. These attentions and regards are immediately *agreeable* to others, abstracted from any consideration of utility or beneficial tendencies : they conciliate affection, promote esteem, and extremely enhance the merit of the person who regulates his behaviour by them.   .

---

[1] It is the nature and, indeed, the definition of virtue, that it is *a quality of the mind agreeable to or approved of by every one who considers or contemplates it*. But some qualities produce pleasure, because they are useful to society, or useful or agreeable to the person himself ; others produce it more immediately, which is the case with the class of virtues here considered.

Many of the forms of breeding are arbitrary and casual; but the thing expressed by them is still the same. A Spaniard goes out of his own house before his guest, to signify that he leaves him master of all. In other countries, the landlord walks out last, as a common mark of deference and regard.

212   But, in order to render a man perfect *good company*, he must have Wit and Ingenuity as well as good manners. What wit is, it may not be easy to define; but it is easy surely to determine that it is a quality immediately *agreeable* to others, and communicating, on its first appearance, a lively joy and satisfaction to every one who has any comprehension of it. The most profound metaphysics, indeed, might be employed in explaining the various kinds and species of wit; and many classes of it, which are now received on the sole testimony of taste and sentiment, might, perhaps, be resolved into more general principles. But this is sufficient for our present purpose, that it does affect taste and sentiment, and bestowing an immediate enjoyment, is a sure source of approbation and affection.

In countries where men pass most of their time in conversation, and visits, and assemblies, these *companionable* qualities, so to speak, are of high estimation, and form a chief part of personal merit. In countries where men live a more domestic life, and either are employed in business, or amuse themselves in a narrower circle of acquaintance, the more solid qualities are chiefly regarded. Thus, I have often observed, that, among the French, the first questions with regard to a stranger are, *Is he polite?* *Has he wit?* In our own country, the chief praise bestowed is always that of a *good-natured, sensible fellow*.

In conversation, the lively spirit of dialogue is *agreeable*, even to those who desire not to have any share in the discourse: hence the teller of long stories, or the pompous declaimer, is very little approved of. But most men desire likewise their turn in the conversation, and regard, with a very evil eye, that *loquacity* which deprives them of a right they are naturally so jealous of.

There is a sort of harmless *liars*, frequently to be met with in company, who deal much in the marvellous. Their usual intention is to please and entertain; but as men are most delighted with what they conceive to be truth, these people mistake extremely the means of pleasing, and incur universal blame. Some indulgence, however, to lying or fiction is given in *humorous* stories; because it is there really agreeable and entertaining, and truth is not of any importance.

Eloquence, genius of all kinds, even good sense, and sound reasoning, when it rises to an eminent degree, and is employed upon subjects of any considerable dignity and nice discernment; all these endowments seem immediately agreeable, and have a merit distinct from their usefulness. Rarity, likewise, which so much enhances the price of every thing, must set an additional value on these noble talents of the human mind.

213 Modesty may be understood in different senses, even abstracted from chastity, which has been already treated of. It sometimes means that tenderness and nicety of honour, that apprehension of blame, that dread of intrusion or injury towards others, that Pudor, which is the proper guardian of every kind of virtue, and a sure preservative against vice and corruption. But its most usual meaning is when it is opposed to *impudence* and *arrogance*, and expresses a diffidence of our own judgement, and a due attention and regard for others. In young men chiefly, this quality is a sure sign of good sense; and is also the certain means of augmenting that endowment, by preserving their ears open to instruction, and making them still grasp after new attainments. But it has a further charm to every spectator; by flattering every man's vanity, and presenting

the appearance of a docile pupil, who receives, with proper attention and respect, every word they utter.

Men have, in general, a much greater propensity to over-value than undervalue themselves; notwithstanding the opinion of Aristotle [1]. This makes us more jealous of the excess on the former side, and causes us to regard, with a peculiar indulgence, all tendency to modesty and self-diffidence; as esteeming the danger less of falling into any vicious extreme of that nature. It is thus in countries where men's bodies are apt to exceed in corpulency, personal beauty is placed in a much greater degree of slenderness, than in countries where that is the most usual defect. Being so often struck with instances of one species of deformity, men think they can never keep at too great a distance from it, and wish always to have a leaning to the opposite side. In like manner, were the door opened to self-praise, and were Montaigne's maxim observed, that one should say as frankly, *I have sense, I have learning, I have courage, beauty, or wit,* as it is sure we often think so; were this the case, I say, every one is sensible that such a flood of impertinence would break in upon us, as would render society wholly intolerable. For this reason custom has established it as a rule, in common societies, that men should not indulge themselves in self-praise, or even speak much of themselves; and it is only among intimate friends or people of very manly behaviour, that one is allowed to do himself justice. Nobody finds fault with Maurice, Prince of Orange, for his reply to one who asked him, whom he esteemed the first general of the age, *The marquis of Spinola,* said he, *is the second.* Though it is observable, that the self-praise implied is here better implied, than if it had been directly expressed, without any cover or disguise.

He must be a very superficial thinker, who imagines

[1] Ethic. ad Nicomachum.

that all instances of mutual deference are to be understood
in earnest, and that a man would be more esteemable for
being ignorant of his own merits and accomplishments.
A small bias towards modesty, even in the internal sentiment, is favourably regarded, especially in young people;
and a strong bias is required in the outward behaviour;
but this excludes not a noble pride and spirit, which may
openly display itself in its full extent, when one lies under
calumny or oppression of any kind. The generous con-
tumacy of Socrates, as Cicero calls it, has been highly
celebrated in all ages; and when joined to the usual
modesty of his behaviour, forms a shining character.
Iphicrates, the Athenian, being accused of betraying the
interests of his country, asked his accuser, *Would you*, says
he, *have, on a like occasion, been guilty of that crime ? By no
means*, replied the other. *And can you then imagine*, cried
the hero, *that* Iphicrates *would be guilty ?*[1] In short,
a generous spirit and self-value, well founded, decently
disguised, and courageously supported under distress and
calumny, is a great excellency, and seems to derive its merit
from the noble elevation of its sentiment, or its immediate
agreeableness to its possessor. In ordinary characters, we
approve of a bias towards modesty, which is a quality
immediately agreeable to others : the vicious excess of the
former virtue, namely, insolence or haughtiness, is immediately disagreeable to others; the excess of the latter
is so to the possessor. Thus are the boundaries of these
duties adjusted.

214   A desire of fame, reputation, or a character with others, is
so far from being blameable, that it seems inseparable from
virtue, genius, capacity, and a generous or noble disposition.
An attention even to trivial matters, in order to please, is
also expected and demanded by society; and no one is
surprised, if he find a man in company to observe a greater

[1] Quinctil. lib. v. cap. 12.

elegance of dress and more pleasant flow of conversation, than when he passes his time at home, and with his own family. Wherein, then, consists Vanity, which is so justly regarded as a fault or imperfection. It seems to consist chiefly in such an intemperate display of our advantages, honours, and accomplishments; in such an importunate and open demand of praise and admiration, as is offensive to others, and encroaches too far on *their* secret vanity and ambition. It is besides a sure symptom of the want of true dignity and elevation of mind, which is so great an ornament in any character. For why that impatient desire of applause; as if you were not justly entitled to it, and might not reasonably expect that it would for ever attend you? Why so anxious to inform us of the great company which you have kept; the obliging things which were said to you; the honours, the distinctions which you met with; as if these were not things of course, and what we could readily, of ourselves, have imagined, without being told of them?

215 Decency, or a proper regard to age, sex, character, and station in the world, may be ranked among the qualities which are immediately agreeable to others, and which, by that means, acquire praise and approbation. An effeminate behaviour in a man, a rough manner in a woman; these are ugly because unsuitable to each character, and different from the qualities which we expect in the sexes. It is as if a tragedy abounded in comic beauties, or a comedy in tragic. The disproportions hurt the eye, and convey a disagreeable sentiment to the spectators, the source of blame and disapprobation. This is that *indecorum*, which is explained so much at large by Cicero in his Offices.

Among the other virtues, we may also give Cleanliness a place; since it naturally renders us agreeable to others, and is no inconsiderable source of love and affection. No one will deny, that a negligence in this particular is a fault; and as faults are nothing but smaller vices, and this fault can have no other origin than the uneasy sensation which it excites in others; we may, in this instance, seemingly so trivial, clearly discover the origin of moral distinctions, about which the learned have involved themselves in such mazes of perplexity and error.

216 But besides all the *agreeable* qualities, the origin of whose beauty we can, in some degree, explain and account for, there still remains something mysterious and inexplicable, which conveys an immediate satisfaction to the spectator, but how, or why, or for what reason, he cannot pretend to determine. There is a manner, a grace, an ease, a genteelness, an I-know-not-what, which some men possess above others, which is very different from external beauty and comeliness, and which, however, catches our affection almost as suddenly and powerfully. And though this *manner* be chiefly talked of in the passion between the sexes, where the concealed magic is easily explained, yet surely much of it prevails in all our estimation of characters, and forms no inconsiderable part of personal merit. This class of accomplishments, therefore, must be trusted entirely to the blind, but sure testimony of taste and sentiment; and must be considered as a part of ethics, left by nature to baffle all the pride of philosophy, and make her sensible of her narrow boundaries and slender acquisitions.

We approve of another, because of his wit, politeness, modesty, decency, or any agreeable quality which he possesses; although he be not of our acquaintance, nor has ever given us any entertainment, by means of these accomplishments. The idea, which we form of their effect on his acquaintance, has an agreeable influence on our imagination, and gives us the sentiment of approbation. This principle enters into all the judgements which we form concerning manners and characters.

SECTION IX.

PART I.

217   IT may justly appear surprising that any man in so late an age, should find it requisite to prove, by elaborate reasoning, that Personal Merit consists altogether in the possession of mental qualities, *useful* or *agreeable* to the *person himself* or to *others*. It might be expected that this principle would have occurred even to the first rude, unpractised enquirers concerning morals, and been received from its own evidence, without any argument or disputation. Whatever is valuable in any kind, so naturally classes itself under the division of *useful* or *agreeable*, the *utile* or the *dulce*, that it is not easy to imagine why we should ever seek further, or consider the question as a matter of nice research or inquiry. And as every thing useful or agreeable must possess these qualities with regard either to the *person himself* or to *others*, the complete delineation or description of merit seems to be performed as naturally as a shadow is cast by the sun, or an image is reflected upon water. If the ground, on which the shadow is cast, be not broken and uneven; nor the surface from which the image is reflected, disturbed and confused; a just figure is immediately presented, without any art or attention. And it seems a reasonable presumption, that systems and hypotheses have perverted our natural understanding, when a theory,

so simple and obvious, could so long have escaped the most elaborate examination.

218 But however the case may have fared with philosophy, in common life these principles are still implicitly maintained; nor is any other topic of praise or blame ever recurred to, when we employ any panegyric or satire, any applause or censure of human action and behaviour. If we observe men, in every intercourse of business or pleasure, in every discourse and conversation, we shall find them nowhere, except in the schools, at any loss upon this subject. What so natural, for instance, as the following dialogue? You are very happy, we shall suppose one to say, addressing himself to another, that you have given your daughter to Cleanthes. He is a man of honour and humanity. Every one, who has any intercourse with him, is sure of *fair* and *kind* treatment[1]. I congratulate you too, says another, on the promising expectations of this son-in-law; whose assiduous application to the study of the laws, whose quick penetration and early knowledge both of men and business, prognosticate the greatest honours and advancement[2]. You surprise me, replies a third, when you talk of Cleanthes as a man of business and application. I met him lately in a circle of the gayest company, and he was the very life and soul of our conversation: so much wit with good manners; so much gallantry without affectation; so much ingenious knowledge so genteelly delivered, I have never before observed in any one[3]. You would admire him still more, says a fourth, if you knew him more familiarly. That cheerfulness, which you might remark in him, is not a sudden flash struck out by company: it runs through the whole tenor of his life, and preserves a perpetual serenity on his countenance, and tranquillity in his soul. He has

---

[1] Qualities useful to others.
[2] Qualities useful to the person himself.
[3] Qualities immediately agreeable to others.

met with severe trials, misfortunes as well as dangers; and by his greatness of mind, was still superior to all of them [1]. The image, gentlemen, which you have here delineated of Cleanthes, cried I, is that of accomplished merit. Each of you has given a stroke of the pencil to his figure; and you have unawares exceeded all the pictures drawn by Gratian or Castiglione. A philosopher might select this character as a model of perfect virtue.

219   And as every quality which is useful or agreeable to ourselves or others is, in common life, allowed to be a part of personal merit; so no other will ever be received, where men judge of things by their natural, unprejudiced reason, without the delusive glosses of superstition and false religion. Celibacy, fasting, penance, mortification, self-denial, humility, silence, solitude, and the whole train of monkish virtues; for what reason are they everywhere rejected by men of sense, but because they serve to no manner of purpose; neither advance a man's fortune in the world, nor render him a more valuable member of society, neither qualify him for the entertainment of company, nor increase his power of self-enjoyment? We observe, on the contrary, that they cross all these desirable ends; stupify the understanding and harden the heart, obscure the fancy and sour the temper. We justly, therefore, transfer them to the opposite column, and place them in the catalogue of vices; nor has any superstition force sufficient among men of the world, to pervert entirely these natural sentiments. A gloomy, hair-brained enthusiast, after his death, may have a place in the calendar; but will scarcely ever be admitted, when alive, into intimacy and society, except by those who are as delirious and dismal as himself.

It seems a happiness in the present theory, that it enters not into that vulgar dispute concerning the *degrees* of benevolence or self-love, which prevail in human nature;

---

[1] Qualities immediately agreeable to the person himself.

a dispute which is never likely to have any issue, both because men, who have taken part, are not easily convinced, and because the phenomena, which can be produced on either side, are so dispersed, so uncertain, and subject to so many interpretations, that it is scarcely possible accurately to compare them, or draw from them any determinate inference or conclusion. It is sufficient for our present purpose, if it be allowed, what surely, without the greatest absurdity cannot be disputed, that there is some benevolence, however small, infused into our bosom; some spark of friendship for human kind; some particle of the dove kneaded into our frame, along with the elements of the wolf and serpent. Let these generous sentiments be supposed ever so weak; let them be insufficient to move even a hand or finger of our body, they must still direct the determinations of our mind, and where everything else is equal, produce a cool preference of what is useful and serviceable to mankind, above what is pernicious and dangerous. A *moral distinction*, therefore, immediately arises; a general sentiment of blame and approbation; a tendency, however faint, to the objects of the one, and a proportionable aversion to those of the other. Nor will those reasoners, who so earnestly maintain the predominant selfishness of human kind, be any wise scandalized at hearing of the weak sentiments of virtue implanted in our nature. On the contrary, they are found as ready to maintain the one tenet as the other; and their spirit of satire (for such it appears, rather than of corruption) naturally gives rise to both opinions; which have, indeed, a great and almost an indissoluble connexion together.

221   Avarice, ambition, vanity, and all passions vulgarly, though improperly, comprised under the denomination of *self-love*, are here excluded from our theory concerning the origin of morals, not because they are too weak, but because they have not a proper direction for that purpose.

The notion of morals implies some sentiment common to all mankind, which recommends the same object to general approbation, and makes every man, or most men, agree in the same opinion or decision concerning it.   It also implies some sentiment, so universal and comprehensive as to extend to all mankind, and render the actions and conduct, even of the persons the most remote, an object of applause or censure, according as they agree or disagree with that rule of right which is established.   These two requisite circumstances belong alone to the sentiment of humanity here insisted on.   The other passions produce in every breast, many strong sentiments of desire and aversion, affection and hatred; but these neither are felt so much in common, nor are so comprehensive, as to be the foundation of any general system and established theory of blame or approbation.

222   When a man denominates another his *enemy*, his *rival*, his *antagonist*, his *adversary*, he is understood to speak the language of self-love, and to express sentiments, peculiar to himself, and arising from his particular circumstances and situation.   But when he bestows on any man the epithets of *vicious* or *odious* or *depraved*, he then speaks another language, and expresses sentiments, in which he expects all his audience are to concur with him.   He must here, therefore, depart from his private and particular situation, and must choose a point of view, common to him with others; he must move some universal principle of the human frame, and touch a string to which all mankind have an accord and symphony.   If he mean, therefore, to express that this man possesses qualities, whose tendency is pernicious to society, he has chosen this common point of view, and has touched the principle of humanity, in which every man, in some degree, concurs.   While the human heart is compounded of the same elements as at present, it will never be wholly indifferent to public good,

nor entirely unaffected with the tendency of characters and manners. And though this affection of humanity may not generally be esteemed so strong as vanity or ambition, yet, being common to all men, it can alone be the foundation of morals, or of any general system of blame or praise. One man's ambition is not another's ambition, nor will the same event or object satisfy both; but the humanity of one man is the humanity of every one, and the same object touches this passion in all human creatures.

223   But the sentiments, which arise from humanity, are not only the same in all human creatures, and produce the same approbation or censure; but they also comprehend all human creatures; nor is there any one whose conduct or character is not, by their means, an object to every one of censure or approbation. On the contrary, those other passions, commonly denominated selfish, both produce different sentiments in each individual, according to his particular situation; and also contemplate the greater part of mankind with the utmost indifference and unconcern. Whoever has a high regard and esteem for me flatters my vanity; whoever expresses contempt mortifies and displeases me; but as my name is known but to a small part of mankind, there are few who come within the sphere of this passion, or excite, on its account, either my affection or disgust. But if you represent a tyrannical, insolent, or barbarous behaviour, in any country or in any age of the world, I soon carry my eye to the pernicious tendency of such a conduct, and feel the sentiment of repugnance and displeasure towards it. No character can be so remote as to be, in this light, wholly indifferent to me. What is beneficial to society or to the person himself must still be preferred. And every quality or action, of every human being, must, by this means, be ranked under some class or denomination, expressive of general censure or applause.

What more, therefore, can we ask to distinguish the

T

sentiments, dependent on humanity, from those connected
with any other passion, or to satisfy us, why the former are
the origin of morals, not the latter? Whatever conduct
gains my approbation, by touching my humanity, procures
also the applause of all mankind, by affecting the same
principle in them; but what serves my avarice or ambition
pleases these passions in me alone, and affects not the
avarice and ambition of the rest of mankind. There is no
circumstance of conduct in any man, provided it have
a beneficial tendency, that is not agreeable to my
humanity, however remote the person; but every man, so
far removed as neither to cross nor serve my avarice
and ambition, is regarded as wholly indifferent by those
passions. The distinction, therefore, between these species
of sentiment being so great and evident, language must
soon be moulded upon it, and must invent a peculiar set of
terms, in order to express those universal sentiments of
censure or approbation, which arise from humanity, or from
views of general usefulness and its contrary. Virtue and
Vice become then known; morals are recognized; certain
general ideas are framed of human conduct and behaviour;
such measures are expected from men in such situations.
This action is determined to be conformable to our abstract rule; that other, contrary. And by such universal
principles are the particular sentiments of self-love frequently
controlled and limited [1].

[1] It seems certain, both from reason and experience, that a rude,
untaught savage regulates chiefly his love and hatred by the ideas of
private utility and injury, and has but faint conceptions of a general rule
or system of behaviour. The man who stands opposite to him in battle,
he hates heartily, not only for the present moment, which is almost
unavoidable, but for ever after; nor is he satisfied without the most
extreme punishment and vengeance. But we, accustomed to society, and
to more enlarged reflections, consider, that this man is serving his own
country and community; that any man, in the same situation, would do
the same; that we ourselves, in like circumstances, observe a like conduct; that, in general, human society is best supported on such maxims.

224   From instances of popular tumults, seditions, factions, panics, and of all passions, which are shared with a multitude, we may learn the influence of society in exciting and supporting any emotion; while the most ungovernable disorders are raised, we find, by that means, from the slightest and most frivolous occasions. Solon was no very cruel, though, perhaps, an unjust legislator, who punished neuters in civil wars; and few, I believe, would, in such cases, incur the penalty, were their affection and discourse allowed sufficient to absolve them. No selfishness, and scarce any philosophy, have there force sufficient to support a total coolness and indifference; and he must be more or less than man, who kindles not in the common blaze. What wonder then, that moral sentiments are found of such influence in life; though springing from principles, which may appear, at first sight, somewhat small and delicate? But these principles, we must remark, are social and universal; they form, in a manner, the *party* of humankind against vice or disorder, its common enemy. And as the benevolent concern for others is diffused, in a greater or less degree, over all men, and is the same in all, it occurs more frequently in discourse, is cherished by society and conversation, and the blame and approbation, consequent on it, are thereby roused from that lethargy into which they are probably lulled, in solitary and uncultivated nature. Other passions, though perhaps originally stronger, yet

and by these suppositions and views, we correct, in some measure, our ruder and narrower passions. And though much of our friendship and enmity be still regulated by private considerations of benefit and harm, we pay, at least, this homage to general rules, which we are accustomed to respect, that we commonly pervert our adversary's conduct, by imputing malice or injustice to him, in order to give vent to those passions, which arise from self-love and private interest. When the heart is full of rage, it never wants pretences of this nature; though sometimes as frivolous, as those from which Horace, being almost crushed by the fall of a tree, affects to accuse of parricide the first planter of it.

being selfish and private, are often overpowered by its force, and yield the dominion of our breast to those social and public principles.

225   Another spring of our constitution, that brings a great addition of force to moral sentiments, is the love of fame; which rules, with such uncontrolled authority, in all generous minds, and is often the grand object of all their designs and undertakings. By our continual and earnest pursuit of a character, a name, a reputation in the world, we bring our own deportment and conduct frequently in review, and consider how they appear in the eyes of those who approach and regard us. This constant habit of surveying ourselves, as it were, in reflection, keeps alive all the sentiments of right and wrong, and begets, in noble natures, a certain reverence for themselves as well as others, which is the surest guardian of every virtue. The animal conveniencies and pleasures sink gradually in their value; while every inward beauty and moral grace is studiously acquired, and the mind is accomplished in every perfection, which can adorn or embellish a rational creature.

Here is the most perfect morality with which we are acquainted: here is displayed the force of many sympathies. Our moral sentiment is itself a feeling chiefly of that nature, and our regard to a character with others seems to arise only from a care of preserving a character with ourselves; and in order to attain this end, we find it necessary to prop our tottering judgement on the correspondent approbation of mankind.

226   But, that we may accommodate matters, and remove if possible every difficulty, let us allow all these reasonings to be false. Let us allow that, when we resolve the pleasure, which arises from views of utility, into the sentiments of humanity and sympathy, we have embraced a wrong hypothesis. Let us confess it necessary to find some other explication of that applause, which is paid to objects, whether

inanimate, animate, or rational, if they have a tendency to promote the welfare and advantage of mankind. However difficult it be to conceive that an object is approved of on account of its tendency to a certain end, while the end itself is totally indifferent: let us swallow this absurdity, and consider what are the consequences. The preceding delineation or definition of Personal Merit must still retain its evidence and authority: it must still be allowed that every quality of the mind, which is *useful* or *agreeable* to the *person himself* or to *others*, communicates a pleasure to the spectator, engages his esteem, and is admitted under the honourable denomination of virtue or merit. Are not justice, fidelity, honour, veracity, allegiance, chastity, esteemed solely on account of their tendency to promote the good of society? Is not that tendency inseparable from humanity, benevolence, lenity, generosity, gratitude, moderation, tenderness, friendship, and all the other social virtues? Can it possibly be doubted that industry, discretion, frugality, secrecy, order, perseverance, forethought, judgement, and this whole class of virtues and accomplishments, of which many pages would not contain the catalogue; can it be doubted, I say, that the tendency of these qualities to promote the interest and happiness of their possessor, is the sole foundation of their merit? Who can dispute that a mind, which supports a perpetual serenity and cheerfulness, a noble dignity and undaunted spirit, a tender affection and good-will to all around; as it has more enjoyment within itself, is also a more animating and rejoicing spectacle, than if dejected with melancholy, tormented with anxiety, irritated with rage, or sunk into the most abject baseness and degeneracy? And as to the qualities, immediately *agreeable to others*, they speak sufficiently for themselves; and he must be unhappy, indeed, either in his own temper, or in his situation and company, who has never perceived the charms of a facetious wit or flowing affability, of a delicate modesty or decent genteelness of address and manner.

227   I am sensible, that nothing can be more unphilosophical than to be positive or dogmatical on any subject; and that, even if *excessive* scepticism could be maintained, it would not be more destructive to all just reasoning and inquiry. I am convinced that, where men are the most sure and arrogant, they are commonly the most mistaken, and have there given reins to passion, without that proper deliberation and suspense, which can alone secure them from the grossest absurdities. Yet, I must confess, that this enumeration puts the matter in so strong a light, that I cannot, *at present*, be more assured of any truth, which I learn from reasoning and argument, than that personal merit consists entirely in the usefulness or agreeableness of qualities to the person himself possessed of them, or to others, who have any intercourse with him. But when I reflect that, though the bulk and figure of the earth have been measured and delineated; though the motions of the tides have been accounted for, the order and economy of the heavenly bodies subjected to their proper laws, and Infinite itself reduced to calculation; yet men still dispute concerning the foundation of their moral duties. When I reflect on this, I say, I fall back into diffidence and scepticism, and suspect that an hypothesis, so obvious, had it been a true one, would, long ere now, have been received by the unanimous suffrage and consent of mankind.

Part II.

228   Having explained the moral *approbation* attending merit or virtue, there remains nothing but briefly to consider our interested *obligation* to it, and to inquire whether every man, who has any regard to his own happiness and welfare, will not best find his account in the practice of every moral duty. If this can be clearly ascertained from the foregoing

theory, we shall have the satisfaction to reflect, that we have advanced principles, which not only, it is hoped, will stand the test of reasoning and inquiry, but may contribute to the amendment of men's lives, and their improvement in morality and social virtue. And though the philosophical truth of any proposition by no means depends on its tendency to promote the interests of society; yet a man has but a bad grace, who delivers a theory, however true, which, he must confess, leads to a practice dangerous and pernicious. Why rake into those corners of nature which spread a nuisance all around? Why dig up the pestilence from the pit in which it is buried? The ingenuity of your researches may be admired, but your systems will be detested; and mankind will agree, if they cannot refute them, to sink them, at least, in eternal silence and oblivion. Truths which are *pernicious* to society, if any such there be, will yield to errors which are salutary and *advantageous.*

But what philosophical truths can be more advantageous to society, than those here delivered, which represent virtue in all her genuine and most engaging charms, and makes us approach her with ease, familiarity, and affection? The dismal dress falls off, with which many divines, and some philosophers, have covered her; and nothing appears but gentleness, humanity beneficence, affability; nay, even at proper intervals, play, frolic, and gaiety. She talks not of useless austerities and rigours, suffering and self-denial. She declares that her sole purpose is to make her votaries and all mankind, during every instant of their existence, if possible, cheerful and happy; nor does she ever willingly part with any pleasure but in hopes of ample compensation in some other period of their lives. The sole trouble which she demands, is that of just calculation, and a steady preference of the greater happiness. And if any austere pretenders approach her, enemies to joy and pleasure, she either rejects them as hypocrites and deceivers; or, if she admit them in her train, they are ranked, however, among the least favoured of her votaries.

And, indeed, to drop all figurative expression, what hopes can we ever have of engaging mankind to a practice which we confess full of austerity and rigour? Or what theory of morals can ever serve any useful purpose, unless it can show, by a particular detail, that all the duties which it recommends, are also the true interest of each individual? The peculiar advantage of the foregoing system seems to be, that it furnishes proper mediums for that purpose.

220   That the virtues which are immediately *useful* or *agreeable* to the person possessed of them, are desirable in a view to self-interest, it would surely be superfluous to prove. Moralists, indeed, may spare themselves all the pains which they often take in recommending these duties. To what purpose collect arguments to evince that temperance is advantageous, and the excesses of pleasure hurtful, when it appears that these excesses are only denominated such, because they are hurtful; and that, if the unlimited use of strong liquors, for instance, no more impaired health or the faculties of mind and body than the use of air or water, it would not be a whit more vicious or blameable?

It seems equally superfluous to prove, that the *companionable* virtues of good manners and wit, decency and genteelness, are more desirable than the contrary qualities. Vanity alone, without any other consideration, is a sufficient motive to make us wish for the possession of these accomplishments. No man was ever willingly deficient in this particular. All our failures here proceed from bad education, want of capacity, or a perverse and unpliable disposition. Would you have your company coveted, admired, followed; rather than hated, despised, avoided? Can any one seriously deliberate in the case? As no enjoyment is sincere, without some reference to company and society; so no society can be agreeable, or even tolerable, where a man feels his presence unwelcome, and discovers all around him symptoms of disgust and aversion.

230   But why, in the greater society or confederacy of mankind, should not the case be the same as in particular clubs and companies? Why is it more doubtful, that the enlarged virtues of humanity, generosity, beneficence, are desirable with a view of happiness and self-interest, than the limited endowments of ingenuity and politeness? Are we apprehensive lest those social affections interfere, in a greater and more immediate degree than any other pursuits, with private utility, and cannot be gratified, without some important sacrifice of honour and advantage? If so, we are but ill-instructed in the nature of the human passions, and are more influenced by verbal distinctions than by real differences.

Whatever contradiction may vulgarly be supposed between the *selfish* and *social* sentiments or dispositions, they are really no more opposite than selfish and ambitious, selfish and revengeful, selfish and vain. It is requisite that there be an original propensity of some kind, in order to be a basis to self-love, by giving a relish to the objects of its pursuit; and none more fit for this purpose than benevolence or humanity. The goods of fortune are spent in one gratification or another: the miser who accumulates his annual income, and lends it out at interest, has really spent it in the gratification of his avarice. And it would be difficult to show why a man is more a loser by a generous action, than by any other method of expense; since the utmost which he can attain by the most elaborate selfishness, is the indulgence of some affection.

231   Now if life, without passion, must be altogether insipid and tiresome; let a man suppose that he has full power of modelling his own disposition, and let him deliberate what appetite or desire he would choose for the foundation of his happiness and enjoyment. Every affection, he would

observe, when gratified by success, gives a satisfaction proportioned to its force and violence ; but besides this advantage, common to all, the immediate feeling of benevolence
and friendship, humanity and kindness, is sweet, smooth,
tender, and agreeable, independent of all fortune and accidents.   These virtues are besides attended with a pleasing
consciousness or remembrance, and keep us in humour with
ourselves as well as others; while we retain the agreeable
reflection of having done our part towards mankind and
society. And though all men show a jealousy of our success in
the pursuits of avarice and ambition ; yet are we almost sure
of their good-will and good wishes, so long as we persevere
in the paths of virtue, and employ ourselves in the execution
of generous plans and purposes.   What other passion is
there where we shall find so many advantages united ; an
agreeable sentiment, a pleasing consciousness, a good reputation ? But of these truths, we may observe, men are, of
themselves, pretty much convinced ; nor are they deficient
in their duty to society, because they would not wish to be
generous, friendly, and humane ; but because they do not
feel themselves such.

232   Treating vice with the greatest candour, and making it all
possible concessions, we must acknowledge that there is
not, in any instance, the smallest pretext for giving it the
preference above virtue, with a view of self-interest ; except,
perhaps, in the case of justice, where a man, taking things in
a certain light, may often seem to be a loser by his integrity.
And though it is allowed that, without a regard to property,
no society could subsist ; yet according to the imperfect
way in which human affairs are conducted, a sensible knave,
in particular incidents, may think that an act of iniquity or
infidelity will make a considerable addition to his fortune,
without causing any considerable breach in the social union
and confederacy.   That *honesty is the best policy*, may be
a good general rule, but is liable to many exceptions ; and

he, it may perhaps be thought, conducts himself with most wisdom, who observes the general rule, and takes advantage of all the exceptions.

233   I must confess that, if a man think that this reasoning much requires an answer, it would be a little difficult to find any which will to him appear satisfactory and convincing. If his heart rebel not against such pernicious maxims, if he feel no reluctance to the thoughts of villainy or baseness, he has indeed lost a considerable motive to virtue; and we may expect that this practice will be answerable to his speculation. But in all ingenuous natures, the antipathy to treachery and roguery is too strong to be counterbalanced by any views of profit or pecuniary advantage. Inward peace of mind, consciousness of integrity, a satisfactory review of our own conduct; these are circumstances, very requisite to happiness, and will be cherished and cultivated by every honest man, who feels the importance of them.

Such a one has, besides, the frequent satisfaction of seeing knaves, with all their pretended cunning and abilities, betrayed by their own maxims; and while they purpose to cheat with moderation and secrecy, a tempting incident occurs, nature is frail, and they give into the snare; whence they can never extricate themselves, without a total loss of reputation, and the forfeiture of all future trust and confidence with mankind.

But were they ever so secret and successful, the honest man, if he has any tincture of philosophy, or even common observation and reflection, will discover that they themselves are, in the end, the greatest dupes, and have sacrificed the invaluable enjoyment of a character, with themselves at least, for the acquisition of worthless toys and gewgaws. How little is requisite to supply the *necessities* of nature? And in a view to *pleasure*, what comparison between the unbought satisfaction of conversation, society, study, even health and the common beauties of nature, but above all the peaceful reflection on one's own conduct; what comparison, I say, between these and the feverish, empty amusements of luxury and expense? These natural pleasures, indeed, are really without price; both because they are below all price in their attainment, and above it in their enjoyment

APPENDIX I.

CONCERNING MORAL SENTIMENT.

234   IF the foregoing hypothesis be received, it will now be easy for us to determine the question first started [1], concerning the general principles of morals; and though we postponed the decision of that question, lest it should then involve us in intricate speculations, which are unfit for moral discourses, we may resume it at present, and examine how far either *reason* or *sentiment* enters into all decisions of praise or censure.

One principal foundation of moral praise being supposed to lie in the usefulness of any quality or action, it is evident that *reason* must enter for a considerable share in all decisions of this kind; since nothing but that faculty can instruct us in the tendency of qualities and actions, and point out their beneficial consequences to society and to their possessor. In many cases this is an affair liable to great controversy: doubts may arise; opposite interests may occur; and a preference must be given to one side, from very nice views, and a small overbalance of utility. This is particularly remarkable in questions with regard to justice; as is, indeed, natural to suppose, from that species of utility which attends this virtue [2]. Were every single instance of justice, like that of benevolence, useful to society; this would be a more simple state of the case, and seldom

---

[1] Sect. I.   [2] See App. III.

liable to great controversy.   But as single instances of
justice are often pernicious in their first and immediate tendency, and as the advantage to society results only from the
observance of the general rule, and from the concurrence
and combination of several persons in the same equitable conduct; the case here becomes more intricate and involved.
The various circumstances of society; the various consequences of any practice; the various interests which may
be proposed; these, on many occasions, are doubtful, and
subject to great discussion and inquiry.   The object of
municipal laws is to fix all the questions with regard to
justice: the debates of civilians; the reflections of politicians; the precedents of history and public records, are all
directed to the same purpose.   And a very accurate *reason*
or *judgement* is often requisite, to give the true determination, amidst such intricate doubts arising from obscure or
opposite utilities.

235   But though reason, when fully assisted and improved, be
sufficient to instruct us in the pernicious or useful tendency
of qualities and actions; it is not alone sufficient to produce
any moral blame or approbation.   Utility is only a tendency
to a certain end; and were the end totally indifferent to us,
we should feel the same indifference towards the means.
It is requisite a *sentiment* should here display itself, in
order to give a preference to the useful above the pernicious
tendencies.   This sentiment can be no other than a feeling
for the happiness of mankind, and a resentment of their
misery; since these are the different ends which virtue and
vice have a tendency to promote.   Here therefore *reason*
instructs us in the several tendencies of actions, and
humanity makes a distinction in favour of those which are
useful and beneficial.

236   This partition between the faculties of understanding and
sentiment, in all moral decisions, seems clear from the
preceding hypothesis. But I shall suppose that hypothesis

false : it will then be requisite to look out for some other theory that may be satisfactory; and I dare venture to affirm that none such will ever be found, so long as we suppose reason to be the sole source of morals. To prove this, it will be proper to weigh the five following considerations.

I. It is easy for a false hypothesis to maintain some appearance of truth, while it keeps wholly in generals, makes use of undefined terms, and employs comparisons, instead of instances. This is particularly remarkable in that philosophy, which ascribes the discernment of all moral distinctions to reason alone, without the concurrence of sentiment. It is impossible that, in any particular instance, this hypothesis can so much as be rendered intelligible, whatever specious figure it may make in general declamations and discourses. Examine the crime of *ingratitude,* for instance ; which has place, wherever we observe good-will, expressed and known, together with good-offices performed, on the one side, and a return of ill-will or indifference, with ill-offices or neglect on the other: anatomize all these circumstances, and examine, by your reason alone, in what consists the demerit or blame. You never will come to any issue or conclusion.

237   Reason judges either of *matter of fact* or of *relations.* Enquire then, *first,* where is that matter of fact which we here call *crime* ; point it out ; determine the time of its existence ; describe its essence or nature ; explain the sense or faculty to which it discovers itself. It resides in the mind of the person who is ungrateful. He must, therefore, feel it, and be conscious of it. But nothing is there, except the passion of ill-will or absolute indifference. You cannot say that these, of themselves, always, and in all circumstances, are crimes. No, they are only crimes when directed towards persons who have before expressed and displayed good-will towards us. Consequently, we may infer, that the crime of ingratitude is not any particular individual *fact*; but arises from a complication of circumstances, which, being presented to the spectator, excites the *sentiment* of blame, by the particular structure and fabric of his mind.

238   This representation, you say, is false. Crime, indeed, consists not in a particular *fact*, of whose reality we are assured by *reason*; but it consists in certain *moral relations*, discovered by reason, in the same manner as we discover by reason the truths of geometry or algebra. But what are the relations, I ask, of which you here talk? In the case stated above, I see first good-will and good-offices in one person; then ill-will and ill-offices in the other. Between these, there is a relation of *contrariety*. Does the crime consist in that relation? But suppose a person bore me ill-will or did me ill-offices; and I, in return, were indifferent towards him, or did him good-offices. Here is the same relation of *contrariety*; and yet my conduct is often highly laudable. Twist and turn this matter as much as you will, you can never rest the morality on relation; . but must have recourse to the decisions of sentiment.

When it is affirmed that two and three are equal to the half of ten, this relation of equality I understand perfectly. I conceive, that if ten be divided into two parts, of which one has as many units as the other; and if any of these parts be compared to two added to three, it will contain as many units as that compound number. But when you draw thence a comparison to moral relations, I own that I am altogether at a loss to understand you. A moral action, a crime, such as ingratitude, is a complicated object. Does the morality consist in the relation of its parts to each other? How? After what manner? Specify the relation : be more particular and explicit in your propositions, and you will easily see their falsehood.

239   No, say you, the morality consists in the relation of actions to the rule of right; and they are denominated good or ill, according as they agree or disagree with it. What then is this rule of right? In what does it consist? How

is it determined? By reason, you say, which examines the moral relations of actions. So that moral relations are determined by the comparison of action to a rule. And that rule is determined by considering the moral relations of objects. Is not this fine reasoning?

All this is metaphysics, you cry. That is enough; there needs nothing more to give a strong presumption of falsehood. Yes, reply I, here are metaphysics surely; but they are all on your side, who advance an abstruse hypothesis, which can never be made intelligible, nor quadrate with any particular instance or illustration. The hypothesis which we embrace is plain. It maintains that morality is determined by sentiment. It defines virtue to be *whatever mental action or quality gives to a spectator the pleasing sentiment of approbation;* and vice the contrary. We then proceed to examine a plain matter of fact, to wit, what actions have this influence. We consider all the circumstances in which these actions agree, and thence endeavour to extract some general observations with regard to these sentiments. If you call this metaphysics, and find anything abstruse here, you need only conclude that your turn of mind is not suited to the moral sciences.

240 II. When a man, at any time, deliberates concerning his own conduct (as, whether he had better, in a particular emergence, assist a brother or a benefactor), he must consider these separate relations, with all the circumstances and situations of the persons, in order to determine the superior duty and obligation; and in order to determine the proportion of lines in any triangle, it is necessary to examine the nature of that figure, and the relation which its several parts bear to each other. But notwithstanding this appearing similarity in the two cases, there is, at bottom, an extreme difference between them. A speculative reasoner concerning triangles or circles considers the several known and given relations of the parts of these figures, and thence infers

U

some unknown relation, which is dependent on the former. But in moral deliberations we must be acquainted beforehand with all the objects, and all their relations to each other ; and from a comparison of the whole, fix our choice or approbation.   No new fact to be ascertained ; no new relation to be discovered.   All the circumstances of the case are supposed to be laid before us, ere we can fix any sentence of blame or approbation.   If any material circumstance be yet unknown or doubtful, we must first employ our inquiry or intellectual faculties to assure us of it ; and must suspend for a time all moral decision or sentiment.   While we are ignorant whether a man were aggressor or not, how can we determine whether the person who killed him be criminal or innocent?   But after every circumstance, every relation is known, the understanding has no further room to operate,_ nor any object on which it could employ itself. The approbation or blame which then ensues, cannot be the work of the judgement, but of the heart ; and is not a speculative proposition or affirmation, but an active feeling or sentiment.   In the disquisitions of the understanding, from known circumstances and relations, we infer some new and unknown.   In moral decisions, all the circumstances and relations must be previously known ; and the mind, from the contemplation of the whole, feels some new impression of affection or disgust, esteem or contempt, approbation or blame.

241   Hence the great difference between a mistake of *fact* and one of *right*; and hence the reason why the one is commonly criminal and not the other.   When Oedipus killed Laius, he was ignorant of the relation, and from circumstances, innocent and involuntary, formed erroneous opinions concerning the action which he committed. But when Nero killed Agrippina, all the relations between himself and the person, and all the circumstances of the fact, were previously known to him ; but the motive of

revenge, or fear, or interest, prevailed in his savage heart over the sentiments of duty and humanity. And when we express that detestation against him to which he himself, in a little time, became insensible, it is not that we see any relations, of which he was ignorant; but that, for the rectitude of our disposition, we feel sentiments against which he was hardened from flattery and a long perseverance in the most enormous crimes. In these sentiments then, not in a discovery of relations of any kind, do all moral determinations consist. Before we can pretend to form any decision of this kind, everything must be known and ascertained on the side of the object or action. Nothing remains but to feel, on our part, some sentiment of blame or approbation; whence we pronounce the action criminal or virtuous.

242 III. This doctrine will become still more evident, if we compare moral beauty with natural, to which in many particulars it bears so near a resemblance. It is on the proportion, relation, and position of parts, that all natural beauty depends; but it would be absurd thence to infer, that the perception of beauty, like that of truth in geometrical problems, consists wholly in the perception of relations, and was performed entirely by the understanding or intellectual faculties. In all the sciences, our mind from the known relations investigates the unknown. But in all decisions of taste or external beauty, all the relations are beforehand obvious to the eye; and we thence proceed to feel a sentiment of complacency or disgust, according to the nature of the object, and disposition of our organs.

Euclid has fully explained all the qualities of the circle; but has not in any proposition said a word of its beauty. The reason is evident. The beauty is not a quality of the circle. It lies not in any part of the line, whose parts are equally distant from a common centre. It is only the effect which that figure produces upon the mind, whose peculiar fabric of structure renders it susceptible of such sentiments. In vain would you look for it in the circle, or seek it, either by your senses or by mathematical reasoning, in all the properties of that figure.

Attend to Palladio and Perrault, while they explain all the parts and proportions of a pillar. They talk of the cornice, and frieze, and base, and entablature, and shaft and architrave; and give the description and position of each of these members. But should you ask the description and position of its beauty, they would readily reply, that the beauty is not in any of the parts or members of a pillar, but results from the whole, when that complicated figure is presented to an intelligent mind, susceptible to those finer sensations. Till such a spectator appear, there is nothing but a figure of such particular dimensions and proportions: from his sentiments alone arise its elegance and beauty.

Again; attend to Cicero, while he paints the crimes of a Verres or a Catiline. You must acknowledge that the moral turpitude results, in the same manner, from the contemplation of the whole, when presented to a being whose organs have such a particular structure and formation. The orator may paint rage, insolence, barbarity on the one side; meekness, suffering, sorrow, innocence on the other. But if you feel no indignation or compassion arise in you from this complication of circumstances, you would in vain ask him, in what consists the crime or villainy, which he so vehemently exclaims against? At what time, or on what subject it first began to exist? And what has a few months afterwards become of it, when every disposition and thought of all the actors is totally altered or annihilated? No satisfactory answer can be given to any of these questions, upon the abstract hypothesis of morals; and we must at last acknowledge, that the crime or immorality is no particular fact or relation, which can be the object of the understanding, but arises entirely from the sentiment of disapprobation, which, by the structure of human nature, we unavoidably feel on the apprehension of barbarity or treachery.

243   IV. Inanimate objects may bear to each other all the same relations which we observe in moral agents; though the former can never be the object of love or hatred, nor are consequently susceptible of merit or iniquity. A young tree, which over-tops and destroys its parent, stands in all the same relations with Nero, when he murdered Agrippina; and if morality consisted merely in relations, would no doubt be equally criminal.

244   V. It appears evident that the ultimate ends of human actions can never, in any case, be accounted for by *reason*, but recommend themselves entirely to the sentiments and affections of mankind, without any dependance on the intellectual faculties. Ask a man *why he uses exercise*; he will answer, *because he desires to keep his health*. If you then enquire, *why he desires health*, he will readily reply, *because sickness is painful*. If you push your enquiries farther, and desire a reason *why he hates pain*, it is impossible he can ever give any. This is an ultimate end, and is never referred to any other object.

Perhaps to your second question, *why he desires health*, he may also reply, that *it is necessary for the exercise of his calling*. If you ask, *why he is anxious on that head*, he will answer, *because he desires to get money*. If you demand *Why? It is the instrument of pleasure*, says he. And beyond this it is an absurdity to ask for a reason. It is impossible there can be a progress *in infinitum*; and that one thing can always be a reason why another is desired. Something must be desirable on its own account, and because of its immediate accord or agreement with human sentiment and affection.

245   Now as virtue is an end, and is desirable on its own

account, without fee and reward, merely for the immediate satisfaction which it conveys; it is requisite that there should be some sentiment which it touches, some internal taste or feeling, or whatever you may please to call it, which distinguishes moral good and evil, and which embraces the one and rejects the other.

246   Thus the distinct boundaries and offices of *reason* and of *taste* are easily ascertained. The former conveys the knowledge of truth and falsehood: the latter gives the sentiment of beauty and deformity, vice and virtue. The one discovers objects as they really stand in nature, without addition or diminution: the other has a productive faculty, and gilding or staining all natural objects with the colours, borrowed from internal sentiment, raises in a manner a new creation. Reason being cool and disengaged, is no motive to action, and directs only the impulse received from appetite or inclination, by showing us the means of attaining happiness or avoiding misery: Taste, as it gives pleasure or pain, and thereby constitutes happiness or misery, becomes a motive to action, and is the first spring or impulse to desire and volition. From circumstances and relations, known or supposed, the former leads us to the discovery of the concealed and unknown: after all circumstances and relations are laid before us, the latter makes us feel from the whole a new sentiment of blame or approbation. The standard of the one, being founded on the nature of things, is eternal and inflexible, even by the will of the Supreme Being: the standard of the other, arising from the eternal frame and constitution of animals, is ultimately derived from that Supreme Will, which bestowed on each being its peculiar nature, and arranged the several classes and orders of existence.

APPENDIX II.

247 THERE is a principle, supposed to prevail among many, which is utterly incompatible with all virtue or moral sentiment; and as it can proceed from nothing but the most depraved disposition, so in its turn it tends still further to encourage that depravity. This principle is, that all *benevolence* is mere hypocrisy, friendship a cheat, public spirit a farce, fidelity a snare to procure trust and confidence; and that while all of us, at bottom, pursue only our private interest, we wear these fair disguises, in order to put others off their guard, and expose them·the more to our wiles and machinations. What heart one must be possessed of who possesses such principles, and who feels no internal sentiment that belies so pernicious a theory, it is easy to imagine: and also what degree of affection and benevolence he can bear to a species whom he represents under such odious colours, and supposes so little susceptible of gratitude or any return of affection. Or if we should not ascribe these principles wholly to a corrupted heart, we must at least account for them from the most careless and precipitate examination. Superficial reasoners, indeed, observing many false pretences among mankind, and feeling, perhaps, no very strong restraint in their own disposition, might draw a general and a hasty conclusion that all is equally corrupted, and that men,

different from all other animals, and indeed from all other
species of existence, admit of no degrees of good or bad,
but are, in every instance, the same creatures under
different disguises and appearances.

248   There is another principle, somewhat resembling the
former; which has been much insisted on by philosophers,
and has been the foundation of many a system; that,
whatever affection one may feel, or imagine he feels
for others, no passion is, or can be disinterested; that
the most generous friendship, however sincere, is a modi-
fication of self-love; and that, even unknown to ourselves,
we seek only our own gratification, while we appear the
most deeply engaged in schemes for the liberty and
happiness of mankind. By a turn of imagination, by
a refinement of reflection, by an enthusiasm of passion,
we seem to take part in the interests of others, and imagine
ourselves divested of all selfish considerations: but, at
bottom, the most generous patriot and most niggardly
miser, the bravest hero and most abject coward, have, in
every action, an equal regard to their own happiness and
welfare.

Whoever concludes from the seeming tendency of this
opinion, that those, who make profession of it, cannot
possibly feel the true sentiments of benevolence, or have
any regard for genuine virtue, will often find himself, in
practice, very much mistaken. Probity and honour were
no strangers to Epicurus and his sect. Atticus and Horace
seem to have enjoyed from nature, and cultivated by
reflection, as generous and friendly dispositions as any
disciple of the austerer schools. And among the modern,
Hobbes and Locke, who maintained the selfish system of
morals, lived irreproachable lives; though the former lay
not under any restraint of religion which might supply the
defects of his philosophy.

249   An epicurean or a Hobbist readily allows, that there is such a thing as a friendship in the world, without hypocrisy or disguise; though he may attempt, by a philosophical chymistry, to resolve the elements of this passion, if I may so speak, into those of another, and explain every affection to be self-love, twisted and moulded, by a particular turn of imagination, into a variety of appearances. But as the same turn of imagination prevails not in every man, nor gives the same direction to the original passion; this is sufficient even according to the selfish system to make the widest difference in human characters, and denominate one man virtuous and humane, another vicious and meanly interested. I esteem the man whose self-love, by whatever means, is so directed as to give him a concern for others, and render him serviceable to society: as I hate or despise him, who has no regard to any thing beyond his own gratifications and enjoyments. In vain would you suggest that these characters, though seemingly opposite, are at bottom the same, and that a very inconsiderable turn of thought forms the whole difference between them. Each character, notwithstanding these inconsiderable differences, appears to me, in practice, pretty durable and untransmutable. And I find not in this more than in other subjects, that the natural sentiments arising from the general appearances of things are easily destroyed by subtile reflections concerning the minute origin of these appearances. Does not the lively, cheerful colour of a countenance inspire me with complacency and pleasure; even though I learn from philosophy that all difference of complexion arises from the most minute differences of thickness, in the most minute parts of the skin; by means of which a superficies is qualified to reflect one of the original colours of light, and absorb the others?

250   But though the question concerning the universal or partial selfishness of man be not so material as is usually imagined to morality and practice, it is certainly of consequence in the speculative science of human nature, and is a proper object

of curiosity and enquiry.   It may not, therefore, be unsuitable, in this place, to bestow a few reflections upon it[1].

The most obvious objection to the selfish hypothesis is,
that, as it is contrary to common feeling and our most unprejudiced notions, there is required the highest stretch of philosophy to establish so extraordinary a paradox.   To the
most careless observer there appear to be such dispositions
as benevolence and generosity; such affections as love, friendship, compassion, gratitude.   These sentiments have their
causes, effects, objects, and operations, marked by common
language and observation, and plainly distinguished from
those of the selfish passions.   And as this is the obvious
appearance of things, it must be admitted, till some hypothesis be discovered, which by penetrating deeper into
human nature, may prove the former affections to be nothing
but modifications of the latter.   All attempts of this kind
have hitherto proved fruitless, and seem to have proceeded
entirely from that love of *simplicity* which has been the
source of much false reasoning in philosophy.   I shall not
here enter into any detail on the present subject.   Many able
philosophers have shown the insufficiency of these systems.
And I shall take for granted what, I believe, the smallest
reflection will make evident to every impartial enquirer.

251   But the nature of the subject furnishes the strongest
presumption, that no better system will ever, for the future,

---

[1] Benevolence naturally divides into two kinds, the *general* and the
particular.   The first is, where we have no friendship or connexion or
esteem for the person, but feel only a general sympathy with him or
a compassion for his pains, and a congratulation with his pleasures.
The other species of benevolence is founded on an opinion of virtue, on
services done us, or on some particular connexions.   Both these sentiments must be allowed real in human nature: but whether they will
resolve into some nice considerations of self-love, is a question more
curious than important.   The former sentiment, to wit, that of general
benevolence, or humanity, or sympathy, we shall have occasion frequently to treat of in the course of this enquiry ; and I assume it as real,
from general experience, without any other proof.

be invented, in order to account for the origin of the benevolent from the selfish affections, and reduce all the various
emotions of the human mind to a perfect simplicity. The
case is not the same in this species of philosophy as in physics.
Many an hypothesis in nature, contrary to first appearances,
has been found, on more accurate scrutiny, solid and satisfactory. Instances of this kind are so frequent that a judicious, as well as witty philosopher[1], has ventured to affirm,
if there be more than one way in which any phenomenon
may be produced, that there is general presumption for its
arising from the causes which are the least obvious and
familiar. But the presumption always lies on the other side,
in all enquiries concerning the origin of our passions, and
of the internal operations of the human mind. The simplest
and most obvious cause which can there be assigned for
any phenomenon, is probably the true one. When a philosopher, in the explication of his system, is obliged to have
recourse to some very intricate and refined reflections, and
to suppose them essential to the production of any passion or
emotion, we have reason to be extremely on our guard against
so fallacious an hypothesis. The affections are not susceptible
of any impression from the refinements of reason or imagination ; and it is always found that a vigorous exertion of the
latter faculties, necessarily, from the narrow capacity of
the human mind, destroys all activity in the former. Our
predominant motive or intention is, indeed, frequently concealed from ourselves when it is mingled and confounded
with other motives which the mind, from vanity or self-
conceit, is desirous of supposing more prevalent : but there is
no instance that a concealment of this nature has ever arisen
from the abstruseness and intricacy of the motive. A man
that has lost a friend and patron may flatter himself that
all his grief arises from generous sentiments, without any
mixture of narrow or interested considerations: but a man that

[1] Mons. Fontenelle.

grieves for a valuable friend, who needed his patronage and protection; how can we suppose, that his passionate tenderness arises from some metaphysical regards to a self-interest, which has no foundation or reality? We may as well imagine that minute wheels and springs, like those of a watch, give motion to a loaded waggon, as account for the origin of passion from such abstruse reflections.

252   Animals are found susceptible of kindness, both to their own species and to ours; nor is there, in this case, the least suspicion of disguise or artifice. Shall we account for all *their* sentiments, too, from refined deductions of self-interest? Or if we admit a disinterested benevolence in the inferior species, by what rule of analogy can we refuse it in the superior?

Love between the sexes begets a complacency and good-will, very distinct from the gratification of an appetite. Tenderness to their offspring, in all sensible beings, is commonly able alone to counter-balance the strongest motives of self-love, and has no manner of dependance on that affection. What interest can a fond mother have in view, who loses her health by assiduous attendance on her sick child, and afterwards languishes and dies of grief, when freed, by its death, from the slavery of that attendance?

Is gratitude no affection of the human breast, or is that a word merely, without any meaning or reality? Have we no satisfaction in one man's company above another's, and no desire of the welfare of our friend, even though absence or death should prevent us from all participation in it? Or what is it commonly, that gives us any participation in it, even while alive and present, but our affection and regard to him?

These and a thousand other instances are marks of a general benevolence in human nature, where no *real* interest binds us to the object. And how an *imaginary* interest known and avowed for such, can be the origin of any passion or emotion, seems difficult to explain. No satisfactory hypothesis of this kind has yet been discovered; nor is there the smallest probability that the future industry of men will ever be attended with more favourable success.

253   But farther, if we consider rightly of the matter, we shall find that the hypothesis which allows of a disinterested benevolence, distinct from self-love, has really more *simplicity* in it, and is more conformable to the analogy of nature than that which pretends to resolve all friendship and humanity into this latter principle.   There are bodily wants or appetites acknowledged by every one, which necessarily precede all sensual enjoyment, and carry us directly to seek possession of the object.   Thus, hunger and thirst have eating and drinking for their end; and from the gratification of these primary appetites arises a pleasure, which may become the object of another species of desire or inclination that is secondary and interested.   In the same manner there are mental passions by which we are impelled immediately to seek particular objects, such as fame or power, or vengeance without any regard to interest; and when these objects are attained a pleasing enjoyment ensues, as the consequence of our indulged affections.   Nature must, by the internal frame and constitution of the mind, give an original propensity to fame, ere we can reap any pleasure from that acquisition, or pursue it from motives of self-love, and desire of happiness. If I have no vanity, I take no delight in praise : if I be void of ambition, power gives me no enjoyment: if I be not angry, the punishment of an adversary is totally indifferent to me.   In all these cases there is a passion which points immediately to the object, and constitutes it our good or happiness;   as there are other secondary passions which afterwards arise and pursue it as a part of our happiness, when once it is constituted such by our original affections. Were there no appetite of any kind antecedent to self-love, that propensity could scarcely ever exert itself; because we should, in that case, have felt few and slender pains or pleasures, and have little misery or happiness to avoid or to pursue.

254   Now where is the difficulty in conceiving, that this may likewise be the case with benevolence and friendship, and that, from the original frame of our temper, we may feel a desire of another's happiness or good, which, by means of that affection, becomes our own good, and is afterwards pursued, from the combined motives of benevolence and self-enjoyments? Who sees not that vengeance, from the force alone of passion, may be so eagerly pursued, as to make us knowingly neglect every consideration of ease, interest, or safety ; and, like some vindictive animals, infuse our very souls into the wounds we give an enemy[1] ; and what a malignant philosophy must it be, that will not allow to humanity and friendship the same privileges which are undisputably granted to the darker passions of enmity and resentment; such a philosophy is more like a satyr than a true delineation or description of human nature ; and may be a good foundation for paradoxical wit and raillery, but is a very bad one for any serious argument or reasoning.

---

[1] Animasque in vulnere ponunt.   VIRG.   Dum alteri noceat, sui negligens, says Seneca of Anger.   De Ira, l. i.

APPENDIX III.

SOME FARTHER CONSIDERATIONS WITH REGARD
TO JUSTICE.

255 THE intention of this Appendix is to give some more
particular explication of the origin and nature of Justice,
and to mark some differences between it and the other
virtues.

The social virtues of humanity and benevolence exert
their influence immediately by a direct tendency or instinct,
which chiefly keeps in view the simple object, moving the
affections, and comprehends not any scheme or system, nor
the consequences resulting from the concurrence, imitation,
or example of others. A parent flies to the relief of his
child; transported by that natural sympathy which actuates
him, and which affords no leisure to reflect on the sentiments or conduct of the rest of mankind in like circumstances. A generous man cheerfully embraces an opportunity of serving his friend; because he then feels himself
under the dominion of the beneficent affections, nor is he
concerned whether any other person in the universe were
ever before actuated by such noble motives, or will ever
afterwards prove their influence. In all these cases the
social passions have in view a single individual object, and
pursue the safety or happiness alone of the person loved
and esteemed. With this they are satisfied: in this they

acquiesce. And as the good, resulting from their benign influence, is in itself complete and entire, it also excites the moral sentiment of approbation, without any reflection on farther consequences, and without any more enlarged views of the concurrence or imitation of the other members of society. On the contrary, were the generous friend or disinterested patriot to stand alone in the practice of beneficence, this would rather inhance his value in our eyes, and join the praise of rarity and novelty to his other more exalted merits.

256   The case is not the same with the social virtues of justice and fidelity. They are highly useful, or indeed absolutely necessary to the well-being of mankind : but the benefit resulting from them is not the consequence of every individual single act; but arises from the whole scheme or system concurred in by the whole, or the greater part of the society. General peace and order are the attendants of justice or a general abstinence from the possessions of others; but a particular regard to the particular right of one individual citizen may frequently, considered in itself, be productive of pernicious consequences. The result of the individual acts is here, in many instances, directly opposite to that of the whole system of actions ; and the former may be extremely hurtful, while the latter is, to the highest degree, advantageous. Riches, inherited from a parent, are, in a bad man's hand, the instrument of mischief. The right of succession may, in one instance, be hurtful. Its benefit arises only from the observance of the general rule ; and it is sufficient, if compensation be thereby made for all the ills and inconveniences which flow from particular characters and situations.

Cyrus, young and unexperienced, considered only the individual case before him, and reflected on a limited fitness and convenience, when he assigned the long coat to the tall boy, and the short coat to the other of smaller size. His

governor instructed him better, while he pointed out more
enlarged views and consequences, and informed his pupil
of the general, inflexible rules, necessary to support general
peace and order in society.

The happiness and prosperity of mankind, arising from
the social virtue of benevolence and its subdivisions, may
be compared to a wall, built by many hands, which still
rises by each stone that is heaped upon it, and receives
increase proportional to the diligence and care of each
workman. The same happiness, raised by the social
virtue of justice and its subdivisions, may be compared to
the building of a vault, where each individual stone would,
of itself, fall to the ground; nor is the whole fabric
supported but by the mutual assistance and combination of
its corresponding parts.

All the laws of nature, which regulate property, as well as
all civil laws, are general, and regard alone some essential
circumstances of the case, without taking into consideration
the characters, situations, and connexions of the person
concerned, or any particular consequences which may result
from the determination of these laws in any particular
case which offers. They deprive, without scruple, a beneficent man of all his possessions, if acquired by mistake,
without a good title; in order to bestow them on a selfish
miser, who has already heaped up immense stores of
superfluous riches. Public utility requires that property
should be regulated by general inflexible rules; and though
such rules are adopted as best serve the same end of public
utility, it is impossible for them to prevent all particular
hardships, or make beneficial consequences result from
every individual case. It is sufficient, if the whole plan
or scheme be necessary to the support of civil society,
and if the balance of good, in the main, do thereby pre-
ponderate much above that of evil. Even the general
laws of the universe, though planned by infinite wisdom,

cannot exclude all evil or inconvenience in every particular operation.

257   It has been asserted by some, that justice arises from Human Conventions, and proceeds from the voluntary choice, consent, or combination of mankind. If by *convention* be here meant a *promise* (which is the most usual sense of the word) nothing can be more absurd than this position. The observance of promises is itself one of the most considerable parts of justice, and we are not surely bound to keep our word because we have given our word to keep it. But if by convention be meant a sense of common interest; which sense each man feels in his own breast, which he remarks in his fellows, and which carries him, in concurrence with others, into a general plan or system of actions, which tends to public utility; it must be owned, that, in this sense, justice arises from human conventions. For if it be allowed (what is, indeed, evident) that the particular consequences of a particular act of justice may be hurtful to the public as well as to individuals; it follows that every man, in embracing that virtue, must have an eye to the whole plan or system, and must expect the concurrence of his fellows in the same conduct and behaviour. Did all his views terminate in the consequences of each act of his own, his benevolence and humanity, as well as his self-love, might often prescribe to him measures of conduct very different from those which are agreeable to the strict rules of right and justice.

Thus, two men pull the oars of a boat by common convention for common interest, without any promise or contract: thus gold and silver are made the measures of exchange; thus speech and words and language are fixed by human convention and agreement. Whatever is advantageous to two or more persons, if all perform their part; but what loses all advantage if only one perform, can arise from no other principle. There would otherwise be no motive for any one of them to enter into that scheme of conduct[1].

258   The word *natural* is commonly taken in so many senses and is of so loose a signification, that it seems vain to dispute whether justice be natural or not. If self-love, if benevolence be natural to man ; if reason and forethought be also natural ; then may the same epithet be applied to justice, order, fidelity, property, society. Men's inclination, their necessities, lead them to combine ; their understanding and experience tell them that this combination is impossible where each governs himself by no rule, and pays no regard to the possessions of others : and from these passions and reflections conjoined, as soon as we observe like passions and reflections in others, the sentiment of justice, throughout all ages, has infallibly and certainly had place to some degree or other in every individual of the human species. In so sagacious an animal, what necessarily arises from the exertion of his intellectual faculties may justly be esteemed natural[2].

---

[1] This theory concerning the origin of property, and consequently of justice, is, in the main, the same with that hinted at and adopted by Grotius. 'Hinc discimus, quae fuerit causa, ob quam a primaeva communione rerum primo mobilium, deinde et immobilium discessum est: nimirum quod cum non contenti homines vesci sponte natis, antra habitare, corpore aut nudo agere, aut corticibus arborum ferarumve pellibus vestito, vitae genus exquisitius delegissent, industria opus fuit, quam singuli rebus singulis adhiberent: Quo minus autem fructus in commune conferrentur, primum obstitit locorum, in quae homines discesserunt, distantia, deinde justitiae et amoris defectus, per quem fiebat, ut nec in labore, nec in consumtione fructuum, quae debebat, aequalitas servaretur. Simul discimus, quomodo res in proprietatem iverint; non animi actu solo, neque enim scire alii poterant, quid alii suum esse vellent, ut eo abstinerent, et idem velle plures poterant; sed pacto quodam aut expresso, ut per divisionem, aut tacito, ut per occupationem ' *De jure belli et pacis.* Lib. ii. cap. 2. § 2. art. 4 and 5.

[2] Natural may be opposed, either to what is *unusual, miraculous,* or *artificial.* In the two former senses, justice and property are undoubtedly natural. But as they suppose reason, forethought, design, and a social union and confederacy among men, perhaps that epithet cannot

259   Among all civilized nations it has been the constant
endeavour to remove everything arbitrary and partial from
the decision of property, and to fix the sentence of judges
by such general views and considerations as may be equal to
every member of society.   For besides, that nothing could
be more dangerous than to accustom the bench, even in the
smallest instance, to regard private friendship or enmity;
it is certain, that men, where they imagine that there was
no other reason for the preference of their adversary but
personal favour, are apt to entertain the strongest ill-will
against the magistrates and judges.   When natural reason,
therefore, points out no fixed view of public utility by which
a controversy of property can be decided, positive laws are
often framed to supply its place, and direct the procedure
of all courts of judicature.   Where these too fail, as often
happens, precedents are called for; and a former decision,
though given itself without any sufficient reason, justly
becomes a sufficient reason for a new decision.   If direct
laws and precedents be wanting, imperfect and indirect ones
are brought in aid; and the controverted case is ranged
under them by analogical reasonings and comparisons, and
similitudes, and correspondencies, which are often more
fanciful than real.   In general, it may safely be affirmed
that jurisprudence is, in this respect, different from all the
sciences; and that in many of its nicer questions, there
cannot properly be said to be truth or falsehood on either
side.   If one pleader bring the case under any former law
or precedent, by a refined analogy or comparison; the
opposite pleader is not at a loss to find an opposite analogy
or comparison: and the preference given by the judge is

strictly, in the last sense, be applied to them.   Had men lived without
society, property had never been known, and neither justice nor injustice
had ever existed.   But society among human creatures had been impossible without reason and forethought.   Inferior animals, that unite, are
guided by instinct, which supplies the place of reason.   But all these
disputes are merely verbal.

often founded more on taste and imagination than on any solid argument. Public utility is the general object of all courts of judicature; and this utility too requires a stable rule in all controversies : but where several rules, nearly equal and indifferent, present themselves, it is a very slight turn of thought which fixes the decision in favour of either party [1].

[1] That there be a separation or distinction of possessions, and that this separation be steady and constant; this is absolutely required by the interests of society, and hence the origin of justice and property. What possessions are assigned to particular persons; this is, generally speaking, pretty indifferent ; and is often determined by very frivolous views and considerations. We shall mention a few particulars.

Were a society formed among several independent members, the most obvious rule, which could be agreed on, would be to annex property to *present* possession, and leave every one a right to what he at present enjoys. The relation of possession, which takes place between the person and the object, naturally draws on the relation of property.

For a like reason, occupation or first possession becomes the foundation of property

Where a man bestows labour and industry upon any object, which before belonged to no body ; as in cutting down and shaping a tree, in cultivating a field, &c., the alterations, which he produces, causes a relation between him and the object, and naturally engages us to annex it to him by the new relation of property. This cause here concurs with the public utility, which consists in the encouragement given to industry and labour.

Perhaps too, private humanity towards the possessor concurs, in this instance, with the other motives, and engages us to leave with him what he has acquired by his sweat and labour; and what he has flattered himself in the constant enjoyment of For though private humanity can, by no means, be the origin of justice; since the latter virtue so often contradicts the former ; yet when the rule of separate and constant possession is once formed by the indispensable necessities of society, private humanity, and an aversion to the doing a hardship to another, may, in a particular instance, give rise to a particular rule of property

I am much inclined to think, that the right of succession or inheritance much depends on those connexions of the imagination, and that the relation to a former proprietor begetting a relation to the object, is the cause why the property is transferred to a man after the death of his kinsman. It is true; industry is more encouraged by the transference of possession to children or near relations: but this con-

260   We may just observe, before we conclude this subject, that after the laws of justice are fixed by views of general utility, the injury, the hardship, the harm, which result to any individual from a violation of them, enter very much into consideration, and are a great source of that universal blame which attends every wrong or iniquity. By the laws of society, this coat, this horse is mine, and *ought* to remain perpetually in my possession : I reckon on the secure enjoyment of it : by depriving me of it, you disappoint my expectations, and doubly displease me, and offend every bystander. It is a public wrong, so far as the rules of equity are violated : it is a private harm, so far as an individual is injured. And though the second consideration could have

siderata will only have place in a cultivated society ; whereas the right of succession is regarded even among the greatest Barbarians.

Acquisition of property by *accession* can be explained no way but by having recourse to the relations and connexions of the imagination.

The property of rivers, by the laws of most nations, and by the natural turn of our thoughts, is attributed to the proprietors of their banks, excepting such vast rivers as the Rhine or the Danube, which seem too large to follow as an accession to the property of the neighbouring fields. Yet even these rivers are considered as the property of that nation, through whose dominions they run ; the idea of a nation being of a suitable bulk to correspond with them, and bear them such a relation in the fancy.

The accessions, which are made to land, bordering upon rivers, follow the land, say the civilians, provided it be made by what they call *alluvion*, that is, insensibly and imperceptibly ; which are circumstances, that assist the imagination in the conjunction.

Where there is any considerable portion torn at once from one bank and added to another, it becomes not *his* property, whose land it falls on, till it unite with the land, and till the trees and plants have spread their roots into both. Before that, the thought does not sufficiently join them.

In short, we must ever distinguish between the necessity of a separation and constancy in men's possession, and the rules, which assign particular objects to particular persons. The first necessity is obvious, strong, and invincible : the latter may depend on a public utility more light and frivolous, on the sentiment of private humanity and aversion to private hardship, on positive laws, on precedents, analogies, and very fine connexions and turns of the imagination.

no place, were not the former previously established : for otherwise the distinction of *mine* and *thine* would be unknown in society : yet there is no question but the regard to general good is much enforced by the respect to particular. What injures the community, without hurting any individual, is often more lightly thought of. But where the greatest public wrong is also conjoined with a considerable private one, no wonder the highest disapprobation attends so iniquitous a behaviour.

APPENDIX IV.

261 NOTHING is more usual than for philosophers to encroach upon the province of grammarians ; and to engage in disputes of words, while they imagine that they are handling controversies of the deepest importance and concern. It was in order to avoid altercations, so frivolous and endless, that I endeavoured to state with the utmost caution the object of our present enquiry ; and proposed simply to collect, on the one hand, a list of those mental qualities which are the object of love or esteem, and form a part of personal merit; and on the other hand, a catalogue of those qualities which are the object of censure or reproach, and which detract from the character of the person possessed of them ; subjoining some reflections concerning the origin of these sentiments of praise or blame. On all occasions, where there might arise the least hesitation, I avoided the terms *virtue* and *vice*; because some of those qualities, which I classed among the objects of praise, receive, in the English language, the appellation of *talents*, rather than of virtues ; as some of the blameable or censurable qualities are often called *defects*, rather than vices. It may now, perhaps, be expected that before we conclude this moral enquiry, we should exactly separate the one from the other ; should mark the precise boundaries of virtues and talents, vices, and defects ; and should explain the reason and origin of that distinction. But in order to excuse myself from this undertaking, which would, at last, prove only a grammatical enquiry, I shall subjoin the four following reflections, which shall contain all that I intend to say on the present subject.

262 *First,* I do not find that in the English, or any other modern tongue, the boundaries are exactly fixed between virtues and talents, vices and defects, or that a precise definition can be given of the one as contradistinguished from the other. Were we to say, for instance, that the esteemable qualities alone, which are voluntary, are entitled to the appellation of virtues; we should soon recollect the qualities of courage, equanimity, patience, self-command; with many others, which almost every language classes under this appellation, though they depend little or not at all on our choice. Should we affirm that the qualities alone, which prompt us to act our part in society, are entitled to that honourable distinction; it must immediately occur that these are indeed the most valuable qualites, and are commonly denominated the *social* virtues; but that this very epithet supposes that there are also virtues of another species. Should we lay hold of the distinction between *intellectual* and *moral* endowments, and affirm the last alone to be the real and genuine virtues, because they alone lead to action; we should find that many of those qualities, usually called intellectual virtues, such as prudence, penetration, discernment, discretion, had also a considerable influence on conduct The distinction between the *heart* and the *head* may also be adopted: the qualities of the first may be defined such as in their immediate exertion are accompanied with a feeling of sentiment; and these alone may be called the genuine virtues: but industry, frugality, temperance, secrecy, perseverance, and many other laudable powers or habits, generally stiled virtues, are exerted without any immediate sentiment in the person possessed of them, and are only known to him by their effects. It is fortunate, amidst all this seeming perplexity, that the question, being merely verbal, cannot possibly be of any importance. A moral, philosophical discourse needs not enter into all these caprices of language, which are so variable in different dialects, and in different ages of the same dialect. But on the whole, it seems to me, that though it is always allowed, that there are virtues of many different kinds, yet, when a man is called *virtuous*, or is denominated a man of virtue, we chiefly regard his social qualities, which are, indeed, the most valuable. It is, at the same time, certain, that any remarkable defect in courage, temperance, economy, industry, understanding, dignity of mind, would bereave even a very good-natured, honest man of this honourable appellation. Who did ever say, except by way of irony, that such a one was a man of great virtue, but an egregious blockhead?

263   But, *secondly*, it is no wonder that languages should not be very precise in marking the boundaries between virtues and talents, vices and defects; since there is so little distinction made in our internal estimation of them. It seems indeed certain, that the *sentiment* of conscious worth, the self-satisfaction proceeding from a review of a man's own conduct and character; it seems certain, I say, that this sentiment, which, though the most common of all others, has no proper name in our language[1], arises from the endowments of courage and capacity, industry and ingenuity, as well as from any other mental excellencies. Who, on the other hand, is not deeply mortified with reflecting on his own folly and dissoluteness, and feels not a secret sting

[1] The term, pride, is commonly taken in a bad sense; but this sentiment seems indifferent, and may be either good or bad, according as it is well or ill founded, and according to the other circumstances which accompany it. The French express this sentiment by the term, *amour propre*, but as they also express self-love as well as vanity by the same term, there arises thence a great confusion in Rochefoucault, and many of their moral writers.

or compunction whenever his memory presents any past occurrence, where he behaved with stupidity of ill-manners? No time can efface the cruel ideas of a man's own foolish conduct, or of affronts, which cowardice or impudence has brought upon him. They still haunt his solitary hours, damp his most aspiring thoughts, and show him, even to himself, in the most contemptible and most odious colours imaginable.

What is there too we are more anxious to conceal from others than such blunders, infirmities, and meannesses, or more dread to have exposed by raillery and satire? And is not the chief object of vanity, our bravery or learning, our wit or breeding, our eloquence or address, our taste or abilities? These we display with care, if not with ostentation; and we commonly show more ambition of excelling in them, than even in the social virtues themselves, which are, in reality, of such superior excellence. Good-nature and honesty, especially the latter, are so indispensably required, that, though the greatest censure attends any violation of these duties, no eminent praise follows such common instances of them, as seem essential to the support of human society. And hence the reason, in my opinion, why, though men often extol so liberally the qualities of their heart, they are shy in commending the endowments of their head: because the latter virtues, being supposed more rare and extraordinary, are observed to be the more usual objects of pride and self-conceit; and when boasted of, beget a strong suspicion of these sentiments.

264   It is hard to tell, whether you hurt a man's character most by calling him a knave or a coward, and whether a beastly glutton or drunkard be not as odious and contemptible, as a selfish, ungenerous miser. Give me my choice, and I would rather, for my own happiness and self-enjoyment, have a friendly, humane heart, than possess all the other virtues of Demosthenes and Philip united: but

I would rather pass with the world for one endowed with extensive genius and intrepid courage, and should thence expect stronger instances of general applause and admiration. The figure which a man makes in life, the reception which he meets with in company, the esteem paid him by his acquaintance ; all these advantages depend as much upon his good sense and judgement, as upon any other part of his character.   Had a man the best intentions in the world, and were the farthest removed from all injustice and violence, he would never be able to make himself be much regarded, without a moderate share, at least, of parts and understanding.

265   What is it then we can here dispute about ? If sense and courage, temperance and industry, wisdom and knowledge confessedly form a considerable part of *personal merit :* if a man, possessed of these qualities, is both better satisfied with himself, and better entitled to the good-will, esteem, and services of others, than one entirely destitute of them ; if, in short, the *sentiments* are similar which arise from these endowments and from the social virtues ; is there any reason for being so extremely scrupulous about a *word,* or disputing whether they be entitled to the denomination of virtues ? It may, indeed, be pretended, that the sentiment of approbation, which those accomplishments produce, besides its being *inferior,* is also somewhat *different* from that which attends the virtues of justice and humanity. But this seems not a sufficient reason for ranking them entirely under different classes and appellations.   The character of Caesar and that of Cato, as drawn by Sallust, are both of them virtuous, in the strictest and most limited sense of the word ; but in a different way : nor are the sentiments entirely the same which arise from them.   The one produces love, the other esteem : the one is amiable, the other awful : we should wish to meet the one character in a friend ; the other we should be ambitious of in

ourselves. In like manner the approbation, which attends temperance or industry or frugality, may be somewhat different from that which is paid to the social virtues, without making them entirely of a different species. And, indeed, we may observé, that these endowments, more than the other virtues, produce not, all of them, the same kind of approbation. Good sense and genius beget esteem and regard : wit and humour excite love and affection [1].

Most people, I believe, will naturally, without premeditation, assent to the definition of the elegant and judicious poet :—

> Virtue (for mere good-nature is a fool)
> Is sense and spirit with humanity [2].

What pretensions has a man to our generous assistance or good offices, who has dissipated his wealth in profuse expenses, idle vanities, chimerical projects, dissolute pleasures or extravagant gaming ? These vices (for we scruple

---

[1] Love and esteem are nearly the same passion, and arise from similar causes. The qualities, which produce both, are such as communicate pleasure. But where this pleasure is severe and serious ; or where its object is great, and makes a strong impression, or where it produces any degree of humility and awe : in all these cases, the passion, which arises from the pleasure, is more properly denominated esteem than love. Benevolence attends both : but is connected with love in a more eminent degree. There seems to be still a stronger mixture of pride in contempt than of humility in esteem ; and the reason would not be difficult to one, who studied accurately the passions. All these various mixtures and compositions and appearances of sentiment form a very curious subject of speculation, but are wide of our present purpose. Throughout this enquiry, we always consider in general, what qualities are a subject of praise or of censure, without entering into all the minute differences of sentiment, which they excite. It is evident, that whatever is contemned, is also disliked, as well as what is hated ; and we here endeavour to take objects, according to their most simple views and appearances. These sciences are but too apt to appear abstract to common readers, even with all the precautions which we can take to clear them from superfluous speculations, and bring them down to every capacity.

[2] The Art of preserving Health. Book 4.

not to call them such) bring misery unpited, and contempt on every one addicted to them.

Achaeus, a wise and prudent prince, fell into a fatal snare, which cost him his crown and life, after having used every reasonable precaution to guard himself against it. On that account, says the historian, he is a just object of regard and compassion: his betrayers alone of hatred and contempt [1].

The precipitate flight and improvident negligence of Pompey, at the beginning of the civil wars, appeared such notorious blunders to Cicero, as quite palled his friendship towards that great man. *In the same manner*, says he, *as want of cleanliness, decency, or discretion in a mistress are found to alienate our affections.* For so he expresses himself, where he talks, not in the character of a philosopher, but in that of a statesman and man of the world, to his friend Atticus [2].

266   But the same Cicero, in imitation of all the ancient moralists, when he reasons as a philosopher, enlarges very much his ideas of virtue, and comprehends every laudable quality or endowment of the mind, under that honourable appellation. This leads to the *third* reflection, which we proposed to make, to wit, that the ancient moralists, the best models, made no material distinction among the different species of mental endowments and defects, but treated all alike under the appellation of virtues and vices, and made them indiscriminately the object of their moral reasonings. The *prudence* explained in Cicero's *Offices* [3], is that sagacity, which leads to the discovery of truth, and preserves us from error and mistake. *Magnanimity, temperance, decency*, are there also at large discoursed of. And as that eloquent moralist followed the common received division of the four cardinal virtues, our social duties

---

[1] Polybius, lib. viii. cap. *i.*

[1] Lib. ix. epist. 10.   [3] Lib. i. cap. 6.

form but one head, in the general distribution of his subject [1].

We need only peruse the titles of chapters in Aristotle's Ethics to be convinced that he ranks courage, temperance, magnificence, magnanimity, modesty, prudence, and a manly openness, among the virtues, as well as justice and friendship.

To *sustain* and to *abstain*, that is, to be patient and continent, appeared to some of the ancients a summary comprehension of all morals.

Epictetus has scarcely ever mentioned the sentiment of humanity and compassion, but in order to put his disciples on their guard against it. The virtue of the *Stoics* seems to consist chiefly in a firm temper and a sound understanding. With them, as with Solomon and the

---

[1] The following passage of Cicero is worth quoting, as being the most clear and express to our purpose, that any thing can be imagined, and, in a dispute, which is chiefly verbal, must, on account of the author, carry an authority, from which there can be no appeal.

'Virtus autem, quae est per se ipsa laudabilis, et sine qua nihil laudari potest, tamen habet plures partes, quarum alia est alia ad laudationem aptior. Sunt enim aliae virtutes, quae videntur in moribus hominum, et quadam comitate ac beneficentia positae : aliae quae in ingenii aliqua facultate, aut animi magnitudine ac robore. Nam clementia, justitia, benignitas, fides, fortitudo in periculis communibus, jucunda est auditu in laudationibus. Omnes enim hae virtutes non tam ipsis, qui eas in se habent, quam generi hominum fructuosae putantur. Sapientia et magnitudo animi, qua omnes res humanae tenues et pro nihilo putantur, et in cogitando vis quaedam ingenii, et ipsa eloquentia admirationis habet non minus, jucunditatis minus. Ipsos enim magis videntur, quos laudamus, quam illos, apud quos laudamus, ornare ac tueri : sed tamen in laudenda jungenda sunt etiam haec genera virtutum. Ferunt enim aures hominum, cum illa quae jucunda et grata, tum etiam illa, quae mirabilia sunt in virtute, laudari.' *De orat.* lib. ii. cap. 84.

I suppose, if Cicero were now alive, it would be found difficult to fetter his moral sentiments by narrow systems ; or persuade him, that no qualities were to be admitted as *virtues*, or acknowledged to be a part of *personal merit*, but what were recommended by *The Whole Duty of Man.*

eastern moralists, folly and wisdom are equivalent to vice and virtue.

Men will praise thee, says David[1], when thou dost well unto thyself. I hate a wise man, says the Greek poet, who is not wise to himself[2].

Plutarch is no more cramped by systems in his philosophy than in his history. Where he compares the great men of Greece and Rome, he fairly sets in opposition all their blemishes and accomplishments of whatever kind, and omits nothing considerable, which can either depress or exalt their characters. His moral discourses contain the same free and natural censure of men and manners.

The character of Hannibal, as drawn by Livy[3], is esteemed partial, but allows him many eminent virtues. Never was there a genius, says the historian, more equally fitted for those opposite offices of commanding and obeying; and it were, therefore, difficult to determine whether he rendered himself *dearer* to the general or to the army. To none would Hasdrubal entrust more willingly the conduct of any dangerous enterprize; under none did the soldiers discover more courage and confidence. Great boldness in facing danger; great prudence in the midst of it. No labour could fatigue his body or subdue his mind. Cold and heat were indifferent to him : meat and drink he sought as supplies to the necessities of nature, not as gratifications of his voluptuous appetites. Waking or rest he used indiscriminately, by night or by day.—These great Virtues were balanced by great Vices : inhuman cruelty; perfidy more than *punic*; no truth, no faith, no regard to oaths, promises, or religion.

The character of Alexander the Sixth, to be found in

[1] Psalm 49th.
[2] Μισῶ σοφιστὴν ὅστις οὐκ αὑτῷ σοφός. EURIPIDES.
[3] Lib. xxi. cap 4.

Guicciardin [1], is pretty similar, but juster; and is a proof that even the moderns, where they speak naturally, hold the same language with the ancients. In this pope, says he, there was a singular capacity and judgement: admirable prudence; a wonderful talent of persuasion; and in all momentous enterprizes a diligence and dexterity incredible. But these *virtues* were infinitely overbalanced by his *vices*; no faith, no religion, insatiable avarice, exorbitant ambition, and a more than barbarous cruelty.

Polybius [2], reprehending Timaeus for his partiality against Agathocles, whom he himself allows to be the most cruel and impious of all tyrants, says: if he took refuge in Syracuse, as asserted by that historian, flying the dirt and smoke and toil of his former profession of a potter; and if proceeding from such slender beginnings, he became master, in a little time, of all Sicily; brought the Carthaginian state into the utmost danger; and at last died in old age, and in possession of sovereign dignity: must he not be allowed something prodigious and extraordinary, and to have possessed great talents and capacity for business and action? His historian, therefore, ought not to have alone related what tended to his reproach and infamy; but also what might redound to his Praise and Honour.

267   In general, we may observe, that the distinction of voluntary or involuntary was little regarded by the ancients in their moral reasonings; where they frequently treated the question as very doubtful, *whether virtue could be taught or not* [3]? They justly considered that cowardice, meanness, levity, anxiety, impatience, folly, and many other qualities of the mind, might appear ridiculous and deformed, contemptible and odious, though independent of the will.   Nor

---

[1] Lib. i.   [2] Lib. xii.

[3] Vid. Plato in Menone, Seneca *de otio sap.* cap. 31. So also Horace, *Virtutem doctrina paret, naturane donet.* Epist. lib. i. ep. 18. Æschines Socraticus, Dial. 1.

could it be supposed, at all times, in every man's power to attain every kind of mental more than of exterior beauty.

268   And here there occurs the *fourth* reflection which I purposed to make, in suggesting the reason why modern philosophers have often followed a course in their moral enquiries so different from that of the ancients. In later times, philosophy of all kinds, especially ethics, have been more closely united with theology than ever they were observed to be among the heathens; and as this latter science admits of no terms of composition, but bends every branch of knowledge to its own purpose, without much regard to the phenomena of nature, or to the unbiassed sentiments of the mind, hence reasoning, and even language, have been warped from their natural course, and distinctions have been endeavoured to be established where the difference of the objects was, in a manner, imperceptible. Philosophers, or rather divines under that disguise, treating all morals as on a like footing with civil laws, guarded by the sanctions of reward and punishment, were necessarily led to render this circumstance, of *voluntary* or *involuntary*, the foundation of their whole theory. Every one may employ *terms* in what sense he pleases: but this, in the mean time, must be allowed, that *sentiments* are every day experienced of blame and praise, which have objects beyond the dominion of the will or choice, and of which it behoves us, if not as moralists, as speculative philosophers at least, to give some satisfactory theory and explication.

A blemish, a fault, a vice, a crime; these expressions seem to denote different degrees of censure and disapprobation; which are, however, all of them, at the bottom, pretty nearly all the same kind of species. The explication of one will easily lead us into a just conception of the others; and it is of greater consequence to attend to things than to verbal appellations. That we owe a duty to ourselves is confessed even in the most vulgar system of morals; and it

must be of consequence to examine that duty, in order to
see whether it bears any affinity to that which we owe to
society. It is probable that the approbation attending the
observance of both is of a similar nature, and arises from
similar principles, whatever appellation we may give to
either of these excellencies.

A DIALOGUE.

My friend, Palamedes, who is as great a rambler in his principles as in his person, who has run over, by study and travel, almost every region of the intellectual and material world, surprized me lately with an account of a nation, with whom, he told me, he had passed a considerable part of his life, and whom, he found, in the main, a people extremely civilized and intelligent.

There is a country, said he, in the world, called Fourli, no matter for its longitude or latitude, whose inhabitants have ways of thinking, in many things. particularly in morals, diametrically opposite to ours. When I came among them, I found that I must submit to double pains; first to learn the meaning of the terms in their language, and then to know the import of those terms, and the praise or blame attached to them. After a word had been explained to me, and the character, which it expressed, had been described, I concluded, that such an epithet must necessarily be the greatest reproach in the world ; and was extremely surprized to find one in a public company, apply it to a person, with whom he lived in the strictest intimacy and friendship. *You fancy*, said I one day, to an acquaintance, *that* Changuis *is your mortal enemy: I love to extinguish quarrels ; and I must, therefore, tell you, that I heard him talk of you in the most obliging manner.* But to my great astonishment, when I repeated Changuis's words, though I had both remembered and understood them perfectly, I found, that they were

taken for the most mortal affront, and that I had very inno-
cently rendered the breach between these persons altogether
irreparable.

As it was my fortune to come among this people on a very
advantageous footing, I was immediately introduced to the
best company; and being desired by Alcheic to live with
him, I readily accepted of his invitation; as I found him
universally esteemed for his personal merit, and indeed
regarded by every one in Fourli, as a perfect character.

One evening he invited me, as an amusement, to bear
him company in a serenade, which he intended to give to
Gulki, with whom, he told me, he was extremely enamoured;
and I soon found that his taste was not singular: For we
met many of his rivals, who had come on the same errand.
I very naturally concluded, that this mistress of his must be
one of the finest women in town; and I already felt a secret
inclination to see her, and be acquainted with her. But as
the moon began to rise, I was much surprized to find, that
we were in the midst of the university, where Gulki studied:
And I was somewhat ashamed for having attended my friend,
on such an errand.

I was afterwards told, that Alcheic's choice of Gulki was
very much approved of by all the good company in town;
and that it was expected, while he gratified his own passion,
he would perform to that young man the same good office,
which he had himself owed to Elcouf. It seems Alcheic had
been very handsome in his youth, had been courted by many
lovers; but had bestowed his favours chiefly on the sage
Elcouf; to whom he was supposed to owe, in great measure,
the astonishing progress which he had made in philosophy
and virtue.

It gave me some surprize, that Alcheic's wife (who by-
the-bye happened also to be his sister) was no wise scandalized at this species of infidelity.

Much about the same time I discovered (for it was not

attempted to be kept a secret from me or any body) that Alcheic was a murderer and a parricide, and had put to death an innocent person, the most nearly connected with him, and whom he was bound to protect and defend by all the ties of nature and humanity. When I asked, with all the caution and deference imaginable, what was his motive for this action ; he replied coolly, that he was not then so much at ease in his circumstances as he is at present, and that he had acted, in that particular, by the advice of all his friends.

Having heard Alcheic's virtue so extremely celebrated, I pretended to join in the general voice of acclamation, and only asked, by way of curiosity, as a stranger, which of all his noble actions was most highly applauded ; and I soon found, that all sentiments were united in giving the preference to the assassination of Usbek. This Usbek had been to the last moment Alcheic's intimate friend, had laid many high obligations upon him, had even saved his life on a certain occasion, and had, by his will, which was found after the murder, made him heir to a considerable part of his fortune. Alcheic, it seems, conspired with about twenty or thirty more, most of them also Usbek's friends ; and falling all together on that unhappy man, when he was not aware, they had torne him with a hundred wounds ; and given him that reward for his past favours and obligations. Usbek, said the general voice of the people, had many great and good qualities : His very vices were shining, magnificent, and generous : But this action of Alcheic's sets him far above Usbek in the eyes of all judges of merit ; and is one of the noblest that ever perhaps the sun shone upon.

Another part of Alcheic's conduct, which I also found highly applauded, was his behaviour towards Calish, with whom he was joined in a project or undertaking of some importance. Calish, being a passionate man, gave Alcheic, one day, a sound drubbing ; which he took very patiently, waited the return of Calish's good-humour, kept still a fair correspondence with him; and by that means brought the affair, in which they were joined, to a happy issue, and gained to himself immortal honour by his remarkable temper and moderation.

I have lately received a letter from a correspondent in Fourli, by which I learn, that, since my departure, Alcheic, falling into a bad state of health, has fairly hanged himself; and has died universally regretted and applauded in that country. So virtuous and noble a life, says each Fourlian, could not be better crowned than by so noble an end; and Alcheic has proved by this, as well as by all his other actions, what he boasted of near his last moments, that a wise man is scarcely inferior to the great god, Vitzli. This is the name of the supreme deity among the Fourlians.

The notions of this people, continued Palamedes, are as extraordinary with regard to good-manners and sociableness, as with regard to morals. My friend Alcheic formed once a party for my entertainment, composed of all the prime wits and philosophers of Fourli; and each of us brought his mess along with him to the place where we assembled. I observed one of them to be worse provided than the rest, and offered him a share of my mess, which happened to be a roasted pullet: And I could not but remark, that he and all the rest of the company smiled at my simplicity. I was told, that Alcheic had once so much interest with this club as to prevail with them to eat in common, and that he had made use of an artifice for that purpose. He persuaded those, whom he observed to be *worst* provided, to offer their mess to the company; after which, the others, who had brought more delicate fare, were ashamed not to make the same offer. This is regarded as so extraordinary an event, that it has since, as I learn, been recorded in the history of Alcheic's life, composed by one of the greatest geniuses of Fourli.

Pray, said I, Palamedes, when you were at Fourli, did you

also learn the art of turning your friends into ridicule, by telling them strange stories, and then laughing at them, if they believed you. I assure you, replied he, had I been disposed to learn such a lesson, there was no place in the world more proper. My friend, so often mentioned, did nothing, from morning to night, but sneer, and banter, and rally; and you could scarcely ever distinguish, whether he were in jest or earnest. But you think then, that my story is improbable; and that I have used, or rather abused the privilege of a traveller. To be sure, said I, you were but in jest. Such barbarous and savage manners are not only incompatible with a civilized, intelligent people, such as you said these were; but scarcely compatible with human nature. They exceed all we ever read of, among the Mingrelians, and Topinamboues.

Have a care, cried he, have a care! You are not aware that you are speaking blasphemy, and are abusing your favourites, the Greeks, especially the Athenians, whom I have couched, all along, under these bizarre names I employed. If you consider aright, there is not one stroke of the foregoing character, which might not be found in the man of highest merit at Athens, without diminishing in the least from the brightness of his character. The amours of the Greeks, their marriages [1], and the exposing of their children cannot but strike you immediately. The death of Usbek is an exact counter-part to that of Caesar.

All to a trifle, said I, interrupting him: You did not mention that Usbek was an usurper.

I did not, replied he; lest you should discover the parallel I aimed at. But even adding this circumstance, we should make no scruple, according to our sentiments of morals, to denominate Brutus, and Cassius, ungrateful

---

[1] The laws of Athens allowed a man to marry his sister by the father. Solon's law forbid paederasty to slaves, as being an act of too great dignity for such mean persons.

traitors and assassins: Though you know, that they are, perhaps, the highest characters of all antiquity; and the Athenians erected statues to them; which they placed near those of Harmodius and Aristogiton, their own deliverers. And if you think this circumstance, which you mention, so material to absolve these patriots, I shall compensate it by another, not mentioned, which will equally aggravate their crime. A few days before the execution of their fatal purpose, they all swore fealty to Caesar; and protesting to hold his person ever sacred, they touched the altar with those hands, which they had already armed for his destruction [1].

I need not remind you of the famous and applauded story of Themistocles, and of his patience towards Eurybiades, the Spartan, his commanding officer, who, heated by debate, lifted his cane to him in a council of war (the same thing as if he had cudgelled him), *Strike!* cries the Athenian, *strike! but hear me.*

You are too good a scholar not to discover the ironical Socrates and his Athenian club in my last story; and you will certainly observe, that it is exactly copied from Xenophon, with a variation only of the names [2]. And I think I have fairly made it appear, that an Athenian man of merit might be such a one as with us would pass for incestuous, a parricide, an assassin, ungrateful, perjured traitor, and something else too abominable to be named; not to mention his rusticity and ill-manners. And having lived in this manner, his death might be entirely suitable: He might conclude the scene by a desperate act of self-murder, and die with the most absurd blasphemies in his mouth. And notwithstanding all this, he shall have statues, if not altars, erected to his memory; poems and orations shall be composed in his praise; great sects shall be proud of calling themselves by his name; and the most distant posterity shall blindly

[1] Appian, Bell. Civ. lib iii. Suetonius in vita Caesaris.
[2] Mem. Soc. lib. iii. sub fine.

continue their admiration : Though were such a one to arise among themselves, they would justly regard him with horror and execration.

I might have been aware, replied I, of your artifice. You seem to take pleasure in this topic : and are indeed the only man I ever knew, who was well acquainted with the ancients, and did not extremely admire them. But instead of attacking their philosophy, their eloquence, or poetry, the usual subjects of controversy between us, you now seem to impeach their morals, and accuse them of ignorance in a science, which is the only one, in my opinion, in which they are not surpassed by the moderns. Geometry, physics, astronomy, anatomy, botany, geography, navigation; in these we justly claim the superiority : But what have we to oppose to their moralists? Your representation of things is fallacious. You have no indulgence for the manners and customs of different ages. Would you try a Greek or Roman by the common law of England? Hear him defend himself by his own maxims ; and then pronounce.

There are no manners so innocent or reasonable, but may be rendered odious or ridiculous, if measured by a standard, unknown to the persons ; especially, if you employ a little art or eloquence, in aggravating some circumstances, and extenuating others, as best suits the purpose of your discourse. All these artifices may easily be retorted on you. Could I inform the Athenians, for instance, that there was a nation, in which adultery, both active and passive, so to speak, was in the highest vogue and esteem : In which every man of education chose for his mistress a married woman, the wife, perhaps, of his friend and companion ; and valued himself upon these infamous conquests, as much as if he had been several times a conqueror in boxing or wrestling at the *Olympic* games : In which every man also took a pride in his tameness and facility with regard to his own wife, and was glad to make friends or gain interest by allowing her to prostitute her charms; and even, without any such motive, gave her full liberty and indulgence: I ask, what sentiments the Athenians would entertain of such a people; they who never mentioned the crime of adultery but in conjunction with robbery and poisoning? Which would they admire most, the villany or the meanness of such a conduct?

Should I add, that the same people were as proud of their slavery and dependance as the Athenians of their liberty; and though a man among them were oppressed, disgraced, impoverished, insulted, or imprisoned by the tyrant, he would still regard it as the highest merit to love, serve, and obey him; and even to die for his smallest glory or satisfaction: These noble Greeks would probably ask me, whether I spoke of a human society, or of some inferior, servile species.

It was then I might inform my Athenian audience, that these people, however, wanted not spirit and bravery. If a man, say I, though their intimate friend, should throw out, in a private company, a raillery against them, nearly approaching any of those, with which your generals and demagogues every day regale each other, in the face of the whole city, they never can forgive him; but in order to revenge themselves, they oblige him immediately to run them through the body, or be himself murdered. And if a man, who is an absolute stranger to them, should desire them, at the peril of their own life, to cut the throat of their bosom-companion, they immediately obey, and think themselves highly obliged and honoured by the commission. These are their maxims of honour: This is their favourite morality.

But though so ready to draw their sword against their friends and countrymen; no disgrace, no infamy, no pain, no poverty will ever engage these people to turn the point of it against their own breast. A man of rank would row in the gallies, would beg his bread, would languish in prison, would suffer any tortures; and still preserve his wretched

life. Rather than escape his enemies by a generous contempt of death, he would infamously receive the same death
from his enemies, aggravated by their triumphant insults,
and by the most exquisite sufferings.

It is very usual too, continue I, among this people to
erect jails, where every art of plaguing and tormenting the
unhappy prisoners is carefully studied and practised: And
in these jails it is usual for a parent voluntarily to shut up
several of his children ; in order, that another child, whom
he owns to have no greater or rather less merit than the
rest, may enjoy his whole fortune, and wallow in every kind
of voluptuousness and pleasure. Nothing so virtuous in
their opinion as this barbarous partiality.

But what is more singular in this whimsical nation, say
I to the Athenians, is, that a frolic of yours during the
Saturnalia [1], when the slaves are served by their masters, is
seriously continued by them throughout the whole year, and
throughout the whole course of their lives ; accompanied
too with some circumstances, which still farther augment
the absurdity and ridicule. Your sport only elevates for
a few days those whom fortune has thrown down, and whom
she too, in sport, may really elevate for ever above you :
But this nation gravely exalts those, whom nature has subjected to them, and whose inferiority and infirmities are
absolutely incurable. The women, though without virtue,
are their masters and sovereigns : These they reverence,
praise, and magnify : To these, they pay the highest deference and respect : And in all places and all times, the
superiority of the females is readily acknowledged and sub-
mitted to by every one, who has the least pretensions to
education and politeness. Scarce any crime would be so
universally detested as an infraction of this rule.

You need go no further, replied Palamedes ; I can easily

[1] The Greeks kept the feast of Saturn or Chronus, as well as the
Romans. See Lucian, Epist. Saturn.

conjecture the people whom you aim at. The strokes, with which you have painted them, are pretty just; and yet you must acknowledge, that scarce any people are to be found, either in ancient or modern times, whose national character is, upon the whole, less liable to exception. But I give you thanks for helping me out with my argument. I had no intention of exalting the moderns at the expence of the ancients. I only meant to represent the uncertainty of all these judgments concerning characters; and to convince you, that fashion, vogue, custom, and law, were the chief foundation of all moral determinations. The Athenians surely, were a civilized, intelligent people, if ever there were one; and yet their man of merit might, in this age, be held in horror and execration. The French are also, without doubt, a very civilized, intelligent people; and yet their man of merit might, with the Athenians, be an object of the highest contempt and ridicule, and even hatred. And what renders the matter more extraordinary: These two people are supposed to be the most similar in their national character of any in ancient and modern times; and while the English flatter themselves that they resemble the Romans, their neighbours on the continent draw the parallel between themselves and those polite Greeks. What wide difference, therefore, in the sentiments of morals, must be found between civilized nations and Barbarians, or between nations whose characters have little in common? How shall we pretend to fix a standard for judgments of this nature?

By tracing matters, replied I, a little higher, and examining the first principles, which each nation establishes, of blame or censure. The Rhine flows north, the Rhone south; yet both spring from the *same* mountain, and are also actuated, in their opposite directions, by the *same* principle of gravity. The different inclinations of the ground, on which they run, cause all the difference of their courses.

In how many circumstances would an Athenian and

a French man of merit certainly resemble each other? Good sense, knowledge, wit, eloquence, humanity, fidelity, truth, justice, courage, temperance, constancy, dignity of mind : These you have all omitted ; in order to insist only on the points, in which they may, by accident, differ. Very well : I am willing to comply with you ; and shall endeavour to account for these differences from the most universal, established principles of morals.

The Greek loves, I care not to examine more particularly. I shall only observe, that, however blameable, they arose from a very innocent cause, the frequency of the gymnastic exercises among that people ; and were recommended, though absurdly, as the source of friendship, sympathy, mutual attachment, and fidelity[1] ; qualities esteemed in all nations and all ages.

The marriage of half-brothers and sisters seems no great difficulty. Love between the nearer relations is contrary to reason and public utility ; but the precise point, where we are to stop, can scarcely be determined by natural reason ; and is therefore a very proper subject for municipal law or custom. If the Athenians went a little too far on the one side, the canon law has surely pushed matters a great way into the other extreme[2].

Had you asked a parent at Athens, why he bereaved his child of that life, which he had so lately given it. It is because I love it, he would reply ; and regard the poverty which it must inherit from me, as a greater evil than death, which it is not capable of dreading, feeling, or resenting[3].

How is public liberty, the most valuable of all blessings, to be recovered from the hands of an usurper or tyrant, if his power shields him from public rebellion, and our scruples from private vengeance? That his crime is capital by law,

[1] Plat. Symp. p. 182, ex edit. Ser.
[2] See Enquiry, Sect. IV.
[3] Plut. de amore prolis, sub fine.

you acknowledge : And must the highest aggravation of his crime, the putting of himself above law, form his full security? You can reply nothing, but by showing the great inconveniences of assassination ; which could any one have proved clearly to the ancients, he had reformed their sentiments in this particular.

Again, to cast your eye on the picture which I have drawn of modern manners ; there is almost as great difficulty, I acknowledge, to justify French as Greek gallantry ; except only, that the former is much more natural and agreeable than the latter. But our neighbours, it seems, have resolved to sacrifice some of the domestic to the sociable pleasures ; and to prefer ease, freedom, and an open commerce, to a strict fidelity and constancy. These ends are both good, and are somewhat difficult to reconcile ; nor need we be surprised, if the customs of nations incline too much, sometimes to the one side, sometimes to the other.

The most inviolable attachment to the laws of our country is every where acknowledged a capital virtue ; and where the people are not so happy, as to have any legislature but a single person, the strictest loyalty is, in that case, the truest patriotism.

Nothing surely can be more absurd and barbarous than the practice of duelling ; but those, who justify it, say, that it begets civility and good-manners. And a duellist, you may observe, always values himself upon his courage, his sense of honour, his fidelity and friendship ; qualities, which are here indeed very oddly directed, but which have been esteemed universally, since the foundation of the world.

Have the gods forbid self-murder? An Athenian allows, that it ought to be forborn. Has the Deity permitted it ? A Frenchman allows, that death is preferable to pain and infamy.

You see then, continued I, that the principles upon which men reason in morals are always the same ; though the

conclusions which they draw are often very different.   That
they all reason aright with regard to this subject, more than
with regard to any other, it is not incumbent on any moralist
to show.   It is sufficient, that the original principles of
censure or blame are uniform, and that erroneous conclusions can be corrected by sounder reasoning and larger
experience.   Though many ages have elapsed since the fall
of Greece and Rome ; though many changes have arrived in
religion, language, laws, and customs ; none of these revolutions has ever produced any considerable innovation in
the primary sentiments of morals, more than in those of
external beauty.   Some minute differences, perhaps, may be
observed in both.   Horace[1] celebrates a low forehead, and
Anacreon joined eye-brows[2] : But the Apollo and the Venus
of antiquity are still our models for male and female beauty ;
in like manner as the character of Scipio continues our
standard for the glory of heroes, and that of Cornelia for
the honour of matrons.

It appears, that there never was any quality recommended
by any one, as a virtue or moral excellence, but on account
of its being *useful,* or *agreeable* to a man *himself,* or to *others.*
For what other reason can ever be assigned for praise or
approbation ?   Or where would be the sense of extolling a
good character or action, which, at the same time, is allowed
to be *good for nothing?*   All the differences, therefore, in
morals, may be reduced to this one general foundation, and
may be accounted for by the different views, which people
take of these circumstances.

Sometimes men differ in their judgment about the usefulness of any habit or action : Sometimes also the peculiar
circumstances of things render one moral quality more useful
than others, and give it a peculiar preference.

[1] Epist. lib. 1. epist. 7.   Also lib. i. ode 3.
[2] Ode 28.   Petronius (cap. 86) joins both these circumstances as
beauties.

It is not surprising, that, during a period of war and disorder, the military virtues should be more celebrated than the pacific, and attract more the admiration and attention of mankind. "How usual is it," says Tully[1], "to find "Cimbrians, Celtiberians, and other Barbarians, who bear, "with inflexible constancy, all the fatigues and dangers of "the field; but are immediately dispirited under the pain "and hazard of a languishing distemper: While, on the "other hand, the Greeks patiently endure the slow ap- "proaches of death, when armed with sickness and disease; "but timorously fly his presence, when he attacks them "violently with swords and falchions!" So different is even the same virtue of courage among warlike or peaceful nations! And indeed, we may observe, that, as the difference between war and peace is the greatest that arises among nations and public societies, it produces also the greatest variations in moral sentiment, and diversifies the most our ideas of virtue and personal merit.

Sometimes too, magnanimity, greatness of mind, disdain of slavery, inflexible rigour and integrity, may better suit the circumstances of one age than those of another, and have a more kindly influence, both on public affairs, and on a man's own safety and advancement. Our idea of merit, therefore, will also vary a little with these variations; and Labeo, perhaps, be censured for the same qualities, which procured Cato the highest approbation.

A degree of luxury may be ruinous and pernicious in a native of Switzerland, which only fosters the arts, and encourages industry in a Frenchman or Englishman. We are not, therefore, to expect, either the same sentiments, or the same laws in Berne, which prevail in London or Paris.

Different customs have also some influence as well as different utilities; and by giving an early bias to the mind, may produce a superior propensity, either to the useful or

---

[1] Tusc. Quaest. lib. ii.

the agreeable qualities; to those which regard self, or those which extend to society. These four sources of moral sentiment still subsist; but particular accidents may, at one time, make any one of them flow with greater abundance than at another.

The customs of some nations shut up the women from all social commerce: Those of others make them so essential a part of society and conversation, that, except where business is transacted, the male-sex alone are supposed almost wholly incapable of mutual discourse and entertainment. As this difference is the most material that can happen in private life, it must also produce the greatest variation in our moral sentiments.

Of all nations in the world, where polygamy was not allowed, the Greeks seem to have been the most reserved in their commerce with the fair sex, and to have imposed on them the strictest laws of modesty and decency. We have a strong instance of this in an oration of Lysias[1]. A widow injured, ruined, undone, calls a meeting of a few of her nearest friends and relations; and though never before accustomed, says the orator, to speak in the presence of men, the distress of her circumstances constrained her to lay the case before them. The very opening of her mouth in such company required, it seems, an apology.

When Demosthenes prosecuted his tutors, to make them refund his patrimony, it became necessary for him, in the course of the law-suit, to prove that the marriage of Aphobus's sister with Oneter was entirely fraudulent, and that, notwithstanding her sham marriage, she had lived with her brother at Athens for two years past, ever since her divorce from her former husband. And it is remarkable, that though these were people of the first fortune and distinction in the city, the orator could prove this fact no way, but by

---

[1] Orat. 33.

calling for her female slaves to be put to the question, and by the evidence of one physician, who had seen her in her brother's house during her illness[1]. So reserved were Greek manners.

We may be assured, that an extreme purity of manners was the consequence of this reserve. Accordingly we find, that, except the fabulous stories of an Helen and a Clytemnestra, there scarcely is an instance of any event in the Greek history, which proceeded from the intrigues of women. On the other hand, in modern times, particularly in a neighbouring nation, the females enter into all transactions and all management of church and state : And no man can expect success, who takes not care to obtain their good graces. Harry the third, by incurring the displeasure of the fair, endangered his crown, and lost his life, as much as by his indulgence to heresy.

It is needless to 'dissemble : The consequence of a very free commerce between the sexes, and of their living much together, will often terminate in intrigues and gallantry. We must sacrifice somewhat of the *useful*, if we be very anxious to obtain all the *agreeable* qualities ; and cannot pretend to reach alike every kind of advantage. Instances of licence, daily multiplying, will weaken the scandal with the one sex, and teach the other by degrees, to adopt the famous maxim of La Fontaine, with regard to female infidelity, *that if one knows it, it is but a small matter ; if one knows it not, it is nothing*[2].

Some people are inclined to think, that the best way of adjusting all differences, and of keeping the proper medium between the *agreeable* and the *useful* qualities of the sex, is to live with them after the manner of the Romans and the English (for the customs of these two nations seem similar

---

[1] In Oneterem.
[2] Quand on le sçait, c'est peu de chose :
Quand on l'ignore, ce n'est rien.

in this respect[1]); that is, without gallantry[2], and without jealousy. By a parity of reason, the customs of the Spaniards and of the Italians of an age ago (for the present are very different) must be the worst of any; because they favour both gallantry and jealousy.

Nor will these different customs of nations affect the one sex only: Their idea of personal merit in the males must also be somewhat different with regard, at least, to conversation, address, and humour. The one nation, where the men live much apart, will naturally more approve of prudence; the other of gaiety. With the one simplicity of manners will be in the highest esteem; with the other, politeness. The one will distinguish themselves by good-sense and judgment; the other, by taste and delicacy. The eloquence of the former will shine most in the senate; that of the other, on the theatre.

These, I say, are the *natural* effects of such customs. For it must be confessed, that chance has a great influence on national manners; and many events happen in society, which are not to be accounted for by general rules. Who could imagine, for instance, that the Romans, who lived freely with their women, should be very indifferent about music, and esteem dancing infamous: While the Greeks, who never almost saw a woman but in their own houses, were continually piping, singing, and dancing?

The differences of moral sentiment, which naturally arise from a republican or monarchical government, are also very obvious; as well as those which proceed from general riches

[1] During the times of the emperors, the Romans seem to have been more given to intrigues and gallantry than the English are at present: And the women of condition, in order to retain their lovers, endeavoured to fix a name of reproach on those who were addicted to wenching and low amours. They were called Ancillarioli. See Seneca de beneficiis, Lib. 1. cap. 9. See also Martial, lib xii. epig. 58.

[2] The gallantry here meant is that of amours and attachments, not that of complaisance, which is as much paid to the fair sex in England as in any other country.

or poverty, union or faction, ignorance or learning. I shall conclude this long discourse with observing, that different customs and situations vary not the original ideas of merit (however they may, some consequences) in any very essential point, and prevail chiefly with regard to young men, who can aspire to the agreeable qualities, and may attempt to please. The Manner, the Ornaments, the Graces, which succeed in this shape, are more arbitrary and casual : But the merit of riper years is almost every where the same ; and consists chiefly in integrity, humanity, ability, knowledge, and the other more solid and useful qualities of the human mind.

What you insist on, replied Palamedes, may have some foundation, when you adhere to the maxims of common life and ordinary conduct. Experience and the practice of the world readily correct any great extravagance on either side. But what say you to *artificial* lives and manners? How do you reconcile the maxims, on which, in different ages and nations, these are founded?

What do you understand by *artificial* lives and manners? said **I**. I explain myself, replied he. You know, that religion had, in ancient times, very little influence on common life, and that, after men had performed their duty in sacrifices and prayers at the temple, they thought, that the gods left the rest of their conduct to themselves, and were little pleased or offended with those virtues or vices, which only affected the peace and happiness of human society. In those ages, it was the business of philosophy alone to regulate men's ordinary behaviour and deportment ; and accordingly, we may observe, that this being the sole principle, by which a man could elevate himself above his fellows, it acquired a mighty ascendant over many, and produced great singularities of maxims and of conduct. At present, when philosophy has lost the allurement of novelty, it has no such extensive influence ; but seems to confine itself mostly to speculations in the closet ; in the same manner, as the ancient religion was limited to sacrifices in the temple. Its place is now supplied by the modern religion, which inspects our whole conduct, and prescribes an universal rule to our actions, to our words, to our very thoughts and inclinations; a rule so much the more austere, as it is guarded by infinite, though distant, rewards and punishments; and no infraction of it can ever be concealed or disguised.

Diogenes is the most celebrated model of extravagant philosophy. Let us seek a parallel to him in modern times. We shall not disgrace any philosophic name by a comparison with the Dominics or Loyolas, or any canonized monk or friar. Let us compare him to Pascal, a man of parts and genius as well as Diogenes himself; and perhaps too, a man of virtue, had he allowed his virtuous inclinations to have exerted and displayed themselves.

The foundation of Diogenes's conduct was an endeavour to render himself an independent being as much as possible, and to confine all his wants and desires and pleasures within himself and his own mind: The aim of Pascal was to keep a perpetual sense of his dependence before his eyes, and never to forget his numberless wants and infirmities. The ancient supported himself by magnanimity, ostentation, pride, and the idea of his own superiority above his fellow-creatures. The modern made constant profession of humility and abasement, of the contempt and hatred of himself; and endeavoured to attain these supposed virtues, as far as they are attainable. The austerities of the Greek were in order to inure himself to hardships, and prevent his ever suffering: Those of the Frenchman were embraced merely for their own sake, and in order to suffer as much as possible. The philosopher indulged himself in the most beastly pleasures, even in public: The saint refused himself the most innocent, even in private. The former thought it his duty to love his friends, and to rail at them, and reprove them, and scold them: The latter endeavoured to be absolutely indifferent towards his nearest relations, and to love and speak well of his enemies. The great object of Diogenes's wit was every kind of superstition, that is every kind of religion known in his time. The mortality of the soul was his standard principle; and even his sentiments of a divine providence seem to have been licentious. The most ridiculous superstitions directed Pascal's faith and practice; and an extreme contempt of this life, in comparison of the future, was the chief foundation of his conduct.

In such a remarkable contrast do these two men stand: Yet both of them have met with general admiration in their different ages, and have been proposed as models of imitation. Where then is the universal standard of morals, which you talk of? And what rule shall we establish for the many different, nay contrary sentiments of mankind?

An experiment, said I, which succeeds in the air, will not always succeed in a vacuum. When men depart from the maxims of common reason, and affect these *artificial* lives, as you call them, no one can answer for what will please or displease them. They are in a different element from the rest of mankind; and the natural principles of their mind play not with the same regularity, as if left to themselves, free from the illusions of religious superstition or philosophical enthusiasm.

ADDITIONAL NOTE TO p. 125, l. 4.

This book was writ by Mons. Montgeron, counsellor or judge of the parliament of Paris, a man of figure and character, who was also a martyr to the cause, and is now said to be somewhere in a dungeon on account of his book.

There is another book in three volumes (called *Recueil des Miracles de l'Abbé* Paris) giving an account of many of these miracles, and accompanied with prefatory discourses, which are very well written. There runs, however, through the whole of these a ridiculous comparison between the miracles of our Saviour and those of the Abbé; wherein it is asserted, that the evidence for the latter is equal to that for the former: As if the testimony of men could ever be put in the balance with that of God himself, who conducted the pen of the inspired writers. If these writers, indeed, were to be considered merely as human testimony, the French author is very moderate in his comparison; since he might, with some appearance of reason, pretend, that the Jansenist miracles much surpass the other in evidence and authority. The following circumstances are drawn from authentic papers, inserted in the above-mentioned book.

Many of the miracles of Abbé Paris were proved immediately by witnesses before the officiality or bishop's court at Paris, under the eye of cardinal Noailles, whose character for integrity and capacity was never contested even by his enemies.

His successor in the archbishopric was an enemy to the Jansenists, and for that reason promoted to the see by the court. Yet 22 rectors or *curés* of Paris, with infinite earnestness, press him to examine those miracles, which they assert to be known to the whole world, and undisputably certain: But he wisely forbore.

The Molinist party had tried to discredit these miracles in one instance, that of Mademoiselle le Franc. But, besides that their proceedings were in many respects the most irregular in the world, particularly in citing only a few of the Jansenist witnesses, whom they tampered with : Besides this, I say, they soon found themselves overwhelmed by a cloud of new witnesses, one hundred and twenty in number, most of them persons of credit and substance in Paris, who gave oath for the miracle. This was accompanied with a solemn and earnest appeal to the parliament. But the parliament were forbidden by authority to meddle in the affair. It was at last observed, that where men are heated by zeal and enthusiasm, there is no degree of human testimony so strong as may not be procured for the greatest absurdity : And those who will be so silly as to examine the affair by that medium, and seek particular flaws in the testimony, are almost sure to be confounded. It must be a miserable imposture, indeed, that does not prevail in that contest.

All who have been in France about that time have heard of the reputation of Mons. Heraut, the *lieutenant de Police*, whose vigilance, penetration, activity, and extensive intelligence have been much talked of. This magistrate, who by the nature of his office is almost absolute, was vested with full powers, on purpose to suppress or discredit these miracles; and he frequently seized immediately, and examined the witnesses and subjects of them : But never could reach any thing satisfactory against them.

In the case of Mademoiselle Thibaut he sent the famous De Sylva to examine her; whose evidence is very curious. The physician declares, that it was impossible she could have been so ill as was proved by witnesses; because it was impossible she could, in so short a time, have recovered so perfectly as he found her. He reasoned, like a man of sense, from natural causes; but the opposite party told him, that the whole was a miracle, and that his evidence was the very best proof of it.

The Molinists were in a sad dilemma. They durst not assert the absolute insufficiency of human evidence, to prove a miracle. They were obliged to say, that these miracles were wrought by witchcraft and the devil. But they were told, that this was the resource of the Jews of old.

No Jansenist was ever embarrassed to account for the cessation of the miracles, when the church-yard was shut up by the king's edict. It was the touch of the tomb, which produced these extraordinary effects; and when no one could approach the tomb, no effects could be expected. God, indeed, could have thrown down the walls in a moment; but he is master of his own graces and works, and it belongs not to us to account for them. He did not throw down the walls of every city like those of Jericho, on the sounding of the rams horns, nor break up the prison of every apostle, like that of St. Paul.

No less a man, than the Duc de Chatillon, a duke and peer of France, of the highest rank and family, gives evidence of a miraculous cure, performed upon a servant of his, who had lived several years in his house with a visible and palpable infirmity.

I shall conclude with observing, that no clergy are more celebrated for strictness of life and manners than the secular clergy of France, particularly the rectors or curés of Paris, who bear testimony to these impostures.

The learning, genius, and probity of the gentlemen, and the austerity of the nuns of Port-Royal, have been much celebrated all over Europe. Yet they all give evidence for a miracle, wrought on the niece of the famous Pascal, whose sanctity of life, as well as extraordinary capacity, is well known. The famous Racine gives an account of this miracle in his famous history of Port-Royal, and fortifies it with all the proofs, which a multitude of nuns, priests, physicians, and men of the world, all of them of undoubted credit, could bestow upon it. Several men of letters, particularly the bishop of Tournay, thought this miracle so certain, as to employ it in the refutation of atheists and free-thinkers. The queen-regent of France, who was extremely prejudiced against the Port-Royal, sent her own physician to examine the miracle, who returned an absolute convert. In short, the supernatural cure was so uncontestable, that it saved, for a time, that famous monastery from the ruin with which it was threatened by the Jesuits. Had it been a cheat, it had certainly been detected by such sagacious and powerful antagonists, and must have hastened the ruin of the contrivers. Our divines, who can build up a formidable castle from such despicable materials ; what a prodigious fabric could they have reared from these and many other circumstances, which I have not mentioned ! How often would the great names of Pascal, Racine, Arnaud, Nicole, have resounded in our ears ? But if they be wise, they had better adopt the miracle, as being more worth, a thousand times, than all the rest of the collection. Besides, it may serve very much to their purpose. For that miracle was really performed by the touch of an authentic holy prickle of the holy thorn, which composed the holy crown, which, &c.

INDEX

—◆—

Abstract—reasonings, 224; ideas, really particular, 125 *n*.
Abstraction—not source of ideas of primary qualities, 122.
Academic—philosophy, 34.
Accession—and property, 259 *n*.
Action—and philosophy, 1, 4, 34, 128; and reasoning, 136.
Addison—4.
Allegiance—164, 188.
Ambition—dist self-love; not source of moral distinctions, 221;
a direct passion terminating on its object, 253.
'Amour-propre'—comprises self-love and vanity, 263 *n*.
Analogy—a species of, the foundation of all reasoning about matter of
fact, 82; appeal to in legal questions, 157, 259.
Animals—the reason of, 82–85; learn from experience and draw in-
ferences, 83; which can only be founded on custom, 84; cause of
difference between men and animals, 84 *n*.
No justice towards, 152; capable of disinterested kindness, 252.
Antiquity—62.
A posteriori—188.
Appearances—to senses must be corrected by reason, 117, 185 (cf. 137).
Appetite—terminating on its object, 253 (*v. Passion, Self-Love*, C, 248–
254).
Approbation—due to sentiment of humanity, 235; not derivable from
Self-love (q. v.), 174–5; of virtue feels different from sense of private
advantage, 175; disinterested, of qualities useful to others, 191 f;
of social virtues feels different from that of accomplishments and
talents, 265 (cf. 172 *n*).
Of benevolence different from that of justice, 255–6.
A priori—25, 36 *n*, 89 *n*, 132, 132 *n*, 187.
Aristotle—4, 266.
Artificial—opp. natural, 258 *n*.
Association—of ideas, three principles of, 18–19, 41–44 (*v. Cause* C).
Atheism—116.
Avarice—221.

Cause.

failure of a cause ascribed to a secret counteracting cause, 47 (cf. 67) ; it is universally allowed that chance when strictly examined is a mere negative word, 74.

D. *Power*—49-57.

Power, force, energy, necessary connexion must either be defined by analysis or explained by production of the impression from which they are copied, 49 ; from the first appearance of an object we cannot foretell its effect : we cannot see the power of a single body : we only see sequence, 50.

Is the idea of power derived from an internal impression and is it an idea of reflection ? 51 ; it is not derived, as Locke said, from reasoning about power of production in nature, 50 *n*; nor from consciousness of influence of will over bodily organs, 52 ; nor from effort to overcome resistance, 52 *n* (cf. 60 *n*); nor from influence of will over mind, 53 ; many philosophers appeal to an invisible intelligent principle, to a volition of the supreme being, and regard causes as only occasions and our mental conceptions as revelations, 54-5 ; thus diminishing the grandeur of God, 56 ; this theory too bold and beyond verification by our faculties, and is no explanation, 57 ; vis inertiae, 57 *n*.

In single instances we only see sequence of loose events which are conjoined and never connected, 58 ; the idea of necessary connexion only arises from a number of similar instances, and the only difference between such a number and a single instance is that the former produces a habit of expecting the usual attendant, 59, 61. This customary transition is the impression from which we form the idea of necessary connexion.

E. *Reasoning from effect to cause and conversely*, 105-115 (*v. Providence*).

In arguing from effect to cause we must not infer more qualities in the cause than are required to produce the effect, nor reason backwards from an inferred cause to new effects, 105-8 ; we can reason back from cause to new effects in the case of human acts by analogy which rests on previous knowledge, 111-2 ; when the effect is entirely singular and does not belong to any species we cannot infer its cause at all, 115.

F. *Definitions of Cause*—60 (cf 74 *n*).

Ceremonies—41.

Chance—ignorance of causes, 46 ; has no existence, 74 (*v. Cause* B).

Chastity—rules of, based on utility, 166-8, 188, 195.

Cheerfulness—great merit of not due to utility, 203.

Cicero—4, 266, 151 *n*, 266 *n*.

Circle—in reasoning, 30.

Civil-law—158 *n* (*v. Justice* B).

Clarke—37 *n*, 158 *n*.

Justice.

like a wall, justice builds it like a vault, 256 (cf. 232, 234); imperfection of human, 109; after the laws of justice are fixed there is a double harmfulness in their violation, 260.

(*b*) Abundance of external conveniences or extensive benevolence would render justice unnecessary, 145–6, 149; so justice suspended by extreme want of necessaries, 147; and in case of criminals and public war, 148; the common situation of man is a mean where justice is useful and therefore meritorious and obligatory, 149; no justice in golden age, 150; nor in state of nature represented as a state of war, 151; no justice towards animals because no inconvenience in injustice towards them, 152, if each man were complete in himself there would be no justice, 153; not so binding between societies as between individuals because not so useful, 165; among robbers, 170.

(*c*) Sentiment of, not derived from instinct, 160; does not arise from a promise, for the observance of promises is a considerable part of justice, 257; arises from a convention as a sense of common interest, e. g. such a convention as exists between two oarsmen, or as establishes currency or language, 257.

Vain to dispute whether it is natural owing to ambiguity of word: it is as natural as self-love, benevolence, reason, and forethought: in so sagacious an animal as man the necessary product of his reason may justly be esteemed natural, 258

(*d*) Why the utility of justice pleases and commands our affection and approbation, 173 f. (*v. Utility*); the affection we have for justice may be due to gratitude, not self-love, 199; the approbation of the social virtues feels different from that of the accomplishments and talents, 265.

B. *Rules of Justice.*

The particular rules by which justice is regulated and property determined only aim at good of mankind, 154; this excludes the principle of proportioning property to merit which would dissolve society, 154; so also the principle of absolute equality is not employed because it is impracticable, 155; all writers on laws of nature end with utility whatever principles they begin with, 156; where utility cannot decide between rival rules analogy is used, and where both fail civil laws supply the place of the natural code, 157, 259; use of precedents which are often fanciful, 259; property altogether subordinate to civil laws which ultimately consider only the happiness of human society, 158; in which respect alone the rules of property differ from superstitions, 159; the rules of property too numerous and various to be derived from instincts, 161; though education and habit make our judgements appear distinctive to us, 162.

General inflexible rules of property are required by public utility,

Mind.

    only mix and compound materials given by inward and outward sentiment, 13; power of will over, 53.

Miracles—86-101.

    Belief in human evidence diminishes according as the event witnessed is unusual or extraordinary, 89; difference between extraordinary and miraculous, 19*n*; if the evidence for a miracle amounted to proof we should have one proof opposed by another proof, for the proof against a miracle is as complete as possible; an event is not miraculous unless there is a uniform experience, that is a proof, against it, 90; definition of miracle, 90 *n*; hence no testimony is sufficient to establish a miracle unless its falsehood would be more miraculous than the event it establishes, 91; as a fact the evidence for a miracle has never amounted to proof, 92; the passion for the wonderful in human nature, 93; prevalence of miracles in savage and early periods and their diminution with civilization, 94; the evidence for miracles in matters of religion opposed by the almost infinite number of witnesses for rival religions, 95; value of human testimony diminished by temptation to pose as a prophet or apostle, 97; no testimony for a miracle has ever amounted to a probability, much less to a proof, and if it did amount to a proof it would be opposed by another perfect proof, 98; so a miracle can never be proved so as to be the foundation of a system of religion, 99; a conclusion which confounds those who base the Christian religion on reason, not on faith, 100; the Christian religion cannot be believed without a miracle which will subvert the principle of a man's understanding and give him a determination to believe what is most contrary to custom and experience, 101.

Mistake—of fact, opp. mistake of right, 241.

Modesty—213.

Monkish—virtues, of celibacy, self-denial, humility, are really vices, 219.

Montesquieu—158, 158*n*.

Moral—evil (q.v.) 80.

    Opp. intellectual endowments, 262 f. (*v. Virtue* A).

Moral distinctions.

    A. *Are they derived from Reason or Feeling?* 134-8, 234-46.

    (*a*) Do they arise from argument or from immediate feeling or finer internal sense? should they be the same for all rational beings or may they vary with particular constitutions, 134 (cf. 246); Ancients said that virtue was conformity to reason and yet derived them from taste and sentiment: Moderns such as Shaftesbury talk of the beauty and virtue, but explain them by metaphysical reasonings and deductions, 134; it is said they must be derived from reason if men reason about them, 135; and again that if based on reason they would produce no actions, 136 (cf. 235); probably reason and sentiment

Moral distinctions.

concur in most moral conclusions : the final sentence is pronounced
by some internal sense which nature has made universal in the whole
species, but this sense, like the sense of beauty, is assisted by such
reasoning, which corrects a false relish ahd enables us to feel the
proper sentiment, 137 (cf. 117, 185) ; if usefulness is the foundation of
praise, much reason is required to show the useful tendencies and
actions, 234 ; but reason alone is not sufficient to produce moral
approbation : there must be a sentiment which prefers the useful
tendencies, and this can only be a feeling of humanity, 235 (cf. 221–2);
the ultimate ends of human actions can never be accounted for by
reason, but only by some desire for which no reason can be given, 244 ;
the boundaries of reason and taste easily ascertained ; reason discovers
truth and falsehood and shows things as they really are ; taste is
a productive faculty and colours its objects : reason is cool and disengaged ; taste, giving pleasure or pain, becomes a motive to action :
the standard of reason is eternal and inflexible even by God ; that of
taste arises from the constitution which is bestowed on men by God,
246 (cf. 134).

(*b*) Reason alone cannot show the demerit in ingratitude, 236 ; it
judges either of matter of fact or of relations : where is the *matter of
fact* which we call ingratitude ? 237 ; if the crime consists in certain
relations, what are they ? there is the same relation of contrariety in
ingratitude and in rewarding good for evil, 238 ; there is a circle in
saying that morality consists in a relation of actions to the rule of
right, and that the rule of right is determined by reason from the
moral relations of actions, 239 ; relations are considered in a different
way by speculative and moral reasoning : in speculation we infer
unknown from known relations ; in morals we require to know all
the relations, and then we award praise or blame without using our
reason, 240 ; hence the great difference between a mistake of fact
and of right, 241 ; natural beauty depends on relations of parts, but
the perception of beauty is not merely the perception of these by
reason, 242 ; inanimate objects may bear the same relations as moral
agents and yet are not praised or blamed, 243.

B. *Reality of Moral distinctions* (*v. Self-Love*, 174–223, 247–254).
Reality of, cannot be seriously denied, 133 ; not the result of education alone but arise from the original constitution of human nature,
173 ; cannot be explained by avarice, ambition, vanity, or other passions vulgarly, though improperly, comprised under self-love, 233 ;
since virtue is an end and desirable in itself without fee or reward there
must be some sentiment which distinguishes it, 245 ; by all the rules
of philosophy we must conclude that the sentiments of morality and
of humanity are originally the same, since they are governed by the
same laws and moved by the same objects, 192 (cf. 183–4) ; can only
be explained by a sentiment common to all men and extending to

Passion.

itself may be such a basis, 231; theory that no passion can be disinterested, 248; this due to false love of simplicity, 250; best explained by most obvious hypothesis, 251; theory of disinterested, more truly simple than selfish theory: there are direct and primary passions, and secondary passions for the pleasure of gratifying the primary: without such primary passions directed immediately to their objects, self-love could not exert itself, 253; benevolence may be a direct desire for another's good, 254.

Calm, confused with Reason, 196.

Life without, insipid and tiresome, 231.

Of benevolence unites more advantages than any other, 231; extraordinary, roused by consideration of fortunes of others, 202 *n.*

Patriotism—a necessary limit to benevolence, 182 *n.*

Perception—and external objects, 119 f. (*v. Scepticism, Impression, Idea*).

Peripatetics—and golden mean, 191.

Perseverance—262.

Philanthropy—natural, 184 (*v Benevolence, Self-love*).

Philosophy—moral, two branches of, abstruse and practical, 1–5; gratifies innocent curiosity, 6; metaphysics tries to deal with matters inaccessible to human understanding, 6.

True, must lay down limits of understanding, 7 (cf 113); a large part of, consists in mental geography, 8; may hope to resolve principles of mind into still more general principles, 9.

Natural, only staves off our ignorance a little longer, as moral or metaphysical philosophy serves only to discover larger portions of it, 26; academical, or sceptical, flatters no bias or passion except love of truth, and so has few partisans, 34; though it destroy speculation, cannot destroy action, for nature steps in and asserts her rights, 34; moral, inferior to mathematics in clearness of ideas, superior in shortness of arguments, 48.

Controversies in, due to ambiguity of terms, 62.

Encroaches on grammar improperly, 261 f.

Disputes in, not be settled by appeal to dangerous consequences of a doctrine, 75 (cf. 228).

Speculative, entirely indifferent to the peace of society and security of government, 104 (cf. 114).

All the philosophy in the world, and all the religion in the world, which is nothing but a species of philosophy, can never carry us beyond the usual course of experience, 113.

Tranquillity of, 206; happiness of, to have originated in an age and country of freedom and toleration, 102; of all kinds, and especially morals, more united with theology in modern than in ancient times, 268.

Pity—202 *n.*

Self-love.

A. Theory that through man's connexion with society and interest in its welfare, he approves of the social virtues from self-love: this theory though held by many is plainly opposed by the voice of nature and experience, 174; we praise actions opposed to our interests or in which we have no interest; we distinguish, both to ourselves and others, laudable from advantageous actions, 175.

A Hobbist says that imagination turns our self-love into a variety of appearances: we reply that at all events we approve those in whom their self-love takes the appearance of benevolence, and disapprove those who appear to seek their own enjoyment: the difference between the two characters cannot be destroyed by minute reflections upon their origin, 249.

To say that we put ourselves by imagination in the place of the persons affected by the actions is a weak subterfuge—imagination of another's interest could not overcome a present view of our own interest, 176; we are not indifferent to others' interest, 177; everything which contributes to the happiness of society recommends itself directly to our approval, 178-188 (*v. Sympathy*); the utility of the social virtues moves us not by any regard of self-interest but by affecting the benevolent principles of our frame, 189.

B. Our approval of qualities useful to the possessor cannot be due to self-love—imagination cannot convert us into another person, still less transport us back into ourselves: all suspicion of selfish regards is here excluded, 191; any man must show a preference for what is useful, 192.

It is still more difficult to resolve the selfish virtues, whose merit consists in their tendency to serve their possessor, into self-love than it is to so resolve the social virtues: every one is really interested in the social virtues, though he approves them rather from gratitude than self-love, but the other virtues can only appeal to a disinterested regard for others. This is a natural and unforced interpretation of the phenomena of human life, 199, 251; the selfish theory is contrary to obvious appearances, and all the systems which maintain it are based on that false love of simplicity which is so dangerous in philosophy, 250; in moral science the presumption is always in favour of the most obvious causes: we cannot account for strong passions by treating them as the result of refined reflections on self-interest, 251; such explanations inapplicable to the kindness of animals, love between the sexes, parental affection and gratitude: there are a thousand marks of a 'general benevolence' in human nature, where no real interest binds us to the object, much less any imaginary interest, 252.

Cannot account for our regard for riches, 201; which beget esteem in us merely because they serve to satisfy the appetites of their possessor, 202.

A. We must own that the interests of society are not even on their own account indifferent to us : everthing which contributes to the happiness of society recommends itself directly to our approbation and good will, 178 ; the very aspect of happiness pleases us, 179 ; we cannot resist sympathetic movements of pleasure or uneasiness, 180 ; hence our great interest in public news, and even ancient history, 181.

Social sympathy is shown in the power of party and factions which excite a concern superior to the narrow attachments of self-love and private interest : so sympathy governs our criticism of style in letters and our judgements of beauty in art, 182.

An unsympathetic man is also indifferent to virtue, a sympathetic man shows a delicate power of drawing moral distinctions, 183.

In all men the principles of humanity give a general approbation of what is useful to society, though in different degrees in different men, 183.

When the natural philanthropy of men is not prevented they prefer the happiness of society and virtue : there is no such thing as disinterested malice, 184.

There are a thousand marks of a 'general benevolence' in human nature, where no real interest binds us to the object, much less any imaginary interest, 252 ; the theory of disinterested benevolence much simpler than the selfish theory, 253.

B. Though our sympathy varies with the distance of objects, we ascribe a uniform merit to actions, because our judgement corrects the inequalities of our internal emotions and perceptions, 185 ; the differences caused by the variations of sympathy are eliminated by our calm judgements through the intercourse of sentiments with other men, and we form some general and unalterable standard, 186 ; so the merit of the social virtues still appears uniform and arises from that regard which the natural sentiment of benevolence engages us to pay to the interests to society : man cannot be indifferent to the well or ill-being of his fellows, though he need not feel any very strong emotion towards virtue which is distant from him, 187–190.

C. The same objects are agreeable to the sentiments of morals and of humanity : these sentiments are therefore originally the same since they are governed by the same laws and moved by the same objects, 192, 220 ; the notion of morals implies some sentiment common to all mankind which recommends the same object to general approbation and extends to the actions of all men however remote : these two circumstances belong to the sentiment of humanity alone, 221 ;

Sympathy.

when a man calls another vicious he expects others to concur in his feeling: he appeals to some universal principle in human nature: this sentiment of humanity being common to all men, can alone be the foundation of a general system of blame and praise : the humanity of one man is the humanity of every one, 222 ; it is also the only sentiment to which no character of man is indifferent, 223.

System—of society, 174, 256, 257.

Talents—opp. virtues, 261.

Taste—in beauty, corrected by reasoning, 137.

A productive faculty, and a motive to action, so depends on the peculiar constitution given by God to particular creatures: opp. reason, 246.

The decision of good manners must be left to the blind but sure testimony of taste and sentiment, being a part of ethics left by nature to baffle the pride of philosophy, 216.

Temperance—229, 262.

Theology—science of, 132 ; influence of, on morals, greater in modern than ancient times: treats moral like civil laws and so lays great stress on voluntariness of actions, 268 (*v. God, Providence*).

Tillotson—argument against real presence, 86.

Time—and space, 124 f.

Tranquillity—philosophical, 206.

Truth—8, 17, 246 (*v. Scepticism*).

Truthfulness—195. '

Understanding—limits of human, 7 ; operations of, to be classified, 8 ; opp. experience, 28 ; weakness of, 126 (*v. Reason, Scepticism*).

Universal—nature of moral judgement and of the sentiment of humanity, 221-2.

Utility.

A. Perceived by reason, 234; not actual utility but tendencies or intentions considered in our moral judgements, 185 *n*; of inanimate objects does not make them virtuous, 172 *n* ; of justice makes it obligatory, 149; no qualities absolutely blameable, but only certain degrees: the happy medium settled by utility, 191-2 ; personal merit must consist in the possession of mental qualities, either useful or agreeable, either to the person himself or to others : there can be no other source of merit, 217 ; a foundation of the chief part of morals, 188.

B. *Qualities useful to others: the social virtues.*

Benevolence and justice, 141-163.

The sole object and standard of justice, 154-163 ; of justice often obscure, 167, 186, 234 ; requires that laws of justice should be inflexible : the utility of justice only arises from the whole system,

Virtue.

and defects, is grammatical ; no such boundaries fixed in English or any other modern tongue, 261 ; the question being merely verbal is of small importance, 262 ; the small verbal distinction made corresponds to the small difference in feeling, 263 ; even if the sentiment of approbation of accomplishments is different from that of justice and humanity, this is not a sufficient reason for ascribing them to entirely different classes, 205 (cf. 172 *n*) ; a blemish, a fault, a vice, a crime, express different degrees of censure which are however all of them at the bottom pretty nearly of the same species, 268.

(i) We cannot limit virtue to voluntary laudable qualities, this excludes many which depend little on our choice—e. g. courage, equanimity, patience, 262 ; the ancients laid little stress on the voluntariness of virtue, 267 , which was emphasized by theology, which treated moral like civil laws, 268.

(ii) Cannot oppose virtues to intellectual endowments, for such as prudence, discernment, discretion, have great influence on conduct : though we call a man virtuous chiefly for his social qualities, no one ever says seriously that such a one is a man of great virtue but an egregious blockhead, 262 ; no man is much regarded, even if he have the best intentions, without a moderate share of parts and understanding, 264 ; the ancient moralists comprised all sorts of mental endowments under the name of virtue, 266.

(iii) Cannot limit virtue to social virtues which by their name imply virtues of another kind, 261

(iv) Cannot limit virtue to qualities which proceed from the heart and are accompanied by a sentiment, for industry, frugality, temperance and perseverance are virtues, but are only known to the possessor by their effects, 262.

Utility of Virtue (*v. Utility, Justice, Benevolence*).

B. Must consist altogether in the possession of mental qualities, either useful or agreeable, either to the person himself or to others, 217 ; nowhere except in the schools is any other doctrine maintained, 218 ; this is the view of natural unprejudiced reason, the monkish virtues rejected by all men of sense because they serve no purpose, 219 ; this theory of virtue only requires of men just calculation and steady preference of the greater happiness, 228 ; treating vice with the greatest candour there is not the smallest pretext for giving it the preference above virtue with a view of self-interest, 232, though it is impossible to convince by argument any one who does not feel that honesty is the best policy, 233 ; men are not deficient in their duty to society, because they would not wish to be generous, friendly, and humane, but because they do not feel themselves such, 231 ; for any one's happiness and self-enjoyment I would sooner have a friendly and human heart than all the other virtues of Demosthenes and Philip, 204

THE END.

OXFORD
PRINTED AT THE CLARENDON PRESS
BY HORACE HART, M.A.
PRINTER TO THE UNIVERSITY

CLARENDON PRESS, OXFORD.
SELECT LIST OF STANDARD WORKS.

1. DICTIONARIES.

A NEW ENGLISH DICTIONARY
ON HISTORICAL PRINCIPLES,

Founded mainly on the materials collected by the Philological Society.

Imperial 4to.

EDITED BY DR. MURRAY.

PRESENT STATE OF THE WORK.

					£	s.	d.
Vol. I.	A, B	By Dr. MURRAY	Half-morocco		2	12	6
Vol. II.	C	By Dr. MURRAY	Half-morocco		2	12	6
Vol. III.	D, E	By Dr. MURRAY and Dr. BRADLEY	Half-morocco		2	12	6
Vol. IV.	F, G	By Dr. BRADLEY	Half-morocco		2	12	6
Vol. V.	H—K	By Dr. MURRAY	Half-morocco		2	12	6
Vol. VI.	L—N	By Dr. BRADLEY . .	L–Lap		0	2	6
			Lap–Leisurely . . .		0	5	0
			Leisureness–Lief . .		0	2	6
			Lief–Lock		0	5	0
			Lock–Lyyn		0	5	0
			M–Mandragon . . .		0	5	0
			Mandragora–Matter .		0	5	0
Vol. VII.	O, P	By Dr. MURRAY . .	O–Onomastic		0	5	0
			Onomastical–Outing.		0	5	0
			Outjet–Ozyat . . .		0	2	6
			P–Pargeted		0	5	0
			Pargeter–Pennached.		0	5	0
			Pennage–Pf		0	5	0
Vol. VIII.	Q—S	By Mr. CRAIGIE . .	Q		0	2	6
			R–Reactive		0	5	0
			Reactively–Ree . . .		0	5	0
			Ree–Reign		0	2	6

The remainder of the work is in active preparation.

Vols. IX, X will contain S–Z with some supplemental matter.

Orders can be given through any bookseller for the delivery of the remainder of the work in complete *Volumes* or in *Half-volumes* or in *Sections* or in *Parts*.

HALF-VOLUMES. The price of half-volumes, bound, with straight-grained persian leather back, cloth sides, gilt top, is £1 7s. 6d. each, or £16 10s. for the twelve now ready, namely, A, B, C–Comm., Comm.–Czech, D, E, F, G, H, I–K, L, O–Pf.

SECTIONS. A single Section of 64 pages at 2s. 6d. or a double Section of 128 pages at 5s. is issued quarterly.

PARTS. A Part (which is generally the equivalent of five single Sections and is priced at 12s. 6d.) is issued whenever ready.

Nearly all the Parts and Sections in which Volumes I–V were first issued are still obtainable in the original covers.

FORTHCOMING ISSUE, Jan. 1906. A portion continuing R, by Mr. CRAIGIE.

A Hebrew and English Lexicon of the Old Testament, with an Appendix containing the Biblical Aramaic, based on the Thesaurus and Lexicon of Gesenius, by Francis Brown, D.D., S. R. Driver, D.D., and C. A. Briggs, D.D. Parts I–XI. Small 4to, 2s. 6d. each.

Thesaurus Syriacus: collegerunt Quatremère, Bernstein, Lorsbach, Arnoldi, Agrell, Field, Roediger: edidit R. Payne Smith, S.T.P. Vol. I (Fasc. I–V), sm. fol., 5l. 5s. Vol. II, completion (Fasc. VI–X), 8l. 8s.

A Compendious Syriac Dictionary, founded upon the above. Edited by Mrs. Margoliouth. Small 4to, complete, 63s. *net.* Part IV, 15s. *net.* *Parts I–III can no longer be supplied.*

A Dictionary of the Dialects of Vernacular Syriac as spoken by the Eastern Syrians of Kurdistan, North-West Persia, and the Plain of Moṣul. By A. J. Maclean, M.A., F.R.G.S. Small 4to, 15s.

An English-Swahili Dictionary. By A. C. Madan, M.A. *Second Edition, Revised.* Extra fcap. 8vo, 7s. 6d. *net.*

Swahili-English Dictionary. By A. C. Madan, M.A. Extra fcap. 8vo. 7s. 6d. *net.*

A Sanskrit-English Dictionary. Etymologically and Philologically arranged, with special reference to cognate Indo-European Languages. By Sir M. Monier-Williams, M.A., K.C.I.E. *New Edition.* Cloth, bevelled edges, 3l. 13s. 6d.; half-morocco, 4l. 4s.

A Greek-English Lexicon. By H. G. Liddell, D.D., and Robert Scott, D.D. *Eighth Edition, Revised.* 4to. 1l. 16s.

An Etymological Dictionary of the English Language, arranged on an Historical Basis. By W. W. Skeat, Litt.D. *Third Edition.* 4to. 2l. 4s.

A Middle-English Dictionary. By F. H. Stratmann. A new edition, by H. Bradley, M.A., Ph.D. 4to, half-morocco. 1l. 11s. 6d.

The Student's Dictionary of Anglo-Saxon. By H. Sweet, M.A., Ph.D., LL.D. Small 4to. 8s. 6d. *net.*

An Anglo-Saxon Dictionary, based on the MS. collections of the late Joseph Bosworth, D.D. Edited and enlarged by Prof. T. N. Toller, M.A. Parts I–III. A–SÁR. 4to, stiff covers, 15s. each. Part IV, § 1, SÁR–SWÍÐRIAN. Stiff covers, 8s. 6d. Part IV, § 2, SWÍÞ-SNEL-ÝTMEST, 18s. 6d.

An Icelandic-English Dictionary, based on the MS. collections of the late Richard Cleasby. Enlarged and completed by G. Vigfússon, M.A. 4to. 3l. 7s.

2. LAW.

Anson. *Principles of the English Law of Contract, and of Agency in its Relation to Contract.* By Sir W. R. Anson, D.C.L. *Tenth Edition.* 8vo. 10s. 6d.

Anson. *Law and Custom of the Constitution.* 2 vols. 8vo.
Part I. Parliament. *Third Edition.* 12s. 6d.
Part II. The Crown. *Second Ed.* 14s.

Bryce. *Studies in History and Jurisprudence.* 2 Vols. 8vo. By the Right Hon J. Bryce, M.P. 25s. *net.*

Goudy. *Von Jhering's Law in Daily Life.* Translated by H. Goudy, D.C.L. Crown 8vo. 3s. 6d. *net.*

Digby. *An Introduction to the History of the Law of Real Property.*

Oxford: Clarendon Press

By Sir Kenelm E. Digby, M.A. *Fifth Edition.* 8vo. 12s. 6d.

Grueber. *Lex Aquilia.* By Erwin Grueber. 8vo. 10s. 6d.

Hall. *International Law.* By W.E.Hall,M.A. *Fifth Edit.* Revised by J. B. Atlay, M.A. 8vo. 21s. *net.*

—— *A Treatise on the Foreign Powers and Jurisdiction of the British Crown.* 8vo. 10s. 6d.

Holland. *Elements of Jurisprudence.* By T. E. Holland, D.C.L. *Ninth Edition.* 8vo. 10s. 6d.

—— *Studies in International Law.* 8vo. 10s. 6d.

—— *Gentilis, Alberici, De Iure Belli Libri Tres.* Small 4to, half-morocco. 21s.

—— *The Institutes of Justinian. Second Edition.* Extra fcap. 8vo. 5s.

—— *The European Concert in the Eastern Question,* a collection of treaties and other public acts. 8vo. 12s. 6d.

Holland and Shadwell. *Select Titles from the Digest of Justinian.* By T. E. Holland, D.C.L., and C. L. Shadwell, D.C.L. 8vo. 14s. Also in Parts, paper covers—I. Introductory Titles. 2s. 6d. II. Family Law. 1s. III. Property Law. 2s.6d. IV. Law of Obligations (No. 1), 3s. 6d. (No. 2), 4s. 6d.

Ilbert. *The Government of India.* Being a Digest of the Statute Law relating thereto. By Sir Courtenay Ilbert, K.C.S.I. 8vo, half-roan. 21s.

—— *Legislative Forms and Methods.* 8vo, half-roan. 16s.

Jenks. *Modern Land Law.* By Edward Jenks, M.A. 8vo. 15s.

Jenkyns. *British Rule and Jurisdiction beyond the Seas.* By the late Sir Henry Jenkyns, K.C.B. 8vo, half-roan. 16s. *net.*

Markby. *Elements of Law* considered with reference to Principles of General Jurisprudence. By Sir William Markby. *Sixth Edition.* 8vo. 12s. 6d.

Moyle. *Imperatoris Iustiniani Institutionum Libri Quattuor,* with Introductions, Commentary, Excursus and Translation. By J. B. Moyle, D.C.L. *Fourth Edition.* 2 vols. 8vo. Vol. I. 16s. Vol. II. 6s.

—— *Contract of Sale in the Civil Law.* 8vo. 10s. 6d.

Pollock and Wright. *An Essay on Possession in the Common Law.* By Sir F. Pollock, Bart., M.A., and Sir R. S. Wright, B.C.L. 8vo. 8s.6d.

Poste. *Gaii Institutionum Juris Civilis Commentarii Quattuor;* or, Elements of Roman Law by Gaius. With a Translation and Commentary by Edward Poste, M.A. *Fourth Edition,* revised and enlarged. 8vo. 16s *net.*

Radcliffe and Miles. *Cases Illustrating the Principles of the Law of Torts.* By F. R. Y. Radcliffe, K.C., and J. C. Miles, M.A. 8vo. 12s.6d. *net.*

Sohm. *The Institutes.* A Text-book of the History and System of Roman Private Law. By Rudolph Sohm. Translated by J. C. Ledlie, B.C.L. *Second Edition,* revised and enlarged. 8vo. 18s.

Stokes. *The Anglo-Indian Codes.* By Whitley Stokes, LL.D. Vol. I. Substantive Law. 8vo. 30s Vol. II. Adjective Law. 8vo. 35s. First and Second Supplements to the above, 1887–1891. 8vo. 6s. 6d. Separately, No.1, 2s.6d.; No. 2, 4s.6d.

Young. *Corps de Droit Ottoman Recueil des Codes, Lois, Règlements, Ordonnances et Actes les plus importants du Droit intérieur, et D'Études sur le Droit coutumier de l'Empire Ottoman.* Par George Young. Part I (Vols. I–III), cloth, 2l. 17s. 6d. net; paper covers, 2l. 12s. 6d. net. Part II (Vols. IV–VII), cloth, 1l. 17s. net; paper covers, 1l. 11s. 6d. The complete Parts I and II separately, will cost 2l. 12s. 6d. net in paper covers, or 2l. 17s. 6d net in cloth each.

3. HISTORY, BIOGRAPHY, ETC.

Asser. *Life of King Alfred,* together with the Annals of St. Noets, erroneously ascribed to Asser. Edited with Introduction and Commentary by W. H. Stevenson, M.A. 2 vols. Crown 8vo. 12s. *net.*

Aubrey. *'Brief Lives,' chiefly of Contemporaries, set down by John Aubrey, between the Years* 1669 *and* 1696. Edited from the Author's MSS., by Andrew Clark, M.A., LL.D. With Facsimiles. 2 vols. 8vo. 25s.

Ballard. *The Domesday Boroughs.* By Adolphus Ballard, B.A., LL.B. 8vo. With four Plans. 6s. 6d. *net.*

Barnard. *Companion to English History (Middle Ages).* With 97 Illustrations. By F. P. Barnard, M.A. Crown 8vo. 8s. 6d. *net.*

Boswell's *Life of Samuel Johnson, LL.D.* Edited by G. Birkbeck Hill, D.C.L. In six volumes, medium 8vo. With Portraits and Facsimiles. Half-bound. 3l. 3s.

Bright. *Chapters of Early English Church History.* By W. Bright, D.D. *Third Edition. Revised and Enlarged.* With a Map. 8vo. 12s.

Bryce. *Studies in History and Jurisprudence.* By J. Bryce, M.P. 2 vols. 8vo. 25s. *net.*

Butler. *The Arab Conquest of Egypt and the last thirty years of the Roman Dominion.* By A. J. Butler, D.Litt., F.S.A. With Maps and Plans. 8vo. 16s. *net.*

Chambers. *The Mediaeval Stage.* By E. K. Chambers. With two illustrations. 2 vols. 8vo. 25s *net.*

Clarendon's *History of the Rebellion and Civil Wars in England.* Re-edited by W. Dunn Macray, M.A., F.S.A. 6 vols. Crown 8vo. 2l. 5s.

Earle and Plummer. *Two of the Saxon Chronicles, Parallel, with Supplementary Extracts from the others.* A Revised Text, edited, with Introduction, Notes, Appendices, and Glossary, by C. Plummer, M.A., on the basis of an edition by J. Earle, M.A. 2 vols. Cr. 8vo, half-roan.
Vol. I. Text, Appendices, and Glossary. 10s. 6d.
Vol. II. Introduction, Notes, and Index. 12s. 6d.

Fisher. *Studies in Napoleonic Statesmanship.— Germany.* By H. A. L. Fisher, M.A. With four Maps. 8vo. 12s. 6d. *net.*

Freeman. *The History of Sicily from the Earliest Times.*
Vols. I and II. 8vo, cloth. 2l. 2s.
Vol. III. The Athenian and Carthaginian Invasions. 24s.
Vol. IV. From the Tyranny of Dionysios to the Death of Agathoklês. Edited by Arthur J. Evans, M.A. 21s.

Freeman. *The Reign of William Rufus and the Accession of Henry the First.* By E. A. Freeman, D.C.L. 2 vols. 8vo. 1l. 16s.

Gardiner. *The Constitutional Documents of the Puritan Revolution,* 1628–1660. By S. R. Gardiner, D.C.L. *Second Edition.* Crown 8vo. 10s. 6d.

Gross. *The Gild Merchant;* a Contribution to British Municipal History. By Charles Gross, Ph.D. 2 vols. 8vo. 24s.

Hill. *Sources for Greek History between the Persian and Peloponnesian Wars.* Collected and arranged by G. F. Hill, M.A. 8vo. 10s. 6d.

Hodgkin. *Italy and her Invaders.* With Plates & Maps. 8 vols. 8vo. By T. Hodgkin, D.C.L.
Vols. I-II. 42s. Vols. III-IV. 36s. Vols. V-VI. 36s. Vols. VII-VIII. 24s.

Johnson. *Letters of Samuel Johnson, LL.D.* Collected and Edited by G Birkbeck Hill, D.C.L. 2 vols. half-roan. 28s.

—— *Johnsonian Miscellanies.* 2 vols. Medium 8vo, half-roan. 28s.

—— *Lives of the Poets.* 3 vols. Medium 8vo (immediately).

Kitchin. *A History of France.*
By G. W. Kitchin, D.D. In three
Volumes. Crown 8vo, each 10s. 6d.
Vol. I. to 1453. Vol. II. 1453–
1624. Vol. III. 1624–1793.

Kyd. *The Works of Thomas
Kyd.* Edited from the original
Texts, with Introduction, Notes,
and Facsimiles, by F. S. Boas,
M.A. 8vo. 15s. net.

Legg. *Select Documents Illus-
trative of the History of the French
Revolution. The Constituent Assembly.*
Edited by L. G. WICKHAM LEGG.
2 vols. Crown 8vo. 12s. net.

Lewis (*Sir G. Cornewall*).
*An Essay on the Government of De-
pendencies.* Edited by C. P. Lucas,
B.A. 8vo, half-roan. 14s.

Lucas. *Historical Geography*
of the British Colonies. By C. P. Lucas,
B.A. With Maps. Cr. 8vo.
  *The Origin and Growth of the
  English Colonies and of their
  System of Government.* By H. E.
  Egerton. 2s. 6d. Also in binding
  uniform with the Series. 3s. 6d.
  Vol. I. The Mediterranean and
    Eastern Colonies (exclusive of
    India). 5s.
  Vol. II. The West Indian Colo-
    nies. Second edition, revised
    to 1905, by C Atchley. 7s. 6d.
  Vol. III. West Africa. *Second
    Edition, revised to the end of* 1899,
    by H. E. Egerton. 7s. 6d.
  Vol. IV. South and East Africa.
    Historical and Geographical.
    9s. 6d. Part I. Historical, 6s. 6d.
    Part II. Geographical, 3s. 6d.
  Vol. V. The History of Canada
    (Part I, New France). 6s.

Ludlow. *The Memoirs of
Edmund Ludlow, Lieutenant-General of
the Horse in the Army of the Commonwealth of England,* 1625–1672. Edited
by C. H. Firth, M.A. 2 vols. 36s.

Lyly. *The Works of John Lyly.*
Collected and edited, with facsimiles, by R. W. Bond, M.A. In 3 vols.
8vo, uniform with *Kyd.* 42s. net.

Machiavelli. *Il Principe.*
Edited by L. Arthur Burd, M.A.
With an Introduction by Lord
Acton. 8vo. 14s.

Merriman. *Life and Letters of
Thomas Cromwell.* With a Portrait
and Facsimile. By R. B. Merriman,
B.Litt. 2 vols. 8vo. 18s. net.

Morris. *The Welsh Wars of
Edward I.* With a Map. By J. E.
Morris, M.A. 8vo. 9s. 6d. net.

Oman. *A History of the Penin-
sular War.* 6 vols. 8vo. With Maps,
Plans, and Portraits. By C. Oman,
M.A. Vol. I, 1807–1809. 14s. net.
Vol. II, Jan.–Sept., 1809 (from the
Battle of Corunna to the end of the
Talavera Campaign). 14s. net.

Payne. *History of the New
World called America.* By E. J.
Payne, M.A. 8vo.
  Vol. I, containing *The Discovery*
    and *Aboriginal America,* 18s.
  Vol. II, *Aboriginal America* (con-
    cluded), 14s.

Plummer. *The Life and Times
of Alfred the Great.* By Charles
Plummer, M.A. Crown 8vo. 5s.
net.

Poole. *Historical Atlas of
Modern Europe from the decline of the
Roman Empire.* Edited by R. L.
Poole, M.A. 5l. 15s. 6d. net. Each
Map can now be bought separately
for 1s. 6d. net.

Prothero. *Select Statutes and
other Constitutional Documents, illustra-
tive of the Reigns of Elizabeth and
James I.* Edited by G. W. Prothero,
M.A. Cr. 8vo. Edition 2. 10s. 6d.

Ramsay (Sir J. H.). *Lancaster
and York* (A.D. 1399–1485). 2 vols.
8vo. With Index. 37s. 6d.

Ramsay (W. M.). *The Cities
and Bishoprics of Phrygia.*
  Vol. I. Part I. The Lycos Valley
    and South-Western Phrygia.
    Royal 8vo. 18s. net.
  Vol. I. Part II. West and West-
    Central Phrygia. 21s. net.

Ranke. *A History of Eng-land, principally in the Seventeenth Century.* By L. von Ranke. Translated under the superintendence of G. W. Kitchin, D.D., and C. W. Boase, M.A. 6 vols. 8vo. 63s. Revised Index, separately, 1s.

Rashdall. *The Universities of Europe in the Middle Ages.* By Hastings Rashdall, M.A. 2 vols. (in 3 Parts) 8vo. With Maps. 2l. 5s. net.

Rhŷs. *Studies in the Arthurian Legend.* By John Rhŷs, M.A. 8vo. 12s. 6d.
—— *Celtic Folklore:* Welsh and Manx. By the same. 2 vols. 8vo. 21s.

Sanday. *Sacred Sites of the Gospels* By W. Sanday, D.D. With many illustrations, including drawings of the Temple by Paul Waterhouse. 8vo. 13s. 6d. net.

Scaccario. *De Necessariis Observantiis Scaccarii Dialogus.* Commonly called Dialogus de Scaccario. Edited by A. Hughes, C. G. Crump, and C. Johnson. 8vo. 12s. 6d. net.

Smith's *Lectures on Justice, Police, Revenue and Arms.* Edited, with Introduction and Notes, by Edwin Cannan. 8vo. 10s. 6d. net.
—— *Wealth of Nations.* With Notes, by J. E. Thorold Rogers, M.A. 2 vols. 8vo. 21s.

Smith (V. A.). *The Early History of India, from 600 B.C. to the Muhammadan Conquest, including the Invasion of Alexander the Great.* By Vincent A. Smith, M.A. 8vo, with Maps and other Illustrations. 14s net.

Stubbs. *Select Charters and other Illustrations of English Constitutional History, from the Earliest Times to the Reign of Edward I.* Arranged and edited by W. Stubbs, D.D. Eighth Edition. Crown 8vo. 8s. 6d.
—— *The Constitutional History of England, in its Origin and Development.* Library Edition. 3 vols. Demy 8vo. 2l. 8s. Also in 3 vols. crown 8vo. 12s. each.
—— *Seventeen Lectures on the Study of Mediaeval and Modern History and kindred subjects.* Crown 8vo. Third Edition. 8s. 6d.
—— *Registrum Sacrum Anglicanum.* Sm. 4to. Ed. 2. 10s. 6d.

Vigfússon and Powell. *Origines Icelandicae.* A Collection of the more important Sagas and other Native Writings relating to the Settlement and Early History of Iceland. Edited and translated by G. Vigfússon and F. York Powell. 2 vols. 8vo. 42s. net.

Vinogradoff. *Villainage in England.* Essays in English Mediaeval History. By Paul Vinogradoff. 8vo, half-bound. 16s.

4. PHILOSOPHY, LOGIC, ETC.

Bacon. *Novum Organum.* Edited, with Introduction, Notes, &c., by T. Fowler, D.D. Second Edition. 8vo. 15s.

Berkeley. *The Works of George Berkeley, D.D., formerly Bishop of Cloyne; including many of his writings hitherto unpublished.* With Prefaces, Annotations, Appendices, and an Account of his Life, by A. Campbell Fraser, Hon. D.C.L., LL.D. New Edition in 4 vols.; cr. 8vo. 24s.
—— *The Life and Letters, with an account of his Philosophy* By A. Campbell Fraser. 8vo. 16s.

Bosanquet. *Logic; or, the Morphology of Knowledge.* By B. Bosanquet, M.A. 8vo. 21s.

Butler. *The Works of Joseph Butler, D C.L.,* sometime Lord Bishop of Durham. Edited by the Right Hon. W. E. Gladstone. 2 vols. Medium 8vo. 14s. each.

Campagnac. *The Cambridge Platonists:* being Selections from the writings of Benjamin Whichcote, John Smith, and Nathanael Culverwel, with Introduction by E. T. Campagnac, M.A. Cr. 8vo. 6s. 6d. net.

Fowler. *Logic;* Deductive and Inductive, combined in a single volume. Extra fcap. 8vo. 7s. 6d.

Fowler and Wilson. *The Principles of Morals.* By T. Fowler, D.D., and J. M. Wilson, B.D. 8vo, cloth. 14s.

Green. *Prolegomena to Ethics.* By T. H. Green, M.A. Edited by A. C. Bradley, M.A. *Fourth Edition.* Crown 8vo. 7s. 6d.

Hegel. *The Logic of Hegel.* Translated from the Encyclopaedia of the Philosophical Sciences. With Prolegomena to the Study of Hegel's Logic and Philosophy. By W. Wallace, M.A. *Second Edition, Revised and Augmented.* 2 vols. Crown 8vo. 10s. 6d. each.

Hegel's *Philosophy of Mind.* Translated from the Encyclopaedia of the Philosophical Sciences. With Five Introductory Essays. By William Wallace, M.A., LL.D. Crown 8vo. 10s. 6d.

Hume's *Treatise of Human Nature.* Edited, with Analytical Index, by L. A. Selby-Bigge, M.A. *Second Edition.* Crown 8vo. 6s. net.

—— *Enquiry concerning the Human Understanding.* Edited by L. A. Selby-Bigge, M.A. *Second Edition.* Crown 8vo. 6s. net.

Leibniz. *The Monadology and other Philosophical Writings.* Translated, with Introduction and Notes, by Robert Latta, M.A., D.Phil. Crown 8vo. 8s. 6d.

Locke. *An Essay Concerning Human Understanding.* By John Locke. Collated and Annotated by A. Campbell Fraser, Hon. D.C.L., LL.D. 2 vols. 8vo. 1l. 12s.

Lotze's *Logic,* in Three Books —of Thought, of Investigation, and of Knowledge. English Translation; edited by B. Bosanquet, M.A. *Second Edition.* 2 vols. Cr. 8vo. 12s.

—— *Metaphysic,* in Three Books—Ontology, Cosmology, and Psychology. English Translation; edited by B. Bosanquet, M.A. *Second Edition.* 2 vols. Cr. 8vo. 12s.

Martineau. *Types of Ethical Theory.* By James Martineau, D.D. *Third Edition.* 2 vols. Cr. 8vo. 15s.

—— *A Study of Religion :* its Sources and Contents. *Second Edition.* 2 vols. Cr. 8vo. 15s.

Selby-Bigge. *British Moralists.* Selections from Writers principally of the Eighteenth Century. Edited by L. A. Selby-Bigge, M.A. 2 vols. Crown 8vo. 12s. net.

Spinoza. *A Study in the Ethics of Spinoza.* By Harold H. Joachim. 8vo. 10s. 6d. net.

Wallace. *Lectures and Essays on Natural Theology and Ethics.* By William Wallace, M.A., LL.D. Edited, with a Biographical Introduction, by Edward Caird, M.A. 8vo, with a Portrait. 12s. 6d.

5. PHYSICAL SCIENCE, ETC.

Chambers. *A Handbook of Descriptive and Practical Astronomy* By G. F. Chambers, F.R.A.S. *Fourth Edition,* in 3 vols. Demy 8vo.
Vol. I. The Sun, Planets, and Comets. 21s.
Vol. II. Instruments and Practical Astronomy. 21s.
Vol. III. The Starry Heavens. 14s.

De Bary. *Comparative Ana-* tomy of the Vegetative Organs of the Phanerogams and Ferns. By Dr. A. de Bary. Translated by F. O. Bower, M.A., and D. H. Scott, M.A. Royal 8vo, half-morocco, 24s. net; cloth, 21s. net.

De Bary. *Comparative Morphology and Biology of Fungi, Mycetozoa and Bacteria.* By Dr. A. de Bary. Translated by H. E. F. Garnsey, M.A. Revised by Isaac Bayley Balfour, M.A., M.D., F.R.S. Royal 8vo, half-morocco, 24s. *net;* cloth, 21s. *net*

De Bary. *Lectures on Bacteria.* By Dr. A. de Bary. *Second Improved Edition.* Translated and revised by Isaac Bayley Balfour, M.A., M.D., F.R.S. Crown 8vo. 5s *net.*

Ewart. *On the Physics and Physiology of Protoplasmic Streaming in Plants.* By A. J. Ewart, D.Sc , Ph.D., F.L.S. With seventeen illustrations. Royal 8vo. 8s. 6d. *net.*

Fischer. *The Structure and Functions of Bacteria.* By Alfred Fischer. Translated into English by A. C. Jones. Royal 8vo. With Twenty-nine Woodcuts. 7s. 6d *net.*

Goebel. *Outlines of Classification and Special Morphology of Plants.* By Dr. K. Goebel. Translated by H. E. F. Garnsey, M.A. Revised by I. B. Balfour, M.A., M.D., F.R.S. Royal 8vo, half-morocco, 22s. 6d. *net;* cloth, 20s. *net.*

—— *Organography of Plants, especially of the Archegoniatae and Spermophyta.* By Dr. K. Goebel. Authorized English Edition, by I. B. Balfour, M.A., M.D., F.R.S. Part I, General Organography. Royal 8vo, half-morocco, 12s. *net;* cloth, 10s. *net.* Pt. II, half-morocco, 24s. *net;* cloth, 21s. *net.*

Miall and Hammond. *The Structure and Life-History of the Harlequin Fly (Chironomus).* By L. C. Miall, F.R.S., and A. R. Hammond, F.L.S. 8vo. With 130 Illustrations. 7s. 6d.

Pfeffer. *The Physiology of Plants. A Treatise upon the Metabolism and Sources of Energy in Plants.* By Prof. Dr. W. Pfeffer. Second fully Revised Edition, translated and edited by A. J. Ewart, D.Sc., Ph.D., F.L.S. Royal 8vo. Vol. I, half-morocco, 26s. *net;* cloth, 23s. *net.* Vol. II, 16s. *net;* cloth, 14s. *net.*

Prestwich. *Geology—Chemical, Physical, and Stratigraphical.* By Sir Joseph Prestwich, M.A., F.R.S. In two Volumes. Royal 8vo. 61s.

Sachs. *A History of Botany.* Translated by H. E. F. Garnsey, M.A. Revised by I. B. Balfour, M.A., M.D., F.R.S. Cr. 8vo. 10s. *net.*

Schimper. *Plant Geography upon a Physiological Basis.* By Dr. A. F. W Schimper. The Authorized English Translation. Royal 8vo. With a photogravure portrait of Dr. Schimper, five collotypes. four maps, and four hundred and ninety-seven other illustrations. Half-morocco, 42s. *net.*

Solms-Laubach. *Fossil Botany. Being an Introduction to Palaeophytology from the Standpoint of the Botanist.* By H. Graf zu Solms-Laubach. Translated and revised by the same. Royal 8vo, half-morocco, 17s. *net;* cloth, 15s. *net.*

OXFORD HISTORY OF MUSIC.

8vo. Edited by W. H. Hadow, M.A. Price 15s. *net* each volume; but upon issue Vols. II and VI will be sold together for 15s. *net*, and the temporary price of the whole set of six volumes will be £3 15s. *net.*

I. *The Polyphonic Period.* Part I (Method of Musical Art, 330–1330). By H. E. Wooldridge, M.A.

III. *The Seventeenth Century.* By Sir C. H. H. Parry, M.A., D.Mus.

IV. *The Age of Bach and Handel.* By J. A Fuller Maitland, M.A.

V. *The Viennese School.* By W. H. Hadow, M.A.

IMMEDIATELY.

II. *The Polyphonic Period.* Part II. By H. E. Wooldridge, M.A.

VI. *The Romantic Period.* By E. Dannreuther, M.A.

OXFORD
AT THE CLARENDON PRESS
LONDON. EDINBURGH. NEW YORK. AND TORONTO